Booth: Reside
and UK

Booth: Residence, Domicile and UK Taxation

Twelfth Edition

Jonathan Schwarz BA, LLB (Witwatersrand), LLM (University of California, Berkeley), FTII
Barrister
Advocate of the High Court of South Africa
Barrister and Solicitor: Alberta, Canada

Tottel publishing

Tottel Publishing, Maxwelton House, 41–43 Boltro Road, Haywards Heath, West Sussex, RH16 1BJ

© Tottel Publishing Ltd 2008

Cover painting © Annette Schwarz 2008

All rights reserved. No part of this publication may be reproduced in any material form (including photocopying or storing it in any medium by electronic means and whether or not transiently or incidentally to some other use of this publication) without the written permission of the copyright owner except in accordance with the provisions of the Copyright, Designs and Patents Act 1988 or under the terms of a licence issued by the Copyright Licensing Agency Ltd, Saffron House, 6–10 Kirby Street, London EC1N 8TS. Applications for the copyright owner's written permission to reproduce any part of this publication should be addressed to the publisher.

Warning: The doing of an unauthorised act in relation to a copyright work may result in both a civil claim for damages and criminal prosecution.

Every effort has been made to ensure the accuracy of the contents of this book. However, the material in this publication is not intended to be, nor is it a substitute for, advice on any matter and neither the author nor the publisher can accept responsibility for any loss occasioned by any person by acting or refraining from acting in reliance on any statement contained in the book.

Crown copyright material is reproduced with the permission of the Controller of HMSO and the Queen's Printer for Scotland. Any European material in this work which has been reproduced from EUR-lex, the official European Communities legislation website, is European Communities copyright.

A CIP Catalogue record for this book is available from the British Library.

ISBN: 978 1 84766 128 9

Typeset by Phoenix Typesetting, Chatham, Kent
Printed and bound in Great Britain by CPI Antony Rowe, Chippenham, Wilts

PREFACE

The law of residence as it relates to individuals and companies has remained remarkably stable for decades. *Unit Construction Co Ltd v Bullock* was decided by the House of Lords in 1959. It took until 2006 for the Court of Appeal in *Wood v Holden* to again express a view on the subject of company residence. Likewise it was over twenty years after decision in *Reed v Clark* in 1985 that the High Court was again asked to consider an appeal on the residence of an individual.

During that period, unprecedented mobility of individuals, capital and business has resulted from technological change in transport and communication as well as a reduction in legal impediments to free movement. The United Kingdom, long an open economy and an open society, has thrived on rules that facilitate this mobility and the pre-eminence of London as a world financial and business centre.

The impact of recent developments in communications technology on company residence has been much discussed but, surprisingly, has not yet given rise to case law in this area. Indeed, Revenue challenges to the residence of companies before the courts have been rather conventional. More importantly, they are taking place against a background of intense debate about the future of residence based taxation for companies.

This debate is expressed in terms of the competitiveness of the UK tax system. It also raises questions as to the proper connection a taxpayer should have with a particular country to justify paying tax there. As with companies, in an era when individuals may be born and educated in one country, work in one or more others and retire or die elsewhere, the answers are less obvious than for a cradle to grave life in a single country.

In the case of individual residence, much of the peaceful co-existence between tax payers and tax administrators had been due to the practice published by HMRC in IR20. Despite criticisms of the statement, it had, until very recently, become viewed by both as a code to be applied virtually as if it was the law. Public signs of Revenue discontent with the way IR20 was applied appeared in a Tax Bulletin article on 'Mobile Workers' in April 2001. Investigation, litigation, a change in the way time spent in the UK is reported on tax returns followed, culminating in the 2008 Finance Act changes to the counting of time spent in the UK. This is not the end of the process, despite assurances given by the Chancellor during the 2008 Budget that there would be no further legislation in this area. The

Preface

beginning of a period of change was signalled in Parliamentary debate on the day count changes in FA 2008 when the Financial Secretary announced that Revenue guidance in this area is to be completely rewritten and the new guidance will be subject to consultation. She also floated the possibility of a statutory residence test for individuals which will also form part of the discussions.

A principled exercise of taxing jurisdiction based on sound connecting factors is likely to be internationally attractive and domestically legitimate in a democratic society, as well as providing a stable revenue base for governments. Grab-what-you-can tax policy encourages escape-what-you-can tax subjects.

Updating and rewriting another author's work is like digging in someone else's flowerbed. After 12 editions, there is bound to be some undergrowth to be pruned back but it is a delicate task to give a fresh view while trying to ensure the original still blooms. I have tried to let the bold and colourful approach of Neil Booth, carefully tended by Denzil Davies MP for a decade, shine through my own more prosaic style as much as possible.

Every book is a collective effort. My thanks go to the Tottel editorial and production team for all their hard work and patience in bringing this edition to fruition which is generally up to date to the beginning of September 2008.

Jonathan Schwarz
Middle Temple
London
September 2008

CONTENTS

Preface	v
Table of Statutes	xiii
Table of Statutory Instruments	xvii
Table of HMRC Material	xix
Table of EC Material and International Conventions	xxi
Table of Cases	xxiii
Abbreviations	xxxiii

Chapter 1	**United Kingdom taxation**	1
1.01	State practice in exercising taxing jurisdiction	1
	QUESTIONS OF SOVEREIGNTY	1
1.02	The right to levy tax	1
1.03	Jurisdictional limitations	2
1.04	Enforcement overseas	3
1.05	Territorial limits	5
	QUESTIONS OF TERRITORY	6
1.06	The territory of the UK	6
1.07	The territorial waters	6
1.08	Territorial extension	7
1.09	The European Community	8
	DETERMINANTS OF CHARGEABILITY	9
1.10	Residence	9
1.11	Ordinary residence	10
1.12	Domicile	10
1.13	Nationality	11
1.14	Source of rules	11
1.15	The remittance basis	12
1.16	Reform of the existing system	12
1.17	Reform of residence rules	12
1.18	Current criticisms of the system	13
1.19	Darling amendments	15
	UK REVENUE LAW	15
1.20	Income tax	15
1.21	Corporation tax	16
1.22	Capital gains tax	17
1.23	Inheritance tax	18
1.24	National Insurance Contributions	18
1.25	Value Added Tax (VAT)	19
1.26	Revenue practices and concessions	19

Chapter 2 Residence of indivduals — 23

2.01 Introduction — 23

THE NATURE OF RESIDENCE — 23
2.02 A qualitative attribute — 23
2.03 A question of fact and degree — 25
2.04 A personal attribute — 26
2.05 An annual attribute — 27
2.06 The judicial principles — 29
2.07 The *Shepherd* synthesis — 29

A PLACE OF ABODE — 31
2.08 Occupation of a dwelling house — 31
2.09 Multiple residence — 32
2.10 Ownership irrelevant — 34

PHYSICAL PRESENCE — 35
2.11 Duration of presence — 35
2.12 Regularity and frequency of visits — 36
2.13 Revenue practice — 38
2.14 Future conduct — 39
2.15 Previous history — 40

CONNECTING FACTORS — 40
2.16 The ties of birth — 40
2.17 The ties of family — 41
2.18 The ties of business — 42
2.19 Other ties — 43

INTENT AND LEGALITY — 44
2.20 Involuntary or unintentional presence — 44
2.21 Unlawful presence — 46
2.22 Residence for tax treaty purposes — 47

Chapter 3 Ordinary residence — 51

3.01 Introduction — 51

CONCEPT AND APPLICATION — 52
3.02 The meaning of ordinary residence — 52
3.03 The relation of residence to ordinary residence — 54

ESSENTIAL ELEMENTS — 56
3.04 A voluntarily adopted place of abode — 56
3.05 Settled purposes — 60
3.06 Regular order of life — 63
3.07 Unlawful residence — 65
3.08 Dual or no ordinary residence — 66

REVENUE PRACTICE — 66
3.09 Year by year residence — 66
3.10 Available accommodation — 68

3.11	Annual visits	69
3.12	Intention	69

Chapter 4 Arrivals and departures — 73

4.01	Introduction	73
4.02	Split tax years	73
4.03	Income Tax Act 2007	74
	PERSONS ARRIVING IN THE UK	74
4.04	Conditional exemption	74
4.05	Temporary purpose	76
4.06	View or intent of establishing residence	78
4.07	A place of abode	79
4.08	Actual residence	80
4.09	Determining presence	82
4.10	The significance of 'the tax year'	86
4.11	The capital gains tax test	86
4.12	TCGA 1992 s 9(3) and ITA 2007 s 831 compared	87
	PERSONS LEAVING THE UK	89
4.13	Residence of individuals temporarily abroad	89
4.14	Occasional residence	89
4.15	A distinct break	93
4.16	Residence of individuals working abroad	97
4.17	Full-time work	97
4.18	Trades and professions	99
4.19	Employments	100
4.20	Incidental duties	101
4.21	Capital gains tax: temporary non-residence	105
4.22	Remittance basis: temporary non-residence	105

Chapter 5 Residence of trusts and estates — 107

5.01	Introduction	107
	TRUSTS	108
5.02	Residence and ordinary residence	108
5.03	Single residence trustees	108
5.04	Mixed residence trustees	108
5.05	Non-resident trustees with a UK permanent establishment	109
5.06	Residence for tax treaties	110
5.07	Residence of estates	111

Chapter 6 Residence of companies — 113

6.01	Introduction	113
6.02	UK incorporated companies	114
6.03	Foreign incorporated companies	115

6.04	The *Untelrab* synthesis	116
6.05	A question of fact	117
6.06	Who exercises central management and control?	118
6.07	Delegated management and control	121
6.08	Shareholder control	122
6.09	Elements of central management and control	125
6.10	Finance as a key element	126
6.11	Degree of activity	127
6.12	Administrative functions	128
6.13	Influence compared with management and control	128
6.14	Location of central management and control	129
6.15	Dual or multiple residence	131
6.16	Residence for tax treaty purposes	135
6.17	Transfer of residence abroad	138
6.18	Treaty non-resident companies	139
6.19	European company	139
6.20	Residence for special statutory purposes	139
6.21	Group relief	140
6.22	Controlled Foreign Companies	140
6.23	Transfer pricing – exemption for small or medium-sized enterprises	141

Chapter 7 **Domicile** 143

7.01	Introduction	143
	THE NATURE OF DOMICILE	144
7.02	Historical background	144
7.03	The two roles of domicile	145
7.04	The five principles of domicile	147
	DOMICILE OF ORIGIN	149
7.05	Acquisition	149
7.06	Displacement and revival	150
	DOMICILE OF DEPENDENCE	152
7.07	Married women	152
7.08	Children	155
7.09	Persons suffering from mental disorder	158
	DOMICILE OF CHOICE	159
7.10	Acquisition	159
7.11	Residence	160
7.12	Intention	164
7.13	Motive as evidence of intention	168
7.14	Proof of intention	171
7.15	Change of domicile of choice	176
7.16	Deemed domicile	180
7.17	Domicile for tax treaty purposes	181

Chapter 8	**Compliance and appeals**	**183**
8.01	Introduction	183
8.02	Assessment of non-residents	185
8.03	Deduction of tax at source – 'usual place of abode'	185
8.04	Claiming not ordinarily resident or non-domiciled status	187
8.05	Appeals	187
8.06	Evidential burden on appeal	188
8.07	Role of court on appeal	189

Chapter 9	**Residence, nationality and discrimination in the European Union**	**191**
9.01	Introduction	191
9.02	Individual nationality and tax residence	193
9.03	Corporate nationality and tax residence	194
9.04	Change of residence and exit taxes	195

Appendix 1
    Inland Revenue Bulletin IR20 (2008)   197

Appendix 2
    Statements of Practice   253

Appendix 3
    Extra-Statutory Concessions   261

Index   263

TABLE OF STATUTES

	PARA
Adoption Act 1976	
s 39(1)	7.08
Adoption (Scotland) Act 1978	
s 39(1)	7.08
Bill of Rights (1688)	1.02, 1.26
Children Act 1975	
Sch 1	
para 3	7.08
Commonwealth Immigrants Act 1962	3.07
Commonwealth Immigrants Act 1968	3.07
Continental Shelf Act 1964	1.08
s 1(1), (7)	1.08
Criminal Law Act 1977	
s 7	2.21
Domicile and Matrimonial Proceedings Act 1973	7.08
s 1	7.07
(1), (2)	7.07
3	7.08
4(1)–(4)	7.08
Education Act 1962	3.05
Finance Act 1910	8.01
Finance (No 2) Act 1915	
s 47(1)	3.04
Finance Act 1951	
s 36	6.02
Finance Act 1953	
s 20	6.06
Finance Act 1956	
s 11	4.20
Sch 2	
para 3	4.08
Finance Act 1968	2.05
Finance Act 1973	1.08
s 38(4)	1.05
Sch 15	1.08

	PARA
Finance Act 1975	
s 45	7.16
Finance (No 2) Act 1983	
s 12	7.16
Finance Act 1986	1.23, 7.03
Finance (No 2) Act 1987	
s 96(2)	1.23
Finance Act 1988	
s 66	6.02, 9.03, App 2
(1)	App 2
66A(2), (3)	6.19
Sch 7	App 2
para 1(1)(c)	App 2
para 5(1)	App 2
Finance Act 1993	
s 208	2.10, 3.10
(1)	4.07
(2)	4.07, 4.12
(3), (4)	4.07
Finance Act 1994	
s 249	6.18
Finance Act 1995	
s 117	2.04
126	8.02
(8)	5.05
128	App 3
Finance Act 1998	
s 127(1)	4.21
Finance Act 2002	
s 134	1.04
Sch 39	1.04
Finance Act 2003	8.02
s 148	5.05
(1)	5.05
150	6.01, 8.02
Finance (No 2) Act 2005	
s 32	4.21

xiii

Table of statutes

	PARA
Finance Act 2006	5.01, 5.07
ss 173–176	1.04
Sch 20	1.23
Finance Act 2008	1.12, 3.01, 4.09, 4.11, 8.04, App 1
s 24	4.09
(6)	4.11
160	1.26
Sch 7	1.03, 1.12, 1.13, 1.15, 4.23
para 23	8.05
para 52	4.22
para 54	8.05
para 77	8.05
Government of Wales Act 1998	1.06
Government of Wales Act 2006	1.06
Highways Act 1980	
s 137	2.21
Income and Corporation Taxes Act 1970	
s 49	4.14, 4.15
50(3)	4.20
122(2)(a)	7.07
482(1)(a)	9.04
Income and Corporation Taxes Act 1988	1.20, 1.21
Pt XVII Ch IV	6.22
s 2(2)	1.20
6(1)	1.21, 6.01
(2)(a)	1.21
8(1)	1.21, 6.01
9	1.21
11(1)	1.20, 5.05, 6.01
(2)	1.20, 6.01
(2A)	6.01
19(4)	1.13, 7.04, 7.14
192	7.04
207	7.04
334	2.07, 4.03, 4.14, 4.14
(a)	4.14
336	2.07, 3.10, 4.03, 4.05, 4.06, 4.09, 4.14, App 2
(1)	4.05
(2)	4.05
403	6.21
404(1)	6.21
(4)	6.21
(b)	6.21
420(2)(b)	4.17
747, 748	1.21
749	1.21
(1)–(3)	6.22
(3)(a)–(e)	6.22
(4), (6)	6.22
750–756	1.21
765(1)(a)	6.02
788	2.22
820	1.20

	PARA
Income and Corporation Taxes Act 1988 – *cont*	
s 825	9.03
832(1)	6.01
Sch 24	1.21
Sch 28AA(1)	6.23
(5A)	6.23
(5B)	6.23
(4), (6)	6.23
(5C), (5D)	6.23
Sch D	4.05, 4.07, 4.08, 5.01
Case I, II	2.05
Case V	6.15
Sch E	1.05
Income Tax Act 1799	
s 8	4.08
Income Tax Act 1806	2.01
s 51	4.06, 4.08
Income Tax Act 1812	
s 39	4.08
Income Tax Act 1842	
s 39	4.14
Income Tax Act 1918	4.14
s 7(3)	8.01
Sch 1	
r 2	2.10, 4.07, 4.08
Schs A–E general rules, r 3	4.14, 4.15
Income Tax Act 1952	
s 132	7.14
Income Tax Act 2007	1.11, 1.20, 4.03, 8.03, 8.05
Pt 13 Ch 2	1.11, 3.01
Pt 14 Ch 2 (ss 829–835)	1.20, 4.03
s 470	5.04
474	5.01
(1), (2)	5.02
475	5.01
(4)–(6)	5.05
476	5.01, 5.04
(2)–(4)	5.04
809B	8.04
811	5.05
829	2.07, 4.03, 4.14, 4.15
(1), (2)	4.13
830	4.03, 4.14, 4.16, 4.17, 4.18, 4.19, 4.20
(1)–(3)	4.16
(4)	4.16, 4.19
(5)	4.16, 4.19, 4.20
(b)	4.20
(6)	4.16
831	2.07, 2.10, 2.11, 2.16, 2.20, 4.03, 4.04, 4.06, 4.08, 4.09, 4.10, 4.11, 4.12, 4.15
(1)	4.04, 4.05, 4.07, 4.08
(a)	4.05
(b)	4.09, 4.11
(1A), 1B)	4.09

Table of statutes

	PARA
Income Tax Act 2007 – *cont*	
s 831(2)	4.04
832	2.10, 2.16, 2.20, 4.03, 4.08, 4.09, 4.10
(1)	4.04, 4.07, 4.08
(b)	4.11
(2)	4.04
832(A)	4.22
833	4.03
834	5.07
874, 906, 971	8.03
Sch 12, Pt 1	5.01
Sch 13	5.01
Income Tax (Earnings and Pensions) Act 2003	1.20, 4.03
Pt 7	3.01
Ch 4	1.20
Ch 5	1.20
s 1(1), (8)	1.20
6, 7	1.20
21–24	3.01
26	3.01
Income Tax (Trading and Other Income) Act 2005	1.20, 4.03
Pt II (ss 3–259)	1.20
Pt II, Ch 6	8.04
Pt III (ss 260–364)	1.20
Pt IV (ss 365–573)	1.20
Pt V	1.20
Pt VIII (ss 829–845)	1.20, 3.01
Pt IX (ss 846–863)	2.04
s 832	1.13
Inheritance Act 1984	
Pt I (ss 1–17)	1.23
s 3	1.23
6(1)	1.23
7	7.03
18, 20, 22–29, 71, 89	1.23
158	7.17
267(1)(a), (b)	7.16
(2)	7.17
(3), (4)	7.16
Inland Revenue Regulations Act 1890	
s 1(2)	1.26
Interpretation Act 1889	
s 3	4.09
Interpretation Act 1978	
s 5	1.06, 6.01
Sch 1	1.06, 6.01
Magna Carta (1215)	
cl 12	1.02
Matrimonial Causes Act 1973	
s 13	7.15
National Assistance Act 1948	
s 24(1)	3.04
Northern Ireland Act 1998	1.06
Public Health Act 1936	
s 49, 269	2.21

	PARA
Representation of the People Act 1983	
s 1(1)	2.21
Royal and Parliamentary Titles Act 1927	1.06
Scotland Act 1998	1.06
s 75	1.10
Social Security Contributions and Benefits Act 1992	
s 1(6)	1.24
Taxation of Chargeable Gains Act 1992	
s 1	1.22
2	1.11
(1)	1.22, 2.05, 3.01, 3.03, 4.11
3	1.22
9	4.09, 5.05
(1)	4.11, 5.07
(2)	8.05
(3)	4.3, 4.09, 4.11, 4.12
(4)	4.12
10	1.22, 4.11
10A	4.11, 4.12, 4.21
12	1.22
(1)	7.04
69(1), (2)	5.01
76	1.22
77–79	App 3
115, 121, 210, 222, 251, 262, 263, 268, 269, 275	1.22
86	App 3
Sch 5	App 3
Taxes Management Act 1970	8.04
s 1	1.26
7	8.01
(2), (3)	8.01
42	8.04
50(6)	8.04, 8.06
56	8.07
(6)	2.03, 8.06
56A	2.03
(1)	8.07
65–68	8.01
115	8.01
Territorial Waters Jurisdiction Act 1878	
s 7	1.07
Town and Country Planning Acts	2.21
Wireless Telegraphy Act 1949	
s 14(7)	1.07
AUSTRALIA	
Domicile Act 1982	
s 7	7.06
NAURU	
Conflict of Laws Act 1974	7.02

xv

Table of statutes

	PARA		PARA
NEW ZEALAND		**US**	
Domicile Act 1976		Federal Internal Revenue Code ...	1.17
s 11	7.06		

TABLE OF STATUTORY INSTRUMENTS

	PARA		PARA
Double Taxation Relief (Taxes on Income) (New Zealand) Order 1984, SI 1984/365	1.04	Social Security (Contributions) Regulations 2001, SI 2001/1004	
Education (Fees and Awards) Regulations 1983		reg 145	1.24
Sch 2(2)	3.05	(1)(a)	1.24
Rules of the Supreme Court 1965, SI 1965/1776	1.03	Territorial Waters Order in Council 1964 arts 2–5	1.07

TABLE OF HMRC MATERIAL

	PARA
Extra-statutory Concessions	
A11 (Residence in the United Kingdom: year of commencement or cessation of residence)	1.26, 4.02, App 3
A78	4.04, 4.16
D2 (Residence in the United Kingdom: year of commencement or cessation of residence: capital gains tax)	1.26, 4.02, App 3
HMRC Brief 01/07	1.26, 2.13, 3.11
HMRC Capital Gains Manual	
CG30650	5.07
HMRC Inspector's Manual	1.26
HMRC International Tax Manual:	8.03
HMRC International Tax Manual	
Ch 3	6.01
INTM 120000 et seq	6.01
INTM 370060	8.03
INTM 505020	8.03
HMRC Property Income Manual	
PIM4800	8.03
PIM4810	8.03
HMRC Savings Income Manual	
SAIM9080	8.03
Statement of Practice A10	4.20
Statement of Practice 3/81	App 2
Statement of Practice on company residence SP 1/90	6.01, 6.06, App 2
para 13	6.06, 6.14
para 14	6.14
para 15	6.06
paras 16, 17	6.08

	PARA
Statement of Practice 2/91 Residence in the UK: visits extended because of exceptional circumstances	App 2
IR 20 (1972)	
para 8	4.09
IR20 (11 April 2000)	
App, para 1.4	2.09
IR20 (July 2008)	1.14, 1.26, 2.02, App 1
para 1.2	2.11, 4.09, 4.14
para 1.3	3.09, 4.14
para 1.4	3.08
para 1.5	4.21
para 1.6	4.21
para 1.7	4.21
Ch 2	4.21
para 2.1	4.14
para 2.2	4.14, 4.17
para 2.10	4.17
Ch 3	4.09, 4.21
para 3.1	3.12
para 3.3	2.13, 4.09
para 3.4	3.09, 3.11, 4.05
para 3.5	3.09, 3.11, 4.05
para 3.8	3.12
para 4.5	7.10, 7.11
para 5.5	4.20
para 5.7	4.19, 4.20
para 5.8	4.20
para 8	3.09
para 11.2	1.24

TABLE OF EC MATERIAL & INTERNATIONAL CONVENTIONS

	PARA
Convention on the Territorial Sea and Contiguous Zone, Cmnd 2511	
art 11	1.07
Council Directive 2006/112 on the common system of value added tax (the VAT Directive)	1.25
Title V, Chs 1–4	1.25
Art 43	1.25
Council Regulation (EC) 2157/2001 on the Statute for a European Company (Societas Europaea):	6.19
Art 8	6.19
Directive 2008/55/EC	1.04
Directive 76/308/EEC of 15 March 1976 on mutual assistance for the recovery of claims relating to certain levies, duties, taxes and other measures	1.04
European Commission Communication 'Exit taxation and the need for co-ordination of Member States' tax policies' COM (2006) 825	9.04
EU Treaty	
Art 12	9.01
(1)	9.01
17	9.01
18	9.04
(1)	9.01
39	9.01
(2)	9.01
43	9.01, 9.04
48	9.01, 9.03
49	9.01
56	9.01
(1)	9.01
58	9.01

	PARA
EU Treaty – cont	
Art 58(a)	9.01
293 [former Art 220]	9.04
Geneva Convention on the Continental Shelf 29 April 1958	1.08
Hague Convention to Regulate Conflicts between the Law of Nationality and the Law of Domicile 1955	
Art 5	7.04
Indonesia-Netherlands Tax Treaty:	6.16
OECD/Council of Europe Convention on Mutual Assistance in Tax Matters, signed by the UK 24 May 2007	1.04
OECD Draft Double Taxation Convention (1963)	2.22
Model Double Taxation Convention on Income and Capital (OECD, Paris 1977)	2.22, 5.06, App 2
Art 4	2.22
(1)	2.22, 5.06, 6.16, 6.21, 6.22
(2)	2.22, 7.17
(a)	2.22
(3)	5.06, 6.16, 6.17, 6.22, App 2
Treaty of Rome	1.03, 1.09
United Kingdom-New Zealand Double Taxation Convention of 4 August 1983	
Protocol of 7 November 2007	1.04
UK/US Double Taxation agreement (1975)	
Art 4(2)	2.22
UK/US Double Taxation Convention	9.03

xxi

TABLE OF CASES

PARA

A

Abdul Manan, Re [1971] 2 All ER 1016, [1971] 1 WLR 859, 115 Sol Jo 289, CA ... 3.07
Absalom v Talbot [1944] AC 204, [1944] 1 All ER 642, (1944) 26 TC 166, 60 TLR 434, HL 1.26
Agassi v Robinson (HMIT) [2006] UKHL 23, [2006] STC 1056, [2006] 3 All ER 97, 77 TC 686, HL 1.05
Agulian & Anor v Cyganik [2006] EWCA Civ 129, [2006] 1 FCR 406, CA .. 7.01, 7.14, 8.07
Aikman v Aikman (1861) 7 Jur NS 1017, 4 LT 374, 3 Macq 854, HL 7.12
American Thread Co v Joyce (Surveyor of Taxes) (1913) 6 TC 163, 57 Sol Jo 321, 108 LT 353, 29 TLR 266, HL 6.07, 6.08, 6.10
Anderson v Laneuville (1854) 9 Moo PCC 325, 2 Ecc & Ad 41, 24 LTOS 281, PC . 7.11
Anderson (executor of Anderson dec'd) v IRC (1997) Sp C 147 .... 7.01
Apthorpe (Surveyor of Taxes) v Peter Schoenhofen Brewing Co Ltd (1899) 4 TC 41, 80 LT 395, 15 TLR 245, CA 6.08
A-G v Coote (1817) 2 TC 385, 4 Price 183 .... 2.08, 2.09, 2.10, 4.06, 4.07
A-G v Kent (1862) 1 H & C 12, 31 LJ Ex 391, 10 WR 722, 6 LT 864 .... 7.13
A-G v Lady Rowe (1862) 1 H & C 31, 31 LJ Ex 314, 8 Jur NS 823, 10 WR 718, 6 LT 438 .... 7.13
A-G v LCC [1900] 1 QB 192, 4 TC 265, CA; revsd sub nom LCC v A-G [1901] AC 26, 4 TC 265, 65 JP 227, 70 LJQB 77, 49 WR 686, 83 LT 605, 17 TLR 131, HL 1.20
A-G v Pottinger (1861) 6 H & N 733, 30 LJ Ex 284, 7 Jur NS 470, 9 WR 578, 4 LT 368 .... 7.12
A-G v Yule and Mercantile Bank of India [1931] All ER Rep 400, 145 LT 9, CA .. 7.14
A-G for Alberta v Huggard Assets Ltd [1953] AC 420, [1953] 2 All ER 951, [1953] 2 WLR 768, 97 Sol Jo 260, PC 1.05
Automatic Self-Cleansing Filter Syndicate Co Ltd v Cunninghame [1906] 2 Ch 34, 75 LJ Ch 437, 13 Mans 156, 50 Sol Jo 359, 94 LT 651, 22 TLR 378, CA 6.08

B

Back (Inspector of Taxes) v Whitlock [1932] 1 KB 747, 16 TC 723, 101 LJKB 698, [1932] All ER Rep 241, 76 Sol Jo 272, 147 LT 172, 48 TLR 289 .... 2.05
Barrett v Revenue & Customs (2007) SpC 639, [2008] STC (SCD) 268 .... 1.18, 4.15
Bayard Brown v Burt (Surveyor of Taxes) (1911) 5 TC 667, 81 LJKB 17, 105 LT 420, 27 TLR 572, CA 2.03, 2.08, 2.10, 2.20, 2.21, 4.08, 8.03
Beaumont, Re [1893] 3 Ch 490, 62 LJ Ch 923, 8 R 9, 42 WR 142, 37 Sol Jo 731 ... 7.08
Bell v Kennedy (1868) LR 1 Sc & Div 307, 5 SLR 566, 6 Macq 69, HL 7.06, 7.10, 7.11, 7.12, 7.14
Bempde v Johnstone (1796) 3 Ves 198, 30 ER 967 .... 7.11
Biehl v Administration des Contributions du Grand-Duché de Luxembourg: C-175/88 [1990] ECR I-1779, [1990] 3 CMLR 143, [1991] STC 575, ECJ 9.02

xxiii

Table of cases

	PARA
Bonaparte (Napoleon) (Late Emperor), Re (1853) 2 Rob Eccl 606, 1 Ecc & Ad 9, 17 Jur 328	7.13
Bowie (or Ramsay) v Liverpool Royal Infirmary [1930] AC 588, 99 LJPC 134, [1930] All ER Rep 127, 143 LT 388, 46 TLR 465, HL	7.11
Bradbury v English Sewing Cotton Co Ltd [1923] AC 744, 8 TC 481, 92 LJKB 736, [1923] All ER Rep 427, 67 Sol Jo 678, 129 LT 546, 39 TLR 590, HL	6.17
Bruce v Bruce (1790) 2 Bos & P 229, 2 Coop temp Cott 510, 6 Bro Parl Cas 566, HL:	7.11
Buchanan (Peter) Ltd and Macharg v McVey [1955] AC 516n, [1954] IR 89	1.04
Bullock (Inspector of Taxes) v Unit Construction Co Ltd [1959] Ch 147, [1958] 3 All ER 186, [1958] 3 WLR 504, 38 TC 712, 37 ATC 292, 51 R & IT 625, [1958] TR 277, 102 Sol Jo 654; on appeal [1959] Ch 315, [1959] 1 All ER 591, [1959] 2 WLR 437, 38 ATC 36, 52 R & IT 194, [1959] TR 37, 103 Sol Jo 238, CA; revsd sub nom Unit Construction Co Ltd v Bullock (Inspector of Taxes) [1960] AC 351, [1959] 3 All ER 831, [1959] 3 WLR 1022, 38 TC 712, 38 ATC 351, 52 R & IT 828, [1959] TR 345, 103 Sol Jo 1027, HL	6.03, 6.06, 6.08, 6.14, 6.15, App 2
Buswell v IRC [1974] 2 All ER 520, [1974] 1 WLR 1631, [1974] STC 266, 49 TC 334, 53 ATC 96, [1974] TR 97, 118 Sol Jo 864, CA	7.14

C

Calcutta Jute Mills Co Ltd v Nicholson (Surveyor of Taxes) (1876) 1 Ex D 428, 1 TC 83, 88, 45 LJQB 821, 25 WR 71, [1874–80] All ER Rep 1102, 35 LT 275	6.01, 6.07, 6.09, 6.10, 6.14
Casdagli v Casdagli [1919] AC 145, 88 LJP 49, [1918–19] All ER Rep 462, 63 Sol Jo 39, 120 LT 52, 35 TLR 30, HL	7.14
Cesena Sulphur Co v Nicholson (1876) 1 Ex D 428, 1 TC 83, 88, 45 LJQB 821, 25 WR 71, [1874–80] All ER Rep 1102, 35 LT 275	6.09, 8.06
Cheney v Conn (Inspector of Taxes) [1968] 1 All ER 779, [1968] 1 WLR 242, 44 TC 217, 46 ATC 192, [1967] TR 177, 111 Sol Jo 562	1.03
Civil Engineer v IRC (2001) Sp C 299	7.01
Clark (Inspector of Taxes) v Oceanic Contractors Inc [1983] 2 AC 130, [1983] 1 All ER 133, [1983] 2 WLR 94, [1983] STC 35, 56 TC 183, 127 Sol Jo 54, HL	1.04, 1.05
Clore (No 2), Re, Official Solicitor v Clore [1984] STC 609, ChD	7.11, 7.13
Colquhoun v Brooks (1889) 14 App Cas 493, 2 TC 490, 54 JP 277, 59 LJQB 53, 38 WR 289, [1886–90] All ER Rep 1063, 61 LT 518, 5 TLR 728, HL	4.04, 4.12
Colquhoun v Heddon (1890) 25 QBD 129, 2 TC 621, 59 LJQB 465, 38 WR 545, 62 LT 853, 6 TLR 331, CA	1.05
Cooke's Trusts, Re (1887) 56 LJ Ch 637, 35 WR 608, 56 LT 737, 3 TLR 558	7.07
Cooper v Cadwalader (1904) 5 TC 101, sub nom IRC v Cadwalader 42 SLR 117, 7 F 146, 12 SLT 449, Ct of Exch (1 Div)	2.07, 2.08, 2.09, 2.10, 4.05, 4.06, 4.07, 6.15

D

D'Etchegoyen v D'Etchegoyen (1888) 13 PD 132, 57 LJP 104, 37 WR 64	7.08
de Lasteyrie du Saillant v Ministère L'Economie, des Finances et de l'Industrie: C-9/02 [2005] STC 1722, [2004] ECR I-2409, 6 ITLR 666, ECJ	9.04
Davis v HMRC [2008] All ER (D) 144 (Jul), CA	1.26
Dawson v IRC [1990] 1 AC 1, [1989] 2 All ER 289, [1989] 2 WLR 858, [1989] STC 473, 62 TC 301, 133 Sol Jo 661, HL	5.01
De Beers Consolidated Mines Ltd v Howe (Surveyor of Taxes) [1905] 2 KB 612, 5 TC 198, 74 LJKB 934, 54 WR 9, 93 LT 63, 21 TLR 578, CA; affd [1906] AC 455, 5 TC 198, 75 LJKB 858, 13 Mans 394, 50 Sol Jo 666, 95 LT 221, 22 TLR 756, HL	6.03, 6.05, 6.10, 6.14, App 2
De Bonneval v De Bonneval (1838) 1 Curt 856, 163 ER 296	7.13
Donaldson (or Nichols) v Donaldson [1949] P 363, [1949] LJR 762, 93 Sol Jo 220, 65 TLR 233, PDA	7.13
Doucet v Geoghegan (1878) 9 Ch D 441, 26 WR 825, CA	7.12
Douglas v Douglas (1871) LR 12 Eq 617, 41 LJ Ch 74, 20 WR 55, 25 LT 530	7.12

Table of cases

PARA

E

EC Commission v France: 270/83 [1986] ECR 273, [1987] 1 CMLR 401, ECJ 9.03
Edwards (Inspector of Taxes) v Bairstow and Harrison (1954) 36 TC 207, 33 ATC 58, 47 R & IT 177, [1954] TR 65, L(TC) 1680; on appeal (1954) 36 TC 207, 33 ATC 131, 47 R & IT 340, [1954] TR 155, L(TC) 1692, CA; revsd [1956] AC 14, [1955] 3 All ER 48, [1955] 3 WLR 410, 36 TC 207, 34 ATC 198, 48 R & IT 534, [1955] TR 209, 99 Sol Jo 558, L(TC) 1742, HL 2.03, 8.07
Egyptian Delta Land and Investment Co Ltd v Todd (Inspector of Taxes). See Todd (Inspector of Taxes) v Egyptian Delta Land and Investment Co Ltd
Egyptian Hotels Ltd v Mitchell (Surveyor of Taxes) [1914] 3 KB 118, 6 TC 542, 83 LJKB 1510, 21 Mans 278, 58 Sol Jo 494, 111 LT 189, 30 TLR 457, CA; affd sub nom Mitchell (Surveyor of Taxes) v Egyptian Hotels Ltd [1915] AC 1022, 6 TC 542, 84 LJKB 1772, 59 Sol Jo 649, 113 LT 882, 31 TLR 546, HL 6.10, 6.15
Erichsen v Last (1881) 1 TC 351; affd (1881) 8 QBD 414, 4 TC 422, 46 JP 357, 51 LJQB 86, 30 WR 301, 45 LT 703, CA 4.18
Executors of Moore dec'd v IRC (2002) Sp C 335 .... 7.01
Executors of Winifred Johnson Dec'd v HMRC (2005) SpC 481, [2005] STC (SCD) 614 .... 7.01, 7.15

F

F (F's (Personal Representatives)) v IRC [2000] STC (SCD) 1, [2000] WTLR 505: 7.14, 7.15
F & Anor (as personal representatives of F deceased) v Commissioners of Inland Revenue (1999) Sp C 219 .... 7.01
Fielden v IRC (1965) 42 TC 501, 44 ATC 210, [1965] TR 221, ChD 7.15
Finanzamt Köln-Altstadt v Schumacker: C-279/93 [1996] QB 28, [1995] All ER (EC) 319, [1995] 3 WLR 498, [1995] ECR I-225, [1996] 2 CMLR 450, [1995] STC 306, ECJ 9.02
Firebrace v Firebrace (1878) 4 PD 63, 47 LJP 41, 26 WR 617, 39 LT 94 .... 7.13
Flynn, Re, Flynn v Flynn [1968] 1 All ER 49, [1968] 1 WLR 103, 112 Sol Jo 93 .... 7.15
Forbes v Forbes (1854) Kay 341, 23 LJ Ch 724, 2 Eq Rep 178, 18 Jur 642, 2 WR 253: 7.08
Foulsham (Inspector of Taxes) v Pickles. See Pickles v Foulsham (Inspector of Taxes)
Fuld's Estate (No 3), Re, Hartley v Fuld [1968] P 675, [1965] 3 All ER 776, [1966] 2 WLR 717, 110 Sol Jo 133 .... 7.10, 7.11, 7.12, 7.14
Furse, Re, Furse v IRC [1980] 3 All ER 838, [1980] STC 596, [1980] TR 275 ..... 7.11, 7.12

G

Gaines-Cooper v Revenue and Customs Comrs [2006] SpC 568, [2007] STC (SCD) 23, [2006] STI 2532, [2007] WTLR 101, 9 ITL Rep 274 .....1.18, 1.26, 2.07, 2.13, 3.11, 4.05, 4.14, 7.01, 8.07
Giovanni Maria Sotgiu v Deutsche Bundespost (Case 152/73) [1974] ECR 153, ECJ 9.02, 9.03
Government of India, Ministry of Finance (Revenue Division) v Taylor [1955] AC 491, [1955] 1 All ER 292, [1955] 2 WLR 303, 34 ATC 10, 48 R & IT 98, [1955] TR 9, 99 Sol Jo 94, HL 1.04
Grace v Revenue and Customs Comrs (2008) Sp C 663, [2008] STC (SCD) 531 .. 1.18, 2.12
Grainger & Son v Gough (Surveyor of Taxes) [1895] 1 QB 71, 3 TC 311, 59 JP 84, 64 LJQB 193, 43 WR 184, 71 LT 802, 11 TLR 39, CA; revsd [1896] AC 325, 3 TC 462, 60 JP 692, 65 LJQB 410, 44 WR 561, 74 LT 435, 12 TLR 364, HL 4.18
Gramophone and Typewriter Ltd v Stanley (Surveyor of Taxes) [1908] 2 KB 89, 77 LJKB 834, 15 Mans 251, [1908–10] All ER Rep 833, 99 LT 39, 24 TLR 480, sub nom Stanley (Surveyor of Taxes) v Gramophone and Typewriter Ltd 5 TC 358, CA 6.08
Green v Russell [1959] 2 QB 226, [1959] 2 All ER 525, [1959] 3 WLR 17, CA 2.04
Greenwood (Surveyor of Taxes) v F L Smidth & Co. See Smidth (F L) & Co v Greenwood (Surveyor of Taxes)

XXV

Table of cases

	PARA
Gubay v Kington (Inspector of Taxes) [1983] 1 WLR 709, [1981] STC 721, 57 TC 601, [1981] TR 291, 125 Sol Jo 590; affd [1983] 2 All ER 976, [1983] 1 WLR 709, [1983] STC 443, 57 TC 601, 127 Sol Jo 411, CA; revsd [1984] 1 All ER 513, [1984] 1 WLR 163, [1984] STC 99, 57 TC 601, 128 Sol Jo 100, [1984] LS Gaz R 900, HL	2.05
Gulbenkian v Gulbenkian [1937] 4 All ER 618, 81 Sol Jo 1003, 158 LT 46, 54 TLR 241	7.12

H

Harrison v Harrison [1953] 1 WLR 865, 97 Sol Jo 456	7.08, 7.15
Haslope v Thorne (1813) 1 M & S 103	8.03
Hellenes (King) v Brostrom (1923) 16 Ll L Rep 167	1.04
Henderson v Henderson [1967] P 77, [1965] 1 All ER 179, [1965] 2 WLR 218, 108 Sol Jo 861	7.10
Hipperson v Newbury District Electoral Registration Officer [1985] QB 1060, [1985] 2 All ER 456, [1985] 3 WLR 61, 83 LGR 638, 129 Sol Jo 432, CA	2.08, 2.21, 8.03
Hodgson v De Beauchesne (1858) 12 Moo PCC 285, 7 WR 397, 33 LTOS 36	7.11, 7.14
Holman v Johnson (1775) 1 Cowp 341, [1775–1802] All ER Rep 98	1.04
Hood (John) & Co Ltd v Magee (Surveyor of Taxes) (1918) 7 TC 327, [1918] 2 IR 34:	6.14
Hoskins v Matthews (1856) 8 De GM & G 13, 25 LJ Ch 689, 2 Jur NS 196, 4 WR 216, 26 LTOS 210	7.13

I

Ideal Film Renting Co v Nielsen [1921] 1 Ch 575, 90 LJ Ch 429, 65 Sol Jo 379, 124 LT 749	6.01
Inchiquin (Lord) v IRC (1948) 31 TC 125, 41 R & IT 570, [1948] TR 343, CA	2.20
Indofood International Finance Ltd v JP Morgan Chase Bank NA [2006] EWCA Civ 158, [2006] STC 1195, 8 ITLR 653	6.16
IRC v Brown (1926) 11 TC 292, KBD	2.07, 4.15
IRC v Bullock [1976] 3 All ER 353, [1976] 1 WLR 1178, [1976] STC 409, 51 TC 522, [1976] TR 179, 120 Sol Jo 591, L(TC) 2598, CA	7.04, 7.11, 7.12
IRC v Cadwalader. See Cooper v Cadwalader	
IRC v Cohen (1937) 21 TC 301, KBD	7.11
IRC v Combe (1932) 17 TC 405, Ct of Sess (1 Div)	2.07, 4.14, 4.15
IRC v Duchess of Portland [1982] Ch 314, [1982] 1 All ER 784, [1982] 2 WLR 367, [1982] STC 149, 54 TC 648, [1981] TR 475, 3 FLR 293, 126 Sol Jo 49	7.07, 7.11
IRC v Fraser (1942) 24 TC 498, 21 ATC 223, 1942 SC 493, 1942 SLT 280, Ct of Sess (1 Div)	2.03
IRC v Hobhouse [1956] 3 All ER 594, [1956] 1 WLR 1393, 36 TC 648, 35 ATC 467, 50 R & IT 20, [1956] TR 347, 100 Sol Jo 818	7.16
IRC v Huni [1923] 2 KB 563, 8 TC 466, 92 LJKB 618, 67 Sol Jo 707, 129 LT 509, 39 TLR 459, KBD	8.01
IRC v Lysaght. See Lysaght v IRC	
IRC v Zorab (1926) 11 TC 289, KBD	2.07, 2.16, 4.05, 4.11
Iveagh (Earl) v Revenue Comrs [1930] IR 386, 1 ITC 316	4.14

J

Johnstone v Beattie (1843) 10 Cl & Fin 42, 7 Jur 1023, [1843-60] All ER Rep 576, 1 LTOS 250, HL	7.08
Jones' Estate, Re 182 NW 227, 192 Iowa 78 (1921), Iowa Supreme Ct	7.06

K

Kinloch v IRC (1929) 14 TC 736, KBD	2.12, 2.17
Koitaki Para Rubber Estates Ltd v Federal Comr of Taxation (1940) 64 CLR 15, [1941] ALR 125	6.15

Table of cases

PARA

L

Lawton, Re (1958) 37 ATC 216, [1958] TR 249, ChD 7.12, 7.14
Leon v Leon [1967] P 275, [1966] 3 All ER 820, [1966] 3 WLR 1164, 110 Sol Jo 546,
 PDA 7.15
Levene v IRC [1927] 2 KB 38, 96 LJKB 457, 71 Sol Jo 253, 137 LT 66, 43 TLR 337,
 CA; affd [1928] AC 217, 13 TC 486, 97 LJKB 377, [1928] All ER Rep 746, 72
 Sol Jo 270, 139 LT 1, 44 TLR 374, HL 2.02, 2.03, 2.05, 2.07, 2.08, 2.09, 2.11,
  2.12, 2.14, 2.15, 2.16, 2.17, 2.18, 2.19,
  3.01, 3.02, 3.03, 3.05, 3.06,
  3.08, 4.08, 4.15
Lloyd v Sulley (Inland Revenue Solicitor) (1884) 2 TC 37, 11 R 687, 21 SLR 482, Ct
 of Exch (1 Div) 2.08, 2.10, 4.12
LCC v A-G. See A-G v LCC
Lowenstein v De Salis (Inspector of Taxes) (1926) 10 TC 424, 161 LT Jo 235,
 KBD 2.03, 2.10, 2.18, 4.07
Lysaght v IRC [1927] 2 KB 55, 6 ATC 326, 96 LJKB 462, 71 Sol Jo 253, 137 LT 70,
 43 TLR 337, CA; revsd sub nom IRC v Lysaght [1928] AC 234, 7 ATC 69, 97
 LJKB 385, [1928] All ER Rep 575, 13 TC 511, 72 Sol Jo 270, 139 LT 6, 44 TLR
 374, HL 2.02, 2.04, 2.07, 2.09, 2.11, 2.13, 2.18,
  2.19, 2.20, 3.02, 3.04, 3.05, 4.05, 4.08

M

Mackenzie, Re [1941] Ch 69, [1940] 4 All ER 310, 19 ATC 399, 110 LJ Ch 28, 84 Sol
 Jo 670, 164 LT 375, 57 TLR 107, ChD 2.20, 3.04
Macreight, Re, Paxton v Macreight (1885) 30 Ch D 165, 55 LJ Ch 28, 33 WR 838,
 53 LT 146 . . . . 7.08
Makins v Elson (Inspector of Taxes) [1977] 1 All ER 572, [1977] 1 WLR 221, [1977]
 STC 46, 51 TC 437, [1976] TR 281, 121 Sol Jo 14, ChD 2.08, 2.10, 8.03
Marrett, Re, Chalmers v Wingfield (1887) 36 Ch D 400, 36 WR 344, [1886–90] All
 ER Rep 816, 57 LT 896, 3 TLR 707, CA 7.11, 7.12, 7.15
Martin, Re, Loustalan v Loustalan [1900] P 211, 69 LJP 75, 48 WR 509, 44 Sol Jo
 449, 82 LT 806, 16 TLR 354, CA 7.04, 7.13
Miesegaes v IRC (1957) 37 TC 493, 36 ATC 201, 50 R & IT 643, [1957] TR 231, 107
 L Jo 298, CA 2.02, 2.15, 2.20, 3.03, 3.04
Mitchell (Surveyor of Taxes) v Egyptian Hotels Ltd. See Egyptian Hotels Ltd v
 Mitchell (Surveyor of Taxes)
Mitchell v IRC (1951) 33 TC 53, 45 R & IT 493, [1951] TR 433, [1952] 1 TLR 497,
 Ct of Sess (1 Div) 2.05
Mohamed v Knott [1969] 1 QB 1, [1968] 2 All ER 563, [1968] 2 WLR 1446, 132 JP
 349, [1968] Crim LR 341, 121 Sol Jo 332, QBD 7.08
Moorhouse v Lord (1863) 10 HL Cas 272, 32 LJ Ch 295, 9 Jur NS 677, 1 New Rep
 555, 11 WR 637, 8 LT 212 . . . . 7.04, 7.12, 7.13
Munro v Munro (1840) 7 Cl & Fin 842, 7 ER 1288, HL 7.11

N

N v Inspecteur van de Belastingdienst Oost/kantoor Almelo (C-470/04) [2008] STC
 436, [2006] ECR I-7409, ECJ 9.04
Navigators and General Insurance Co Ltd v Ringrose [1962] 1 All ER 97, [1962] 1
 WLR 173, [1961] 2 Lloyd's Rep 415, 106 Sol Jo 135, CA 1.06
Neubergh v IRC [1978] STC 181, 52 TC 79, [1977] TR 263, L(TC) 2655, ChD 2.05
News Datacom Ltd & News Data Security Products Ltd v Revenue & Customs
 (2006) SpC 561, [2006] STC (SCD) 732 . . . . 6.07, 6.12, 6.14, 6.20, 8.06
Norris, Re, ex p Reynolds (1888) 5 Morr 111, 4 TLR 452, CA 3.08

P

Palmer v Maloney [1999] STC 890, 71 TC 502, [1999] BTC 357, (1999) 96(34) LSG
 34, (1999) 149 NLJ 1515, CA 4.17

Table of cases

	PARA
Patten's Goods, Re (1860) 24 JP 150, 6 Jur NS 151	7.13
Pickles v Foulsham (Inspector of Taxes) [1923] 2 KB 413, 9 TC 261; on appeal [1924] 1 KB 323, 9 TC 261, 93 LJKB 197, 68 Sol Jo 185, 130 LT 492, 40 TLR 107, CA; affd sub nom Foulsham (Inspector of Taxes) v Pickles [1925] AC 458, 94 LJKB 418, [1925] All ER Rep 706, 69 Sol Jo 411, 133 LT 5, 41 TLR 323, sub nom Pickles v Foulsham (Inspector of Taxes) 9 TC 261, HL	2.02
Pilkington v Randall (Inspector of Taxes) (1965) 42 TC 662, 44 ATC 228, [1965] TR 241, 109 Sol Jo 666; on appeal (1966) 42 TC 662, 45 ATC 32, [1966] TR 33, 110 Sol Jo 132, CA	2.03
Post Office v Estuary Radio Ltd [1968] 2 QB 740, [1967] 3 All ER 663, [1967] 1 WLR 1396, [1967] 2 Lloyd's Rep 299, 111 Sol Jo 636, CA	1.07
Potinger v Wightman (1817) 3 Mer 67, 36 ER 26, [1814-23] All ER Rep 786, Rolls Ct	7.08

Q

Qureshi v Qureshi [1972] Fam 173, [1971] 1 All ER 325, [1971] 2 WLR 518, 114 Sol Jo 908, PDA	7.12, 7.15

R

R v Barnet London Borough, ex p Shah [1982] QB 688, [1980] 3 All ER 679, [1981] 2 WLR 86, 79 LGR 210, 145 JP 50, 125 Sol Jo 64; affd [1982] QB 688, [1982] 1 All ER 698, [1982] 2 WLR 474, 80 LGR 571, 125 Sol Jo 828, CA; revsd sub nom Shah v Barnet London Borough Council [1983] 2 AC 309, [1983] 1 All ER 226, [1983] 2 WLR 16, 81 LGR 305, 127 Sol Jo 36, HL	2.07, 3.01, 3.02, 3.03, 3.04, 3.05, 3.06, 3.07, 3.12
R v Bundy [1977] 2 All ER 382, [1977] 1 WLR 914, [1977] RTR 357, 65 Cr App Rep 239, 141 JP 345, 121 Sol Jo 252, CA	2.08, 8.03
R v Hammond (1852) 17 QB 772, 16 JP 312, 21 LJQB 153, 16 Jur 194, 19 LTOS 21	2.22, 8.03
R v HM Treasury and Commissioners of Inland Revenue, ex parte Daily Mail and General Trust plc (Case 81/87) [1989] 1 QB 446, [1988] STC 787, [1989] 1 All ER 328, [1989] 2 WLR 908, [1988] BCLC 206, [1988] ECR 273, ECJ	9.04
R v Holden (Inspector of Taxes) and related appeals. See Wood v Holden (Inspector of Taxes)	
R v ICR Haulage Ltd [1944] KB 551, [1944] 1 All ER 691, 42 LGR 226, 30 Cr App Rep 31, 108 JP 181, 113 LJKB 492, 171 LT 180, 60 TLR 399, CCA	6.01
R v IRC, ex p Commerzbank AG: C-330/91 [1994] QB 219, [1993] 4 All ER 37, [1994] 2 WLR 128, [1993] ECR I-4017, [1993] 3 CMLR 457, [1993] STC 605, (1995) 68 TC 252, ECJ	9.03
R v IRC ex parte Fulford-Dobson [1987] QB 978, [1987] 3 WLR 227, [1987] STC 334, (1987) 131 SJ 975, (1987) 84 LS Gaz 2197, QBD	1.26
R v IRC ex parte Wilkinson [2005] UKHL 30, [2006] STC 270, [2006] 1 All ER 529, 77 TC 78, HL	1.26
R v J G Hammond & Co Ltd [1914] 2 KB 866, 83 LJKB 1221, 58 Sol Jo 513, 111 LT 206, 30 TLR 491, DC	6.01
R v Kent Justices, ex p Lye [1967] 2 QB 153, [1967] 1 All ER 560, [1967] 2 WLR 765, 131 JP 212, sub nom R v St Augustine, Kent, Justices, ex p Lye [1967] 1 Lloyd's Rep 154, 110 Sol Jo 979	1.07
R v Secretary of State for the Home Department, ex p Margueritte [1983] QB 180, [1982] 3 All ER 909, [1982] 3 WLR 754, 126 Sol Jo 641, CA	3.07
R v Waltham Forest London Borough Council, ex p Vale (1985) Times, 25 February	3.04, 3.09, 3.12
Raffenel's Goods, Re (1863) 32 LJPM & A 203, 9 Jur NS 386, 1 New Rep 569, 3 Sw & Tr 49, 11 WR 549, 8 LT 211	7.15
Ramsay v Liverpool Royal Infirmary. See Bowie (or Ramsay) v Liverpool Royal Infirmary	

Table of cases

PARA

Reed (Inspector of Taxes) v Clark [1986] Ch 1, [1985] 3 WLR 142, [1985] STC 323,
    58 TC 528, 129 Sol Jo 469, [1985] LS Gaz R 2016, ChD 1.26, 2.03, 2.07, 3.05,
                                                                                          3.06, 3.09, 4.14, 4.15
Regazzoni v K C Sethia (1944) Ltd [1958] AC 301, [1957] 3 All ER 286, [1957] 3
    WLR 752, [1957] 2 Lloyd's Rep 289, 101 Sol Jo 848, HL 1.04
Reid v IRC (1926) 10 TC 673, 5 ATC 357, 1926 SC 589, 1926 SLT 365, Ct of Sess (1
    Div) . . . .
                                           2.11, 2.16, 2.17, 2.18, 2.19, 3.02, 3.03, 3.05, 3.08
Robson v Dixon (Inspector of Taxes) [1972] 3 All ER 671, [1972] 1 WLR 1493, 48
    TC 527, 51 ATC 179, [1972] TR 163, 116 Sol Jo 863 . . . . 4.19, 4.20
Rogers v IRC (1879) 1 TC 225, Ct of Exch (1 Div) 4.14

S

Salomon v A Salomon & Co Ltd [1897] AC 22, 66 LJ Ch 35, 4 Mans 89, 45 WR 193,
    [1895–9] All ER Rep 33, 41 Sol Jo 63, 75 LT 426, 13 TLR 46, HL 6.01
Sawyers, Re, ex p Blain (1879) 12 Ch D 522, [1874–80] All ER Rep 708, CA 1.03
Scullard, Re, Smith v Brock [1957] Ch 107, [1956] 3 All ER 898, [1956] 3 WLR 1060,
    100 Sol Jo 928 . . . .   7.07
Shah v Barnet London Borough Council. See R v Barnet London Borough, ex p
    Shah
Sharpe v Crispin (1869) LR 1 P & D 611, 38 LJP & M 17, 17 WR 368, 20 LT 41:   7.09, 7.13
Shekleton v Shekleton [1972] 2 NSWR 675 . . . .   7.08
Shepherd v Revenue and Customs Comrs (2005)Sp C 484, [2005] STC (SCD) 644;
    [2006] EWHC 1512 (Ch), [2006] STC 1821 . . . . 1.18, 1.26, 2.07, 2.10, 2.12, 4.14
Smidth (F L) & Co v Greenwood (Surveyor of Taxes) [1921] 3 KB 583, 8 TC 193, 37
    TLR 949, CA; affd sub nom Greenwood (Surveyor of Taxes) v F L Smidth &
    Co [1922] 1 AC 417, 8 TC 193, 91 LJKB 349, 66 Sol Jo 349, 127 LT 68, 38 TLR
    421, HL 4.18
Squirrell v Revenue and Customs (2005) Sp C 493, [2005] STC (SCD) 717 . . . .   2.22
Stanley v Bernes (1830) 3 Hag Ecc 373, 162 ER 1190 . . . .   7.11
Stanley (Surveyor of Taxes) v Gramophone and Typewriter Ltd. See Gramophone
    and Typewriter Ltd v Stanley (Surveyor of Taxes)
Steer, Re (1858) 3 H & N 594, 28 LJ Ex 22, 32 LTOS 130 . . . . 7.12, 7.14
Steiner v IRC [1973] STC 547, 49 TC 13, 52 ATC 224, [1973] TR 177, CA 7.13
Sulley v A-G (1860) 2 TC 149, 24 JP 676, 5 H & N 711, 29 LJ Ex 464, 6 Jur NS 1018,
    8 WR 472, 2 LT 439 . . . .   4.18
Surveyor v IRC (2002) Sp C 339 . . . .   7.01
Swedish Central Rly Co Ltd v Thompson (Inspector of Taxes) [1925] AC 495, 9 TC
    342, 4 ATC 163, 94 LJKB 527, [1924] All ER Rep 710, 133 LT 97, 41 TLR 385,
    HL 6.12, 6.15

T

Tee v Tee [1973] 3 All ER 1105, [1974] 1 WLR 213, 118 Sol Jo 116, CA 7.15
Thomson v Bensted (Surveyor of Taxes) (1918) 7 TC 137, Ct of Sess (2 Div) 2.05, 2.10
Thomson v Minister of National Revenue [1946] SCR 209, [1946] 1 DLR 689, [1946]
    CTC 51 . . . .   2.02
Todd (Inspector of Taxes) v Egyptian Delta Land and Investment Co Ltd [1928] 1
    KB 152, 14 TC 119, 6 ATC 33, 96 LJKB 554, 136 LT 786, 43 TLR 275, CA;
    revsd sub nom Egyptian Delta Land and Investment Co Ltd v Todd (Inspector
    of Taxes) [1929] AC 1, 14 TC 119, 7 ATC 355, 98 LJKB 1, 72 Sol Jo 545, 140 LT
    50, 44 TLR747, HL 2.04, 2.20, 6.12, 6.15, 6.17
Travers v Holley [1953] P 246, [1953] 2 All ER 794, [1953] 3 WLR 507, 97 Sol Jo 555,
    CA 7.04
Trevor Smallwood Trust, Re; Smallwood and another v IRC (2008) Sp C 669, [2008]
    STC (SCD) 629 . . . . 5.06, 6.16
Trustees of Wensleydale's Settlement v IR Commissioners (1996) Sp C 73 . . . .   5.06
Turnbull v Foster (Surveyor of Taxes) (1904) 6 TC 206, Exch Ct (2 Div) 4.14

Table of cases

PARA

U

Udny v Udny (1869) LR 1 Sc & Div 441, 7 Macq 89, HL 7.04, 7.05, 7.06, 7.10, 7.11, 7.12, 7.13, 7.15
Union Corpn Ltd v IRC [1951] WN 448, 34 TC 207, 44 R & IT 560, [1951] TR 271, 95 Sol Jo 484, [1951] 2 TLR 582; on appeal [1952] 1 All ER 646, 34 TC 207, 31 ATC 99, 45 R & IT 189, [1952] TR 69, 96 Sol Jo 150, [1952] 1 TLR 651, CA; affd [1953] AC 482, [1953] 1 All ER 729, [1953] 2 WLR 615, 34 TC 207, 32 ATC 73, 46 R & IT 190, [1953] TR 61, 97 Sol Jo 206, HL 6.15
Unit Construction Co Ltd v Bullock (Inspector of Taxes). See Bullock (Inspector of Taxes) v Unit Construction Co Ltd
University College London v Newman (1986) Times, 8 January, CA 3.05, 3.08
Untelrab Ltd & Ors v McGregor (1995) Sp C 55 .... 6.04, 6.08, 8.06

W

Wahl v A-G [1932] All ER Rep 922, 147 LT 382, HL 7.14
Werle & Co v Colquhoun (1888) 20 QBD 753, 2 TC 402, 52 JP 644, 57 LJQB 323, 36 WR 613, 58 LT 756, 4 TLR 396, CA 4.18
Whicker v Hume (1858) 22 JP 591, 7 HL Cas 124, 28 LJ Ch 396, 4 Jur NS 933, 6 WR 813, [1843-60] All ER Rep 450, 31 LTOS 319 .... 7.04, 7.12
Whitney v IRC [1924] 2 KB 602, 10 TC 88, 93 LJKB 833, 68 Sol Jo 735, 131 LT 813, 40 TLR 705, CA; affd [1926] AC 37, 10 TC 88, 95 LJKB 165, 134 LT 98, 42 TLR 58, HL 8.01
Wilkie v IRC [1952] Ch 153, [1952] 1 All ER 92, 32 TC 495, 31 ATC 442, 45 R & IT 29, [1951] TR 371, 95 Sol Jo 817, [1952] 1 TLR 22, L(TC) 1565, ChD 4.08, 4.09
Winans v A-G [1904] AC 287, 73 LJKB 613, [1904-7] All ER Rep 410, 90 LT 721, 20 TLR 510, HL 7.14, 7.15
Withers (Inspector of Taxes) v Wynyard (1938) 21 TC 724, 82 Sol Jo 274, KBD .. 2.19, 4.06
Wood v Holden (Inspector of Taxes) sub nom R v Holden (Inspector of Taxes) [2006] EWCA Civ 26, [2006] STC 443, [2006] 1 WLR 1393, [2006] BTC 208, 8 ITL Rep 468, [2006] STI 236, (2006) 150 SJLB 127, (2006) Times, 20 February, CA; [2005] EWHC 547 (Ch), [2005] STC 789, ChD; sub nom R v Holden (Inspector of Taxes) and related appeals SpC 422, (2004) [2004] STC (SCD) 416 .... 6.04, 6.06, 6.08, 6.11, 6.13, 6.14, 6.16

Y

Young, Re (1875) 1 TC 57, Exch Ct 2.07

Z

Zanelli v Zanelli [1948] WN 381, 92 Sol Jo 646, 64 TLR 556, CA 7.15

Decisions of the European Court of Justice are listed below numerically. These decisions are also included in the preceding alphabetical list.

152/73: Giovanni Maria Sotgiu v Deutsche Bundespost [1974] ECR 153, ECJ ... 9.02, 9.03
270/83: EC Commission v France [1986] ECR 273, [1987]1 CMLR 401, ECJ 9.03
81/87: R v HM Treasury and Commissioners of Inland Revenue, ex parte Daily Mail and General Trust plc [1989] 1 QB 446, [1988] STC 787, [1989] 1 All ER 328, [1989] 2 WLR 908, [1988] BCLC 206, [1988] ECR 273, ECJ 9.04
C-175/88: Biehl v Administration des Contributions du Grand-Duché de Luxembourg [1990] ECR I-1779, [1990] 3 CMLR 143, [1991] STC 575, ECJ .. 9.02
C-330/91: R v IRC, ex p Commerzbank AG [1994] QB 219, [1993] 4 All ER 37, [1994] 2 WLR 128, [1993] ECR I-4017, [1993] 3 CMLR 457, [1993] STC 605, ECJ; affd (1995) 68 TC 252 .... 9.03

Table of cases

	PARA
C-279/93: Finanzamt Köln-Altstadt v Schumacker [1996] QB 28, [1995] All ER (EC) 319, [1995] 3 WLR 498, [1995] ECR I-225, [1996] 2 CMLR 450, [1995] STC 306, ECJ	9.02
C-9/02: de Lasteyrie du Saillant v Ministère de l'Economie, des Finances et de l'Industrie [2004] ECR I-2409, ECJ	9.04
C-470/04: N v Inspecteur van de Belastingdienst Oost/kantoor Almelo [2008] STC 436, [2006] ECR I-7409, ECJ	9.04

ABBREVIATIONS

CPR	Civil Procedure Rules
DMPA 1973	Domicile and Matrimonial Proceedings Act 1973
FA	Finance Act
HMRC	Her Majesty's Revenue and Customs
ICTA 1970	Income and Corporation Taxes Act 1970
ICTA 1988	Income and Corporation Taxes Act 1988
IHTA 1984	Inheritance Tax Act 1984
IR	Inland Revenue
ITA 1918	Income Tax Act 1918
ITA 2007	Income Tax Act 2007
ITEPA 2003	Income Tax (Earnings and Pensions) Act 2003
ITTOIA 2005	Income Tax (Trading and Other Income) Act 2005
OECD	Organisation for Economic Co-operation and Development
PCTA 1968	Provisional Collection of Taxes Act 1968
TCGA 1992	Taxation and Chargeable Gains Act 1992
TMA 1970	Taxes Management Act 1970

CHAPTER 1

United Kingdom taxation

> *I am a stranger and a sojourner with you*
> Genesis ch 23 v 4

1.01 State practice in exercising taxing jurisdiction

In the field of direct taxation, state practice in exercising taxing jurisdiction universally recognises that either the person subject to taxation, or the item of income (or gain), that is the object of taxation, must be within the territory of the taxing state. Taxation by the country of the source of the income is often described as 'limited taxation', in that the liability is limited to income (and gains) from sources within that state's territory. 'Unlimited liability', on the other hand, applies to persons whose personal connection, typically residence, is within the state's territory, because the liability is in respect of income (or gains) regardless of where they arise.[1]

Most states adopt a single factor connecting persons with their territory, namely residence. The UK has long adopted a more nuanced approach in relation to individuals, applying instead several connecting factors: residence, ordinary residence, domicile and nationality. In general, the more connected the person is to the UK, the greater the exposure to UK taxation. This approach, has contributed to, and is a product of, an open economy, a diverse and tolerant society and a central position as a leading centre of international commerce, finance and creativity.

---

[1] For a recent examination of these issues worldwide see, 'Source and residence: new configuration of their principles' *Cahiers de droit international*, Vol 90a (International Fiscal Association, 2005).

Questions of sovereignty

1.02 The right to levy tax

It was 1199 when King John began to convert the elaborate and well-ordered fiscal system he had inherited from Henry I and Henry II into an instrument of arbitrary and merciless extortion, but it was not until 15 June 1215 that 'in a Thames-side meadow called Runnymede, ... the taxpayers ... combined to control the tax-imposer'[1] by forcing the monarch to set his seal to Magna Carta. Clause 12 of the charter provided that 'no scutage or aid shall be imposed in our Kingdom unless by the Common Council of our Realm' but, even then, the control was incomplete. In the fourteenth century, Edward III imposed massive taxation to finance his long war with France and the price of the people's consent to such taxation was that future taxation would be conditional on the 'common consent of prelates, earls, barons and other lords and commons of the realm'.[2]

Although this was 'a major step on the road to parliamentary control of taxation',[3] it was not until 1689 that the prerogative rights of the British monarchy were finally and completely abrogated in that regard. In 1681, Charles II had dissolved the Parliament and begun to rule absolutely. In 1685, he was succeeded by his brother James II and, in 1689, upon the accession to the throne of William and Mary, Parliament secured the passing of the Bill of Rights which vouchsafed for it ultimate supremacy. Ever since then, the British monarch has reigned but not ruled, so that today, just as in 1689, 'levying moneys for or to the use of the Crowne by pretence of prerogative without grant of Parlyament ... is illegal'.[4]

In recent years, as the sophistication, complexity and volume of tax legislation has grown, concerns have been expressed about the reality of Parliamentary control. A 2005 International Monetary Fund working paper found that the UK had some of the weakest powers in the world for budget scrutiny. The Tax Law Review Committee of the Institute for Fiscal Studies said in 2003, 'The truth of the matter is that the House of Commons has neither the time nor the expertise nor, apparently the inclination, to undertake any systematic or effective examination of whatever tax rules the government of the day places before it for approval.' A Confederation of British Industry task force report in 2008 concluded, 'it would not be unreasonable to say... there is no genuine scrutiny of the finance bill under the present system.' To illustrate, Schedule 7 to the Finance Act 2008 (the Remittance Basis) is some 50 pages in lengh and had 135 Government amendments introduced at the committee stage but received the attention of the Public Bills Committee for less than an full day.

---

1 Arthur Bryant, *Set in a Silver Sea* (Collins) pp 130–132.
2 Bryant, p 226.
3 Bryant, p 226.
4 Bill of Rights 1688.

1.03 Jurisdictional limitations

It is a matter of constitutional law that, because the sovereign power of Parliament is absolute, unless Parliament chooses voluntarily to abrogate its powers,[1] it may legislate contrary to the requirements of international law, for 'international law ... yields to statute'[2] and, 'if the language of the statute is clear, it must be followed notwithstanding the conflict between municipal and international law which results'.[3]

The primary characteristic of law is that it is enforceable by sanction (ie fine, suspension of rights, imprisonment, etc). Before a court may order enforcement, however, it must be competent to hear and determine the alleged non-compliance, and, in the English courts, such competence rests solely on whether a claim has been served on the defendant in person. This – following from the fact that a writ is essentially an assertion of sovereignty and that sovereignty itself is territorial – gives rise to the

> '... broad general universal proposition that English legislation ... is applicable only to English subjects or to foreigners who by coming into this country, whether for a long or a short time, have made themselves during that time subject to English jurisdiction.'[4]

It may, at this point, be objected that the court has, in fact, power to go beyond the common law principle described and, in certain circumstances, to enlarge its jurisdiction by summoning absent defendants – even foreign ones – under the Rules of the Supreme Court. This is so, but – as the court's discretionary power may be exercised only in specific cases, none of which can conceivably be so construed as to embrace the enforcement of a UK tax liability against foreigners who have no connection with the UK – the court's jurisdiction remains nonetheless limited by common law principles in relation to the matters with which this book is concerned.

---

1 As, for example, when, on 1 January 1973, Britain acceded to the Treaty of Rome and became bound, as a European Community Member State, by certain Community legislation.
2 *Cheney v Conn* (1967) 44 TC 217 at 221, per Ungoed-Thomas J.
3 *Maxwell on the Interpretation of Statutes* (12th edn) p 183.
4 *Re Sawyers, ex p Blain* [1874–80] All ER Rep 708 at 710, per James LJ.

1.04 Enforcement overseas

Although the requirement of service of process on a defendant personally may prevent an action for the recovery of taxes from a person abroad being brought before an English court, what is to prevent such an action being brought before the court of the foreign state in which that person is present and being heard there in accordance with the principles of international law? The short answer is simply that 'it is the practice of nations not to enforce the fiscal legislation of other nations'.[1]

The principle on which this practice is based emerged over two centuries ago when, in upholding a French individual's claim for the purchase moneys due in respect of goods which were to be smuggled into England by their purchaser in violation of English revenue laws, Lord Mansfield enunciated the proposition that 'no country ever takes notice of the revenue laws of another'.[2] Stated thus, the proposition may be too wide – and may, indeed, no longer even be of application in the circumstances

1.04 *United Kingdom taxation*

with which Lord Mansfield was concerned.[3] What may be said, however, is that:

> '... a foreign government cannot come here – nor will the Courts of other countries allow our government to go there – and sue a person found in that jurisdiction for taxes levied and which he is declared to be liable to by the country to which he belongs.'[4]

The rationale behind the principle thus stated is that:

> '... a claim for taxes is but an extension of the sovereign power which imposed the taxes, and ... an assertion of sovereign authority by one State within the territory of another ... is (treaty or convention apart) contrary to all concepts of independent sovereignties.'[5]

Were the payment of tax a contractual obligation, the situation would, of course, be different and the contract would be not only recognised but enforced if necessary by the courts of a foreign state in accordance with the principles of private international law. Tax collection is, however, 'not a matter of contract, but of authority and administration as between the State and those within its jurisdiction'.[6] Accordingly, foreign courts will not entertain a suit for the direct or indirect[7] enforcement of UK revenue laws and, this being so, the limitation implicitly imposed on the legislature's legislative power by the principle of action *in personam* cannot be circumvented (at least so far as revenue laws are concerned) by recourse to a foreign forum.

This principle is now increasingly limited by European Community law and international treaties. The EC Mutual Assisitance in Recovery of Taxes Directive[8] reguires Member States to collect unpaid taxes of all kinds on behalf of each other. Authority to extend this assistance beyond the European Union by treaty has existed since 2006.[9] In 2007 the UK signed the Multilateral OECD/Council of Europe Convention on Mutual Assistance in Tax Matters, which, likewise, facilitates collection of taxes by one signatory state for the others.[10] The UK has also started to include such provisions in its bilateral tax treaties.[11]

---

1 *Clark v Oceanic Contractors Inc* [1983] STC 35 at 41, per Lord Scarman.
2 *Holman v Johnson* (1775) 1 Cowp 341.
3 In *Regazzoni v K C Sethia (1944) Ltd* [1957] 3 All ER 286 at 292, Viscount Simonds said: 'It does not follow from the fact that today the court will not enforce a revenue law at the suit of a foreign state that today it will enforce a contract which requires the doing of an act in a foreign country which violates the Revenue laws of that country.'
4 *King of the Hellenes v Brostrom* (1923) 16 Ll L Rep 167, per Rowlatt J.
5 *Government of India v Taylor* [1955] 1 All ER 292, per Lord Keith of Avonholm.
6 *Government of India v Taylor* [1955] 1 All ER 292, per Lord Somervell of Harrow.
7 In *Peter Buchanan Ltd and Macharg v McVey* [1954] IR 89, the director of a Scottish company made a deal with the Inland Revenue on which the Revenue authorities subsequently reneged. The director promptly stripped the company of its assets and removed them – along with his private assets and himself – to the Republic of Ireland where he proceeded to 'snap his hands in the face of the disgruntled Scottish Revenue'. The Inland Revenue, realising that a direct attempt to recover taxes through the courts of Eire would fail, attempted to do so indirectly by suing the director on the grounds that he

had acted in breach of his duties as a director. The court looked beyond the action, however, and, seeing that it was no more than an indirect attempt to enforce UK revenue laws in the Republic of Ireland, dismissed it.
8 Directive 2008/55/EC (repeals and replaces Directive 76/308/EEC) on mutual assistance for the recovery of claims relating to certain levies, duties, taxes and other measures; implemented in the UK by FA 2002 s 134 and Sch 39.
9 FA 2006 ss 173–176.
10 OECD/Council of Europe Convention on Mutual Assistance in Tax Matters signed by the UK on 24 May 2007.
11 See Protocol of 7 November 2007 to United Kingdom-New Zealand Double Taxation Convention of 4 August 1983 (SI 1984/365 as amended).

1.05 Territorial limits

In interpreting a Parliamentary enactment, however, the courts have been committed to carrying the principle of territorial sovereignty no further than they need. Almost a century ago, Lord Esher MR expressed his conviction that:

> 'Parliament ought not to deal in any way, either by regulation or otherwise, directly or indirectly, with any foreign matter or person which is outside the jurisdiction of our Parliament, and ... the Courts ought always to construe ... general words to apply only to the person or thing which will answer the description in them, but which person or thing is also within the jurisdiction of our Parliament.'[1]

Those same sentiments have been echoed by Lord Asquith, who was adamant that:

> '... an Act of the Imperial Parliament today, unless it provides otherwise, applies ... to nothing outside the United Kingdom: not even to the Channel Islands or the Isle of Man, let alone a remote overseas colony or possession.'[2]

In the context of taxation, in *Clark v Oceanic Contractors Inc*[3], the House of Lords held that, because Oceanic, a non-resident company, had an address for service in the UK and carried out operations in the designated areas of the North Sea (the profits of which were to be treated under FA 1973 s 38(4) as profits from a trade carried on by it in the UK and, as such, to be liable to corporation tax,, it had a trading presence in the UK and that such a trading presence was sufficient to impose an obligation on the company to operate a PAYE scheme for the collection of tax in respect of emoluments chargeable to tax under Schedule E.

Lord Scarman also noted in that case that 'the principle is a rule of construction only' and that 'British tax liability has never been exclusively limited to British subjects and foreigners resident within the jurisdiction'. Lord Wilberforce[4] referred to the 'territorial principle' as being 'really a rule of construction of statutes expressed in general terms'.

On the other hand in *Agassi v Robinson (HM Inspector of Taxes)*[5], a non-resident company, set up by the famous tennis star, entered into endorsement contracts with two manufacturers of sports clothing and

1.05 *United Kingdom taxation*

equipment, neither of which was resident or had a tax presence in the UK. The company received payments abroad from the manufacturers pursuant to the contracts. The House of Lords by a majority concluded that the foreign entertainers' tax applied to the payments as a matter of legislative intendment.

1 *Colquhoun v Heddon* (1890) 2 TC 621 at 626.
2 *A-G for the Province of Alberta v Huggard Assets Ltd* [1953] 2 All ER 951.
3 [1983] STC 35.
4 At p 427; 152.
5 [2006] UKHL 23.

Questions of territory

1.06 The territory of the UK

The UK has three constituent units, each subject to the ultimate sovereignty of the common Parliament at Westminster. The three units are England and Wales, Scotland, and Northern Ireland. Legislation has now been passed which establishes a Parliament for Scotland with powers of primary legislation in some areas, including a limited power to vary income tax; a National Assembly for Wales which has, jointly with Westminster, some powers of primary legislation; and an Assembly for Northern Ireland with powers of legislation in certain areas.[1] England, Wales and Scotland are described collectively as Great Britain,[2] and the UK consists of Great Britain and Northern Ireland.[3] The Isle of Man and the islands of Jersey, Guernsey, Alderney, Sark, Herm and Jethou (ie the Channel Islands) are British Isles outside the UK[4] and have their own systems of private law and taxation.

1 Scotland Act 1998, Government of Wales Acts 1998 and 2006, and Northern Ireland Act 1998.
2 Royal and Parliamentary Titles Act 1927.
3 Interpretation Act 1978 s 5 and Sch 1.
4 As to the Channel Islands not being part of the UK, see *Navigators and General Insurance Co Ltd v Ringrose* [1962] 1 All ER 97.

1.07 The territorial waters

In addition to the land mass described at **1.06** above, the UK includes territorial waters. These include internal waters such as rivers, lakes and the area of sea which lies upon the landward side of the low-water line along the coast (including the coast of all islands and low-tide elevations comprised in the territory) or, in the case of a bay, the area of sea which lies on the landward side of a straight line (not more than 24 miles in length) joining the low-water lines of the natural entrance points of the bay.[1] They include also the territorial sea which consists of those parts of the sea over which the UK's sovereignty is subject to the right of innocent passage by foreign ships[2] being any part of the open sea which lies within one marine league[3] on the seaward side of the base-line from which the areas of internal waters are determined.[4]

The relevance of territorial waters in the context of revenue law may not be immediately obvious. As we shall see, however, the precise time at which a person leaves the UK may be critical in the context of the establishment of non-resident tax status,[5] and that time is the time at which a person moves out of the UK's territorial waters (or out of the air space above them).

Another possible area of application is suggested by two cases brought by the Post Office under the Wireless Telegraphy Act 1949 s 14(7) against a so-called 'pirate' radio station in the Thames estuary. The defendants, who operated from Red Sands Tower, a structure which rests on the seabed more than three nautical miles from the nearest low-water lines of the Kent and Essex coasts, contended that their operations were performed on the high seas outside the UK's territorial waters and that they did not, therefore, come within the UK's jurisdiction. It was held, however, that the Red Sands Tower lies within the bay contained by a straight line drawn between the Naze and Foreness Point (the natural entrance points of that coastal indentation which forms part of the Thames estuary) and is accordingly within the internal waters of the UK.[6] Had Estuary Radio Ltd sought to escape UK taxation on the grounds advanced in its defence, it would, it seems, have been bound to fail for identical reasons.

It is worth noting that one of the questions raised in the cases described was whether or not the jurisdiction of a magistrates' court could extend over an area of territorial water. As the territorial waters in question adjoined the county of Kent, it was held that the Kent justices did indeed have jurisdiction. On the same premise, therefore, it seems clear that, where matters of revenue law are concerned in relation to persons or sources of income or gains within territorial waters, the General Commissioners (whose function is similar in connection with revenue law to that of the justices in connection with criminal law) appointed for the adjoining tax division will have jurisdiction to the same extent as they would have jurisdiction were the person or source located on the area of land contained within that division.

---

1 Territorial Waters Order in Council 1964, arts 2–5.
2 Convention on the Territorial Sea and Contiguous Zone, Cmnd 2511, art 11.
3 Ie three nautical miles.
4 Territorial Waters Jurisdiction Act 1878 s 7.
5 See **4.08** below. See also **7.16** below in relation to domicile.
6 *Post Office v Estuary Radio Ltd* [1967] 1 WLR 1396 and *R v Kent Justices, ex p Lye* [1967] 2 WLR 765.

1.08 Territorial extension

Although Parliament is not, for all the reasons stated thus far, presumed to generally legislate beyond the limits of the territory over which it has sovereignty, there is nothing to prevent it so doing if the inhibiting constraints of international law are removed by international treaty. This will, of course, happen only rarely, but one instance of its occurrence may be cited.

In 1958, the Geneva Convention on the Continental Shelf[1] secured agreement at international level concerning exploration or exploitation rights in relation to all resources in the seabed and subsoil of the North Sea continental shelf. Certain of that Convention's provisions were brought within the municipal law of the UK[2] by the Continental Shelf Act 1964 and that Act provided that areas of the continental shelf outside the UK's territorial waters[3] might be designated by Order in Council[3] as areas within which the UK might exercise rights of exploration and exploitation.[4] The Act recognised that any areas so designated would not thereby become part of the UK[5] and, implicitly, that the sovereignty of Parliament would not extend to them.

Once the Order in Council had been made, however, Parliament decided to extend its revenue legislation so as to bring within the scope of the Taxes Acts any profits or gains from exploration or exploitation activities carried on in the designated areas. This territorial extension of the charge to tax was achieved by the Finance Act 1973.[6]

1 29 April 1958.
2 See **1.07** above.
3 Orders have been made in relation to the sea around the Orkneys and Shetlands, the sea west and north-west of the Shetlands, the sea off the west coast of Scotland, the Irish Sea, St George's Channel, the Bristol Channel, the sea south of Cornwall, the south-western approaches to the English Channel, the English Channel, the North Sea and the southern North Sea.
4 Continental Shelf Act 1964 s 1(7).
5 Continental Shelf Act 1964 s 1(1).
6 FA 1973 Sch 15.

1.09 The European Community

On 1 January 1973, the UK acceded to the Treaty of Rome which had come into effect on 1 January 1959 and had provided for the establishment of a European Economic Community. While the European Community does not have a specific jurisdiction over direct taxation, EC law places limitations on the freedom of action of Member States in the field of direct taxation as a consequence of the duty of Member States to conform to the requirements of EC law.

There is an increasing number of cases going to the European Court of Justice over recent years, where taxpayers resident within a Member State have sought to challenge a Member State's residence-based rules on the ground that they are alleged to infringe the prohibitions in EU law against discrimination on grounds of nationality or the fundamental freedoms conferred by Community law. Chapter 9 below considers jurisprudence of the European Court in this regard in relation to residence.

Determinants of chargeability

1.10 Residence

Residence is the central pillar of personal taxing jurisdiction in the UK. It is the common thread found in relation to all taxes identifed in this work. It is applied to natural persons (individuals), legal persons (companies) and notional persons (trusts or settlements). Despite this centrality, there is no proper statutory definition of residenceas such for individuals or companies. The task of giving meaning to the expression has been largely left to the courts,with legislation addressing only limited issues.

This may be contrasted with the position in relation to Scotland, the only country within the UK that has an element of autonomy in relation to income tax. The expression 'Scottish taxpayer'[1] is used rather than 'Scottish resident' although the defintion bears the hallmarks of residence:

'75. Scottish taxpayers.—
(1) For the purposes of this Part a person is a Scottish taxpayer in relation to any year of assessment if—
    (a) he is an individual who, for income tax purposes, is treated as resident in the UK in that year, and
    (b) Scotland is the part of the UK with which he has the closest connection during that year.
(2) For the purposes of this section an individual who is treated for income tax purposes as resident in the UK in any year of assessment has his closest connection with Scotland during that year if, but only if, one or more of the following paragraphs applies in his case—
    (a) he is an individual to whom subsection (3) applies for that year,
    (b) the number of days which he spends in Scotland in that year is equal to or exceeds the number of days in that year which he spends elsewhere in the United Kingdom,
    (c) he is an individual who, for the whole or any part of that year, is a member of Parliament for a constituency in Scotland, a member of the European Parliament for Scotland or a member of the Scottish Parliament.
(3) This subsection applies to an individual for a year of assessment if—
    (a) he spends at least a part of that year in Scotland,
    (b) for at least a part of the time that he spends in Scotland in that year, his principal UK home is located in Scotland and he makes use of it as a place of residence, and
    (c) the times in that year when Scotland is where his principal UK home is located comprise (in aggregate) at least as much of that year as the times (if any) in that year when the location of his principal UK home is not in Scotland.
(4) For the purposes of this section—
    (a) an individual spends a day in Scotland if, but only if, he is in Scotland at the end of that day, and
    (b) an individual spends a day elsewhere in the UK if, but only if, he is in the UK at the end of that day and it is not a day that he spends in Scotland.
(5) For the purposes of this section an individual's principal UK home at any time is located in Scotland if at that time—

(a) he is an individual with a place of residence in Scotland, and
(b) in the case of an individual with two or more places of residence in the United Kingdom, Scotland is the location of such one of those places as at that time is his main place of residence in the United Kingdom.
(6) In this section 'place' includes a place on board a vessel or other means of transport.'

While, these Scottish tests raise issues of interpretation, the legislation does at least attempt an all embracing defintion. Residence of individuals in the international context is analysed in Chapter 2, of trusts in Chapter 5 and of companies in Chapter 6.

1 Scotland Act 1998

1.11 Ordinary residence

Ordinary residence only applies to individuals for the purposes of income tax, capital gains tax and national insurance contributions. In some cases it serves to extend taxing jurisdiction. Liability to capital gains tax arises even where the individual, though not resident, is ordinarily resident in the UK.[1] In other cases it may limit taxing jurusdiction. The anti-avoidance provisions of ITA 2007 relating to transfers of assets only apply to individuals ordinarily resident in the UK.[2] It has an uneasy relationship with simple residence, requiring as it does a degree of settled purpose. Ordinary residence is considered in Chapter 3.

1 TCGA 1992 s 2.
2 ITA 2007 Pt 13 Ch 2.

1.12 Domicile

Domicile is frequently used to identify the personal law applicable to an individual. It may be described as the country in which the person has his (to use a neutral term) 'permanent home'. It is universally recognised that, though a person may change his shores, this personal law remains the same – except in certain extreme circumstances.

Questions of status and succession are determined according to the law of the domicile and it has been adopted as the criterion for determining the chargeability of a person to inheritance tax on a worldwide basis. The use of this ultimate, long-term connecting factor as a determinant of liability to income tax and capital gains tax has been a key factor in making the UK attractive to foreigners as a place to live and work. It has been widely regarded as an important contributor to the success of the UK, and London in particular, as the centre of international trade finance, investment, and of artistic and scientific creativity. The scope of domicile as a determining factor for tax purposes has been dramatically narrowed by the Finance Act 2008, Schedule 7. Only time will tell if the restriction the remittance basis for longer-term non-domiciled residents wealthy enough to pay the £30,000 minimum tax on foreign income and related measures will result in the fairer tax system its advocates claim, or, be seen as a hubristic tax grab aimed at income and gains tenuously linked to the UK by the territoriality principle. The concept of domicile is examined in Chapter 7.

1.13 Nationality

Nationality now has only a modest impact on taxing jurisdiction. As from the tax year 2005–06 and subsequent years and in consequence of the tax law rewrite project as explained at **1.20** below, the citizenship conditions which were contained in ICTA 1988 s 65(4), limiting the remittance basis for individuals resident but not ordinarily resident to Commonwealth or Irish citizens, have been removed so that any person who is resident but not ordinarily resident in the UK is entitled to claim to be taxable on the remittance basis as described in Finance Act 2008 Schedule 7[1]

---

1 ITTOIA 2005 s 832.

1.14 Sources of rules

The present system has over the years become increasingly complex and outcomes less certain. The three factors of residence, ordinary residence and domicile can, as this work bears witness, make the determination of an individual's liability and claim to relief a difficult and time-consuming matter.

Although all authority to tax must come from Parliament, the tax statutes offer only the most modest guidance on the meaning of the affiliation factors. The law on residence is an amalgam of a small amount of statute law and case law dating mostly from the early twentieth century. Domicile is largely a common law concept overlayed by brief statutory provisions. HMRC practice has historicaly played a central part in addressing these questions. Earlier editions of this work treated published guidelines as an integral part of the law in this area. Recent decisions of the Special Commissioners illustrate that the law and HMRC published practice are parallel regimes. The guidelines, the latest of which were published in 2008,[1] do not have the force of law, but a taxpayer ignores the guidelines at his peril.

Application of HMRC guidance and its relationship with the legal position has itself become a complex issue.[2]

---

1 HMRC Booklet IR20 (July 2008); see **Appendix 1** below.
2 See **1.26** below.

1.15 The remittance basis

Some individuals are charged to income tax and capital gains tax on certain kinds of income and gains on the remittance basis; tax liability is charged only on the income and gains which are remitted to the UK. Usually the remittance basis applies where the income or gains arise outside the UK and where the individuals are not domiciled and in some cases not ordinarily resident in the UK. The remittance basis dates from 1803 and remained largely unchanged over the last 90 years. The meaning of remittance is now the subject of detailed and lengthy statutory provisions introduced by Finance Act 2008, Schedule 7.

1.16 Reform of the existing system

The remittance basis itself remained largely unchanged for over 80 years, although the scope of its application has become restricted over time. By 1974, only non-domiciled individuals and trustees benefited from the remittance basis, and, for income other than employment income, non-ordinarily resident Commonwealth and Irish citizens. In 1974 a proposal to end the remittance basis completely for non-domiciled taxpayers who had been ordinarily resident for five out of the six previous years of assessment, by deeming such persons to be domiciled was abandoned.

1.17 Reform of residence rules

The only serious attempt to reform the definition of residence itself was in 1988 when the Inland Revenue published *Residence in the United Kingdom, The Scope of UK Taxation for Individuals, A Consultation Document*. In it a comprehensive reform was proposed under which residence would be determined only by physical presence in the UK.

Residence based on physical presence

The proposals were based on the US Federal Internal Revenue Code. An individual who was present in the UK for 183 days or more would, as now, be resident in that year for income tax and capital gains tax. An individual who was present for 30 days or less in a year would not be resident in that year. When an individual was present for between 30 and 183 days in a year, his residence would be determined by including not only the days spent in the UK during the year in question but also one-third and one-sixth of the days spent in the UK in the preceding year and the year before that respectively. Presence for any part of a day would count as presence for the whole day.[1]

Intermediate basis of taxation

Although the reform project was originally conceived only as a review of the residence tests, enthusiastic drafters of the document also proposed abolition of the remittance basis for non-domiciled residents. Residence would be the only affiliation test and an intermediate basis of taxation which would be applied to an individual's worldwide income depending on the length of an individual's residence in the UK. A graduated charge would apply to individuals who had been resident for seven out of fourteen years and only to those who had not previously been resident in this country for a continuous period of, say, 10 or 15 years.

The intermediate charge would apply to an individual's income and gains arising outside the UK. Liability would be based not on remittance but on a percentage of the total of worldwide income and gains, the percentage being determined by the number of years during which the individual had been resident in the UK in the previous, say, 14 years. The Inland Revenue suggested 15 per cent in the case of one year's residence in the 14 years, increasing to 100 per cent where the individual has resided for seven years out of the previous fourteen years. The percentage would be applied to the individual's liability to tax on worldwide income and gains, taking account of any overseas tax paid. If the resultant figure were higher than the amount of tax payable on income and gains arising within the UK calculated in the normal way, then the individual's total tax charge for that year would be that higher figure. Otherwise total tax liability would be the amount of tax payable on the individual's income and gains arising within the UK.

Political unacceptability of the changes for non-domiciled residents effectively scuppered the project. No further changes in this area emerged during the period of Conservative government which ended in 1997.

---

[1] *Residence in the United Kingdom, The Scope of UK Taxation for Individuals, a Consultation Document,* (Inland Revenue, July 1988).

1.18 Current criticisms of the system

In November 1994, the Rt Hon Gordon Brown MP, then the Shadow Chancellor of the Exchequer, issued a document entitled *Tackling Abuses – Tackling Unemployment.* It stated, inter alia, that:

> 'Taxation of non-residents, non-domiciles and those with off-shore accounts should be overhauled in line with the recommendations of the Inland Revenue. It is not fair that a wealthy few be allowed to work or live in the UK without making a fair contribution through taxation ... In Britain it is easy for a few, even if they live or work here to avoid substantial amounts of tax through claiming to be non-resident or non-domiciled. The Tories have even widened the loopholes by scrapping the "available accommodation test" ... Today it is possible for an individual to fly into Britain every day of the year and not be treated as resident as long as he is absent for a few hours of each day ... People wishing to avoid substantial capital gains arrange to be non-resident for a year.

1.18 *United Kingdom taxation*

Those who are non-domiciled are able to live in the UK free of tax ... In 1988 the Inland Revenue recommended a radical new approach to residents and domiciles.'

Included in the materials of Chancellor Gordon Brown's 2003 Budget, was a document entitled *Reviewing the residence and domicile rules as they affect the taxation of individuals: a background paper* (published jointly by HM Treasury and Inland Revenue in April 2003). Through the use of a series of examples the paper identified a number of issues where there was unhappiness with the existing system. Most related to the benefits enjoyed by non-domiciled individuals and to somewhat anomalous results that can flow from various circumstances where residence is determined by counting days present in the UK.

The principles, it stated, which underpin the review are that the rules:

(a) should be fair;
(b) should support the competitiveness of the UK economy; and
(c) should be clear, and easy to operate.

The questions that the Government stated in the document that it was considering, and welcomed comments from others upon, were whether the current rules:

(a) successfully identify those with a long-term connection to the UK who have an obligation to help support the UK exchequer on the basis of their worldwide income;

(b) successfully identify those with a temporary connection to the UK, and ensure an appropriate contribution to the UK exchequer from those individuals;

(c) provide objective criteria for determining when a long-term or temporary connection is severed, suspended or restored;

(d) establish an appropriate divide between long-term and temporary connections to the UK;

(e) play an appropriate role, alongside other policy instruments, in supporting the internationalisation of labour markets, and ensuring the competitiveness of UK firms in the international market for skills, entrepreneurship and expertise;

(f) ensure that any difference in treatment between UK locals and visitors, and long- and short-term residents have a clear economic rationale;

(g) take into account the equivalent arrangements in other countries;

(h) are transparent, provide clear and unambiguous outcomes, and minimise the compliance burden on individuals and their employers; and

(i) present minimal opportunities for exploitation or avoidance.

Again, these proposals seemed to be kicked into the political long grass, at least at the legislative level during the Brown Chancellorship. At an administrative level there were stirrings of action, tackling taxpayers regularly flying in and out of the UK who claimed not to be resident which have thus far produced four decisions of the Special Commissioners.[1]

---

1 Inland Revenue Tax Bulletin, 52, April 2001, Page 836 "Mobile Workers"; *Shepherd v Revenue and Customs* [2005] UKSPC 484; *Gaines-Cooper v HMRC* [2006] UKSPC SPC568; *Barrett v Revenue & Customs* [2007] UKSPC SPC 639 and *Grace v Revenue & Customs* [2008] UKSPC SPC 663. See generally Chaps 2 and 4.

1.19 Darling amendments

In his first Pre-Budget Report in November 2007, Chancellor Alistair Darling announced sweeping changes limiting the availability of the remittance basis, expanding the meaning of remittance and a change to the method of counting days in the UK for the purpose of determining residence. This was followed by a further consultation exercise launched by a document entitled *Paying a fairer share: a consultation on residence and domicile* on 6 December 2007 and ending on 28 February 2008. It sought views on whether the application of the remittance basis should be further limited. In the March 2008 Budget the Chancellor confirmed that there would be no more legislation in this area during the life of the present Parliament.

UK revenue law

1.20 Income tax

There are four UK direct taxes whose incidence is, to some extent, governed by the residence or domicile status of the person on whom the liability will fall: income tax, corporation tax, capital gains tax and inheritance tax. A detailed consideration of each of those taxes is beyond the scope of this work but, in this and the three subsequent paragraphs, the relevance to each of territoriality and of a person's residence and domicile is noted. Income tax is the first to be considered.

Although income tax is 'one tax, not a collection of taxes essentially distinct',[1] it has, since 1803, been charged under one or other of a number of schedules each of which specifies a chargeable source of income. Income tax is now charged in accordance with the Income Tax Act 2007 (ITA), effective from 6 April 2007, the Income Tax (Earnings and Pensions) Act 2003 (ITEPA), effective from 6 April 2003, and the Income Tax (Trading and Other Income) Act 2005 (ITTOIA), effective from 6 April 2005. These Acts were passed by the UK Parliament as part of the Tax Law Rewrite Project, whose aim is to rewrite tax law in plain English and modern legislative drafting structure without changing the law. The

Act repeals or replaces those parts and sections of ICTA 1988 which relate to earnings and pensions. Some minor changes in the laws have been made but case law which used to appertain to the old Schedular system may still be relevant in interpreting the new legislation.

Income tax is an annual tax, being reimposed for each new year of assessment[2] (ie a year which runs from 6 April in one calendar year to 5 April in the next following calendar year)[3] and thus, in principle, if income is to be charged to tax for say, 2008–09, income must arise in the year ended 5 April 2009.

The Income Tax (Earnings and Pensions) Act imposes a charge to income tax on employment income, being a charge which is described as a charge on general earnings and a charge on special employment income.[4] Chapter 4 of the Act sets out the rules applying to employees who are resident, ordinarily resident and domiciled in the UK, while Ch 5 of the Act sets out the rules applying to employees not resident, ordinarily resident and domiciled in the UK.

The Income Tax (Trading and Other Income) Act 2005 deals with sources of income other than employment and pensions: Pt 2 of ITTOIA 2005 deals with trading profits; Pt 3 with property income; Pt 4 with saving and investment income; Pt 5 miscellaneous income; and Pt 8 specifically with foreign income.

The latest product of the Rewrite Project is the Income Tax Act 2007 which rewrites, and in some cases repeals, various provisions relating to income tax not dealt with by the two Acts mentioned above. The rules regarding residence are contained in Pt 14 of Ch 2. The Act came into force on 5 April 2007.

---

1 *A-G v LCC* (1900) 4 TC 265 at 293, per Lord Macnaghten.
2 The continuing structure is preserved by ICTA 1988 s 820 but the tax itself requires an annual parliamentary resolution (invested with statutory authority by PCTA 1968) to keep it alive pending the enactment of the annual Finance Act.
3 ICTA 1988 s 2(2).
4 Income Tax (Earnings and Pensions) Act 2003 ss 1(1), (8), 6, 7.

1.21 Corporation tax

Corporation tax is chargeable on the worldwide profits of any company resident in the UK.[1] A non-resident company is, however, chargeable to corporation tax only if it carries on a trade in the UK through a permanent establishment in the UK, and, in that event, the profits brought into charge to corporation tax are those of, or attributable to, the permanent establishment.[2]

The profits chargeable to corporation tax are to be arrived at by aggregating with its chargeable gains (if any) its income computed on income tax principles.[3] The income tax principles set out in the schedules (abolished for individuals by the Tax Law Rewrite project) contained in the Income and Corporation Taxes Act 1988 continue to apply to companies.

UK-resident companies are also liable to the controlled foreign companies' charge. This charge is analagous to corporation tax but is imposed by apportioning among UK-resident corporate shareholders with an interest in a non-resident company, the profits of the non-resident company (computed on the basis of it being a company resident in the UK) if that company is controlled by persons resident in the UK, but is resident in a country where its profits are subject to a level of taxation lower than that to which they would be subject in the UK.[4] Company residence is examined in Chap 6.

1 ICTA 1988 ss 6(1), (2)(a) and 8(1).
2 ICTA 1988 s 11(1), (2).
3 ICTA 1988 s 9.
4 ICTA 1988 ss 747–756 and Sch 24;. See **6.22** below.

1.22 Capital gains tax

A charge to capital gains tax arises when a gain accrues to an individual on the disposal or deemed disposal of a chargeable asset in a year of assessment during any part of which he is resident or during which he is ordinarily resident in the UK.[1] A chargeable gain accruing to a company is included in its profits for corporation tax purposes.[2]

A disposal occurs whenever the owner of the asset disposes (or is deemed to dispose) of his ownership, absolute and beneficial, of the whole or part of the asset; a chargeable asset is any asset (including incorporeal property) other than an individual's principal private residence,[3] gilt-edged securities and qualifying corporate bonds,[4] savings certificates and non-marketable securities,[5] life policies, and deferred annuities,[6] tangible moveable assets disposed of for £6,000 or less,[7] private motor vehicles,[8] certain interests under settlements,[9] decorations for valour etc,[10] debts other than debts on a security,[11] and foreign currency for personal expenditure.[12]

There is an annual exemption for individuals.[13] For the year 2008–09 it is £9,600.

Where a person has a foreign domicile, no capital gains tax is to be charged on a gain accruing to him from the disposal of an asset situated outside the UK except to the extent of any amounts received in the UK in respect of that gain.[14] Whether an asset is situated outside the UK or not is determined by the provisions of TCGA 1992, s 275.

Where a person is neither resident nor ordinarily resident in the UK but carries on a trade in the UK through a branch or agency, he is to be charged to tax on gains accruing to him from the disposal of assets situated in the UK and either held by the branch, or used in connection with the trade.[15]

1 TCGA 1992 ss 1 and 2(1).
2 See **1.21** above.
3 TCGA 1992 s 222.
4 TCGA 1992 s 115.
5 TCGA 1992 s 121.
6 TCGA 1992 s 210.
7 TCGA 1992 s 262.

8   TCGA 1992 s 263.
9   TCGA 1992 s 76.
10 TCGA 1992 s 268.
11 TCGA 1992 s 251.
12 TCGA 1992 s 269.
13 TCGA 1992 s 3.
14 TCGA 1992 s 12.
15 TCGA 1992 s 10.

1.23   Inheritance tax

Inheritance tax is a direct tax on transfers of value made on, or (at a tapered rate) during the seven years preceding, a person's death;[1] and on transfers by a close company or by an individual (during his life) into certain trusts.[2]

Transfers to a spouse are exempt from tax, provided that the spouse is domiciled in the UK,[3] as are gifts of £250 or less,[4] certain gifts in consideration of marriage,[5] and gifts to charities etc.[6] Where lifetime transfers by an individual are chargeable to tax, the amount brought into charge is to be reduced by an annual exemption.

Domicile is a key concept in relation to inheritance tax. If a person is domiciled in the UK, the transfer, during the last seven years of his life or upon his death, of any property to which he is beneficially entitled, wherever situated, is within the charge to tax. If, however, a person is domiciled outside the UK, only transfers of property situated in the UK will be within the charge.[7] Domicile has, however, an extended meaning for the purpose of inheritance tax as explained in Chapter 7 below.

1 IHTA 1984 Pt I as amended by FA 1986.
2 IHTA 1984 ss 3, 71 and 89; F(No 2)A 1987 s 96(2); FA 2006, Sch 20.
3 IHTA 1984 s 18.
4 IHTA 1984 s 20.
5 IHTA 1984 s 22.
6 IHTA 1984 ss 23–29.
7 IHTA 1984 s 6(1).

1.24   National Insurance Contributions

While not strictly a tax, National Insurance Contributions are often thought of by both those who pay and collect them in the same way as tax. In the international context, they share some of the same jurisdictional issues with income tax. Liability to pay Class 1, Class 1A, Class 1B or Class 2 contributions generally only falls on persons who fulfil prescribed conditions as to residence or presence in Great Britain.[1] The prescribed conditions refer to both residence and ordinary residence (but not domicile).[2] Unlike the income tax rules, mere presence by an employed earner at the time of employment may be sufficient to establish liability.[3] These expressions are undefined in the social security legislation and thus the case law on the meaning of those expressions is relevant to this area of law. HMRC however ascribe a different meaning to the expressions for National Insurance Contributions purposes and do not apply their practice set out in IR20.[4]

1 Social Security Contributions And Benefits Act 1992 s 1(6).
2 Social Security (Contributions) Regulations 2001 (SI 2001/1004) Reg 145.
3 Reg 145(1)(a).
4 IR20 (July 2008) para 11.2, see Appendix 1 below.

1.25 Value Added Tax (VAT)

Member States of the European Union are required to impose Value Added Tax (VAT) under the VAT Directive.[1] Residential concepts are again relevant in determining taxing jurisdiction. While the place of supply of goods for VAT purposes is decided by reference to the goods supplied,[2] the place of supply of services is generally by reference to the location of the supplier or customer.[3] Thus, for example, the place of supply of services is the place where the supplier has established his business or has a fixed establishment from which the service is supplied, or, in the absence of such a place of business or fixed establishment, the place where he has his permanent address or usually resides.[4]

1 Council Directive 2006/112 on the common system of value added tax (the VAT Directive).
2 VAT Directive Title V, Chs 1, 2 and 4.
3 VAT Directive Title V, Ch 3.
4 VAT Directive, Art 43.

1.26 Revenue practices and concessions

The operation of the UK system of taxation has included concessions whereby the Revenue do not enforce the letter of the law and published practices as to how they apply the law. At first, it was thought that the authority for such concessions and practices lay in the Inland Revenue Regulations Act 1890 s 1(2) which provided that the Commissioners of Inland Revenue ('the Board') 'shall have all necessary powers for carrying into execution every Act of Parliament relating to inland revenue', but when, in 1947, three years after the first list of concessions had been published, Sir Stafford Cripps MP, the then Chancellor of the Exchequer, was asked to state their basis in law, he replied that they had been brought into existence 'without any particular legal authority under any Act of Parliament, but by the Inland Revenue under my authority'.[1]

From this clear admission of the fact that HMRC concessions and practices have no statutory foundation but represent merely the will of the Executive, it follows that – whether they work in favour of the Crown or the subject – they have no place in the law for 'the pretended power of suspending laws or the execution of laws by regall authoritie without consent of Parlyament is illegal'.[2]

In areas of law that are unclear or where its application can be

1.26 *United Kingdom taxation*

uncertain, such as the subject of this work, the way in which the law is administered is of particular importance. There are few areas where Revenue practice is more significant than in relation to the residence and ordinary residence of individuals. Revenue booklet IR20 (the most recent version was published in July 2008) which is reproduced in Appendix 1 is the central statement of practice and concessions on individual residence, ordinary residence and domicile. The judicial attitude towards this code is plain. When, in *Reed v Clark*,[3] Nicholls J was referred to IR20, he dismissed its authority in a single sentence: 'I do not see', he said, 'how this booklet affects any matter I have to decide.'[4]

Although IR20 is merely a statement of HMRC practice and, in certain respects, concessions, it had for some time been widely regarded almost as a codification of the rules. There had been no cases before the Courts on residence for some 20 years after *Reed v Clark* in 1985. The first case to disabuse taxpayers from this notion was *Shepherd v Revenue and Customs*.[5] In that case, Captain Shepherd, a British Airways pilot, knew that he would have to retire on 22 April 2000 when he attained the age of 55 years. He started to plan for his retirement in 1997 when he wrote to the Revenue and asked for guidance on retirement overseas; he did not mention any particular country. In reply he received a copy of the Revenue publication IR20 'Residents and non-residents'. On 17 September 1998 he wrote to the Revenue to say that, with one year and seven months to go before his retirement, he was considering moving abroad to minimise his tax liabilities. He understood that his time in the UK had to average less than 91 days over four years. He had applied for Cyprus residency and would move there when permission was granted. However, this would take a considerable time and so he might move to Switzerland or Eire in the meantime. The Revenue replied to say that he was responsible for determining his residency status but if he was in the UK for 183 days or more in a tax year then he would be regarded as resident here. He spent less than 91 days a year in the UK. When the question of his residence came before the Special Commissioners it was determined without reference to IR20. While the case was not about the application of IR20, it neatly illustrates the special credence given to it.

In the *Shepherd* case as well as in *Gaines-Cooper v HMRC*[6], the taxpayers offered calculations of the number of days they had spent in the UK based on the practice in IR20 that the days of arrival and departure should be ignored. In *Gaines-Cooper* these calculations were not disputed for years from 1976 to 1979. They were disputed during the period 1992 to 2004. The Revenue calculations included the days of arrival and departure and recorded the number of visits and visits of more than one night. These gave a very different picture of the presence of Mr Gaines-Cooper. The Special Commissioner noted that on appeal the law rather than IR20 should apply.[7]

Following the decision in *Gaines-Cooper*, HMRC issued a statement aimed at clarifying the application of IR20.[8] It noted that some commentators had suggested that the decision in *Gaines-Cooper* means that HMRC has changed the basis on which it calculates the '91-day test' and declared this to be incorrect. It stated further that there has been no change to the HMRC practice in relation to residence and the '91-day test' and that HMRC would,

> 'continue to:
> - follow its published guidance on residence issues, and apply this guidance fairly and consistently;
> - treat an individual who has not left the United Kingdom as remaining resident here;
> - consider all the relevant evidence, including the pattern of presence in the United Kingdom and elsewhere, in deciding whether or not an individual has left the United Kingdom;
> - apply the '91-day test' (where HMRC is satisfied that an individual has actually left the United Kingdom) as outlined in booklet IR20, normally disregarding days of arrival and departure in calculating days under this "test".'

It restated that:

> 'The guidance provided by booklet IR20 is general in nature. If, on the facts of the matter, a dispute arises over the application of this general guidance and the parties cannot resolve their dispute by agreement, the Commissioners will determine any appeals. The Commissioners are bound to decide the legal issues by reference to statute and case law principles rather than HMRC guidance. Where a dispute relates to particular facts the Commissioners will consider the evidence and make findings of fact to which they will apply the law.'

At the same time in January 2007 the long-standing Inspector's Manual was withdrawn. While parts of that manual have migrated to other more recently written HMRC manuals, the individual residence parts which elaborated on IR20 have yet to appear elsewhere in the manuals.

Two extra-statutory concessions address the treatment of individuals, coming to or leaving the UK part way through a tax year as there is no legal rule splitting a tax year between periods of residence and non-residence. In the *Shepherd* case, at the hearing, Captain Shepherd had to accept that the Special Commissioners had no jurisdiction to consider the possible application of extra-statutory concession A11 (*Residence in the United Kingdom: year of commencement or cessation of residence*) which provided for the splitting of a tax year where an individual ceased to reside in the UK during a year of assessment.

Given the state of the law, taxpayers will often seek to rely on published practice or concession. Since such matters cannot form the basis of an appeal, the only remedy open to taxpayers where HMRC do not apply published practice or concessions is under administrative law principles on judicial review. Administrative law gives wide discretion to the Revenue in the application of concessions and administrative practice.

In *R v IRC, Ex Parte Fulford-Dobson*[9] the taxpayer sought application of the ESC D2 dealing with split tax years in relation to capital gains. Shortly before he left the UK mid-way through a tax year, his wife, who remained resident, gave capital assets to him which he sold after departing. The Court declined to interfere with a Revenue refusal to apply the concession on the basis that it was used for a tax avoidance purpose.

The broad effect illustrated by this case is that where taxpayers need to rely on concessions they are governed by administrative discretion rather than legal rights. This unsatisfactory approach has been criticised by the courts. In *Absolom v Talbot*,[10] Scott LJ observed: 'The fact that such extra-legal concessions have to be made to avoid unjust hardships is conclusive that there is something wrong with the legislation.' Perhaps the final death blow to extra-statutory concessions was the decision of the House of Lords in *R v Inland Revenue Commissioners, ex p Wilkinson*[11] where Lord Hoffmann said of the power to make such concessions:

> 'This discretion enables the Commissioners to formulate policy in the interstices of the tax legislation, dealing pragmatically with minor or transitory anomalies, cases of hardship at the margins or cases in which a statutory rule is difficult to formulate or its enactment would take up a disproportionate amount of Parliamentary time. The Commissioners publish extra-statutory concessions for the guidance of the public and Miss Rose drew attention to some which she said went beyond mere management of the efficient collection of the Revenue. I express no view on whether she is right about this, but if she is, it means that the Commissioners may have exceeded their powers under section 1 of TMA .'[12]

In light of the uncertainty now surrounding concessions, Finance Act 2008 s 160 now authorises HM Treasury by order to make provision for and in connection with giving effect to any existing HMRC concession.[13]

The procedural complexities where HMRC refuse to apply IR 20 are well illustrated in *Davis v HMRC*.[14] There HMRC asserted that the taxpayers were UK resident in 2001–02. The claimants challenged this both as a matter of law by appeal to the Special Commissioners and an application to the High Court for judicial review, arguing that they had a legitimate expectation to be treated in accordance with IR20. The judge stayed the application pending the appeal to the Special Commissioners. The Court of Appeal however restored the application for judicial review on the basis that, assuming it was well founded it might be pre-empted if the special Commissioners determination proceeded before it. It would also create a significant obstacle to the taxpayers in pursuing the judicial review claim as there was a real risk that a decision by the special Commissioners might be seen as ruling out a claim on the basis of legitimate expectation.

---

1 446 HC Official Report (5th Series) col 2266.
2 Bill of Rights 1688.
3 [1985] STC 323.
4 [1985] STC 323 at 347.
5 [2005] UKSPC 484.
6 [2006] UKSPC SPC568
7 At para 99.
8 HMRC Brief 01/07.
9 [1987] STC 334.
10 (1944) 26 TC 166 at p 181.
11 [2005] UKHL 30.
12 at para [21].
13 At the time of publication, no such order has been made.
14 [2008] EWCA (Civ) 10 July 2008.

CHAPTER 2

Residence of individuals

Come, give us a taste of your quality.
Shakespeare *Hamlet* Act 2 Sc 2

2.01 Introduction

The Income Tax Act 1806 (which is the foundation on which the present system of direct taxation rests) accorded clear recognition to this limitation by making 'residence' in Great Britain (now the UK) the chief determinant of chargeability where there would not otherwise be a sufficient connection between the sovereign territory and the source of the profits or gains which Parliament had resolved to tax. Residence is, as we shall see, a concept rooted in, but of greater durability and more nuanced than, the concept of presence[1] and, as a determinant of chargeability to tax, has survived to the present day.

---

1 As to whether it follows from this that a person cannot be regarded as resident in the UK for a tax year during which he has at no time been physically present within the territorial bounds of the UK, see **4.14** below.

The nature of residence

2.02 A qualitative attribute

It has often been observed that, in legislating for the imposition of taxation on the basis of 'residence', Parliament omitted, or declined, to give the term 'residence' any statutory definition. That omission created an immediate difficulty which very soon required judicial resolution for, in the absence of a statutory definition, the word 'residence' has 'no technical or special meaning'[1] and must, therefore, according to accepted principles of construction, be given the meaning it would bear 'in the speech of plain men'.[2] To put it another way: if Parliament uses a word without explaining what it means by that word, it must be assumed to be using that word 'in

2.02 *Residence of individuals*

its common sense'.[3] But what *is* the common sense of 'residence' or any of its variants? As Rowlatt J has said:

> 'When you speak of a person residing, do you mean that he has attributed to himself a quality which makes him describable in that way with reference to a place, or do you mean that he is really there?'[4]

If 'residing' means no more than 'is really there', 'residence' becomes a mere synonym for 'physical presence' and that, as we saw in Chapter 1, is what Parliament sought to avoid. Presence is an attribute which is far too easily acquired or shed for it to serve as an adequate determinant of chargeability to tax, and residence instead of presence was chosen to fill that role because of its ability to provide a more enduring territorial link. Residence can play the part assigned to it, however, only if it carries the *first* of the two senses which Rowlatt J has indicated it may bear and, accordingly, the judiciary has consistently held that, in the context of fiscal legislation, 'residence' is to be regarded only 'as signifying an attribute of the person'.[5] Therefore, one must never, in the context of a fiscal statute, 'think of 'residence' in the sense of a house or place of residence',[6] and the same is true of all the variants – 'resident', 'reside', 'resides', 'residing', etc. 'Resident', for example, 'indicates a quality of the person and is not descriptive of ... property, real or personal'.[7]

Attributes or qualities of the person defy encompassment in a form of words. They have no concrete reality. Their existence may only be inferred or deduced from a person's particular pattern of behaviour in particular circumstances, and rarely, if ever, will the pattern or the circumstances in any two cases be quite the same. 'Residence', taken as a term expressing a quality of the person,

> '... is not a term of invariable elements, all of which must be satisfied in each instance. It is quite impossible to give it a precise and inclusive definition. It is highly flexible, and its many shades of meaning vary not only in the contexts of different matters, but also in different aspects of the same matter. In one case it is satisfied by certain elements, in another by others, some common, some new.'[8]

To bring a person within, or to exclude a person from, the charging sections of a taxing statute solely by reference to a determinant of such inexactitude is, clearly, far from satisfactory and, indeed, brings the Taxes Acts close to defeating the maxim that a taxing statute must impose a charge in clear terms or fail. As Viscount Sumner has pointed out, however, 'the words are plain and it is only their application that is haphazard and beyond all forecast'.[9]

The Royal Commission on the Taxation of Profits and Income[10] believed that a precise defintion would benefit the Inland Revenue. The Commission's report concluded by recommending further statutory provisions in this area but, apart from legislation introduced in 1956 in relation to persons working abroad,[11] that recommendation was never implemented.

Instead, the Inland Revenue further developed its own code of practice[12] which, though of no legal standing,[13] has been generally applied with a degree of inflexibility normally accorded only to statutory instruments.

This has placed the taxpayer in the worst of all possible positions for though the code is far from being comprehensive or the balanced summary of case law principles which the Inland Revenue held it out to be, the taxpayer will frequently find that he has no option but to employ the appeal machinery, applying the law, if he wishes to challenge the code on any point.

1 *Lysaght v IRC* (1928) 13 TC 511 at 536, per Lord Warrington of Clyffe.
2 *Lysaght v IRC* (1928) 13 TC 511 at 529, per Viscount Sumner.
3 *Lysaght v IRC* (1928) 13 TC 511 at 534, per Lord Buckmaster.
4 *Levene v IRC* (1928) 13 TC 486 at 492.
5 *Pickles v Foulsham* (1923) 9 TC 261 at 274, per Rowlatt J.
6 *Pickles v Foulsham* (1923) 9 TC 261 at 274, per Rowlatt J.
7 *Lysaght v IRC* (1928) 13 TC 511 at 528, per Viscount Sumner.
8 *Thompson v Minister of National Revenue* [1946] SCR 209 at 224, per Rand J, quoted with approval by Wynn-Perry J in *Miesegaes v IRC* (1957) 37 TC 493 at 497.
9 *Levene v IRC* (1928) 13 TC 486 at 502.
10 Final Report, 1955, Cmd 9474, para 292.
11 See **4.16–4.20** below.
12 Now contained in Booklet IR20 (July 2008), 'Residents and non-residents: liability to tax in the UK'. See **Appendix 1** below.
13 See **1.26** above.

2.03 A question of fact and degree

The absence of a statutory definition of the term 'residence' is yet more far-reaching in its consequences than even the foregoing paragraphs might suggest. If the Taxes Act contained such a definition, then it would be open to the courts[1] to decide whether or not a person had come within that definition, for 'a proper construction of ... statutory language is a matter of law'.[2]

As we have seen, however, the Taxes Acts give no definition of the word 'residence' and the judiciary has inclined to the view that 'it is not possible to frame one'.[3] Accordingly, whether a person is resident or not is, within the present state of affairs, a question not of law but of fact.

Because of the way in which the appeal procedure operates, however, it falls not to the courts but to the Commissioners to consider what Rowlatt J called the 'bundle of actual facts'[4] and to form from those facts the 'impression or opinion' in accordance with which a finding of 'resident' or 'non-resident' will be made. As Nicholls J put it in *Reed v Clark*:[5]

> 'The key word "residing" is not defined by statute ... Thus the task of the fact-finding tribunal in the present case was to consider and weigh all the evidence and then, giving the word 'residing' its natural and ordinary meaning, reach a conclusion on the factual question of whether or not the taxpayer was residing in the UK in the year of assessment.'[6]

Once such a conclusion has been reached, the appellate court's powers of intervention become very limited. Its role is restricted by statute[7] to the hearing and determination only of questions of law arising on the case stated by the General Commissioners for its opinion or on appeal from the Special Commissioners which means that:

2.03 *Residence of individuals*

'... when commissioners have made findings of fact, their decision is not open to review provided (a) they had before them evidence from which such findings could properly be made and (b) they did not misdirect themselves in law.'[8]

Thus, a finding by the Commissioners that a person is resident in the UK in a year of assessment 'only raises a question of law if it can be contended that it is impossible to draw that conclusion of fact as to residence in the United Kingdom from the facts set out in the case'.[9] By reason of the very inexactitude of the term 'resident', such a contention will rarely be upheld, and this places the taxpayer in an unenviable position.

The facts on which the Commissioners make their findings as to residence or non-residence differ from case to case, but have tended to be facts concerning a person's physical presence in the UK or absence from it, facts concerning his history of residence or non-residence, facts concerning his present habits and manner of life, facts as to his nationality, facts as to the purpose, frequency, regularity and duration of his visits to the UK or to places overseas, facts as to ties of family and ties of business in the UK, and facts as to the maintenance or availability of a place of abode in the UK.

Such facts do not all carry equal weight and, indeed, facts which in one case carry no weight at all may, in another case, be so significant as to completely tip the scales. This is what is meant when residence is referred to (as, from time to time, it has been) as a 'question of degree'. A visit to the UK this year may signify little, a visit next year may signify not much more, but visits year after year may, in the context of the particular circumstances of a case, push the needle to that point on the Commissioners' scale which reads 'resident'. It is then that the questions of degree resolve themselves into a finding of fact and it is that finding of fact which the courts are powerless to disturb unless 'no person acting judicially and properly instructed as to the relevant law could have come to the determination under appeal'[10] or 'no reasonable person could have arrived at the same conclusion as the Commissioners'.[11]

---

1 Ie, on an appeal from a decision of the Commissioners.
2 *IRC v Fraser* (1942) 24 TC 498 at 501, per Lord Normand LP.
3 *Levene v IRC* (1928) 13 TC 486 at 497, per Lord Hanworth MR.
4 *Lowenstein v De Salis* (1926) 10 TC 424 at 437.
5 [1985] STC 323.
6 [1985] STC 323 at 338.
7 TMA 1970 ss 56(6), 56A.
8 *Reed v Clark* [1985] STC 323 at 336–337, per Nicholls J.
9 *Bayard Brown v Burt* (1911) 5 TC 667 at 670, per Hamilton J.
10 *Edwards v Bairstow and Harrison* (1955) 36 TC 207 at 229, per Lord Radcliffe.
11 *Pilkington v Randall* (1966) 42 TC 662 at 674, per Salmon LJ.

2.04 A personal attribute

Because residence is a 'quality of the person'[1] and, therefore, a 'question ... of degree',[2] it follows that a spouse's residence status is not governed by her co-spouse's status but is determined by her own circumstances.

Recognition as a person as a matter of law carries with it the implication that residential status is capable of being conferred. Because corporate bodies such as limited companies are legal persons independent of their members under English law, they too will either possess or lack UK residence status. 'Resident' is, however, 'a term exceedingly unsuited to describe a statutory "person"'[3] and, accordingly, a corporation's residence status can be determined only 'by analogy from natural persons'.[4] So it has been with partnerships during the years in which they were given quasi personality for income and corporation tax purposes.[5] A partnership is not a legal entity under English law and its residence status, too, was arrived at by analogy. Trusts and settlements present even greater conceptual difficulties, for a trust or a settlement is a proprietary relationship.[6] It does become necessary in some circumstances to determine its residence status. All these matters are discussed in depth in Chapters 5 and 6.

1 *IRC v Lysaght* (1928) 13 TC 511 at 528, per Viscount Sumner.
2 *IRC v Lysaght* (1928) 13 TC 511 at 536, per Lord Warrington of Clyffe.
3 *Todd v Egyptian Delta Land and Investment Co Ltd* (1928) 14 TC 119 at 140, per Viscount Sumner.
4 *Todd v Egyptian Delta Land and Investment Co Ltd* (1928) 14 TC 119 at 140, per Viscount Sumner.
5 Repealed by FA 1995 s 117; see now ITTOIA 2005 Pt 9.
6 See for example *Green v Russell* [1959] 2 Q.B. 226 (CA) per Romer LJ, at 241.

2.05 An annual attribute

In *Levene v IRC*,[1] Viscount Sumner said that 'the taxpayer's chargeability in each year of charge constitutes a separate issue',[2] and, in so saying, gave recognition to the fact that income tax is an annual tax. It is an annual tax in that the charge must be reimposed by Parliament in the Finance Act each year and it is an annual tax in that the charge is made upon the annual income, ie, the income of the year of charge. As was noted in Chapter 1, however, residence is a principal determinant of chargeability and it will come as no surprise, therefore, to learn that residence is an annual attribute, ie, an attribute which endures for a year.

This was brought out very clearly in the case of *Thomson v Bensted*[3] where it was held that, although during the year 1911–12 Mr Thomson had actually spent only four or so months at his home in Scotland and had spent the remainder of the year in West Africa, he was resident in the UK 'during the whole year, in the sense of the ... Acts'.[4]

It is quite possible to argue that what was being recognised in the *Thomson* case was not so much that residence is an annual attribute but simply that Mr Thomson had a quality of residence which, because it had been acquired at some time in the past and because it extended into the foreseeable future, was not disturbed or impaired by the periods of time he spent abroad. That argument did not hold good, however, in the case of *Back v Whitlock*.[5] There, Rowlatt J said that if a person were to become a new permanent resident in the UK only two days before the end of a year of assessment he would be just as chargeable to tax as would someone who had resided here throughout the year. It could surely not be contended that such a person, *de facto*, had the quality of residence prior to the date on which his period of actual residence began and, indeed, Rowlatt J did not base his statement on that ground. It was rather that:

> '... there is no question under the Income Tax Acts of any apportionment or adjustment for Income Tax in time, with regard to the date when a person became resident and so became taxable.'[6]

This same principle emerged more clearly, but in relation to a person who had permanently left the UK, in *Neubergh v IRC*[7] when Brightman J had to decide whether a Mr Felix Neubergh, who had lived in the UK since 1919 but had permanently departed on 26 January 1968, was nevertheless liable to the special charge on investment income imposed by the Finance Act 1968 on persons domiciled in the UK in the year 1967–68 or resident in the UK in that fiscal year and throughout the nine preceding years. Having first asked the question: 'Was the taxpayer resident in the UK in the year 1967–68 and throughout the nine preceding years?',[8] he declared that 'the answer to that question can only be Yes'.[9] His grounds for such a conclusion were that, in accordance with the reasoning in *Mitchell v IRC*[10] 'residence during a part of the year is clearly sufficient'.[11]

It was in the case of *Gubay v Kington*,[12] that the point was finally made clear. The case concerned the chargeability or otherwise of Mr Gubay to capital gains tax on the disposal of shares to his non-resident wife in a tax year during only part of which he was *de facto* resident in the UK. The argument with which Mr Gubay succeeded before the House of Lords was not the argument on which he had gone to the High Court and then to the Court of Appeal. In the lower courts, he had argued that, as he was actually resident in the UK for only six and a half months in the tax year 1972–73 he could not be said to be resident 'for the year of assessment' 1972–73 and could not, therefore, be charged with capital gains tax on the notional gain accruing to him on the disposal of shares made to his non-resident wife during that year. This argument was dismissed in both courts. In the High Court, Vinelott J said:

> 'The words "resident in the UK for a year of assessment" are frequently used by judges and textbook writers to describe the situation of a taxpayer who, because he was resident in the UK for part of a year of assessment, is assessable to tax from all sources of income arising during that year of assessment. In effect, the words "resident in the UK for a year of assessment" are used to predicate of the taxpayer that he had the status or quality of being a resident in the UK for tax purposes during the year of assessment.'[13]

In the Court of Appeal, Sir John Donaldson MR, said:

> 'Being resident in the UK may be a status or a fact. Where it is a status, it is something which is either enjoyed (if that be the right word) or not enjoyed for a whole tax year.'[14]

It has thus been placed beyond doubt that any person who possesses or acquires the attribute of residence for part of a tax year will, unless a statute or an extra-statutory concession or a rule of practice dictates otherwise,[15] be regarded as being resident for the whole of that year; and both residence and its related concept of ordinary residence[16] may, therefore, in general terms, be said to be annual attributes, enduring for the whole of any fiscal year in which they are enjoyed, however briefly.

1 *Levene v IRC* (1928) 13 TC 486.
2 *Levene v IRC* (1928) 13 TC 486 at 501.
3 (1918) 7 TC 137.
4 (1918) 7 TC 137 at 145, per the Lord President.
5 (1932) 16 TC 723.
6 (1932) 16 TC 723 at 726.
7 [1978] STC 181.
8 [1978] STC 181 at 184.
9 [1978] STC 181 at 185.
10 (1951) 33 TC 53.
11 *Neubergh v IRC* [1978] STC 181 at 185.
12 [1983] STC 443.
13 *Gubay v Kington* [1981] STC 721 at 735.
14 *Gubay v Kington* [1983] STC 443 at 451.
15 No statute other than TCGA 1992 s 2(1) presently so provides, but extra-statutory concessions and HMRC f practice do. See **4.21** below.
16 See Ch 3.

2.06 The judicial principles

Although, as has been explained, the question of whether or not a person possesses the quality of residence is a question of fact, and although the task of the judiciary is limited to that of examining the facts on which the Commissioners reach their decisions and seeing whether anyone acting judicially and properly instructed as to the relevant law could have arrived at the decisions at which the Commissioners have arrived,[1] judges have, in the course of carrying out their examinations, tended to underline significant facts, formulate principles and outline approaches which would lead them to one conclusion or another – even if, at the end of the day, they are obliged, in the absence of any obvious error of law on the part of the Commissioners, to uphold a decision which they themselves might not have reached. It is these general principles which will now be considered.

1 See **2.03** above.

2.07 The *Shepherd* synthesis

As the size of this work indicates, explaining the undefined statutory expression and distilling the cases is no easy or brief task. From a practical perspective, a brief statement of principles is most desirable. In *Shepherd v HMRC*,[1] the first published decision of the Special Commissioners dealing with residence, an attempt was made to synthesise the principles thus:

2.07 *Residence of individuals*

- that the concept of residence and ordinary residence are not defined in the legislation; the words therefore should be given their natural and ordinary meanings (*Levene*);
- that the word 'residence' and 'to reside' mean 'to dwell permanently or for a considerable time, to have one's settled or usual abode, to live in or at a particular place' (*Levene*);
- that the concept of 'ordinary residence' requires more than mere residence; it connotes residence in a place with some degree of continuity (*Levene*); 'ordinary' means normal and part of everyday life (*Lysaght*) or a regular, habitual mode of life in a particular place which has persisted despite temporary absences and which is voluntary and has a degree of settled purpose (*Shah*);
- that the question whether a person is or is not resident in the UK is a question of fact for the Special Commissioners (*Zorab*);
- that no duration is prescribed by statute and it is necessary to take into account all the facts of the case; the duration of an individual's presence in the UK and the regularity and frequency of visits are facts to be taken into account; also, birth, family and business ties, the nature of visits and the connections with this country, may all be relevant (*Zorab*; *Brown*);
- that a reduced presence in the UK of a person whose absences are caused by his employment and so are temporary absences does not necessarily mean that the person is not residing in the UK (*Young*);
- that the availability of living accommodation in the UK is a factor to be borne in mind in deciding if a person is resident here (*Cooper*) (although that is subject to ICTA 1988 s 336 (now ITA 2007 s 831);
- that the fact that an individual has a home elsewhere is of no consequence; a person may reside in two places but if one of those places is the UK he is chargeable to tax here (*Cooper* and *Levene*);
- that there is a difference between the case where a British subject has established a residence in the UK and then has absences from it (*Levene*) and the case where a person has never had a residence in the UK at all (*Zorab*; *Brown*);
- that if there is evidence that a move abroad is a distinct break that could be a relevant factor in treating an individual as non-resident (*Combe*); and
- that a person could become non-resident even if his intention was to mitigate tax (*Reed v Clark*).[2]

On appeal to the High Court[3] only the statutory provisions of ICTA 1988 ss 334 and 336 (now ITA 2007 ss 829 and 831) were addressed. However Lewison J 'detected no error of law' in the Special Commissioner's conclusion[4] This synthesis was restated in *Gaines-Cooper*.[5] While undoubtedly a handy list, caution must be exercised in treating the synthesis as a comprehensive statement of the law. Indeed, it may be questioned the extent to which some cases establish principles of law at all, or whether they are merely illustrations of a very broad test based on facts and circumstances.

1 *Shepherd v Revenue and Customs* [2005] UKSPC 484.
2 *Shepherd* para 58.
3 [2006] EWHC 1512 (CH); STC 1821.
4 At para [23].
5 *Gaines-Cooper v Revenue and Customs Comrs* [2007] UKSPC 568 at para 165.

A place of abode

2.08 Occupation of a dwelling house

In *Levene v IRC*,[1] Lord Cave said:

> 'The word "reside" is a familiar English word and is defined in the Oxford English Dictionary as meaning "to dwell permanently or for a considerable time, to have one's settled or usual abode, to live in or at a particular place". No doubt this definition must for present purposes be taken subject to any modification which may result from the terms of the Income Tax Act and Schedules; but subject to that observation, it may be accepted as an accurate indication of the meaning of the word "reside"'.[2]

Those words are a useful reminder that, although, as has been pointed out,[3] we must not think of residence in terms of bricks and mortar, we must not overlook the fact that the primary meaning of residence is to do with a person's inhabitation of bricks and mortar – or their equivalent.[4] Thus, in *Lloyd v Sulley*,[5] the President of the Court of the Exchequer said of Mr Lloyd's castle in Scotland and his town house and country villa in Italy:

> 'They are places to which it is quite easy for [him] to resort as his dwelling place whenever he thinks fit, and to set himself down there with his family and establishment. That is a place of residence, and if he occupies that place of residence for a portion of a year he is then within the meaning of the Clause as I read it, residing there in the course of that year.'[6]

The same was true of Sir C H Coote. He had a house in Ireland which he occupied for the greater part of each year and a house in Connaught Place, London, in which he stayed from time to time for a few weeks. The Court of the Exchequer held that he was resident in Great Britain and 'clearly within the Act'.[7]

Both these judgments were followed in the case of *Cooper v Cadwalader*.[8] Mr Cadwalader was an American citizen who had a house in New York but spent two months of each year in occupation of Millden Lodge, a furnished house in Forfar in Scotland, which he leased and kept available for his use throughout each year. Was Mr Cadwalader resident in the UK? Lord Adam was in no doubt as to the answer:

> 'Can it be said that during ... these two months in which he is residing continuously in Millden Lodge that he is not residing there? Where is he

residing? He is residing ... in Millden Lodge, and therefore residing in the UK; and if that be so, then it humbly appears to me that he is a person in the sense of the Act residing in the UK, and assessable under the Act.'[9]

---

1 (1929) 13 TC 486.
2 (1929) 13 TC 486 at 505.
3 At **2.02** above.
4 In *Bayard Brown v Burt* (1911) 5 TC 667, it was accepted that an ocean-going yacht anchored in territorial waters was Mr Bayard Brown's place of abode, and in *Hipperson v Electoral Registration Officer for the District of Newbury* [1985] 2 All ER 456, Sir John Donaldson MR (at 462) rejected the submission that women living in tents, vehicles and benders (a form of tent) on Greenham Common in furtherance of their protest concerning cruise missiles could not be said to have a home in the camp: 'It may be unusual to make one's home in a tent, bender or vehicle, but we can see no reason in law why it should be impossible.' In *Makins v Elson* [1977] STC 46, it was further held that a wheeled caravan, jacked up and resting on bricks, with water, electricity and telephone services installed, was a dwelling house, while in *R v Bundy* [1977] 2 All ER 382, even a motor car in which a certain Mr Bundy had been living rough was held to be his place of abode when sited – though not while in transit.
5 (1884) 2 TC 37.
6 (1884) 2 TC 37 at 41.
7 *A-G v Coote* (1817) 2 TC 385.
8 (1904) 5 TC 101.
9 (1904) 5 TC 101 at 107.

2.09 Multiple residence

The cases cited at **2.08** above not only 'determine that when the individual has a home here in the ordinary sense he is taxable',[1] but also that it is of no consequence that he may also have a home elsewhere.

In *A-G v Coote*,[2] for instance, one of the questions was whether Sir C H Coote could possess the quality of UK residence for a year of assessment during which he undoubtedly possessed the quality of Irish residence. The court found his Irish residence to be no barrier at all. Baron Wood said:

> 'It is no uncommon thing for a gentleman to have two permanent residences at the same time, in either of which he may establish his abode at any period, and for any length of time. This is just such a case.'[3]

The same question arose in *Cooper v Cadwalader*.[4] The fact that Mr Cadwalader was clearly resident in New York did not prevent him being found to be resident in the UK also.

It must be understood that these cases did not establish that a person may be resident *consecutively* in two or more places during a year, but that a person may *simultaneously* be resident (ie possess the quality of residence) in two or more places for the same year. This both follows from and supports the proposition that residence is an annual quality which endures for the whole of any tax year in which it is enjoyed, however briefly.

This proposition was implicitly confirmed by Viscount Cave LC when, in *Levene v IRC*,[5] he said:

'A man may reside in more than one place ... he may have a home abroad and a home in the UK, and in that case he is held to reside in both places and to be chargeable with tax in this country.'[6]

In *Lysaght v IRC*,[7] Viscount Sumner admitted that it runs counter to our normal mode of thought to think of such people as Mr Cadwalader[8] as being resident in the UK:

'Who in New York would have said of Mr Cadwalader: "His home's in the Highlands; his home is not here?" ... One thinks of a man's settled and usual place of abode as his residence, but the truth is that in many cases in ordinary speech one residence at a time is the underlying assumption and though a man may be the occupier of two houses, he is thought of as only resident in the one he lives in at the time in question. For Income Tax purposes such meanings are misleading. Residence here may be multiple and manifold.'[9]

It is now an established principle, therefore, that the possession of residence status in relation to some foreign place or country is not on its own sufficient to prevent a person becoming attributed with UK residence status.

Revenue guidance on this matter is true to the decided cases in this respect and is that:

'It is possible to be resident ... in both the UK and some other country (or countries) at the same time. If you are resident ... in another country, this does not mean that you cannot also be resident ... in the UK.'[10]

This notion involves residence in more than one country in accordance with UK principles. In closing this examination of the concept of multiple residence, it should be noted that, as the HMRC booklet points out in relation to residence under both UK and foreign tax principles:

'Where, however, you are resident both in the UK and in a country with which the UK has a double taxation agreement, there may be special provisions in the agreement for treating you as a resident of only one of the countries for the purposes of the agreement.'[11]

This aspect of residence is dealt with at **2.22** below.

---

1 *Levene v IRC* (1928) 13 TC 486 at 499, per Sargant LJ.
2 (1817) 2 TC 385.
3 (1817) 2 TC 385 at 386.
4 (1904) 5 TC 101.
5 (1928) 13 TC 486.
6 (1928) 13 TC 486 at 505.
7 (1928) 13 TC 511.
8 *Cooper v Cadwalader* (1904) 5 TC 101. See **2.08** above.
9 *Lysaght v IRC* (1928) 13 TC 511 at 528 and 529.
10 Appendix IR20 (11 April 2000) para 1.4.
11 Appendix IR20 (11 April 2000) para 1.4.

2.10 Ownership irrelevant

The general principle which has been discussed in the foregoing paragraphs is that a person cannot possess a dwelling place in the UK and occupy it, however briefly, during a tax year without becoming resident in the UK for that tax year. But is 'possess' the correct word? Sir C H Coote owned his house in London,[1] Thomas Lloyd owned his castle in Minard,[2] Robert Thomson owned his house in Hawick,[3] and John Cadwalader leased Millden Lodge from the Earl of Dalhousie.[4] Captain Loewenstein did not possess his accommodation.[5] He was a Belgian subject with a home in Brussels, who visited 'Pinfold', a furnished hunting box at Melton Mowbray in Leicestershire, each year for the purpose of fox hunting. The property was owned by the Belgian Breeding Stock Farm Company Ltd, a company in which he had a controlling interest and of which he was a director. In no year did he spend as many as six months in the UK and he claimed, therefore, that, on the basis of ITA 1918 Sch 1, Rule 2 of the Miscellaneous Rules of Schedule D (now ITA 2007 s 831),[6] he was exempt from tax under Schedule D. That exemption is discussed in Chapter 4 and does not concern us here, but Rowlatt J's view of Captain Loewenstein's central argument is of present concern. On the question of the necessity of a 'proprietorial interest', Rowlatt J said:

> 'I cannot see what difference that makes ... this man had this house at his disposal, with everything in it or for his convenience, kept going all the year round, although he only wanted it for a short time. Luckily, he was in relation with a Company who were the owners of it, and he could do that without owning it. It is an accident. It might well have been that he could do that with a relation, or a friend, or a philanthropist, or anybody; but in fact there was this house for him ... He has got this house to come to when he likes; he does not own it; he has got no proprietary interest in it, but it is just as good as if he had for the purpose of having it for a residence, and there it is.'

In the light of this pronouncement, the general principle may be more accurately stated to be that an individual may be held to be resident here notwithstanding that he does not possess the accommodation, provided that the accommodation is available for the individual throughout the tax year even though he occupies it only briefly during that year.

It should be noted that the precise form which the accommodation takes is irrelevant. An ocean-going yacht permanently moored in the UK's territorial waters has been held to be a dwelling-house for these purposes[7] and so, too, in other circumstances, has a wheeled but immobilised caravan to which electricity, water and telephone services had been supplied.[8]

The entry of a person's name on an electoral roll may be evidence of the availability of accommodation.[9]

The effect of ITA 2007 ss 831 and 832,[10] which provides that the existence or otherwise of available accommodation must be disregarded in determining whether, for the purpose of those provisions, an individual is in the UK for some temporary purpose and not with a view to or intent of establishing his residence here will be considered at **4.06** below.[11] The presence or otherwise of available accommodation can still be relevant to assist in determining whether an individual is generally resident in the UK or not.[12]

---

1   *A-G v Coote* (1817) 2 TC 385. See **2.07** above.
2   *Lloyd v Sulley* (1884) 2 TC 37. See **2.07** above.
3   *Thomson v Bensted* (1918) 7 TC 137.
4   *Cooper v Cadwalader* (1904) 5 TC 101. See **2.07** above.
5   *Loewenstein v De Salis* (1926) 10 TC 424 at 438.
6   See **4.02** below.
7   *Bayard Brown v Burt* (1911) 5 TC 667.
8   *Makins v Elson* [1977] STC 46.
9   See paras 6 and 5 respectively of the cases stated by the Commissioners in *Lloyd v Sulley* (1884) 2 TC 37 at 38 and *Cooper v Cadwalader* (1904) 5 TC 101 at 103.
10 Originally enacted as FA 1993 s 208.
11 ITA 2007 s 831 and s 832.
12 See *Shepherd v HMRC* at paras 49 and 58 relying on *Cooper v Cadwalader* in this respect.

Physical presence

2.11   Duration of presence

There are many situations in which the principle of occupation of available accommodation is of no application. If residence is not synonymous with mere physical presence, then the mere fact of presence in the UK ought not to constitute residence there. However, a person may be in the UK without ever acquiring a 'settled or usual abode'[1] but that will not necessarily prevent him from being attributed with the status of UK residence. As Viscount Sumner has said:

> 'Although setting up an establishment in this country, available for residence at any time throughout the year of charge, even though used but little, may be good ground for finding its master to be 'resident' here, it does not follow that keeping up an establishment abroad and none here is incompatible with being 'resident here' if there is other sufficient evidence of it.'[2]

The point is graphically made in *Reid v IRC*[3] by Lord Clyde, the Lord President of the Court of Session:

> '... take the case of a homeless tramp, who shelters to-night under a bridge, to-morrow in the greenwood and as the unwelcome occupant of a farm outhouse the night after. He wanders in this way all over the United Kingdom. But will anyone say he does not *live* in the United Kingdom? – and will anyone regard it as a misuse of language to say he *resides* in the United Kingdom. In his case there may be no relations with family or friends, no business ties, and none of the ordinary circumstances which create a link between the life of a British subject and the United Kingdom; but, even so, I do not think it could be disputed that he *resides* in the United Kingdom. There are other and very different kinds of tramps, who – being possessed of ample means, and having the ordinary ties of birth, family, and affairs with the United Kingdom or some part of it – yet prefer to enjoy those means without undertaking the domestic

2.11 *Residence of individuals*

responsibility of a home, and who move about from one house of public entertainment to another – in London today, in the provinces to-morrow, and in the Highlands the day after. They too are homeless wanderers in the United Kingdom. But surely it is true to say they *live* in the United Kingdom, and *reside* there? The Section of the Act of Parliament with which we are dealing speaks of persons 'residing', not at a particular locality, but in a region so extensive as the United Kingdom.'[4]

Although the person at the centre of the *Reid* case was a woman who possessed many links with the UK other than mere presence, the principal point which the Lord President was making was that the duration of a person's presence may alone in exceptional cases be sufficient to transform mere presence into residence. Nothing but presence attaches the homeless tramp to the UK, yet if that presence endures for a significant length of time, the whole of his time in the example given by Lord Clyde, it alone will be sufficient to imbue the tramp with UK residence status.[5] Lord Blackburn, in a concurring judgment, referred to a person spending 365 days a year, each in a different hotel,[6] and while accepting the Special Commissioners' decision on the facts, regarded residing outwith the UK for the greater part of the year as inconsistent with residence.[7]

If the case falls within ITA 2007 s 831,[8] 183 days within a tax year will be a significant length of time, but if the case does not fall within that section the question what is a significant length of time will be one for the Commissioners to decide.

HMRC believes that 183 days will, in any case, be decisive[9] and with that the Commissioners may or may not agree. In the reported cases, the physical presence which has resulted in the attribution of residence has always been for periods amounting to less than 183 days, but in each case there has been some element other than time to which weight has also had to be given.

---

1 See **2.08** above for the *Oxford English Dictionary* definition of residence quoted by Lord Cave in *Levene v IRC* (1928) 13 TC 486.
2 *Lysaght v IRC* (1928) 13 TC 511 at 528.
3 (1926) 10 TC 673.
4 (1926) 10 TC 673 at 679.
5 As to whether a person can be attributed with residence status without ever setting foot in the UK during a tax year, see **4.14** below.
6 At p 6810.
7 At p 682.
8 See **4.03** and **4.09–4.10** below.
9 See IR20 (July 2008) para 1.2, at Appendix 1 below.

2.12 Regularity and frequency of visits

Closely linked to the element of time or duration is the element of regularity and frequency. The duration of a person's physical presence in the UK during any one tax year may not be sufficiently significant for it to transform the presence into residence, but presence of insignificant duration in a succession of tax years may be sufficient to effect the transformation. This principle is well-illustrated by the case of *Kinloch v IRC*.[1] Although Mrs Kinloch spent the greater part of her time abroad, she visited the UK each year, sometimes for only a few days, other times for weeks or even months. The pattern of her visits from 1921–22 to 1927–28 was as follows: 66 days in 1921–22, 40 days over three visits in 1922–23, 177 days over five visits in 1923–24, five months, twelve days over three visits in 1924–25, 145 days over four visits in 1925–26, 141 days over five visits in 1926–27, and 156 days over four visits in 1927–28. In 1924–25, the Inland Revenue challenged Mrs Kinloch's assertion that she was not resident in the UK and the question was taken before the Special Commissioners. They decided that Mrs Kinloch was correct: she was not resident in the UK; and, accordingly, for the following two years the Inland Revenue followed the Commissioners' ruling. In 1927–28, however, the Inland Revenue again challenged Mrs Kinloch's non-resident status, and this time the Inland Revenue's contention was upheld: the Commissioners found that:

'... having regard to the continuance through the series of years of the regular and lengthy visits to the United Kingdom the circumstances were different from those under consideration when the appeal for the earlier year was heard,'[2]

and that Mrs Kinloch was resident in the UK. In 1927–28, she 'crossed the line, and ... now she is resident here'.[3] But what was the line Mrs Kinloch had crossed? Rowlatt J seems to have thought it was the line of duration of presence. He said that in 1927–28 Mrs Kinloch had stayed in the UK rather longer than previously; but that was not so: her visits in 1927–28 were of shorter duration than her visits in either 1923–24 or 1924–25. The line can only have been the line of frequency and regularity. Although a pattern had begun to emerge by the third year of Mrs Kinloch's visits, that pattern was neither sufficiently clear nor sufficiently well-established for it to have transformed her presence into residence; but, by the fifth year, her continued visits had remedied those defects. In the case of *Levene v IRC*[4] a similar pattern had emerged. Mr Levene, whose circumstances are fully described at **4.15** below, had

'... elected in each [of the four years from 1920–21 to 1924–25] to adopt a regular system of life in accordance with which he and his wife made their abode and lived in this country for a period of between four and five months in each year, and ... they were therefore resident in the United Kingdom not merely in the sense of being present here but in the fuller sense of making their home here.'[5]

Two recent decisions involving airline pilots flying in and out of the UK illustrate how similar patterns of presence may produce differing outcomes. In *Shepherd*[6] the Special Commissioner found that in 1998/99 the taxpayer was in the UK (not including the days of arrival and departure) for 92 days and in 1999/2000 for 80 days. By comparison, in *Grace*[7] it was found that he was present in 1997/1998 for 41 days, in 1998/1999 for 71 days and in 1999/2000 for 70 days (not including the days of arrival and departure). This translated into 86, 146 and 136 days

2.12 *Residence of individuals*

including the days of arrival and departure in each of those years. Shepherd was found to be resident while Grace was not.

1 (1929) 14 TC 736.
2 (1929) 14 TC 736 at 738.
3 (1929) 14 TC 736 at 738, per Rowlatt J.
4 (1928) 13 TC 486.
5 (1928) 13 TC 486 at 499.
6 *Shepherd v Revenue and Customs* [2005] UKSPC 484.
7 *Grace v Revenue & Customs* [2008] UKSPC SPC 663.

2.13 Revenue practice

Perhaps the most extreme case bearing on the principle of regular visits is that of *Lysaght v IRC*.[1] Since 1920, Mr Lysaght had lived in Ireland with his wife and family and had had no definite place of abode in the UK. Each month, however, he visited England to attend a meeting of the directors of John Lysaght Ltd and remained here on company business for about a week on each occasion. During his visits to the UK he stayed either at the home of his brother or in hotels. The total number of days spent in the UK for the three years 1922–23, 1923–24 and 1924–25 were 101, 94 and 84 respectively. The Special Commissioners held that Mr Lysaght was resident in the UK for each of those years and the House of Lords felt itself bound to uphold their decision on the grounds that the question of residence is a question of degree and fact and not a question of law.[2] Their Lordships' support for the Commissioners was by no means unqualified, however, and Viscount Cave LC went so far as to say:

> 'There appears to me to be no reason whatever for holding that [Mr Lysaght] is resident . . . in this country. It is true that he comes here at regular intervals and for recurrent business purposes; but these facts, while they explain the frequency of his visits, do not make them more than temporary visits or give them the character of residence in this country.'[3]

For reasons such as these, Viscount Cave thought the Crown's appeal should have been dismissed; Lord Warrington of Clyffe doubted that he would have come to the Commissioners' conclusion; Viscount Sumner could see several points in Mr Lysaght's favour but could find no error of law which would enable him to interfere with the Commissioners' decision; and only Lord Atkinson and Lord Buckmaster clearly felt that the Commissioners' decision was the correct one. For all this, however, it is the *Lysaght* case, tainted with uncertainty and stretching the concept of residence almost to its breaking point, on which the Inland Revenue has built its rule concerning the frequency and regularity of visits to the UK.[4]

As explained at **4.05** below, HMRC regards three months as equivalent to 92 days, and it may easily be calculated that Mr Lysaght's annual average was that less only one day! Although, as we shall see later,[5] it was Mr Lysaght's strong business link with the UK which, clearly, combined with the frequency and regularity of his visits so as to give his presence here the quality which transformed it into residence, the Revenue rule betrays no recognition that any such link is a necessary ingredient in the transformational process.

Following the decision in *Gaines-Cooper*, HMRC issued a statement aimed at clarifying the application of IR20 on the question as to when it regards the counting of days present to be relevant as follows:[6]

> 'In considering the issues of residence, ordinary residence and domicile in the Gaines-Cooper case, the Commissioners needed to build up a full picture of Mr Gaines-Cooper's life. A very important element of the picture was the pattern of his presence in the UK compared to the pattern of his presence overseas. The Commissioners decided that, in looking at these patterns, it would be misleading to wholly disregard days of arrival and departure. They used Mr Gaines-Cooper's patterns of presence in the UK as part of the evidence of his lifestyle and habits during the years in question. Based on this, and a wide range of other evidence, the Commissioners found that he had been continuously resident in the UK. From HMRC's perspective, therefore, the '91-day test' was not relevant to the Gaines-Cooper case since Mr Gaines-Cooper did not leave the UK.'

1 (1928) 13 TC 511.
2 See **2.03** above.
3 *Lysaght v IRC* (1928) 13 TC 511 at 532.
4 IR20 (July 2008), para 3.3, at Appendix 1 below.
5 At **2.18** below.
6 HMRC Brief 01/07.

2.14 Future conduct

Before leaving this discussion of the acquisition of residence status through regular and frequent visits, something must be said about the fact that a determination of residence status on those grounds in many cases involves the simultaneous consideration of a number of tax years. In the *Levene* case, it was objected that such a global consideration was wrong in law since it involved the taking into account in earlier years of conduct which only occurred subsequently. Viscount Sumner did not accept that this was at all erroneous:

> 'I agree that the taxpayer's chargeability in each year of charge constitutes a separate issue, even though several years are included in one appeal, but I do not think any error of law is committed if the facts applicable to the whole of the time are found in one continuous story. Light may be thrown on the purpose with which the first departure from the United Kingdom took place, by looking at his proceedings in a series of subsequent years. They go to show method and system and so remove doubt which might be entertained if the years were examined in isolation from one another.'[1]

1 *Levene v IRC* (1928) 13 TC 486 at 501.

2.15 Previous history

If it is permissible to look at a person's conduct in years subsequent to the year for which a determination of residence status is being sought,[1] it is certainly permissible to look at a person's conduct in previous years, and this was Viscount Sumner's initial approach in the *Levene* case.[2] Having decided that for the first year in question, 1920–21, Mr Levene was resident in the UK, Viscount Sumner took Mr Levene's conduct in that year as a reference against which to examine each of the subsequent years in question and concluded that 'no material change occurred in his way of living'.[3] It followed, therefore, that Mr Levene was resident in each of the subsequent years also.

This same approach was adopted by the Special Commissioners in the case of *Miesegaes v IRC*.[4] Stanley Miesegaes was a Dutch national who was at boarding school in Harrow from 1939 until July 1951. The years for which his residence status was in question were 1947–48 to 1951–52. Having found that Mr Miesegaes was resident for the years 1947–48 to 1950–51, the Special Commissioners had still to decide his residence status for the year 1951–52. At the start of that tax year, Mr Miesegaes was in Holland but he was in the UK from 15 April to 17 August. On 17 August he left the UK to continue his education in Switzerland. The Commissioners decided the question for 1951–52 by looking back to the previous years. The four months' presence in 1951–52 was, they said, 'in continuation of what we found to be his residence here for the previous four years and we found that he was resident in the UK for 1951–52 also'.[5] The Commissioners' decision was upheld by both the High Court and the Court of Appeal, and it is clear, therefore, that the principle applied by the Commissioners will stand: UK residence status, once acquired, will endure in succeeding years unless there is some change in a person's manner of life of such significance as to throw the question of his residence status into doubt.

---

1 See **2.14** above.
2 *Levene v IRC* (1928) 13 TC 486.
3 *Levene v IRC* (1928) 13 TC 486 at 501.
4 (1957) 37 TC 493.
5 (1957) 37 TC 493 at 495.

Connecting factors

2.16 The ties of birth

Clearly, the less conclusive the elements of duration, frequency and regularity of presence where a person's residence status has been called into question are, the more important will be the other elements that may, in any particular case, be indicative of that status. One element which obviously carried some weight with the Lord President in the case of *Reid v IRC*[1] was the tie of nationality. Miss Reid, he said 'is a British subject',[2] and the suggestion would seem to be that the link thus subsisting between Miss Reid and the UK must necessarily have tinged her periods of presence here with the hue of residence – though the tie of nationality can never alone do more than that. Prior to the enactment of ITA 2007 ss 831 and 832, a British subject whose ordinary residence had been in the UK found it more difficult than a foreign national to divest himself of UK residence status[3] and, the possible rationale behind that section – that a British subject may be supposed to wish to cultivate and preserve, rather than sever, his links with the UK – has had a place in the approach to questions of residence even where the statutory provisions were of no direct application. Viscount Cave recognised this in the *Levene* case when he said:

> 'The most difficult case is that of a wanderer who, having no home in any country, spends a part only of his time in hotels in the United Kingdom and the remaining and greater part of his time in hotels abroad ... If ... such a man is a foreigner who has never resided in this country, there may be great difficulty in holding that he is resident here. But if he is a British subject the Commissioners are entitled to take into account all the facts of the case.'[4]

The link of nationality is, then, of greater importance than it is often acknowledged to be for, if a person is found to be joined to the UK by that link, the Commissioners have not only the right but also the duty to look much more closely at the circumstances surrounding that person's presence here than would otherwise be the case. A practical example of the difference in approach is given by the *Zorab* case which is described at **4.05** below. Mr Zorab had been born in India and had spent all his life there until his retirement from the Indian Civil Service. Upon his retirement, however, he began to spend almost half of each year in the UK, yet, despite the duration and regularity of his visits, the Commissioners found that he was not resident here. His nationality was a decisive factor. 'This gentleman,' said Rowlatt J, 'is a native of India'.[5]

1 (1926) 10 TC 673.
2 (1926) 10 TC 673 at 679.
3 See **4.14** ff below.
4 *Levene v IRC* (1928) 13 TC 486 at 506.
5 *IRC v Zorab* (1926) 11 TC 289 at 292.

2.17 The ties of family

As well as being a British subject, Miss Reid[1] had a sister who lived in London. Viewed in isolation, that fact may not seem of particular significance but it was one of the elements listed by Lord Clyde as contributing to the finding that she was resident in the UK. 'Her family ties', he said, 'are with this country'.[2]

So it was, too, with Mr Levene and his wife:

2.17 *Residence of individuals*

> 'They ... came to visit their relatives in England, and (on one occasion) to make arrangements for the care of a brother of [Mr Levene] who is mentally afflicted [and] to visit the graves of his parents.[3]
>
> His family ties are in this country, his wife having five sisters and he himself six brothers and sisters residing here.'[4]

In the *Levene* case, Lord Hanworth MR had said in the Court of Appeal that an important characteristic factor to look for in determining whether or not a man possesses the quality of residence is 'if he returns to and seeks his own fatherland in order to enjoy a sojourn in proximity to his relations and friends',[5] and this characteristic was very much in evidence in the *Kinloch* case referred to at **2.12** above. Mrs Kinloch was a British subject and a widow who had lived in India from 1909 to 1919. From 1919 onwards she made frequent and regular visits to the UK in each tax year but her presence here throughout was coloured by the fact that her son was attending boarding schools in England and that:

> '... her various objects in coming to the United Kingdom were to take her son to and from school, to attend to his outfitting, to consult with his doctor, dentist and oculist, to interview those having charge of him, to be with him during illness and to attend his confirmation.'[6]

Although, as has been noted,[7] the decisive factor in the Commissioners' decision that Mrs Kinloch was resident in the UK was the frequency and regularity of Mrs Kinloch's visits here, her family ties with this country were undoubtedly of weight and had a bearing on their determination for here was a lady:

> '... who spends a good deal of her time in this country but without any settled home, living in hotels here and abroad, but having a reason for coming here, because she has a son who is being educated here and who is sometimes ill, and so on.'[8]

---

1 *Reid v IRC* (1926) 10 TC 673.
2 *Reid v IRC* (1926) 10 TC 673 at 679.
3 *Levene v IRC* (1928) 13 TC 486 at 504, per Viscount Cave LC.
4 *Levene v IRC* (1928) 13 TC 486 at 508, per Lord Warrington of Clyffe.
5 *Levene v IRC* (1928) 13 TC 486 at 497.
6 *Kinloch v IRC* (1929) 14 TC 736 at 738.
7 At **2.12** above.
8 *Kinloch v IRC* (1929) 14 TC 736 at 739, per Rowlatt J.

2.18 The ties of business

Another factor which, in the *Reid* case,[1] Lord Clyde singled out as being relevant to the finding that the taxpayer possessed UK residence status was that 'her business matters (including her banking) are conducted here'.[2] That tie was of particular importance in the case of Mr Lysaght. It has already been explained[3] that the element of frequency and regularity in Mr Lysaght's visits to the UK was thought by the House of Lords to be barely sufficient to justify the finding of residence returned by the Commissioners. This feeling was present in each of the lower courts, too, and it seems clear that it was only the strong business link between Mr Lysaght and the UK which, in the view of Lawrence LJ, added a support which would enable the Commissioners' decision to stand:

> 'The case is near the line but in my opinion the determining factor is that the post which [Mr Lysaght] holds in John Lysaght Ltd causes him to come regularly to England and to stay in the UK for a substantial period in each year. The fact that [Mr Lysaght] stays regularly in England for about three months of the year for the discharge of his duties as the servant of an English company in my opinion constitutes him a person who is ... resident ... in the UK.'[4]

Mr Levene, too, had ties of business which contributed to the finding that he was resident in the UK:

> 'He had gone out of business in England and had broken up his establishment, but he still had in England business interests connected with his Income Tax assessments.'[5]

Included in ties of business may be ties of communication. People wishing to get in touch with Miss Reid did so 'c/o Commercial Bank, Glasgow', thus 'the address by which she can be found at any time is in this country'[6] and this factor too was added to the list of those which weighed in favour of Miss Reid's residence in the UK.

The insertion of a UK address for Captain Loewenstein[7] in the annual return of The Belgian Breeding Stock Farm Company Ltd weighed against his assertion that he was not resident in the UK:

> 'At any rate this gentleman's return to the Registrar of Joint Stock Companies shows him as a Director and having his usual residence at 'Pinfold'. Now it is said that this was only done for convenience ... The Commissioners say they do not accept that view, and they certainly are entitled to say that, and I am bound by it.'[8]

---

1 *Reid v IRC* (1926) 10 TC 673.
2 *Reid v IRC* (1926) 10 TC 673 at 679.
3 At **2.12** above.
4 *Lysaght v IRC* (1928) 13 TC 511 at 525.
5 *Levene v IRC* (1928) 13 TC 486 at 500, per Viscount Sumner.
6 *Reid v IRC* (1926) 10 TC 673 at 679, per the Lord President.
7 *Loewenstein v De Salis* (1926) 10 TC 424. See **2.10** above.
8 *Loewenstein v De Salis* (1926) 10 TC 424 at 436, per Rowlatt J.

2.19 Other ties

In the *Reid* case,[1] the Commissioners noted that, when the house in Glasgow in which Miss Reid had once lived was given up, Miss Reid 'sent three trunks with clothes, jewellery, and a few other personal effects to a store in London and has since, on one or two occasions, been to the store

2.19 *Residence of individuals*

to fetch or put back various articles',[2] and this fact, that 'her personal belongings not required when she is travelling are kept in store in London',[3] duly weighed against her when the question of her residence status was decided.

The ties of religious observance also may weigh against a person's claim to be non-resident. Mr Levene, on occasions, visited the UK 'to take part in certain Jewish religious observances'.[4] This, accordingly, became a factor in the determination of his residence status.

Membership of clubs and societies in the UK will also be a factor of importance.[5] Continued membership will indicate an intention to return and will weigh against any claim that ties with the UK have been broken.

The list of possible links with the UK which may so colour a person's presence here as to transform it into residence is inexhaustible. All such links will be of importance, however, should it ever become necessary for the question of a person's residence status to be determined.

---

1 *Reid v IRC* (1926) 10 TC 673.
2 *Reid v IRC* (1926) 10 TC 673 at 676.
3 *Reid v IRC* (1926) 10 TC 673 at 679, per the Lord President.
4 *Levene v IRC* (1928) 13 TC 486 at 509, per Lord Warrington of Clyffe.
5 See paras 2(6) and 2(m) respectively of the cases stated by the Commissioners in *Lysaght v IRC* (1928) 13 TC 511 at 514 and *Withers v Wynyard* (1938) 21 TC 724 at 727.

Intent and legality

2.20 Involuntary or unintentional presence

While positive intentions may contribute to the transformation of presence into residence, negative intentions will not prevent such a transformation taking place if other indicia would lead to the conclusion that a person is resident in the UK.

In *Bayard Brown v Burt*,[1] Mr Brown, who had lived on an ocean-going yacht in UK territorial waters for the last 20 years, contended that 'it was the intention to go to sea at any moment, and the ship could be steamed out of port at an hour's notice',[2] but he was nonetheless held to be resident in the UK.

In *Lysaght v IRC*[3] it was shown that Mr Lysaght visited the UK only in fulfilment of his business obligations and not from personal choice. Lord Buckmaster held, however, that this was no bar to residence:

> 'A man might well be compelled to reside here completely against his will; the exigencies of business often forbid the choice of residence and though a man may make his home elsewhere and stay in this country only because business compels him, yet none the less, if the periods for which and the conditions under which he stays are such that they may be regarded as constituting residence, it is open to the Commissioners to find that in fact he does so reside.'[4]

During the years for which his residence status was in question, Stanley Miesegaes was a schoolboy boarding at Harrow. His counsel argued that a stay at a boarding school could not constitute residence because 'it is not voluntary residence; and it is institutional. If one asked a schoolboy ... where he lived, he would never say that he lived at his public school'.[5] Pearce LJ could not accept that argument, however:

> 'Lord Buckmaster's remarks [in the *Lysaght* case] as to the exigencies of business seem equally applicable to the exigencies of education. Education is a large, necessary and normal ingredient in the lives of adolescent members of the community, just as work or business is in the lives of its adult members ... In this case the school terms at Harrow dictated the main residential pattern of the boy's life ... It would be erroneous to endow educational residence with some esoteric quality that must as a matter of law, remove it from the category of residence.'[6]

It was neither business nor education that constrained Lord Inchiquin to stay in the UK for most of 1940–41 and 1941–42: 'The only reason he was there was because his military duties kept him there.'[7] He had, furthermore, before the outbreak of the Second World War, formed the intention of returning to Dromoland Castle, his ancestral home in Eire, and had carried out that intention as soon as he managed to obtain indefinite release from active service. None of this was, however, of the least effect:

> 'I am quite unable to say that where you find a man has at all times before the war been resident in this country and you find him continuing to serve in this country in His Majesty's Forces during the war, the mere fact that he had, before the outbreak of war, formed the intention of going to live elsewhere makes it impossible to say, as the Commissioners have found, that he was resident in this country during the period of his military service.'[8]

In *Re Mackenzie*[9] it was held that an Australian lady who, four months after arriving in England in 1885, was certified to be insane and detained in an asylum for the 54 years ending with her death in 1939, was resident in the UK for each of those years:

> 'Her residence in England became permanent, no doubt, by reason of her mental condition and the fact that she required care and attention, but I think it may fairly be said that, in the ordinary course of her life as events happened, she resided in England.'[10]

The same would, it seems, be true of a person imprisoned in the UK. In *Todd v Egyptian Delta Land and Investment Co Ltd*,[11] Viscount Sumner said:

> 'A man may change his residence at will, except that a certain duration of time or fixity of decision is requisite, and, but for the peculiar cases of a convict in gaol or a lunatic lawfully detained in a madhouse, I do not think that residence is ever determined for a natural person simply by law.'[12]

The rationale behind all the decisions referred to above is very simply put. Residence depends upon the fact of residing not (except in the context of ITA 2007 ss 831 and 832)[13] upon the intent or wish to reside. Just as a man is none the less present for not wanting to be where he is, so he cannot be the less resident for not wishing to be where he resides. It must be noted,

2.20 *Residence of individuals*

however, that this does not hold true in questions of ordinary residence. There, as explained in Chapter 3, the voluntary adoption of an abode in a particular place or country is essential.

---

1   (1911) 5 TC 667.
2   (1911) 5 TC 667 at 672.
3   (1928) 13 TC 511.
4   (1928) 13 TC 511 at 534.
5   *Miesegaes v IRC* (1957) 37 TC 493 at 500, per Pearce LJ.
6   *Miesegaes v IRC* (1957) 37 TC 493 at 501.
7   *Inchiquin v IRC* (1948) 31 TC 125 at 130, per Singleton J.
8   *Inchiquin v IRC* (1948) 31 TC 125 at 134 and 135.
9   (1940) 19 ATC 399.
10 (1940) 19 ATC 399 at 404, per Morton J.
11 (1928) 14 TC 119.
12 (1928) 14 TC 119 at 140.
13 See **4.05** below.

2.21 Unlawful presence

If, as has been demonstrated at **2.20** above, residence is not necessarily a matter of volition, neither is it necessarily a matter of lawful presence. Mr Bayard Brown[1] had no right to anchor his yacht in the tidal waters off Brightlingsea but that did not alter the fact that he was residing there:

> 'Residence is something which depends upon the fact of residing and not upon the legal right to reside.'[2]

The question of the effect of unlawful or illegal presence on residence status was fully explored by Sir John Donaldson MR in the case of *Hipperson v Electoral Registration Officer for the District of Newbury*.[3] The case concerned the right of women living in tents and vehicles on Greenham Common, in the furtherance of their protest against the presence of cruise missiles, to be placed on the electoral register of the District of Newbury. Under the Representation of the People Act 1983 s 1(1), such a right rests on a person being 'resident' in the relevant district on a specified date, and it was contended that the Greenham women could not be resident in the District of Newbury as they were present there in breach of the byelaws and of the Highways Act 1980 s 137. In rejecting this submission, Sir John Donaldson MR pointed out that:

> '... the consequences of holding that ... residence must not involve the commission of a criminal offence and, a fortiori, that the residence must be lawful in the sense of not involving a breach of the civil rights of others are startling in the extreme. A whole range of citizens would be disqualified. The county court judge gave, as an example, the occupation as a living room or workroom of a room which is immediately over a cesspool, midden or ashpit contrary to s 49 of the Public Health Act 1936. He could also have referred to breach of conditions relating to the use of caravans under s 269 of the same Act, to the continued occupation of premises to which a closing order has been applied under the Housing Acts, to the use of premises for residential purposes in breach of an enforcement notice under the Town and Country Planning Acts

and to adverse possession of residential premises contrary to s 7 of the Criminal Law Act 1977. If the scope of the disqualification is to be extended from the illegal to the unlawful, all those who remain in occupation of residential premises when a possession order has been made would be disqualified.'[4]

The Master of the Rolls concluded his rejection of the submission by declaring that 'residence ... does not depend on law for its existence'.[5]

---

1 See **4.08** below.
2 *Bayard Brown v Burt* (1911) 5 TC 667 at 672, per Kennedy LJ.
3 [1985] 2 All ER 456.
4 [1985] 2 All ER 456 at 463.
5 [1985] 2 All ER 456 at 463.

2.22 Residence for tax treaty purposes

It will be apparent that an individual may be resident in the UK for tax purposes although also living elsewhere. In most, but not all cases, residence in another country will entail a liability to tax in that country as well. The UK has entered into over 100 treaties with the objective of the prevention of, or relief from, double taxation, ie the taxation of the same income or gains by both the UK and the foreign state concerned.[1] A double tax treaty generally protects a person against double taxation by allocating taxing jurisdiction between the contacting states and providing that income arising in one state is not to be charged to tax in the hands of a resident of the other state, or affords him relief by providing that, where he is charged to tax on income accruing to him in the source state, he is to be given exemption or a credit for that tax in the state of which he is resident.

Included in the mechanisms for allocating taxing jurisdiction are rules for determining which residence status of the two is to prevail for the purposes of the treaty where both states claim taxing rights on the basis that the taxpayer is resident in each state.

Most modern treaties to which the UK is a party follow the Model Double Taxation Convention on Income and Capital published by the Organisation for Economic Co-operation and Development, Paris. Although the model has been amended several times, the provisons dealing with residence have in essence remained constant since the 1963 OECD Draft Double Taxation Convention. The current form, as it applies to individuals reads as follows:

'**Article 4: Residence**
(1) For the purposes of this Convention, the term 'resident of a Contracting State' means any person who, under the laws of that State, is liable to tax therein by reason of his domicile, residence, ...or any other criterion of a similar nature; the term does not include any person who is liable to tax in that Contracting State only if he derives income or capital gains from sources therein.
(2) Where by reason of the provisions of paragraph (1) of this Article an individual is a resident of both Contracting States, then his status shall be determined in accordance with the following rules:

2.22 *Residence of individuals*

    (a) he shall be deemed to be a resident of the Contracting State in which he has a permanent home available to him; if he has a permanent home available to him in both Contracting States, he shall be deemed to be a resident of the Contracting State with which his personal and economic relations are closer (centre of vital interests);
    (b) if the Contracting State in which he has his centre of vital interests cannot be determined, or if he has not a permanent home available to him in either Contracting State, he shall be deemed to be a resident of the Contracting State in which he has an habitual abode;
    (c) if he has an habitual abode in both Contracting States or in neither of them, he shall be deemed to be a resident of the Contracting State of which he is a national;
    (d) if he is a national of both Contracting States or of neither of them, the competent authorities of the Contracting States shall settle the question by mutual agreement.'

Consequently, if an individual is regarded as a resident for tax purposes by both contracting states under their respective domestic laws, then Art 4(2) provides that his status is to be determined by applying in sequence each of the listed rules.[2]

The first of these is that he is deemed to be a resident of the State in which he has a permanent home available to him. According to the OECD Commentary to the Model Convention 'any form of home may be taken into account (house or apartment belonging to or rented by the individual, rented furnished room).[3] If that is to be so, 'home', in the context of Art 4(2)(a), may be taken to be similar to 'place of abode' as described at **2.08** to **2.10** above.[4] Permanence is however essential. According to the commentary, this means that 'the individual must have arranged to have the dwelling available to him at all times, continuously, and not occasionally and retained [the home] for his permanent use as opposed to staying at a particular place under such conditions that it is evident that the stay is intended to be of short duration'. This rules out the possibility that a house etc which is let between visits might be a 'permanent home' for tie-breaker purposes.

If a person has a permanent home in both states (but not if he has a permanent home in neither), then he shall be deemed to be a resident of the State with which his personal and economic relations are closer (centre of vital interests).

The meaning of the words in parentheses is by no means clear, but the OECD Commentary provides some guidance by stating that:

> '... regard will be had to his family and social relations, his occupations, his political, cultural or other activities, his place of business, the place from which he administers his property etc ... but ... considerations based on the personal acts of the individual must receive special attention'.[5]

If a person's centre of vital interests are divided equally between the two states concerned, or if the person concerned has no permanent home, then the person is to be regarded as resident in the state 'in which he has an habitual abode'. The OECD Commentary suggest that the place where he spends more time tips the balance in favour of that state.[6] Furthermore, the

Intent and legality **2.22**

French version of the text is '*où elle séjourne de façon habituelle*', which indicates that what is being referred to is the state in which a person habitually *stays*.

Where, even after the application of these tests, the question of a person's residence remains unresolved, nationality becomes the deciding factor. If the person is a national of both states or of neither of them, then the competent authorities of the contracting states are required to settle the question by mutual agreement.

---

1 Such treaties are given effect in domestic law by Order in Council made under the authority of ICTA 1988 s 788.
2 The only case in the UK where the residence tie-breaker provisions of Art 4(2) were invoked is *Squirrell v Revenue and Customs* [2005] UKSPC SPC 00493 (23 June 2005). The taxpayer left the UK on October 2000, moving to the US where he was treated as resident for the whole of 2000. He was resident in the UK in the tax year 1999–2000 when he received a termination payment from his UK employer. Although Art 4(2) of the US-UK treaty was referred to, no claim had been made in either country to determine his residence status for the purposes of the treaty by going through the tie-breaker provisions in turn. In any event the Special Commissioner concluded that the taxpayer's UK tax treatment was the same regardless of where he was resident for purposes of the treaty.
3 Commmentary to Art 4, para 13.
4 It is interesting to note that, in *R v Hammond* (1852) 17 QB 772, Lord Campbell CJ said (at 780 and 781) that 'a man's residence, where he lives with his family and sleeps at night, is always his place of abode in the full sense of that expression'.
5 Commentary to Art 4 para 15.
6 Commentary to Art 4 para 17.

CHAPTER 3

Ordinary residence

> '*Sark.*'
> '*Yes, sir,*' *said the man in the little quayside hut.* '*A return fare. Six shillings.*'
> '*A single, my friend,*' *said Mr Harold Pye.*
>
> Mervyn Peake *Mr Pye* Ch 1

3.01 Introduction

It has been noted at **1.10** above that residence *simpliciter* as interpreted by the Courts as a determinant of chargeability is an attribute more difficult to acquire and less easy to shed than the attribute of mere presence. Ordinary residence may be seen as that same principle carried one stage further. However, ordinary residence is 'a more elusive concept than simple residence. It can also be more adhesive, in that a person can remain ordinarily resident even though physically absent from the country throughout the year (and, accordingly, not resident)'.[1] Ordinary residence is, in fact,

> '... a point on a scale which ranges from mere presence in this country through "resident" ... to "domicile" which is widely used to specify the nature and quality of the association between person and place which brings the person within the scope of that particular enactment.[2]

In the context of the Taxes Acts, the term 'ordinarily resident', like the term 'resident', has 'no ... technical or special meaning'[3] and must, therefore, be given its natural and ordinary meaning.[4] The courts have, however, found some difficulty in deciding not only what that natural meaning might be but also how ordinary residence differs from residence *simpliciter* – though the fact that there is a difference between the two terms is evident from the legislation itself.

While residence is the central determinant of liability, ordinary residence is a determinant of liability only in certain special cases. In some circumstances it limits liability to UK taxation for those whose connection with the UK is more tenuous. Thus, Pt 8 of ITTOIA 2005 charges the 'relevant foreign income' of individuals who are resident but not ordinarily resident. Employment earnings of such individuals from duties performed

3.01 *Ordinary residence*

outside the UK are likewise chargeable on the remittance basis.[5] A further graduation is found in the case of employees who are both resident and ordinarily resident but not domiciled in the UK. The 'overseas earnings' of such individuals are taxable on the remittance basis.[6] The parallel limited application of ITEPA 2003 Pt 7 (Employment Related Securities) to such individuals was modified by Finance Act 2008.[7]

On the other hand, the higher degree of connection with the UK is required before certain anti-avoidance legislation is applicable. ITA 2007 Pt 13 (Tax Avoidance), Chapter 2 (Transfer of Assets Abroad) is only applicable to individuals ordinarily resident in the UK at the material time.

Ordinary residence is also perhaps used to extend taxing jurisdiction. It is apparent that ordinary residence is a more enduring personal attribute than residence *simpliciter*, and TCGA 1992 s 2(1) may suggest that Parliament has sought to rely on it to impose a charge on a wider range of person:

> 'Subject to any exceptions provided by this Act, a person shall be chargeable to capital gains tax in respect of chargeable gains accruing to him in a year of assessment during any part of which he is resident in the United Kingdom, or during which he is ordinarily resident in the United Kingdom.'

In other words, on this approach a person who succeeds in divesting himself of the quality of residence *simpliciter* (by, perhaps, absence from the UK for an entire tax year) would, if he remains ordinarily resident here, remain within the charge to capital gains tax on any disposals made during that year.[8]

Because 'ordinary residence' is a term which is undefined by statute, the question whether or not a person possesses the attribute which that term signifies is a question not of law but of fact. The discussion at **2.03** above concerning the determination of questions of fact is, therefore, of equal relevance whether residence *simpliciter* or ordinary residence is the attribute in question.

---

1 Inland Revenue explanatory note relating to a proposed amendment to Finance Bill 1974, cl 18.
2 *R v Barnet London Borough, ex p Shah* [1980] 3 All ER 679 at 681, per Ormrod J.
3 *Levene v IRC* (1928) 13 TC 486 at 507, per Lord Warrington of Clyffe.
4 See **2.02** above.
5 ITEPA s 26.
6 ITEPA ss 21–24.
7 Schedule 7 paragraph 22.
8 But see further para **3.03** below.

Concept and application

3.02 The meaning of ordinary residence

Although the question of whether a person is 'ordinarily residing in the UK' is a question of fact, the meaning of those words is a matter of statutory interpretation and thus a matter of law. As such, the words were given careful consideration by the Court of Session in 1926 and by the House of Lords in two leading tax cases decided in 1928. In each case the court made it clear that it was construing the words as bearing their natural and ordinary meaning.

In the case of *Reid v IRC*[1] Lord Clyde LP firmly rejected Miss Reid's argument that, even if she was resident in the UK by reason of her visits and the various ties which bound her to this country, she could not be ordinarily resident since she had always spent the greater part of each year abroad:

> 'The argument was that the meaning of the word "ordinarily" is governed – wholly or mainly – by the test of time or duration. I think it is a test, and an important one; but I think it is only one among many. From the point of view of time, "ordinarily" would stand in contrast to "casually". But [Miss Reid] is not a "casual" visitor to her home country; on the contrary she regularly returns to it, and "resides" in it for a part – albeit the smaller part – of every year. I hesitate to give the word "ordinarily" any more precise interpretation than "in the customary course of events", and anyhow I cannot think that the element of time so predominates in its meaning that, unless [Miss Reid] "resided" in the United Kingdom for at least six months and a day, she could not be said "ordinarily" to reside there in the year in question.'[2]

This point was taken up in the case of *Levene v IRC*[3] by Rowlatt J who said:

> '"Ordinarily" may mean either preponderatingly in point of time or time plus importance, or it may mean habitually as a matter of course, as one might say: in the ordinary course of a man's life, although in time it might be insignificant ... I think that "ordinary" does not mean preponderatingly, I think it means ordinary in the sense that it is habitual in the ordinary course of a man's life, and I think a man is ordinarily resident in the United Kingdom when the ordinary course of his life is such that it discloses a residence in the United Kingdom ...'[4]

In the House of Lords, Lord Warrington of Clyffe affirmed this view, saying of ordinary residence that it is:

> "... impossible to restrict its connotation to its duration. A member of this House may well be said to be ordinarily resident in London during the Parliamentary session and in the country during the recess. If it has any definite meaning I should say it means according to the way in which a man's life is usually ordered.'[5]

In that same case, the Lord Chancellor, Viscount Cave, said:

> 'The expression "ordinary residence" ... is contrasted with ... occasional or temporary residence; and I think it connotes residence in a place with some degree of continuity and apart from accidental or temporary absences. So understood, the expression differs little in meaning from the word "residence" ...'[6]

In *Lysaght v IRC*[7] Viscount Sumner said:

> 'I think the converse to "ordinarily" is "extraordinarily", and that part of the regular order of a man's life, adopted voluntarily and for settled purposes, is not "extraordinary".'[8]

3.02 Ordinary residence

In 1981, the words 'ordinarily resident' again fell to be construed by the courts and, in *R v Barnet London Borough, ex p Shah*,[9] Lord Denning MR said:

> 'The words "ordinarily resident" mean that the person must be habitually and normally resident here, apart from temporary or occasional absences of long or short duration.'[10]

---

1 (1926) 10 TC 673.
2 (1926) 10 TC 673 at 680.
3 (1928) 13 TC 486.
4 (1928) 13 TC 486 at 493.
5 (1928) 13 TC 486 at 509.
6 (1928) 13 TC 486 at 507.
7 (1928) 13 TC 511.
8 (1928) 13 TC 511 at 528.
9 [1982] 1 All ER 698.
10 [1982] 1 All ER 698 at 704.

3.03 The relation of residence to ordinary residence

Lord Denning's interpretation of the words 'ordinarily resident'[1] expands Viscount Cave's phrase 'with some degree of continuity' into 'habitually and normally' and takes ordinary residence to be residence *simpliciter* which is customary, usual and confirmed by habit. Thus, Miss Reid was ordinarily resident because the residence status she attracted to herself by reason of the regularity of her visits to the UK[2] and her various links with this country[3] was confirmed by habit as being residence of a customary and usual kind rather than residence which was exceptional, unusual or accidental.

Although Miss Reid undoubtedly had engaged in a great deal of wandering – one month in France, next month in Spain, the month after in Austria, the month after that in Portugal – the Commissioners decided no: Miss Reid every year, without fail (though only for some three and a half months) returned to the UK and it was this factor which added the quality of ordinariness to her residence *simpliciter*.

It should be noted, however, that had the regularity of Miss Reid's visits to the UK and her links with this country not, in the opinion of the Commissioners, been sufficient to imbue her with the quality of UK residence *simpliciter*, she could not, within either Viscount Sumner's, Viscount Cave's or Lord Denning's understanding of the term, have been attributed with the quality of being ordinarily resident during the years in question. In law, ordinary residence springs from residence *simpliciter*, and if residence *simpliciter* is never acquired then ordinary residence cannot be acquired either. Viscount Cave said:

> 'I find it difficult to imagine a case in which a man while not resident here is yet ordinarily resident here.'[4]

As is explained below, such a case *could* have arisen under the law as it stood in Viscount Cave's day, and can certainly arise under the law as it stands today; but this does not invalidate the linking of ordinary residence with residence *simpliciter* in the manner described. In the *Miesegaes* case,[5] the Special Commissioners considered that they had:

> '... first [to] decide whether [Mr Miesegaes] was resident in the United Kingdom in each of the years in question, and, second, if he was so resident, whether his residence had the quality of ordinary residence,'[6]

and Morris LJ commented:

> 'It seems to me that the Special Commissioners were correct in their approach when they decided that first they should consider whether [Mr Miesegaes] was resident in the United Kingdom in each of the years in question and, in the second place, whether his residence had the quality of ordinary residence.'[7]

This approach will still be helpful provided it is borne in mind that, where it leads to the conclusion that a person is not resident *simpliciter*, the additional question, 'But is he not resident *simpliciter* merely by reason of a temporary absence extending over the entire tax year or by reason of the special rules concerning persons working abroad full-time in a trade, profession or vocation?'[8] Except in the case of a person who goes abroad for a period of full-time service under a contract of service,[9] neither of these circumstances will result in the loss of ordinary residence status if that status was possessed immediately prior to the departure which led to the loss of resident *simpliciter* status.

TCGA 1992 s 2(1) is drafted on the assumption that a person may be ordinarily resident in the UK without being resident *simpliciter* here, which provides that, subject to certain exceptions:

> '... a person shall be chargeable to capital gains tax in respect of chargeable gains accruing to him in a year of assessment during any part of which he is resident in the UK, or during which he is ordinarily resident in the UK.'

The contrary is the basis for the income tax legislation discussed in **3.01** above. If a person can be ordinarily resident while not resident, it must be most exceptional. It is important to note that, although (subject to what has been said in the preceding paragraphs) a person cannot be ordinarily resident in the UK unless he is also resident *simpliciter* here, a person may, in certain circumstances (and contrary to all current Revenue guidance),[10] be resident *simpliciter* in the UK, year after year, without being ordinarily resident here. Those circumstances will subsist where a person's residence *simpliciter* lacks one or more of the elements emphasised by Lord Scarman when he said:

> 'I unhesitatingly subscribe to the view that 'ordinarily resident' refers to a man's abode in a particular place or country which he has adopted voluntarily and for settled purposes as part of the regular order of his life for the time being, whether of short or long duration.'[11]

It is to these three key features of voluntary adoption, settled purpose and the regular order of life – none of which is essential to the acquisition of residence *simpliciter* status but all of which are essential to the acquisition of ordinary residence status – that we must now turn our attention.

3.03 *Ordinary residence*

1 See **3.02** above.
2 See **3.02** above.
3 See **2.16–2.19** above.
4 *Levene v IRC* (1928) 13 TC 486 at 507.
5 *Miesegaes v IRC* (1957) 37 TC 493.
6 *Miesegaes v IRC* (1957) 37 TC 493 at 495.
7 *Miesegaes v IRC* (1957) 37 TC 493 at 502.
8 See **4.13–4.17** below.
9 See **4.17** below.
10 See **3.09–3.12** below.
11 *Shah v Barnet London Borough Council* [1983] 1 All ER 226 at 235.

Essential elements

3.04 A voluntarily adopted place of abode

It is clear from the facts of the case in which Viscount Sumner gave his interpretation of the words 'ordinarily residing' that he cannot have used the words 'adopted voluntarily' in the sense of 'free of any kind of external constraint' for Mr Lysaght was in Great Britain only because his business commitments compelled him to be here. He would, no doubt, have preferred to be at home in Ireland rather than in the Spa Hotel in Bath, but in choosing to be a director of John Lysaght Ltd he had accepted that he would have to spend one week or so of each month in the UK. The phrase 'adopted voluntarily' must, therefore, have been understood by Viscount Sumner as being not inconsistent with submission to such constraints as a person's chosen order of life imposed upon him.

On the face of it, however, the first case which came before the courts following the *Lysaght* case and which centred on the phrase 'adopted voluntarily' took the meaning of those words some way beyond that. It concerned Miss Mackenzie, an Australian, who, at the age of 28, came on a visit to England with her mother. There was no evidence as to how long the visit was intended to last but, in the event, Miss Mackenzie, having stayed here four months, remained here until her death at the age of 82 because, after spending those four months here, she was, in 1885, certified as insane and detained, first in Holloway Mental Hospital until 1893, then in the Coppice Lunatic Hospital at Nottingham until her death. The case was an estate duty case which arose because of a disagreement over the meaning of the words 'ordinarily resident' in F(No 2)A 1915 s 47(1), and counsel for the administrator of Miss Mackenzie's estate submitted that:

> 'Miss Mackenzie could not be said to be ordinarily resident in September, 1885, when she was certified as of unsound mind, and that during the whole of the rest of her life she was under constraint and unable to exercise any will of her own, and that that period, the last 54 years of her life, cannot be taken into account at all as making her ordinarily resident in this country ... [T]he words of Viscount Sumner "adopted voluntarily" indicate that no residence can be treated as ordinary residence unless it is the result of a voluntary act on the part of the person residing there.'[1]

Morton J could not agree:

> 'The matter does not wholly depend on choice ... I do not understand Viscount Sumner ... as saying that a period of residence in this country which is involuntary must be wholly disregarded for the purpose of ascertaining whether or not a person is ordinarily resident, and it must not be left out of account that Miss Mackenzie came to this country, one presumes, voluntarily at the age of 28, and, as a result of the circumstances ... described, never left it.'[2]

Morton J then went on to comment on some hypothetical case submitted by counsel for the administrator of Miss Mackenzie's estate:

> 'They put the case of a prisoner of war who has come to this country and been detained here, it might be, for a year. They say that he would not be ordinarily resident, because the element of constraint is present. They take again the case of a foreigner with a home abroad, who comes to this country on a visit and commits some crime or offence against the laws of this country, and is imprisoned for a considerable time, and ultimately dies in this country. There, they say, he would not be held to be ordinarily resident ... [S]uch cases must be dealt with on their particular facts, if and when they arise, but I can well imagine, in the case of a prisoner of war, that, if a man had a permanent residence in Germany and came over here in an aeroplane to attack this country, and was captured and kept here for a considerable period, it might well be held that his ordinary residence was his home in Germany.'[3]

Comparing Morton J's judgment as regards Miss Mackenzie and his views on the hypothetical case of the German prisoner of war, it is clear that it was in Miss Mackenzie's initial voluntary entry to the UK for an indefinite period that he found a justification for holding her to have been ordinarily resident here throughout all the years which followed. What he seems to have been saying is that the words are 'voluntarily adopted' not 'voluntarily continued and pursued'. If the beginning is a voluntary matter it is of no consequence that the continuance is enforced. Thus, the hypothetical German could not be ordinarily resident in the UK since his initial entry to this country would not be a matter of free will but of military orders emanating from those in command over him. Indeed, during the 1939–45 war, members of the allied forces who became resident in the UK were generally treated by the Inland Revenue as not ordinarily resident and so, too, were refugees and displaced persons.

This understanding of Viscount Sumner's words seems perfectly reasonable and the implicit rephrasing of 'adopted voluntarily' as 'adopted (but not necessarily continued) voluntarily' does them no violence.

It has been suggested, however, that in *Shah v Barnet London Borough Council*[4] Lord Scarman rejected this approach and, despite his explicit acceptance of the authority of Viscount Sumner's dictum,[5] so qualified Viscount Sumner's words as to rob them of any meaning. What Lord Scarman said was this:

> 'The residence must be voluntarily adopted. Enforced presence by reason of kidnapping or imprisonment, or a Robinson Crusoe existence on a desert island with no opportunity of escape, may be so overwhelming a factor as to negative the will to be where one is.'[6]

3.04 *Ordinary residence*

The relation of the second sentence to the first in this quotation is by no means clear, but if, as one writer has suggested,[7] it is to be taken as meaning that:

'... to be ordinarily resident an individual must have adopted his residence voluntarily, except for extreme cases such as imprisonment or a desert island existence with no opportunity to escape where the imposed circumstances will override the individual's intention,'

then 'adopted (but not necessarily continued) voluntarily' has become 'adopted voluntarily or involuntarily', which is a quite different matter. It must surely be, however, that the writer of those words is misunderstanding the force of Lord Scarman's dictum. His way of reading Lord Scarman's remarks implies the insertion of an additional and somewhat nonsensical clause at the end of the first sentence quoted so that the passage reads as follows:

'The residence must be voluntarily adopted [except where it is *in*voluntarily adopted]. Enforced presence by reason of kidnapping or imprisonment, or a Robinson Crusoe existence on a desert island with no opportunity of escape, may be so overwhelming a factor as to negative the will to be where one is.'

Only then would the second sentence of the quotation be what the writer of the passage takes it to be: a list of typical circumstances in which voluntary adoption of a place of residence is *not* a prerequisite of ordinary residence. Is it credible, however, that, having been at such pains to impress upon us the continuing relevance and authority of Viscount Sumner's remarks, Lord Scarman should, with his next breath, have set out to render those remarks meaningless? Surely not. It is suggested, therefore, that the correct approach to Lord Scarman's second sentence must be to take it as a list of circumstances in which a place of abode will be involuntarily adopted and in which, accordingly, the attribution of ordinary residence will *not* ensue. This alternative way of reading Lord Scarman's remarks implies the insertion of a perfectly logical additional sentence between the two quoted so that the passage reads as follows:

'The residence must be voluntarily adopted. [Only if a person is where he is because at some point he has chosen to be there can the kind of residence known as ordinary residence ensue; but being where one is is not always a matter of choice.] Enforced presence by reason of kidnapping or imprisonment, or a Robinson Crusoe existence on a desert island with no opportunity of escape, may be so overwhelming a factor as to negative the will to be where one is.'

The *Mackenzie* case discussed above is not the only case where, on the face of it, the court appeared to set aside Viscount Sumner's requirement that residence must be voluntarily adopted before it can become ordinary residence. *Miesegaes v IRC*[8] concerned the residence status of Stanley Miesegaes who, during the years 1947–48 to 1951–52, had been a schoolboy boarding at Harrow. Counsel for Mr Miesegaes argued that even if Mr

Miesegaes had been resident *simpliciter* in the UK during those years, such residence could not have constituted ordinary residence because it had not been voluntary residence; it had been institutional. Pearce LJ could not accept that argument. Referring to Viscount Sumner's interpretation of the words 'ordinarily resident' which he later quoted, he said:

> 'Education is too extensive and universal a phase to justify such descriptions as "unusual" and "extraordinary" ... The argument based on the institutional or compulsory nature of a boy's life at school is misleading. The compulsion is merely the will of his parents who voluntarily send him to that school. It would be hazardous, and in my opinion irrelevant, to investigate whether adolescents are residing voluntarily where their lot is cast and how far they approve of their parents' choice of a home or school.'[9]

Far from constituting a rejection of Viscount Sumner's test, however, those words are a strong affirmation of it. Pearce LJ is saying not that one can set aside Viscount Sumner's words but that, in order to give them due weight in circumstances where the person concerned is not a person of full capacity, one must have regard to the will of the person's parents, trustees or guardians in determining whether or not his place of abode has been adopted voluntarily. That is because, in law, an *incapax* has no will but the will of those who are legally responsible for him.[10] Accordingly, during the years 1947–48 to 1951–52, Stanley Miesegaes was ordinarily resident in Harrow because he was resident *simpliciter* in Harrow for each of those years for the settled purpose of being educated and cared for there and Harrow had been voluntarily adopted *by his father* (who, until his death on 10 July 1948, had custody and control of Stanley at all material times) as Stanley's place of abode.

These two principles concerning the ordinary residence status of a person who, in law, has no will of his own were brought together in the case of *R v Waltham Forest London Borough Council, ex p Vale*.[11] Judith Vale, a severely mentally handicapped child born in London in 1956, was, in 1961, moved by her parents to Dublin where, because of her handicap, she was, until May 1984, boarded at various rural community homes. The last of these was Camp Hill at Wexford. In 1978, her parents returned to England and took up residence in the London Borough of Waltham Forest, visiting Judith two or three times a year. In 1984, Judith became so severely disturbed that, on 6 May, her parents brought her from Ireland to live with them until such time as she could be accommodated at Stoke Place, a residential home in Buckinghamshire. In the event, Judith was placed there just one month later on 6 June 1984. Judith's parents sought the funding of this placement from the London borough in which they lived but this was refused on the ground that Judith was not ordinarily resident within the borough at the time of her placement in the home in Buckinghamshire and that, under the National Assistance Act 1948 s 24(1), this relieved the borough of responsibility. Judith's parents sought a judicial review of that decision and Taylor J held that:

> 'Where the propositus ... is so mentally handicapped as to be totally dependent upon a parent or guardian, the concept of her having an independent ordinary

residence of her own which she has adopted voluntarily and for which she has a settled purpose does not arise. She is in the same position as a small child. Her ordinary residence is that of her parents because that is her "base" ... It may well be that if the parents delegate their guardianship of her to a school or home for greater or shorter periods she will acquire a second ordinary residence at that establishment ... It may well be therefore that in the present case Judith, although ordinarily resident with her parents throughout, had a second ordinary residence at Camp Hill for the duration of her stay there, and again acquired a second ordinary residence when she went to Stoke Place. For the period May to June 1984, however, she had only one ordinary residence: at home.'[12]

It would seem to be established, therefore, that an infant or incapacitated person will be ordinarily resident wherever his parents, trustees or guardians are ordinarily resident and, if the person resides elsewhere in accordance with the will of those having legal responsibility for him and as part of the settled order of his life, in that other place also. In cases where there is no incapacity, however, a person's residence must be voluntarily adopted by the person himself before it can acquire the character of ordinary residence.

---

1 *Re Mackenzie* (1940) 19 ATC 399 at 402 and 403.
2 *Re Mackenzie* (1940) 19 ATC 399 at 403 and 404.
3 *Re Mackenzie* (1940) 19 ATC 399 at 403 and 404.
4 [1983] 1 All ER 226.
5 See **3.03** above.
6 *Shah v Barnet London Borough Council* [1983] 1 All ER 226 at 235.
7 J L Wosner, 'Ordinary Residence, the Law and Practice' [1983] *British Tax Review* 347 at 348.
8 (1957) 37 TC 493.
9 (1957) 37 TC 493 at 501.
10 Had this principle been invoked in the *Mackenzie* case, Miss Mackenzie's ordinary residence status could have been established on grounds far more convincing than those on which it was established.
11 QB, 11 February 1985. Unreported except in (1985) *The Times,* 25 February.
12 (1985) *The Times*, 25 February, QB.

3.05 Settled purposes

In *Shah v Barnet London Borough Council*,[1] Lord Scarman said that ordinary residence was dependent not only on a person's voluntary adoption of an abode in some place or country, but also on,

'... a degree of settled purpose. The purpose may be one or there may be several. It may be specific or general. All the law requires is that there is a settled purpose. This is not to say that the propositus intends to stay where he is indefinitely; indeed his purpose, while settled, may be for a limited period. Education, business or profession, employment, health, family or mere love of the place spring to mind as common reasons for a choice of regular abode. And there may well be many others. All that is necessary is that the purpose of living where one does has a sufficient degree of continuity to be properly described as settled.'[2]

In *Reid v IRC*,[3] the settled purpose of Miss Reid in spending some three and a half months in the UK each year was chiefly, it seems, to visit her homeland and her sister.

In *Lysaght v IRC*,[4] the settled purpose of Mr Lysaght's three months' residence in the UK each year was business. He came here to attend directors' meetings of John Lysaght Ltd and to deal with business matters arising in connection with that company.

In *Levene v IRC*,[5] the settled purposes of Mr Levene's regular periods of residence in the UK were to obtain medical advice, to visit relatives, to take part in Jewish religious observances, to visit the graves of his parents and to deal with his tax affairs.

In *Reed v Clark*,[6] the settled purpose of Dave Clark in going to Los Angeles and staying there throughout the tax year 1978–79 was to work there and to avoid a UK tax liability on income of $450,000. In his judgment of the case, Nicholls J said:

'Artificial tax avoidance schemes do not find much favour with the courts today. In this case the position, as I see it, is that when deciding issues of residence, ordinary residence and occasional residence all the reasons (including any desire to avoid a liability to UK income tax) underlying a person's being in a particular place are part of the overall picture. They are part of the material to be looked at and considered when deciding those issues. The presence of a tax avoidance intention may help to show, for instance, why a person went abroad at all, or at the particular time he did, how long he intended to remain away, or where his home in fact was in the year of assessment. But residence abroad for a carefully chosen limited period of work there ... is no less residence abroad for that period just because the major reason for it was the avoidance of tax. Likewise with ordinary residence.'[7]

Although the cases cited above provide examples of settled purposes, they provide no detailed explanation of the term itself. Thus, the question what is meant by 'settled purpose' remained unanswered until it came to the fore in the case of *Shah v Barnet London Borough Council*.[8] That case concerned the eligibility of students for local authority grants in connection with their education. Such eligibility depends on whether or not a student is 'ordinarily resident' in the UK, but, in the Education Act 1962, as in the Taxes Acts, the term 'ordinarily resident' is undefined. Several of the education authorities involved tried to suggest that education could not be a settled purpose for the purposes of establishing ordinary residence and that, to establish a settled purpose:

'... there must be shown an intention to live here on a permanent basis as part of the general community; if a person's presence here was for a 'specific or limited purpose only', eg to pursue a course of study, he would not be ordinarily resident.'[9]

Lord Scarman, however, firmly rebutted that suggestion:

'A man's settled purpose will be different at different ages. Education in adolescence or early adulthood can be as settled a purpose as a profession or business in later years ... study can be as settled a purpose as business or pleasure. And the notion of permanent or indefinitely enduring purpose as an element in ordinary residence derives not from the natural and ordinary meaning of the words "ordinarily resident" but from a confusion of it with domicile.[10]

Earlier,[11] Lord Scarman had said, 'all that is necessary is that the purpose of living where one does has a sufficient degree of continuity to be properly described as settled'. A settled purpose is, therefore, a purpose which, though it need not provide a person with a motivation for becoming permanently or indefinitely present in a particular place, will provide him with the motivation to be more than transitorily or fleetingly present there. The purpose must, in other words, have a certain intrinsic durability. The difference between the two kinds of purpose may be illustrated by contrasting the motivation of the man who takes a holiday in the Cotswolds with that of the man who makes being in the Cotswolds part of his life; or the motivation of the woman who pays a visit to her invalid mother with that of the woman who makes caring for her invalid mother part of her life. In the first of both cases, the purpose is essentially transitory and results in a deviation from the person's normal mode of life; but in the second of both cases the purpose has an inbuilt element of continuity which results in the normal mode of life itself being modified so as to accommodate the presence of the person in the place in question. In either case the purpose which possesses an intrinsic element of continuity may, of course, be terminated very shortly after the mode of life has been altered to accommodate that purpose: the man may discover a preferred alternative to the Cotswolds and may further modify his mode of life so as to exclude presence in the Cotswolds and allow for presence in Tenerife, and the woman's mother may die. But in neither case can the early termination of the purpose change the settled nature it once possessed or retrospectively divest the person of the ordinary residence status to which it will have given rise.

How small a degree of continuity of purpose is needed for a purpose to be settled is well illustrated in *University College London v Newman*.[12] Edward Newman was a New Zealand citizen who, in 1977, left New Zealand and, after travelling extensively, arrived in the European Community in August 1978 whereupon, using France as his base, he became,

'... a rather aimless drifter who has spent his time in what is inelegantly but descriptively called colloquially "bumming" around Europe.'[13]

In October 1983, however, he embarked upon a degree course at University College London and claimed to be eligible for lower rate fees on the grounds of having been ordinarily resident within the European Community during the course of the three years ended 1 September 1983 within the terms of the Education (Fees and Awards) Regulations 1983 Sch 2(2). In the Westminster County Court, McDonnell J held that he had not been ordinarily resident as claimed, but, in the Court of Appeal, his judgment was reversed. Croom-Johnson LJ said that Mr Newman,

'... had been living in the EC for the necessary three years. But was he "ordinarily resident"? He has put down roots nowhere. He used France "as my base for travelling". He went from country to country, in short spells, returning again and again. His work record is spasmodic, and was described by the judge as "the token effort required to ensure that he receives social security payments".'[14]

Nevertheless, Croom-Johnson LJ concluded that if McDonnell J had asked himself 'Has Mr Newman been shown to have been ordinarily resident in the EEC for the three qualifying years'? and had he applied Lord Scarman's test (ie, had Mr Newman's purpose of living where he did a sufficient degree of continuity to be properly described as settled?), the answer would have to be 'yes ... Mr Newman was ordinarily resident, after his casual fashion, somewhere in the EC for the whole of the qualifying three years'.[15]

It was accepted in the Court of Appeal that Mr Newman had not been ordinarily resident in any particular European Community Member State during the three-year period, but that is not relevant to the point being made. On the basis of the court's judgment, Mr Newman would have been ordinarily resident in the UK had he confined himself to merely 'bumming around' England, Scotland, Wales and Northern Ireland. 'Bumming around' may be a settled purpose.

---

1 [1983] 1 All ER 226.
2 [1983] 1 All ER 226 at 235.
3 (1926) 10 TC 673.
4 (1928) 13 TC 511.
5 (1928) 13 TC 486.
6 [1985] STC 323.
7 [1985] STC 323 at 346.
8 [1983] 1 All ER 226.
9 [1983] 1 All ER 226 at 237.
10 [1983] 1 All ER 226 at 236, 238 and 239.
11 [1983] 1 All ER 226 at 235.
12 CA, 19 December 1985. Unreported except in (1986) *The Times*, 8 January.
13 (1986) *The Times*, 8 January, CA.
14 (1986) *The Times*, 8 January, CA.
15 (1986) *The Times*, 8 January, CA.

3.06 Regular order of life

Given that a person voluntarily adopts the UK as a place of abode and comes here in pursuit of one or more settled purposes, over what period must he be present here in pursuit of those purposes before his presence becomes part of the 'regular order' of his life and before he can thus be attributed with ordinary residence status? The body of case law preceding the *Shah* case[1] had suggested that the answer is three or more years – not because any of the judges hearing the cases concerned had declared that that was the required period but because, in every instance, the appellants had, in fact, visited the UK in three or more consecutive years before the Inland Revenue chose to assert that the status of ordinary residence had

3.06 *Ordinary residence*

been acquired and before the Commissioners (subsequently supported by the courts) upheld its assertion that that was so. Where the settled purpose involves but a single visit to the UK in each tax year, that answer will no doubt be correct: common sense would dictate that three such visits are the minimum required to give those visits regularity and habituality, but – by the same logic – where the settled purpose involves monthly or weekly visits, will surely have become regular and habitual once the third or fourth such monthly or weekly visit has been made.

Where the settled purpose involves not merely visits to the UK but continuous presence here, a person's presence in the UK will necessarily have become part of the regular order of his life after only a few days have elapsed, and – just as early termination or fulfilment of the purpose will not retrospectively rob that purpose of any settled nature it possessed[2] – early termination or fulfilment of the purpose will not prevent the person's presence here from being presence as part of the regular order of his life. In the *Shah* case, Lord Scarman had said:

> 'If there be proved a regular, habitual mode of life in a particular place, the continuity of which has persisted despite temporary absences, ordinary residence is established provided only it is adopted voluntarily and for a settled purpose.'[3]

Likewise, in *Reed v Clark*,[4] Nicholls J was satisfied that a period of just over a year abroad was not too short a period for a person to have established an ordinary residence overseas.

The test which Nicholls J would (following Lord Scarman) seem to have been applying, however, was: did the period of residence in question, however long or short, represent an intrusion into or a deviation from the person's regular and habitual mode of life, or was it, in fact, a component part of the person's regular and habitual mode of life for the time being? If it was intrusive or deviatory it could not be ordinary residence, but if it was a component part of the normal pattern it could not be other than ordinary residence.

This would seem to bring the matter round full circle. In the *Levene* case, Lord Hanworth had said:

> 'I find it difficult to attach any distinction of meaning to the word "ordinarily" as affecting the term "resident", unless it be to prevent facts which would amount to residence being so estimated on the ground that they arose from some fortuitous cause, such as illness of the so-called resident or of some other person, which demanded his continuance at a place for a special purpose otherwise than in accordance with his own usual arrangements and shaping of his movements . . .'[5]

In other words, residence always will be ordinary residence unless it either lacks settled purpose or is enforced. That was the stance of the courts in 1928 and that, despite Revenue insistence (not always to the taxpayer's detriment) during the intervening years that ordinary residence necessitates the establishment of an annually recurrent pattern of residence *simpliciter*, has now been affirmed by the courts as being their stance today.

One further point must be made. Viscount Cave,[6] Lord Denning[7] and Lord Scarman[8] all made reference to the irrelevance of temporary absences in the context of the 'regular order of life' which is under discussion here. What each was saying is that once a person has, by reason of his voluntary presence in the UK in pursuit of one or more settled purposes, made his presence here part of the regular order of his life for the time being and thus attracted to himself the status of ordinary residence, his absence from the UK will not affect that status provided that the absences are temporary, occasional or accidental. This will be so even where an absence extends over an entire tax year – though in such an instance residence *simpliciter* status may be lost.

It is worth observing that this principle of disregarding temporary absences provides additional support for the proposition that a person who makes voluntary regular visits to the UK in pursuit of settled purposes is ordinarily resident here. If the periods between visits are treated as temporary absences from the UK and are disregarded, the visitor's periodic presence in the UK is, effectively, transformed into a continuous presence.

1 *Shah v Barnet London Borough Council* [1983] 1 All ER 226 at 236.
2 See **3.05** above.
3 *Shah v Barnet London Borough Council* [1983] 1 All ER 226 at 236.
4 [1985] STC 323.
5 *Levene v IRC* (1928) 13 TC 486 at 496.
6 *Levene v IRC* (1928) 13 TC 486 at 507.
7 *R v Barnet London Borough, ex p Shah* [1982] 1 All ER 698 at 704.
8 *Shah v Barnet London Borough Council* [1983] 1 All ER 226 at 236.

3.07 Unlawful residence

It has already been explained that residence is a question of fact not of law[1] so that, unless an Act contains specific provision to the contrary, residence does not need to be lawful for it to be residence which is voluntarily adopted and for a settled purpose as part of the regular order of a person's life. Thus although a deserting seaman who is living in the UK in breach of the immigration laws cannot be ordinarily resident here for the purposes of the Commonwealth Immigration Acts since those Acts make specific provision to that effect,[2] he may be ordinarily resident here for tax purposes since the Taxes Acts contain no such prohibiting provision. The principle underlying these rules is that a person who would appear to be ordinarily resident to anyone observing the way in which he is living but who is not entitled lawfully so to live cannot be allowed to benefit from his apparent status but 'for the purposes of taxation he will not be allowed to deny his apparent status'.[3] This, according to Oliver LJ in *R v Secretary of State for Home Department, ex p Margueritte*[4] made 'good common sense'.

1 See **2.21** above.
2 *Re Abdul Manan* [1971] 2 All ER 1016.
3 *R v Barnet London Borough Council, ex p Shah* [1982] 1 All ER 698 at 706, per Eveleigh LJ.
4 [1982] 3 All ER 909.

3.08 Dual or no ordinary residence

That a person may be ordinarily resident nowhere was affirmed in *University College London v Newman*.[1] Croom-Johnston LJ said:

> 'I agree that it is possible for someone to be ordinarily resident nowhere. People who spend their lives sailing about the world are such. So are the well-known class of tax-evaders who move on from country to country, always one move ahead of the tax man.'[2]

And that a man may be ordinarily resident in two places at one and the same time was established in bankruptcy law in *Re Norris, ex p Reynolds*[3] and has been admitted in tax law also:

> 'I am not sure there is anything impossible in a person "ordinarily residing" in two places.'[4]

> 'I think ... that a man can have two ordinary residences not because he commonly is to be found at those places, but because the ordinary course of his life is such that he acquires the attribute of residence at those two places.'[5]

HMRC agrees that this is so and states this in its guidance.[6]

---

1 CA, 19 December 1985. Unreported except in (1986) *The Times*, 8 January.
2 (1986) *The Times*, 8 January, CA.
3 (1888) 4 TLR 452.
4 *Reid v IRC* (1926) 10 TC 673 at 680, per Lord Clyde LP.
5 *Levene v IRC* (1928) 13 TC 486 at 494, per Rowlatt J.
6 IR20 (July 2008), para 1.4, see **Appendix 1** below.

Revenue practice

3.09 Year by year residence

In its guidance, HMRC states that:

> 'If you are resident in the United Kingdom year after year, you are treated as ordinarily resident here.'[1]

As will become increasingly clear, that sentence is the maxim upon which HMRC has based its entire code of practice concerning the attribution or otherwise of ordinary residence status; and it is, therefore, unfortunate, to say the least, that that maxim does not accurately reflect the principle which the courts have established as being applicable in the determination of a person's ordinary residence status. It may be faulted on two counts.

First, it disregards the fact that before the year-by-year residence to which it refers can acquire the character of ordinary residence it must have resulted from the voluntary adoption of the UK as a place of abode[2] and must relate to one or more settled (as opposed to casual or temporary) purposes.[3] By its silence on these points, the Revenue statement implies that the possession of residence *simpliciter* in each of a number of successive years will alone be sufficient to transform residence *simpliciter* into ordinary residence and that the 'year after year' element will override the need to have regard to any other factors; but such is not the case.

Secondly, the statement betrays no recognition of the fact that, although a person's possession of residence *simpliciter* year after year will (subject to the conditions described above being met) result in his being attributed with ordinary residence status, residence which is of only short duration and which results in the attribution of residence *simpliciter* in only a single tax year will also, in law, take on the character of ordinary residence if the three judicially prescribed conditions referred to earlier[4] are met. This assertion runs counter to the Revenue statement that:

> 'You may be resident but not ordinarily resident in the United Kingdom for a tax year if, for example, you normally live outside the United Kingdom but are in this country for 183 days or more in the year'.[5]

Yet the *Vale* case[6] provides a striking affirmation of its truth.

Because this second defect, the principle adopted by HMRC will invariably work in the taxpayer's favour by resulting in the non-attribution of ordinary residence status in certain instances where such attribution is due, it is tempting to regard those Revenue rules which rest on this defect as concessions of which the taxpayer may take advantage. This would be a dangerous attitude. Almost all the Revenue rules are qualified by the insertion of the word 'normally' or by the use of 'may' rather than 'will' and, as the *Clark* case[7] demonstrates, HMRC will have no hesitation in relying on those qualifications and setting aside a rule if it is thus enabled to pursue a taxpayer for a significant amount of tax which, under the rule, would be avoided.

Thus the Revenue statement at paras 3.4–3.5 of IR20 (July 2008)[8] and the Revenue statement quoted above must both be viewed with a certain amount of caution. Any voluntary visitor to the UK who comes here with more than a casual or temporary purpose and whose presence here becomes for the time being part of the regular order of his life will, in law, be liable to be regarded as ordinarily resident here from the outset irrespective of the number of weeks, months or years spanned by his visit.

Contrariwise, no visitor to the UK whose presence here is enforced or who is here in pursuit of a purpose which is merely temporary or casual can, in law, be regarded as ordinarily resident, even in the unlikely event of his visit extending beyond the third anniversary of his arrival.

It was said earlier that HMRC has based its entire code of practice concerning the attribution or otherwise of ordinary residence status on the maxim under discussion here, namely that if a person is resident in the UK year after year, he is ordinarily resident here. That is not immediately apparent when one reads the Revenue guide for, on the face of it, the guide appears to be asserting that the attribution of ordinary residence status is

3.09 *Ordinary residence*

dependent on factors such as periodic visits here of a certain average length,[9] and a person's future intentions.[10] A closer examination will reveal, however, that the guide is relating these factors to ordinary residence only in so far as it is relating them to the establishment, on a year-by-year basis, of the status of residence *simpliciter*. Again, in the mind of the Revenue, it is the year after year attribution of residence *simpliciter* status which is critical and which will inevitably result in the attribution of ordinary residence status.

---

1 IR20 (July 2008), para 1.3, see **Appendix 1** below.
2 See **3.04** above.
3 See **3.05** above.
4 See **3.04, 3.05** and **3.06** above.
5 IR20 (July 2008), para 1.3, see **Appendix 1** below.
6 *R v Waltham Forest London Borough Council, ex p Vale* QB, 11 February 1985. Unreported except in (1985) *The Times*, 25 February. See **3.04** above.
7 *Reed v Clark* [1985] STC 323. Despite the Revenue's assertion in para 8 of its booklet IR20 that 'If a person is to be regarded as resident in the UK for a given tax year he must normally be present in the country for at least part of that year', the Revenue assessed Clark to tax on £275,700 for 1978–79 although he had been absent from the UK throughout the whole of that year. The Revenue case was that, notwithstanding his absence, Clark was resident in the UK.
8 See **Appendix 1** below.
9 See **3.11** below.
10 See **3.12** below.

3.10 Available accommodation

It has been explained at **2.08** to **2.10** above that a person who has accommodation available to him in the UK and who occupies that accommodation, however briefly, during the course of a tax year, will (unless he is working full-time overseas)[1] fall to be attributed with residence *simpliciter* for the whole of that tax year. It follows from this that, if the Revenue maxim discussed at **3.09** above (namely, that 'if a person is resident in the UK year after year, he is ordinarily resident here') is taken as a valid principle of law, anyone who has accommodation available to him in the UK and who occupies that accommodation, however briefly, in each of a number of successive tax years will be not only resident *simpliciter* for each of those years but ordinarily resident here also. The effect of FA 1993 s 208 which provides that for the purposes of ICTA 1988 s 336 the existence or otherwise of available accommodation must be disregarded in determining whether an individual is in the UK for some temporary purpose and not with a view to or intent of establishing his residence here will be considered at **4.06** below. While s 208 alters the law in respect of the application of s 336, it is submitted that the presence or otherwise of available accommodation can still be relevant in assisting in determining whether an individual is generally ordinarily resident in the UK or not.

---

1 See **4.16** ff below.

3.11 Annual visits

Persons who come to the UK regularly on annual visits, and where those visits average 91 days or more in a tax year, will be treated as short-term visitors for the purpose of determining whether they are ordinarily resident in the UK according to the long standingpractice of HMRC.[1] The practice is only applicable where the taxpayer has 'left' the UK,[2] that is where he is not resident or ordinarily resident according to general principles and case law.[3]

Short-term visitors are treated as ordinarily resident where visits average 91 days or more in a tax year – days which are spent in the UK for exceptional circumstances beyond the visitor's control, for example through the illness of the visitor or a member of the visitor's immediate family, are, however, not normally counted for the purpose of arriving at the 91 days.

For all tax years before 1993–94, a short-term visitor who came regularly to the UK and had accommodation available in the UK for the visitor's use is treated as ordinarily resident even if the visitor averaged less than 91 days in a tax year.

HMRC couples physical presence with intention.[4] A short-term visitor who fulfils the criteria for physical presence as explained above is treated as being ordinarily resident from a date which is determined by the visitor's intentions.

The visitor will be treated as ordinarily resident from 6 April of the tax year of his first arrival if it is clear at that period that the visitor intended visiting the UK regularly for at least four tax years. If the visitor came originally with no definite plans about the number of years for which the visitor would visit, he is treated as ordinarily resident from 6 April of the fifth tax year after he has visited the UK for four years. If the decision to visit the UK regularly is made before the start of the fifth tax year, then the visitor is treated as being ordinarily resident from 6 April of the tax year in which that decision is taken.[5]

---

1 IR20 (July 2008), para 3.4, see **Appendix 1** below.
2 HMRC Brief 01/07.
3 *Gaines-Cooper v Revenue and Customs Commrs* [2007] UKSPC 568.
4 IR20 (July 2008), para 3.5, see **Appendix 1** below.
5 IR20 (July 2008), para 3.5, see **Appendix 1** below.

3.12 Intention

It will have been noted that the first of the Revenue rules described at **3.11** above involves the use of a continuous base period of four years in assessing whether the length of an overseas visitor's visits to the UK have been of sufficient average length to trigger the attribution to him of residence and ordinary residence status. The first rule is expressed as an intention to visit the UK regularly. In formulating a rule based on intention HMRC has ventured onto shaky ground. In the *Vale* case,[1] for instance, Taylor J said that, in considering the question of a person's ordinary residence:

3.12 Ordinary residence

'... future intention is to be left out of account,'[2]

and in taking that line he was quite properly following Lord Scarman who, in the *Shah* case,[3] had said that:

> '... ordinary residence ... lays emphasis not on intention or expectation for the future ... but on immediately past events, namely the usual order of the [person's] way of life ....'[4]

In law, therefore, a person who comes to the UK from overseas may be attributed with ordinary residence status only if he has come here voluntarily and with one or more settled (as opposed to temporary or casual) purposes and only when his presence here has, despite any temporary absences of long or short duration, acquired a degree of continuity and become a part of (rather than a deviation from) his regular and habitual mode of life. As the *Vale* case[5] demonstrates, this need not take long if the person has no ordinary residence elsewhere – a month may be sufficient; but if the person has an ordinary residence elsewhere and merely makes short intermittent visits here it may take several years before the characteristics of continuity, regularity and habituality are sufficiently pronounced for attribution of ordinary residence status validly to take place. The fact that the establishment of ordinary residence status may take several years does not, however, justify HMRC in setting aside established judicial principles in favour of its own; and it is submitted that HMRC will find no support in law should it, by applying the rules under discussion here, anticipate a person's acquisition of ordinary residence status by having regard to his future intent rather than to his immediate past mode of life.

The factor of intent or expectation is irrelevant and four years is an arbitrary length of time which has no special significance in law.

Reliance on a person's future intent lies behind two other rules in the Revenue's code of practice concerning ordinary residence. The first states that:

> 'You are treated as resident and ordinarily resident from the date you arrive if your home has been abroad and you intend –
> – to come to the UK to live here permanently, or
> – to come and remain here for three years or more ...'[6]

and the second states that:

> 'You will be treated as ordinarily resident in the UK from the date you arrive, whether to work here or not, if it is clear that you intend to stay for at least three years.'[7]

It will be clear from the foregoing discussion that mere intent to settle permanently in the UK is not in itself sufficient to imbue with ordinary residence status either the new arrival to these shores or the hitherto undecided visitor. Although both will possess a settled purpose and will have voluntarily adopted the UK as their place of residence, it will still

Revenue practice **3.12**

remain for each to establish a regular and habitual mode of life here which displays a certain degree of continuity. Until that has taken place, any judgment as to their residence status will be premature. This, as pointed out above, may not take long – particularly if their arrival here or decision to stay here coincides with their severing of ties with elsewhere – but until it has taken place, attribution of ordinary residence status will have no foundation in law. Having made the point that these rules are wrong in principle, however, it is conceded that, in almost every case in which HMRC, by application of these rules, attributes a person with ordinary residence status, the qualities of life which a person's presence here must display for him validly to be regarded as ordinarily resident will have emerged by the time the attribution of ordinary residence status is made.

1 *R v Waltham Forest London Borough Council, ex p Vale*, QB, 11 February 1985. Unreported except in (1985) *The Times*, 25 February.
2 (1985) *The Times*, 25 February, QB.
3 *Shah v Barnet London Borough Council* [1983] 1 All ER 226.
4 [1983] 1 All ER 226 at 236.
5 *R v Waltham Forest London Borough Council, ex p Vale*, QB, 11 February 1985. Unreported except in (1985) *The Times*, 25 February.
6 IR20 (July 2008), para 3.1, see **Appendix 1** below.
7 IR20 (July 2008), para 3.8, see **Appendix 1** below.

CHAPTER 4

Arrivals and departures

They sailed away for a year and a day,
To the land where the Bong-tree grows.

Edward Lear *The Owl and the Pussy-Cat*

4.01 Introduction

It might be supposed that, in the light of the discussion in Chapters 2 and 3, the question of the residence and ordinary residence status of a person who arrives on the shores of the UK or leaves them for other shores across the sea is determined merely by reference to the factors discussed in those chapters. This is not the case, however. Although none of those factors cease to be relevant, Parliament has enacted limited but important provisions which deal specifically with the determination of residence status in circumstances of arrival in and departure from the UK, and those impose certain overriding tests and rules. Furthermore, HMRC has adopted certain extra-statutory concessions whose impact is significant on mobile individuals.

4.02 Split tax years

As has been repeatedly noted, the Taxes Acts do not recognise that a person may be resident in the UK for part of a tax year and non-resident for the balance. The consequence of this extraordinarily blinkered view is that a person leaving the UK on 7 April and returning on the following 4 April is nonetheless resident for the whole of the tax year running from 6 April to the following 5 April.[1]

There has been no inclination to allow taxpayers moving to or from the UK to divide a tax year between periods of non-residence by statute. Instead, the Revenue has allowed this split by concession in the case of individuals. This concessionary treatment is unique among concessions in that provision is made for claiming this treatment appears on the individual's self-assessment form.[2] Separate concessions apply for income tax[3] and capital gains tax[4] and the conditions for their application are not

4.02 *Arrivals and departures*

identical. Neither treats the individual as non-resident for all purposes during the relevant part of the tax year. Furthermore the concessionary treatment described in the two ESCs is not identical with that described in IR20.

1 See a more extreme illustration in *Reviewing the residence and domicile rules as they affect the taxation of individuals: a background paper* (published jointly by HM Treasury and Inland Revenue in April 2003), Example 4.
2 See Non-resident etc pages box 9.3.
3 Extra-statutory Concession A11.
4 Extra-statutory Concession D2.

4.03 Income Tax Act 2007

The Income Tax Act 2007 (ITA) became law from 5 April 2007. It is the latest product of the Tax Law Rewrite Project.[1] ITA 2007 rewrites, and in some cases repeals, various provisions covering most of the rules relating to income tax which were not dealt with by the project's two previous Acts: the Income Tax (Earnings and Pensions) Act 2003 (ITEPA) and the Income Tax (Trading and Other Income) Act 2005 (ITTOIA). The rules regarding residence are contained in ITA 2007, Pt 14, Ch 2.[2]

Although the project is intended to produce a restatement of existing law, acknowledged changes have been made. Thus, the reference in ICTA 1988, s 336 (Persons arriving in the UK) and to 'six months' in s 336 is replaced by a reference to '183 days' in the sucessor provisions (ITA 2007 ss 831 and 832).[3] ICTA 1988, s 334 (Persons leaving the UK) is replaced by ITA 2007, s 829. This new section expands the scope of the rule beyound Commonwealth and Irish citizens who were the only subjects of the predecessor rules in ICTA 1988, s 334.[4] Despite the changes, much of the case law pertaining to the previous, now repealed legislation, it is submitted, will still be relevant in the application of the new sections.

1 See **1.20** above.
2 Section 829 Residence of individuals temporarily abroad; s 830 Residence of individuals working abroad; s 831 Foreign income of individuals in the UK for temporary purpose; s 832 Employment income of individuals in the UK for temporary purpose; s 832 Employment income of individuals in the UK for temporary purpose and s 833 Visiting forces and staff of designated allied headquarters.)
3 Rewrite:Explanatory Notes, Annex 1, Change 124.
4 Rewrite:Explanatory Notes, Annex 1, Change 123.

Persons arriving in the UK

4.04 Conditional exemption

In 1889, Sir E Clarke who was at that time the Solicitor General, had the task of replying to a clearly astonished and disbelieving Lord Chancellor (Halsbury, no less) who had asked him:

'Do you contend that a subject of a foreign state residing here, carrying on a business abroad from which profits are derived, but not one farthing of which is earned in this country or ever comes here, is liable to pay Income Tax thereon in consequence of simply residing here?'

His answer was,

'Yes, subject to this limitation: he must be residing here; he must not be here merely for a temporary purpose. If he is residing here there is no hardship. Persons residing here and enjoying the protection of the laws of this country ought to bear its burdens.'[1]

It was just such sentiment that guided Parliament when it included in the taxing statutes the predecessors of ITA 2007, s 831. The function of this rule is to keep out of the income tax net the foreign income of any genuine short-term visitor who might otherwise find himself attributed with the quality of residence in the UK by reason of his visits here or other factors. TCGA 1992 s 9(3) which, on the face of it, has the same objectives with regards to capital gains tax presents special difficulties and is discussed at **4.11** and **4.12** below.

Separate provisions apply to employment income[2] and other income from other sources[3] but are identical (except for the wording in italics). ITA 2007 s 831(1)[4] reads:

'Subsection (2) applies in relation to an individual if–
(a) the individual is in the United Kingdom for some temporary purpose only and with no *view to* establishing the individual's residence in the United Kingdom, and
(b) in the tax year in question the individual has not *actually resided in the United Kingdom at one or several times for a total period equal to 183 days (or more)*.
In determining whether an individual is within paragraph (a) ignore any living accommodation available in the United Kingdom for the individual's use.'

If both (a) and (b) are satisfied, the individual's liability to income tax is determined according to ITA 2007 s 831(2) by treating the individual generally as non-UK resident. If (a) is satisfied but (b) is not, then the individual is treated as resident for s 831 purposes.

In relation to employment income section 832(1) reads:

'Subsection (2) applies in relation to an individual if–
(a) the individual is in the United Kingdom for some temporary purpose only and with no *intention of* establishing the individual's residence in the United Kingdom, and
(b) during the tax year in question the individual *spends (in total) less than 183 days in the United Kingdom.*
In determining whether an individual is within paragraph (a) ignore any living accommodation available in the UK for the individual's use.'

which is governed by s 832(2).

Similarly, if both (a) and (b) are satisfied, the individual's liability to income tax is determined according to ITA 2007 s 832(2) by treating the individual as non-UK resident. If (a) is satisfied but (b) is not, then the individual is treated as resident for s 832 purposes.

The benefit of s 832 is extended by concession to determine the status of an individual accompanying or later joining a spouse who goes abroad for full-time employment.[5]

---

1 *Colquhoun v Brooks* (1889) 2 TC 490 at 492.
2 Section 831(1).
3 Section 831(1).
4 See **4.03** above.
5 Extra statutory Concession A 78.

4.05 Temporary purpose

The expression 'temporary purpose' in ITA 2007, s 831(1)(a) and its predecessor ICTA 1988 s 336(1) and (2) is not without difficulty as is illustrated by the case of Mr Cadwalader, an American citizen, who was ordinarily resident in New York but who rented a house and shooting rights in Scotland and there spent some two months of each year. Was visiting Scotland each year for the shooting season a temporary purpose? The Commissioners seem to have been of the opinion that it was for they found against the Crown. The Court of Exchequer, however, reversed their decision. Lord McLaren said:

> 'I don't think that Mr Cadwalader is in a position to affirm, when he comes year after year during the currency of his lease to spend the shooting season in Scotland, that he is here for a temporary purpose only. I don't mean that you might not frame a definition which would bring this within the scope of temporary purposes, but taking the ordinary meaning of the word, I should say that temporary purposes means casual purposes as distinguished from the case of a person who is here in the pursuance of his regular habits of life ... [The word] "temporary" ... means that it is casual or transitory residence, as distinguished from a residence, of which there may be more than one, but which may be habitual or permanent.'[1]

In the previous chapter, we saw that a purpose which results in a person becoming present in the UK as part of the regular order of his life is properly describable as a 'settled purpose'.[2] What Lord McLaren is saying, therefore (in the current vocabulary of the law of residence), is that the terms 'settled purpose' and 'temporary purpose' are mutually exclusive and that for a purpose to be a temporary purpose it must be a non-settled purpose, ie a purpose which, if it brings a person to the UK, does so only in deviation from the regular order of his life.

The Inland Revenue was quick to take up Lord McLaren's definition and, over the years following the *Cadwalader* case, the Crown's rejection of many an individual's claim to exemption was based on a contention that the person 'was in this country in pursuance of his regular habits of life and therefore not "for some temporary purpose only"'. Thus it was in the case of Mr Zorab.[3]

Mr Zorab was a native of India who had lived there all his life and held office in the Indian Civil Service. In May 1920, however, he left India on two years' furlough at the end of which he intended to (and did) retire from the Indian Civil Service. In 1920–21 he spent a little over five months in the UK, just short of six months in 1921–22, 1922–23 and 1923–24, and a little short of five months in 1924–25. The remainder of each year he spent in Paris or Belgium. He had no business interests in the UK and his visits here were made solely with the object of seeing his friends. The Crown contended that Mr Zorab's visits were not 'for some temporary purpose only' within the meaning of rule 2 of the Miscellaneous Rules of Schedule D but that he was 'in this country in pursuance of his regular habits of life'. The Commissioners found against the Crown, however, and Rowlatt J upheld their decision. Contrasting the case of Mr Zorab with that of someone who, when absent from the UK, has links here which perpetuate and particularise his attachment to the UK (a house, a bank account, stored furniture and the like),[4] he said of Mr Zorab:

> 'This gentleman seems to be a mere traveller ... He is a native of India, he has retired from his work there and he really travels in Europe. All that can be said about it is that in the course of his habitual travels he spends a considerable period every year in England.'[5]

This judgment reinforces what has been said earlier,[6] namely, that mere recurrence of visits is by no means conclusive proof of the existence of a settled purpose. A person may visit the UK in each of a succession of years and yet each visit may (to use Lord McLaren's words in the *Cadwalader* case) be only 'casual or transitory' and possess a temporary character. Indeed, Viscount Cave LC argued in *Lysaght v IRC*[7] that although Mr Lysaght made monthly visits from Ireland to England for the purpose of attending directors' meetings and stayed for about one week on each occasion, that did not make his visits 'more than temporary visits or give them the character of residence in this country'.[8] Again, presumably, in Viscount Cave's view, the visits were merely 'casual or transitory' despite their regularity and frequency.

In *Gaines-Cooper v Revenue and Customs Comrs*[9] the Special Commissioners held that s 336 did not apply because a decision to visit the UK on a large number of days each year to be with one's wife and child was not a 'temporary purpose'. The Special Commissoner expressed the rule as follows:

> 'We conclude that a temporary purpose is a purpose lasting for a limited time; a purpose existing or valid for a time; a purpose which is not permanent but transient; a purpose which is to supply a passing need. "Temporary purpose" means a casual purpose as distinguished from the case of a person who is here in pursuance of his regular habits of life. Temporary purpose means the opposite of continuous purpose. A decision to visit the United Kingdom for a few months each year to shoot (ignoring the availability of living accommodation) is not a temporary purpose (*Cadwalader*).'[10]

The Special Commissioner also rejected the general proposition that because a visit is short it must necessarily be for a temporary purpose. In the author's

4.05 *Arrivals and departures*

view, neither of these statements meet the exposition of Lord McLaren in *Cadwalader* cited above.

In IR20, HMRC stipulates '91 days or more'. Any days spent in the UK for exceptional circumstances such as the illness of the individual or a member of his family will not normally be counted.[11]

For the purposes of whether a person is in the UK for a temporary purpose and not with any view or intent of establishing residence here the question whether the person has available accommodation here must be disregarded.[12]

---

1 *Cooper v Cadwalader* (1904) 5 TC 101 at 109.
2 See **3.05** and **3.06** above.
3 *IRC v Zorab* (1926) 11 TC 289.
4 See Ch 2 above.
5 *IRC v Zorab* (1926) 11 TC 289 at 292.
6 See **3.05** above.
7 (1928) 13 TC 511. Viscount Sumner, on the other hand, saw Mr Lysaght's commitment to monthly attendance at directors' meetings in the UK as a settled purpose (a term which Viscount Sumner coined in the *Lysaght* case) and, accordingly, he held that Mr Lysaght's visits to the UK were precluded from possessing the temporary character which might have brought them within the scope of what is now ICTA 1988 s 336(1).
8 (1928) 13 TC 511 at 532.
9 [2007] UKSPC 568.
10 At para 178.
11 At para 181.
11 IR20 (July 2008) paras 3.4, 3.5, at **Appendix 1** below.
12 ITA 2007, s 831(1); **4.06** below.

4.06 View or intent of establishing residence

In *A-G v Coote*[1] the court had to decide whether Sir C H Coote, who was domiciled in Ireland and spent most of his time there but visited a furnished house which he owned in Connaught Place, London, for a few weeks each year, fell within the excepting provisions of ITA 1806 s 51. It was held that:

> 'The fact of the defendant's domicile has nothing to do with the question, nor has the time of his residence any effect on the construction of the words of the Act; for if the defendant came here for the purpose of establishing a residence it were enough, although he should reside here only two weeks.'[2]

As Baron Graham made clear, the availability of the accommodation was the all-important fact, not the actual duration of Sir C H Coote's stay in it:

> 'At any period of the year he might have come to Connaught Place, where he would have found his house ready for him,'[3]

and this point was taken up almost a century later by Lord McLaren who said of the phrase 'not with any view or intent of establishing his residence':

> 'The words are somewhat vague, but they seem to me to recognise what may be called a constructive residence as distinguished from actual residence.'[4]

In the case of Mr Cadwalader, this meant leasing a furnished house which, though he actually occupied it for only two months in each year, was maintained for him and placed at his disposal so that he was able to occupy it whenever he chose. As in the *Coote* case, the essence of constructive residence was held to be that a person 'has a residence always ready for him if he should choose to come to it',[5] not that when in the UK he necessarily ever does set foot there. As Lord McLaren has said:

> 'If you are looking forward to it ... that makes you liable to taxation, because in order to get the benefit of the exemption you must say that you have no view and no intention of acquiring a residence there.'[6]

Lord McLaren was there using the term 'looking forward' not in its modern sense of 'anticipating with pleasure' but in its plain sense of seeing oneself in occupation of the dwelling place in question at some future time. In ICTA 1988 s 336 (now ITA 2007, s 831) and its predecessors, the 'view or intent of establishing ... residence' is not necessarily a view or intent in relation to the particular visit in question. So long as a person has a dwelling place maintained and available for his use in the UK, he cannot be free of a view or intent of establishing his residence here. If a man has no such view, he will not acquire or have made available to him a dwelling place in the UK. If he once had such a view but has now abandoned it, he will dispose of the accommodation[7] or in some way negate its availability – by, for example, renting it out to another – and if he does not do so the presumption must be that a view or intent to reside there, at some time in the future, remains.

---

1 (1817) 2 TC 385.
2 (1817) 2 TC 385 at 385, per Richards CB.
3 (1817) 2 TC 385 at 385.
4 *Cooper v Cadwalader* (1904) 5 TC 101 at 109.
5 *Cooper v Cadwalader* (1904) 5 TC 101 at 106, per the Lord President.
6 *Cooper v Cadwalader* (1904) 5 TC 101 at 109, per Lord McLaren.
7 Or attempt to dispose of it. See *Withers v Wynyard* (1938) 21 TC 724.

4.07 A place of abode

The principle that no one who has a place of residence in the UK, maintained and available for his use, can be free of a view or intent of establishing his residence in the UK, was, in 1926, challenged by a certain Captain Loewenstein.[1] He noted that in both the *Coote* case and the *Cadwalader* case the persons attributed with a view or intent of establishing residence had proprietary interests in the dwelling houses concerned and he contended that unless there was such a proprietary interest the principle was of no application.

As has been noted at **2.10** above, Captain Loewenstein was a Belgian subject, resident in Brussels, who visited a property at Melton Mowbray in Leicestershire each year for the purpose of fox hunting. The property was a furnished hunting box called 'Pinfold' which was owned by The Belgian

4.07 *Arrivals and departures*

Breeding Stock Farm Company Ltd, a company in which Captain Loewenstein had a controlling interest and of which he was a director. In no year did he spend as many as six months in the UK and he claimed, therefore, that, on the basis of ITA 1918 1 Sch, rule 2 of the Miscellaneous Rules of Schedule D (now ITA 2007, s 831(1)), he was exempt from tax under Schedule D. Rowlatt J did not agree. Taking up the question of the application of rule 2, he said:

> 'It really comes to this, – whether it is of the essence of the case that a man should be treated under the Rule ... as coming here with a view to establishing his residence, and not for a temporary purpose only, that he should have at any rate a proprietary interest, such as a lease or something of that sort, in the house. I cannot see what difference that makes ... this man had this house at his disposal, with everything in it or for his convenience, kept going all the year round, although he only wanted it for a short time. Luckily, he was in relation with a Company who were the owners of it, and he could do that without owning it. It is an accident. It might well have been that he could do that with a relation, or a friend, or a philanthropist, or anybody; but in fact there was this house for him ... He has got this house to come to when he likes; he does not own it; he has got no proprietary interest in it, but it is just as good as if he had for the purpose of having it for a residence, and there it is.'[2]

The *Loewenstein* case therefore established that to have a place of abode in the UK at one's disposal *de facto* was sufficient, if a person set foot in the UK, to attribute that person with a view or intent of establishing residence here, whether the place of abode was *actually* occupied or not. The 'place of abode' test was pressed to its fullest extent by the Inland Revenue until the law was changed by FA 1993 s 208(1)(4). It requires that 'in determining whether an individual is within paragraph (a) ignore any living accommodation available in the UK for the individual's use'.

From 1993–94 *Loewenstein* ceases to be applicable law for the purposes of what is now ss 831(1) and 832(1). It should be realised that the availability of accommodation in the UK may still be one of the relevant conditions that may have to be taken into account, along with other conditions, in determining the general question whether a person is resident or ordinarily resident in the UK. See **2.10** and **3.10** above.

---

1 *Loewenstein v De Salis* (1926) 10 TC 424.
2 *Loewenstein v De Salis* (1926) 10 TC 424 at 437 and 438.

4.08 Actual residence

As emphasised at **4.04** above, anyone who is in the UK for a settled (ie nontemporary) purpose or who is here with a view or intent of establishing his residence is beyond the scope of ITA 2007 s 831(1) and his residence and ordinary residence status will fall to be determined in accordance with the general principles discussed in Chapters 2 and 3. Anyone who establishes that his purpose in being here was temporary and that he had no view or intent of establishing his residence here is, however, then to be subjected to a '183 day maximum' test in order that it may be determined whether he is to be treated as resident or non-resident.[1] The terms in which this test is framed are, however, not without their difficulties of construction.

In relation to the question of chargeability to tax in respect of profits or gains received in respect of possessions or securities out of the UK, the test asks whether a person who is in the UK for some temporary purpose only has not actually resided in the UK at one time or several times for a total period equal to 183 days or more[2] in the year of assessment, whereas for the purposes of employment income[3] the test is whether a person who is in the UK for some temporary purpose only spends (in total) less than 183 days in the UK in the year of assessment.[4]

The ambiguity lies in the words 'actually resided' in s 831(1) and 'spends' in s 832(1).[5] Are the two terms synonymous and do both, or does only the second, refer to physical presence?

Whereas the legislation antecedent to s 832 first appeared comparatively recently, originating as FA 1956 Sch 2, para 3, the antecedents of ITA 2007 s 831 first appeared as ITA 1799 s 8 and then being re-enacted, first as ITA 1806 s 51, then as ITA 1812 s 39 and then as ITA 1918 Sch 1, rule 2 of the Miscellaneous Rules applicable to Schedule D. It was in that guise that they became the subject of comment by Lawrence LJ who considered them to mean that 'a person actually staying in the United Kingdom for 6 months is resident therein for the purposes of the charge to tax under Schedule D'.[6] 'Actually residing' has, it will be noted, been paraphrased as 'actually staying' and, clearly, in the view of Lawrence LJ, refers to nothing more than physical presence. Rowlatt J was more direct. He considered the force of rule 2 to be that 'if the person is in the United Kingdom for six months, then that is enough, if you have no other ground to make him chargeable as a person residing'[7] and with this Sargant LJ agreed:

> 'The language of this Rule draws a marked distinction between mere physical presence, called 'actual residence', which by the final words of the Rule makes a person chargeable if he is actually resident for six months, and that presence which is in the course of being at home and therefore amounts to residence in the ordinary sense.'[8]

On the basis of such pronouncements, Donovan J held, in the case of *Wilkie v IRC*[9] that "actual' means 'truly' and 'in fact', and is the reverse of notional',[10] and paraphrased 'actually resided in the United Kingdom as 'was here'. He concerned himself with the time Mr Wilkie 'spent' in the UK, and declared that the point at issue in rule 2 was the length of a person's 'stay' in the UK. It would seem, therefore, that Lawrence LJ, Rowlatt J, Sargant LJ and Donovan J have, between them, satisfactorily eliminated any distinction that might otherwise be drawn between the terms 'actually resided' and 'spends', and that for either term we may safely read 'was physically present'.

It is worth noting that the 'physical presence' of 183 days' duration which will result in a visitor to the UK becoming attributed with residence status for the purposes of ITA 2007 ss 831 and 832 need not be on-shore physical presence. The UK consists of territorial land and territorial waters, and the territorial waters include both inland waters and the

4.08 *Arrivals and departures*

territorial sea. It was this fact which Mr Bayard Brown, an American citizen living on a yacht anchored in the tidal waters off Brightlingsea within the Port of Colchester, appears to have overlooked when he sought to avoid UK taxation. The yacht had, under the harbour-master's sufferance, been anchored off the Essex coast for some 20 years and though it had no lawful right to be there, the Court of Appeal recognised that, in point of fact, it *was* there and that Mr Bayard Brown was upon it 'for more than six months' in the year 1908–09. Accordingly, as the yacht was within the UK's territorial waters, 'in the body of the County of Essex', Mr Bayard was chargeable to income tax 'as a person residing in the UK'.[11]

---

1 See **1.20**; **4.04** above
2 ITA 2007 s 832(1).
3 See also **1.20**.
4 ITA 2007 s 832(1).
5 See **1.20**; **4.04** above.
6 *Lysaght v IRC* (1928) 13 TC 511 at 524.
7 *Levene v IRC* (1928) 13 TC 486 at 492.
8 *Levene v IRC* (1928) 13 TC 486 at 498.
9 (1952) 32 TC 493.
10 (1952) 32 TC 495 at 511.
11 *Bayard Brown v Burt* (1911) 5 TC 667.

4.09 Detemining presence

The *Wilkie* case has already been referred to at **4.08** above in connection with the meaning of the words 'actually resides'. The case's real importance lies, however, in the fact that it gave a judicial answer to the question of what was meant by 'six months'. As stated at **4.03** above, the 'six month test' as provided in ICTA 1988 s 336, is replaced in ITA 2007 ss 831 and 832 as well as TCGA 1992 s 9(3) by the '183 day test'.[1]

Mr Wilkie, a Scotsman, had spent his working life in India but visited the UK when on leave every few years. At 2pm on 2 June 1947, he and his wife arrived in England by air for one such visit, intending to return to India not later than the end of November, but, unfortunately, Mr Wilkie had to undergo a medical operation in October and was not discharged from hospital until 10 November. Thereupon he booked a flight from Poole for 30 November – the earliest date on which a flight to India was available – but, on 14 November, those flight arrangements were cancelled by the airline and, in consequence, he was unable to actually leave the UK until 10am on 2 December 1947.

The Crown contended (a) that a fraction of a day falls to be treated as a full day, and (b) that 'six months' means six lunar months of 28 days each. By Inland Revenue reckoning, therefore, Mr Wilkie had actually resided in the UK for 184 days and had fallen to be treated as resident (by reason of his actual residence for a period equal in the whole to six months in 1947–48) after 168 days.

Mr Wilkie, on the other hand, contended (a) that fractions of a day fall to be taken account of as fractions, and (b) that 'six months' means six calendar months. By his reckoning, therefore, he had actually resided in the UK for 182 days and 20 hours and would not have fallen to be treated as resident (on the grounds of actual residence equal in the whole to six months in 1947–48) unless he had stayed in the UK for 183 days, ie until 2pm on 2 December, four hours after his actual time of departure.

Donovan J allowed Mr Wilkie's appeal, holding that, because under the Interpretation Act 1889 s 3, 'month' in all Acts passed since 1850 means calendar month unless a contrary intention appears, '"six months" ... means six calendar months'[2] and that when computing the length of a person's stay in the UK,

'... there is nothing in the language of the Rule to prevent hours being taken into the computation; but that, on the other hand, since what has to be determined is the period of actual residence it is legitimate to do so.'[3]

Accordingly, in order to determine whether or not a person falls to be treated as resident under the six-month rule, one has simply to

'... look at complete days of actual residence ... and at the hours in the case of days when the Appellant was here for a part of the day and elsewhere for the rest; and then see whether or not it all adds up to the amount of time that there is in six months.'[4]

Revenue guidance on the six-month rule is that:

'To be regarded as resident in the UK you must normally be physically present in the country at some time in the tax year. You will always be resident if you are here for 183 days or more in the tax year. There are no exceptions to this. A count is made of the total number of days you spend in the UK – it does not matter if you come and go several times during the year or if you are here for one stay of 183 days or more. If you are here for less than 183 days you may still be treated as resident for the year under other tests.'[5]

In a letter to the Consultative Committee of Accountancy Bodies dated 4 March 1983, the Inland Revenue commented that:

'The treatment for residence purposes, as outlined in paragraph 8 of Booklet IR20, was adopted in 1972 following a review of our practice in the light of the decision in *Wilkie v IRC* (1952) 32 TC 495. That case established the principle that, in deciding whether a temporary visitor had actually resided in the UK for a period equal to six months, periods of time in terms of hours were relevant for days of less than total residence. In view of the difficulties which would arise in following the strict rule it was decided to regard 183 days as equal to six months and to disregard days of arrival and departure in making the count.'[6]

The boundary has been shifted to limit the time that an individual might spend in the UK without becoming resident by the Finance Act 2008. Measurement of days spent in the UK from 6 April 2008 is determined by detailed statutory rules added by FA 2008 s 24 amending ITA ss 831 and 832 as well as TCGA s 9 by the addition of the following:

'(1A) In determining whether an individual is within subsection (1)(b) treat a day as a day spent by the individual in the United Kingdom if (and only if) the individual is present in the United Kingdom at the end of the day.

(1B) But in determining that issue do not treat as a day spent by the individual in the United Kingdom any day on which the individual arrives in the United Kingdom as a passenger if—
(a) the individual departs from the United Kingdom on the next day, and
(b) during the time between arrival and departure the individual does not engage in activities that are to a substantial extent unrelated to the individual's passage through the United Kingdom.'

The changes to the legislation introduced in the clause are in respect of the 183-day test only. However, HMRC have stated that where their practice requires the use of day-counting to determine residence for tax purposes, that practice will also be changed in line with the statutory amendment introduced in this clause. All day counting tests, such as the non-statutory 91-day test, will follow the same principle that any day where the individual is in the UK at the end of the day will be included as a day of residence. The same exception from that general rule will apply where the individual is a passenger in transit and their activities whilst in the UK are not substantially unrelated to that travel.[7]

Whether an individual is present in the UK at the end of a day (presumably ending at midnight) is a straightforward question of fact. Individuals staying overnight and departing the next day will face detailed examination of minute and subtle fact relating to their presence as illustrated by HMRC examples.

Example 1

Peter works for the Jersey arm of HSBC and is travelling from Jersey to Frankfurt. He flies from Jersey to Gatwick and will catch his onward flight the next day to Frankfurt from London City airport. He travels from Gatwick to Canary Wharf for a meeting with several other HSBC colleagues before staying overnight in a nearby hotel. The meeting with colleagues is not an activity substantially related to completing travel to a foreign destination. The transit passenger provisions will not apply.

Example 2

John works for the Jersey arm of HSBC and is travelling from Jersey to Frankfurt via Gatwick and London City airport. In the lobby of his hotel near London City Airport, he unexpectedly spots another colleague who has just arrived from Paris. They have a couple of pints together and their conversation covers a number of business-related issues. Peter then travels to London City airport to catch his onward connection. This meeting was not planned and therefore it can be considered that John's activities in the UK substantially related to completing travel to a foreign destination. The transit passenger provisions will apply.

Example 3

Shirley lives in Guernsey and is travelling to New Zealand by way of Gatwick and Heathrow. She has planned to spend most of the day with her daughter and grandchildren, who live in Crawley and will also spend the night there before travelling to Heathrow for her onward flight. Her visit is not an activity substantially related to completing travel to a foreign destination. The transit passenger provisions will not apply.

Example 4

Phil lives in Guernsey and is travelling to New Zealand by way of Gatwick and Heathrow. His flight from Guernsey is delayed by fog and he arrives too late to make his onward connection to New Zealand that day. His son had already arranged to meet him at Gatwick and drive him to Heathrow, now he drives him to a hotel near Heathrow instead where Phil will stay overnight before catching his rearranged flight. At the hotel they have a snack together. These activities are substantially related to completing travel to a foreign destination – Phil would have eaten in the hotel even if he had been unaccompanied. The transit passenger provisions will apply.

Example 5

George lives in the Isle of Man and is flying to New York on business via Manchester. He has made an appointment with a consultant orthopaedic surgeon based in Manchester to carry out a number of tests. He will stay in the clinic overnight before travelling on to New York the following afternoon. The appointment is not an activity substantially related to completing travel to a foreign destination. The transit passenger provisions will not apply.

Example 6

George lives in Jersey and is travelling to Stavanger. He does not fly and travels to the UK by ferry before continuing to London by train. He stays overnight at a West End hotel, having prearranged dinner and a trip to the theatre with friends. The next day he travels to Newcastle by train, where he boards a ferry to Stavanger. His activities in the UK are not substantially related to completing travel to a foreign destination. The transit passenger provisions will not apply

---

1 See **4.11** below.
2 *Wilkie v IRC* (1951) 32 TC 495 at 508.
3 *Wilkie v IRC* (1951) 32 TC 495 at 511.
4 *Wilkie v IRC* (1951) 32 TC 495 at 511.
5 IR20 (July 2008) para 1.2 and Ch 3 and in particular para 3.3, see **Appendix 1** below.
6 CCAB Notes (TR 508) on Taxation Anomalies and Practical Difficulties.
7 Explanatory Notes to Clause 22 of 2008 Finance Bill, paragraph 17.

4.10 *Arrivals and departures*

4.10 The significance of 'the tax year'

ITA 2007 s 831 refers to actual residence of a total period equal to 183 days (or more) 'in the tax year in question' while s 832 refers to 'during the tax year in question'. It is perfectly possible, therefore, for a person to arrive in the UK on 5 October in one year and to leave on 5 October in the following year (4 October if that year is a leap year) and thus spend a full twelve months in the UK without exceeding the maximum permitted time for the purpose of the provisions of that section. Although 364 days will have been spent in the UK, only 182 days will have been spent in each of two consecutive but separate tax years. In the *Zorab* case,[1] Mr Zorab arrived in the UK on 1 November 1920 and departed on 3 October 1921 thus spending 337 consecutive days in the UK. Of those 337 days, only 156 were spent here in 1920–21 and only 181 were spent here in 1921–22 in consequence of which no challenge on 'six-month rule' grounds was raised against his non-resident status.

Any temporary visitor whose visits follow this pattern may, of course, find himself attributed with the status of residence on one or more of the circumstantial grounds described in Chapter 2, above. Although presence for 183 days of the tax year will ensure that he is treated as resident for the purposes of ITA 2007, ss 831 and 832, presence for less than 183 days will not ensure that he is *not* attributed with the quality of residence for those or any other purposes under the Taxes Acts.

---

1 *IRC v Zorab* (1926) 11 TC 289. See **4.05** above.

4.11 The capital gains tax test

TCGA 1992 s 2(1) provides that, subject to certain exceptions:

> '... a person shall be chargeable to capital gains tax in respect of chargeable gains accruing to him in a year of assessment during any part of which he is resident in the United Kingdom, or during which he is ordinarily resident in the UK,'

and goes on to provide in s 9(3) that subject to s 10 (non-residents with UK branch or agency) and subject to s 10A (temporary non-residents):

> '... an individual who is in the United Kingdom for some temporary purpose only and not with any view or intent to establish his residence in the United Kingdom shall be charged to capital gains tax on chargeable gains accruing in any year of assessment if and only if the individual spends (in total) at least 183 days in the UK.'

Finance Act 2008 s 24(6) amended the wording of s 9(3) of TCGA so that the former reference in that provision to 'six months' is replaced by a reference to '183 days'. The amended wording mirrors the existing wording in ITA 2007 s 832(1)(b), and the revised wording to be inserted in ITA 2007 s 831(1)(b). It brings some consistency to the statutory language used in the relevant provisions in this respect for both capital gains tax and income tax purposes.

It seems beyond doubt that the terms 'temporary purpose', 'view or intent to establish his residence' and '183 days' fall to be construed in the manner indicated at **4.05**, **4.06** and **4.09** above.

Only two subsections earlier TCGA 1992 s 9(1) states that "resident' and 'ordinarily resident' have the same meanings as in the Income Tax Acts'.

These provisons do not sit together perfectly. That being so, is not TCGA 1992 s 9(3) simply stating that, in order to alleviate such a burden in the case of individuals who have come to the UK for some temporary purpose but have become attributed with residence status, no charge to capital gains tax is to be made unless the total period for which residence status is possessed exceeds six months? The fact that residence is an annual attribute for taxation purposes is no bar to such a construction. As has been explained at **2.05** above (and as is, indeed, implied in the wording of TCGA 1992 s 2(1) itself), a person may acquire or lose the quality of residence at any time; its predication to him throughout the year is merely an expedient to which the annual nature of income tax gives rise.

This interpretation of TCGA 1992 s 9(3) necessitates rejection of the idea that it and ITA 2007 s 831 are parallel provisions – though HMRC is likely to treat them as such.[1] It sees TCGA 1992 s 9(3) as a relieving provision; and the words 'and only if' within the section affirm that that is so. The only charge intended by TCGA 1992 or referred to in s 9(3) is the charge imposed by s 2(1). TCGA 1992 s 9(3) is not extending that charge to anyone not already within the reach of s 2(1). On the contrary, it has been enacted to extricate from the charge under s 2(1) anyone who, though in the UK for a short visit only, is trapped by that section. It is for that reason that s 9(3) (the relieving section) did not prior to FA 2008 use the terminology of 'presence' but uses instead the same terminology of 'residence' as is used in s 2(1) (the charging section). That, surely, was as it should be, for, had Parliament couched the exempting provisions of s 9(3) in terms of physical presence, it would have made the exemption wider than the charge and would be setting free certain individuals who were not even caught!

---

1 See **4.12** below.

4.12 TCGA 1992 s 9(3) and ITA 2007 s 831 compared

TCGA 1992 s 9(3) and ITA 2007 s 831 serve different purposes. The object of s 831 is not only to remove from the charge imposed under ITTOIA and ITEPA[1] certain persons who would otherwise unjustifiably be trapped there, but also to draw into the charge certain persons who would otherwise be beyond its reach. Although s 831 is, in part, a relieving section, it is, therefore, also, in part (and unlike TCGA 1992 s 9(3)), a charging section. An occasional visitor to the UK might, in the light of all his personal circumstances, succeed in satisfying the court (if not HMRC) that he does

4.12 *Arrivals and departures*

not possess such status. However, he will then have to contend with ITA 2007 s 831. That section fills the gap which the longer-term casual visitor might walk through unscathed and, provided the period for which the visitor is physically present in the UK during the year of assessment is, in aggregate, 183 days or more, permits HMRC to *treat* him as resident and to impose on him the charge which would be imposed were he *actually* in possession of such status. As Lord Shand said in *Lloyd v Sulley*:[2]

> 'Although the provision ... is in the language of exemption ... it rather appears to me to be a section which is intended to impose liability,'[3]

and, as Sir R Webster A-G put it even more positively in *Colquhoun v Brooks*,[4] the section is

> '... not an exempting section in the proper sense of the word; it is a special charging section under limited circumstances.'

In short, ITA 2007 s 831 is saying (in this author's view) that, once a temporary visitor has been here for a total of 183 days, he must, if he is found not to possess residence status on general grounds, be attributed with quasi-residence status and charged to tax accordingly; while TCGA 1992 s 9(3) is saying (again, in this author's view) that if a temporary visitor has acquired residence status on general grounds and would therefore fall to be charged to capital gains tax, he must be excused from the charge provided he possesses that status for less than 183 days in the year.

The construction of TCGA 1992 s 9(3) propounded at **4.11** and **4.12** above is not (as one might expect) the construction placed on it by HMRC. HMRC would like to believe that the effect of TCGA 1992 s 9(3) is that *actual* residence of 183 days' duration in a tax year will automatically bring a temporary visitor into charge to capital gains tax, and it is Revenue practice to treat such actual residence as doing so. It must be questioned, however, whether that practice is within the law.

Section 208(2) of the FA 1993 inserted subsection (4) into s 9 of TCGA 1992. It provides that in determining whether for capital gains tax, as for income tax, a person is in the UK for some temporary purpose only and not with any view or intent to establish residence no regard shall be taken of any living accommodation available in the UK for that person's use. The new s 9(4) applies with effect for the year 1993–94 and subsequent years of assessment.

Section 10A of the TCGA 1992 affects certain individuals who arrive in the UK following a period when they have left the UK for a temporary purpose, such as to dispose of assets which otherwise would be chargable to capital gains tax.[5]

---

1 See **1.20**; **4.04** above.
2 (1884) 2 TC 37.
3 (1884) 2 TC 37 at 44.
4 (1899) 2 TC 490.
5 See **4.21** below.

Persons leaving the UK

4.13 Residence of individuals temporarily abroad

ICT 2007 s 829(1) states:

'(1) This section applies if –
 (a) an individual has left the United Kingdom for the purpose only of occasional residence abroad, and
 (b) at the time of leaving the individual was both UK resident and ordinarily UK resident.'

ICT 2007 s 829(2) states:

'(2) Treat the individual as UK resident for the purpose of determining the individual's liability for income tax for any tax year during the whole or a part of which the individual remains outside the United Kingdom for the purpose only of occasional residence abroad.'

4.14 Occasional residence

ITA 2007 s 829 is concerned with persons who are both resident and ordinarily resident in the UK. If any such person leaves the UK for the purpose 'only of occasional residence abroad' he is, despite his absence, to be treated as resident here. The words in quotation marks are of very great importance since, most UK taxpayers remain within its ambit and, whenever one of them claims to have become non-resident by reason of taking up residence abroad, the Crown, if it wishes to resist that claim, will attempt to do so by contending that the residence abroad is occasional residence only.

Although the term 'occasional residence abroad' may suggest only short periods of absence, it was, in one of the earliest cases on the subject of residence,[1] held to include a temporary absence which extended over an entire tax year. This should immediately alert us to the fact that the words have been construed as possessing a far wider meaning than we might otherwise suppose. The case concerned the validity of a charge to tax within the context of the first part of ITA 1842 s 39 – one of the predecessors of ITA 2007 s 829 – which provided that:

'... any subject of Her Majesty whose ordinary residence shall have been in Great Britain, and who shall have departed from Great Britain and gone into any parts beyond the seas, for the purpose only of occasional residence ... shall be deemed, notwithstanding such temporary absence, a person chargeable to the duties granted by this Act as a person actually residing in Great Britain.'

The case concerned a master mariner who, because he was absent from the UK throughout the whole of 1878–79, contended that his residence abroad was not merely 'occasional' and that he was, therefore, beyond the

4.14 *Arrivals and departures*

scope of s 39 and thus not liable to tax for that year. The Lord President Inglis did not agree:

> 'The circumstance that Captain Rogers has been absent from the country during the whole year to which the assessment applies does not seem to me to be a speciality of the least consequence. That is a mere accident. He is not a bit the less a resident of Great Britain because the exigencies of his business have happened to carry him away for a somewhat longer time than usual during this particular voyage.'[2]

Captain Rogers was a British subject, commanded a British ship, owned a house at Innerleven in the county of Fife in which his wife and children dwelt throughout the year in question, owned no house elsewhere, and was absent merely by reason of following his vocation of master mariner. Despite the fact that he was not physically present for even a single day in the tax year 1878–79, he was, therefore, qualitatively resident in the UK throughout that tax year.[3]

The principle – that occasional residence abroad may extend to absences in excess of an entire tax year – remained unchanged and, indeed, was reiterated a quarter of a century later in the Irish case of *Iveagh v Revenue Comrs*[4] when, in the course of expressing his opinion on the application of what had then become rule 3 of the General Rules applicable to Schedules A, B, C, D and E under ITA 1918, Hanna J declared:

> 'It may well be that under this rule a citizen absent through illness for a lengthy period, even two years, may be liable to tax ...'[5]

and when, in that same case, it was held that the Special Commissioners had not misdirected themselves in point of law in holding that

> '... there must be personal presence ... at some time during the year of assessment, except in a case coming within the terms of Rule 3 of the General Rules.'[6]

Anyone who is 'resident in the United Kingdom for a year of assessment, but ... absent from the United Kingdom throughout that year' can clearly only be someone who has been attributed with the quality of residence in the UK for a particular tax year without ever having been physically present in the UK during any part of that year. This was noted by Nicholls J in *Reed v Clark*[7] who later confirmed that:

> 'There is nothing in the language or in my view the context of s 49 to show that regardless of the circumstances a person can never be said to have left for the purpose of occasional residence abroad if his residence abroad extends throughout an entire tax year. A man ordinarily resident here may go to live abroad in March intending to return some months later but through serious illness of himself or others or other unforeseen change of circumstances not return until the end of the following March. I can see no reason why, depending on all the facts, such a man may not fall within s 49. If that is right, it would be absurd that such a man should fall outside s 49 if the emergency which kept him

abroad should chance to last for a week or two longer and not permit his return until after 5 April.'[8]

In the eyes of HMRC, however, 'residence is essentially related to physical presence'[9] so that 'to be regarded as resident in the United Kingdom you must normally be physically present in the country at some time in the tax year'[10] and even if he usually lives in the UK but has gone abroad for a long holiday and does not set foot in the UK during the year,[11] he will be regarded as non-resident for that year. HMRC shows consistency, therefore, when it equates 'occasional residence abroad' with absence of 'short periods'[12] only, but it must be emphasised that this view of the meaning of occasional residence is unsupported by case law and that the strict position of any British subject or citizen of the Irish Republic falling within the provisions of ICTA 1988 s 334 (previously TA 1970 s 49) is as it was in Captain Rogers' day. Furthermore, the rule of practice does, it should be noted, include the qualification 'normally' which leaves it open to the Revenue to decide in any particular case that a person is resident in the UK for a tax year throughout the whole of which he has been physically absent. This was the Revenue stance in *Reed v Clark*[13] where Dave Clark's absence was admittedly motivated by tax avoidance considerations. In *IRC v Combe*,[14] Lord Clyde LP said that:

'..."occasional residence" is residence taken up or happening as passing opportunity requires, in one case, or admits in another, and contrasts with the residence, or ordinary residence, of a person who ... is "resident" or "ordinarily resident" in some place or country,'[15]

and in *Reed v Clark*[16] Nicholls J, commenting on s 49, said:

'In this section occasional residence is the converse of ordinary residence.'[17]

The duration of the physical absence from the UK of a person falling within ITA 2007 s 829 (previously ICTA 1988 s 334) is of relevance, therefore, only to the extent to which it bears on whether or not that person has, in fact, become resident or ordinarily resident elsewhere. If he has, then his residence in that other place or country cannot be 'occasional residence' abroad, for one cannot be resident and occasionally resident in one and the same place at one and the same time.[18] If a person has *not* become resident or ordinarily resident elsewhere, however, but, having been ordinarily resident in the UK, has left these shores, his residence overseas *is* 'occasional residence'. In short, a person within the category prescribed by ITA 2007 s 829 *will* be attributed with the status of residence in accordance with that section unless there is evidence of 'a distinct break'[19] with the UK. Although general Revenue practice is to treat physical absence which extends over a whole tax year as creating such a break, such absence alone is, as the earlier cases show, not conclusive evidence in law of such a break, and although even the courts have conceded that the attribution of residential status to a person who 'during a whole year, the year of assessment ... has never been in this country ... would require a pretty strong case indeed',[20] that is not to say that there are

4.14 *Arrivals and departures*

no circumstances in which such a case could be made by the Revenue – as *Reed v Clark*[21] plainly shows.

In *Shepherd v Revenue and Customs Comrs*[22] the taxpayer was an airline pilot who was domiciled in the UK. He bought a flat in Cyprus and from then on spent only 80 days a year in the UK. He therefore fell within the 90 days 'test' set out in HMRC's booklet IR20 at para 2.2. The rest of the year he was either living in Cyprus, working abroad or on holiday abroad. He had a home in the UK and stayed in it with his wife when here. The High Court upheld the Commissioners' decision that he was abroad only for the purpose of 'occasional residence' under ICTA 1988 s 334(a) and therefore remained ordinarily resident in the UK.

The Special Commissioners in *Gaines-Cooper v Revenue and Customs Comrs*[23] held that the taxpayer was also resident within the terms of s 334. They did not regard him as a 'temporary resident' although those words are not contained in s 334. Since however they had held that he was not in the UK for some 'temporary purpose' within s 336, they may have felt that he could not be said to have left the UK otherwise than for an 'occasional residence' – the actual words of s 334 – abroad. If therefore he was not a temporary resident here he could be nothing more than an occasional resident abroad.

---

1 *Rogers v IRC* (1879) 1 TC 225.
2 *Rogers v IRC* (1879) 1 TC 225 at 227.
3 It is unlikely that any present-day Captain Rogers would be regarded as resident in the circumstances described, but this would be because of the application of ITA 2007 s 830 – see **4.15** below – not because of any change in the judicial view of the meaning of 'occasional residence abroad'.
4 (1930) 1 ITC 316.
5 (1930) 1 ITC 316 at 349.
6 (1930) 1 ITC 316 at 356–357.
7 [1985] STC 323.
8 [1985] STC 323 at 344.
9 Inland Revenue explanatory note relating to a proposed amendment to Finance Bill 1974, cl 18.
10 IR20 (July 2008), para 1.2, see **Appendix 1** below.
11 IR20 (July 2008), para 1.3, see **Appendix 1** below.
12 IR20 (July 2008), para 2.1, see **Appendix 1** below.
13 [1985] STC 323.
14 (1932) 17 TC 405.
15 (1932) 17 TC 405 at 410.
16 [1985] STC 323.
17 [1985] STC 323, at 345.
18 One can, however, be resident in two or more places at the same time – see **2.09** above – and the fact that a person may escape the provisions of ITA 2007 s 829 by proving that his residence overseas is not merely occasional, does not necessarily mean, therefore, that he cannot exceptionally be found to be nonetheless resident in the UK as well as resident elsewhere and thus to be liable for UK taxes.
19 *IRC v Combe* (1932) 17 TC 405 at 411, per Lord Sands.
20 *Turnbull v Foster* (1904) 6 TC 206 at 209, per Clerk LJ.
21 [1985] STC 323.
22 [2005] UKSPC 484.
23 [2007] UKSPC 568.

4.15 A distinct break

The foregoing discussion should have served to illustrate how adhesive the quality of residence is in the case of an individual whose ordinary residence has been in the UK. Indeed, nothing less than a distinct break with the UK will suffice to divest a person of that quality, as the leading case[1] concerning the application of ITA 1918 Sch 1, rule 3 of the General Rules applicable to Schedules A, B, C, D and E (the predecessor of ICTA 1988 s 334) makes very plain.

Until March 1918, Mr Louis Levene, a British subject, leased a house in Curzon Street, London. On that date he surrendered the lease, sold his furniture and, until January 1925, was of no fixed abode but stayed at hotels either in the UK or abroad. Until December 1919, he stayed in England and was, on his own admission, resident and ordinarily resident in the UK until that date. In December 1919, however, he went abroad but returned to the UK in July 1920 and, from then until January 1925, spent between four and five months here in each tax year. The purpose of his annual visits to the UK was to obtain medical advice for himself and his wife, to visit relatives and the graves of his parents, to take part in certain Jewish religious observances and to deal with his tax affairs. In January 1925 he took a nine-year lease on a flat in Monaco.

Mr Levene contended that for the years 1920–21 to 1924–25 he was neither resident nor ordinarily resident in the UK and that, in consequence, he was entitled to exemption from tax on certain interest and dividends from securities. The Special Commissioners did not agree and the High Court, the Court of Appeal and finally the House of Lords upheld the Commissioners' decision. Key passages from Viscount Sumner's lucid judgment are given below.

> 'My Lords, early in 1918 Mr Levene, a British subject, formed the intention to 'live abroad'. He sold his house in Mayfair, sold such furniture as was not in settlement, and then lived in hotels in England for the best part of two years. I will assume that, but for passport difficulties and the condition of his wife's health, he would have gone abroad sooner. He left England in December, 1919.
>
> Accordingly on 6 April 1920, at the beginning of the five years of charge now in question, he was, in the words of Rule 3 of the General Rules, 'a British subject, whose ordinary residence has been in the UK' and so he remained chargeable to tax notwithstanding, if he had left the United Kingdom for the purpose only of occasional residence abroad. Was that the only purpose of his leaving so far as residence is concerned?
>
> The Special Commissioners found that it was, and I think it is clear that they had evidence before them on which they could so find. His only declaration was that he meant to live abroad, not saying whether it was to be an occasional or a constant, a part time or a whole time sojourn. He was advised by his doctor to seek a better climate, which is consistent with returning to England when English weather mends. He had gone out of business in England and broken up his establishment, but he still had in England business interests connected with his Income Tax assessments, and ties of filial piety and religious observance, for his father was buried at Southampton and he was himself a member of the English community of Jews. What he actually did was to come back to England after an absence of about seven months, and he remained for nearly five. In the

4.15 Arrivals and departures

meantime he had not set up an establishment abroad but had lived in hotels. This, however, was only what he had done in England from March, 1918, to December, 1919. I think there was ample evidence before the Commissioners to show that a man, who left England to live abroad as he had been living here, and when warm weather came returned to his native country and to his permanent associations, had in 1919 'left the United Kingdom for the purposes of occasional residence only'. If so, he remained chargeable.

So much for the year of charge 1920–21. In the following years he was a bird of passage of almost mechanical regularity. No material change occurred in his way of living, for his enquiries for a permanent flat came to nothing until so late as not to affect his life and residence for the period in question ... The evidence as a whole disclosed that Mr Levene continued to go to and fro during the years in question, leaving at the beginning of winter and coming back in summer, his home thus remaining as before. He changed his sky but not his home.[2] On this I see no error in law in saying of each year that his purpose in leaving the United Kingdom was occasional residence abroad only. The occasion was the approach of an English winter and when with the promise of summer here that occasion passed away, back came Mr Levene to attend the calls of interest, of friendship and of piety.[3]

Not until January 1925 was there evidence of a distinct break with Mr Levene's former residence in the UK and, accordingly, not until 1925 could his periods of residence abroad be anything other than occasional residence within the context of ICTA 1988 s 334 (the predecessor of ITA 2007 s 829) despite the fact that for a period of five years Mr Levene had no fixed abode in this country and consistently spent the greater part of each year overseas.

The case of Mr Levene may usefully be compared and contrasted with that of Mr F L Brown.[4] Mr Brown was a British subject whose ordinary residence had been in the UK from 1893 until February 1918. On that date he, like Mr Levene, gave up his house in Folkestone, stored his furniture and, until October 1919, lived at hotels in various places in the UK. In October 1919, however, he departed for a hotel in Menton on the French Riviera where he had habitually stayed for two or three months every winter since 1906, and from October 1919 his ordinary and usual habit of life was to spend seven months of each year in the same suite of rooms in that hotel (ie practically the whole of the hotel's open season), two months in Switzerland or at the Italian lakes, and three months in the UK. Mr Brown had four sons living in the UK and his visits to the UK were to see them, other relations and friends, and for a change. Sometimes he stayed with friends or relatives, other times he stayed at hotels or boarding houses. He had no business ties in the UK but he had a banking account here into which dividends were paid. The Inland Revenue contended that Mr Brown, being a British subject whose ordinary residence had been in the UK, had gone abroad for the purpose of occasional residence only within the meaning of rule 3 of the General Rules, but the Special Commissioners did not agree. They held that 'there had been a definite break in his habit of life in February 1918, when the house in the UK was given up'.[5] In a remarkably brief judgment, Rowlatt J dismissed the Crown's appeal on the grounds that he could see no error of law in the Commissioners' finding and could not, therefore, interfere with it. Nevertheless, he made his reservations plain: Mr Brown 'had some furniture and a banking account and he had connections with England, and if the Commissioners had found the other way I should not have disturbed them'.[6] There was a break, but one which, clearly, was not as clean as Rowlatt J would have liked to find it. Because of that break, however, Mr Brown became non-resident from 6 April 1918 and his residence status for 1924–25, the tax year in question, was determined by the Commissioners under the statutory provisions now contained in ITA 2007 s 831which relate to visitors in the UK.[7] Because the Commissioners considered that Mr Levene had made no such break prior to January 1925, however, his residence status for the years 1920–21 to 1924–25 could not be determined under those provisions. Hence the difference in outcome of what, on the face of them, were very similar cases.

The principle that once there is a 'distinct break' in a person's residence in the UK, the overseas residence that ensues will necessarily be more than 'occasional' residence, was emphasised some six years later by Lord Sands in *IRC v Combe*.[8] Captain Combe, a British subject, left the UK for America and there served an apprenticeship under a New York employer with a view to becoming that employer's European representative. During each of the three years following his departure, he made visits here on his employer's business but, having no place of abode in the UK, stayed in hotels. The Crown claimed that Captain Combe had remained resident in the UK throughout the three years in question as, within the terms of ICTA 1988 s 334 (the precedessor of ITA 2007 s 829), he had left the UK for the purpose only of occasional residence abroad. This claim was, however, rejected by the Commissioners and, on appeal, by the Court of Session. Lord Sands, referring to the fact that Captain Combe had left the UK on 24 April 1926 and had not returned for a visit until 4 March 1927, said:

> 'There was a distinct break. Any residence in the first year in this country was what might have been accounted for by simply not very prolonged holidays.'[9]

It was that opinion on which, in part, Nicholls J based his judgment in *Reed v Clark*.[10] Dave Clark was a British subject whose ordinary residence had been in England until, on 3 April 1978, he left England to live and work in Los Angeles for 13 months. The 13 months intentionally spanned the tax year 1978–79 because Dave Clark had been advised that, by staying abroad throughout that year, he would avoid tax on $450,000 received in the previous year from the sale of Polydor Ltd – a German recording company – of the right to make and sell certain recordings of the 'Dave Clark Five' – a band which he had formed and which had enjoyed considerable success in the 1960s.

Mr Clark was unmarried and, before leaving for America, he lived with his mother in a house he had bought for her in North London. Upon returning to the UK on 2 May 1979 he resumed residence there. Throughout the period, Dave Clark (London) Ltd – a company of which Mr Clark was sole director – owned the lease of a flat in Mayfair and, until leaving for America, Mr Clark had an office and bedroom there. A firm of estate agents were instructed to sub-let the flat during the period of his absence but they were unable to do so. Mr Clark had, however, packed away his files and other belongings and the flat was in a state of readiness for a sub-tenant had one been found.

In contending that Mr Clark's residence in America was merely occasional residence abroad, the Crown stressed the fact that it was, from the outset, Mr Clark's intention to return to the UK after 13 months; the fact that during his absence his established domestic and business arrangements in this country were maintained to such a degree that, immediately upon his return, his ordinary pattern of life could be resumed without any significant disruption; and the fact that his absence was contrived for tax avoidance purposes.

Nicholls J was of the opinion that none of those facts brought Mr Clark's residence within the term 'occasional residence' as used in TA 1970 s 49. He said:

> 'In this case there was a distinct break in the pattern of the taxpayer's life which lasted (as from the outset he intended) for just over a year. He ceased living in London and for that year he lived in or near Los Angeles, mostly in one fixed place of abode, and he worked from there. For that year Los Angeles was his headquarters. He did not visit this country at all. On the whole I do not think he can be said to have left the UK for the purpose only of occasional residence abroad. In my judgment the conclusion of the commissioners on this was correct.'[11]

In *Barrett v Revenue & Customs*,[12] the taxpayers' contention that there was a distinct break was rejected on the basis that there was no change in his circumstances. Mr Barrett continued to be employed by the same employer under the same contract of employment and seemed to have been doing much what he was doing before. He was looking for a musical act or acts to manage through his employer and had worked abroad before for them. He did not establish a permanent home or 'HQ' abroad. His partner and family continued to be in the UK in the family home where they still live. He paid the UK bills from his UK accounts and made no special financial arrangement for his time abroad (such as bank account, credit card, medical insurance etc). No special arrangements seem to have been made as to his car, driving licence, residence permits, foreign identity card or similar matters. There was a lack of certainty as to when he went abroad, which the Special Commissioner found surprising if it was a distinct break in the pattern of his life. It was also surprising that there was no ticket or boarding pass stub or similar evidence if this was so different from what had gone on before so as to be a distinct break in the pattern of his life. If he went abroad for tax reasons to escape the UK tax net, having taken advice from well-known advisers, one would have expected him to have been advised of the importance of objective evidence to show this.

---

1 *Levene v IRC* (1928) 13 TC 486.
2 Although Viscount Sumner is generally credited with the coining of this striking phrase, it seems clear that he was, in fact, either consciously or unconsciously, misquoting the Latin poet Horace who centuries earlier had written 'caelum non animum mutant qui

trans mare currunt' (Epist I.xi.27) – 'they change their sky but not their soul who speed across the sea'.
3   *Levene v IRC* (1928) 13 TC 486 at 501.
4   *IRC v Brown* (1926) 11 TC 292.
5   *IRC v Brown* (1926) 11 TC 292 at 295.
6   *IRC v Brown* (1926) 11 TC 292 at 296.
7   See **4.04–4.10** above.
8   (1932) 17 TC 405.
9   (1932) 17 TC 405 at 411.
10 [1985] STC 323.
11 [1985] STC 323 at 346.
12 [2007] UKSPC SPC639.

4.16 Residence of individuals working abroad

The statutory provision concerning residence which next falls to be discussed is that contained in ITA 2007 s 830:

(1) This section applies for income tax purposes if an individual works full-time in one or both of –
   (a) a foreign trade, and
   (b) a foreign employment.
(2) In determining whether the individual is UK resident ignore any living accommodation available in the UK for the individual's use.
(3) A trade is foreign if no part of it is carried on in the UK.
(4) An employment is foreign if all of its duties are performed outside the UK.
(5) An employment is also foreign if in the tax year in question –
   (a) the duties of the employment are in substance performed outside the UK, and
   (b) the only duties of the employment performed in the UK are duties which are merely incidental to the duties of the employment performed outside the UK in the year.
(6) In this section –
   'employment' includes an office, and
   'trade' includes profession and vocation.

By concession this is extended to determine the status of an individual accompanying or later joining a spouse who goes abroad for full-time employment.[1]

1   Extra statutory Concession A 78.

4.17 Full-time work

ITA 2007 s 830 is of no application to anyone who does not work full-time in one, or more than one, trade, profession, vocation, office or employment. 'Full-time' is, however, a term which is undefined in the statute and which must, therefore, be given its ordinary, accepted meaning. This, according to *Chambers Dictionary*[1] is: 'occupied during or extending over the whole working day, week etc', but HMRC may, in practice, be

4.17 *Arrivals and departures*

expected to interpret it more liberally than that dictionary definition would suggest. The words 'works full-time' appear in only one other place in the Taxes Acts and that is in relation to loans to participators by close companies.[2] In that context, it is Revenue practice to treat a director or employee as working full-time if his hours of work are equivalent to at least three-quarters of the company's normal working hours.

Even if we take s 830 as being directed, therefore, only at those who, apart from periods of holiday, leave, sickness etc, are occupied in their work throughout substantially the whole (ie at least 25 hours) of each working week, the term 'full-time' has not, however, been cleared of all its difficulties of construction. Although the term is clearly intended to contrast full-time work with part-time work, the words 'in one or more of the following, that is to say, a trade, profession, vocation, office or employment' do not, on a strict construction, exclude a person who, although working only part-time in relation to any one trade, profession, employment or the like, does so in relation to more than one trade, profession, employment or the like so that his various part-time occupations extend over the whole of each working week. The Revenue now appears to accept this view.[3]

ITA 2007 s 830 is silent as to whether the full-time occupation to which it refers must extend over an entire tax year in order that its provisions might be effective for that tax year but there would seem to be no strong argument in favour of such a construction. The section is not granting a full-time overseas worker non-resident status; it is merely saying that his residence status is to be decided without regard to any place of abode he maintains in the UK. Disregard of a person's maintained place of abode in the UK will, however, in the majority of cases, not prevent the attribution of residence status to a person whose period of full-time work abroad does not span an entire tax year. The various connecting factors described at **2.16** to **2.19** above will alone be sufficient, in most cases, to imbue the person with residence status upon his return to the UK and, as explained at **2.05** above, that status will, in law, be attributed to him for the whole of the tax year in which the return takes place. It is HMRC practice to refuse non-resident status to a person working overseas unless

> '...your absence from the United Kingdom and your employment abroad both last for at least a whole tax year; during your absence any visits you make to the United Kingdom (i) total less than 183 days in any tax year, and (ii) average less than 91 days a tax year (the average is taken over a period of absence up to a maximum of four years;[4] any days spent in the United Kingdom because of exceptional circumstances beyond your control, for example the illness of yourself or a member of your immediate family are not normally counted for this purpose).'[5]

Clearly, the timing of relatively short overseas assignments can assume great importance in the light of these considerations.

---

1 1998 edition.
2 TA 1988 s 420(2)(b).
3 Revenue Interpretation, Tax Bulletin 40 (February) 1993. See also *Pamer v Maloney* [1999] STC 890 (CA).

4 IR20 (July 2008), para 2.10 at **Appendix 1** below.
5 IR20 (July 2008), para 2.2 at **Appendix 1** below.

4.18 Trades and professions

It has been stressed[1] that unless a person works full-time in a trade, profession, vocation, office or employment, he cannot bring himself within the ambit of ITA 2007 s 830. The fact that a person may so work is, however, not sufficient, on its own, to guarantee his inclusion within the ambit of the section, for there is an additional condition which must first be fulfilled.

In the case of a person working full-time in a trade, profession or vocation, that condition is that no part of the trade, profession or vocation is carried on in the UK. If any part of it is carried on then the person is beyond the scope of the section and the question of whether he himself ever actually works in the UK is completely irrelevant.

The consequences of this may be severe. Anyone who carries on a trade, profession or vocation partly in the UK and partly overseas will, if he is attributed with UK residence status, find himself chargeable to tax on the *whole* of his profits or gains irrespective of whether they have arisen from activities inside the UK or abroad. Only if he is able to obtain or maintain non-resident status will assessments be restricted to such of his profits or gains as may be attributed to activities in the UK.

In order to determine where a trade is carried on, one must ask the question: 'Where do the operations take place from which the profits in substance arise?'[2] If the answer to that question is partly within and partly outside the UK, then it follows that 'part of the trade ... is carried on in the United Kingdom' within ITA 2007 s 830.

The test is a very broad one and necessitates a detailed examination of all the facts in any particular case, but a number of decided cases have given rise to certain general principles. In *Sully v A-G*,[3] for instance, it was decided that merely contracting to purchase goods in the UK for subsequent resale abroad cannot constitute the carrying on of trade in the UK. Nor, according to the decision in *Grainger & Son v Gough*,[4] can the mere soliciting of sales orders which are then actually entered into overseas amount to trading in the UK. (In that case, the now-familiar distinction between trading *in* the UK and trading *with* the UK was drawn.) Similarly, in *Smidth & Co v Greenwood*,[5] it was decided that assistance given in the UK in relation to the negotiation and execution of sales contracts concluded overseas did not amount to trading here. Where, however, contracts are actually and habitually made in the UK, by a person not resident here, he may, according to the decision in *Erichsen v Last*,[6] be regarded as trading in the UK, even though the fulfilment of the contracts made in the UK takes place overseas. The importance which the place of the making of sales contracts has assumed in these matters may be traced back to *Werle & Co v Colquhoun*[7] where Esher MR said:

'... the contract is the very foundation of the trade. It is the trade really ... If the trade consists in making contracts which are profitable contracts, if those contracts are made in England, then the trade is carried on in England, because the making of the contracts is the very substance and essence of the trade.'[8]

It must be remembered, however, that those words were spoken in the context of a case which concerned the merchanting of wine, and that even there, the place of delivery and the place of payment were held to be important matters for consideration. Where the trade involves manufacture, and the manufacture takes place in the UK, the place at which contracts of sale are made will be of much less significance. As Atkin LJ said in the *Smidth* case:[9]

'The contracts in this case were made abroad. But I am not prepared to hold that this test is decisive. I can imagine cases where the contract of re-sale is made abroad and yet the manufacture of the goods, some negotiation of the terms and complete execution of the contract take place here under such circumstances that the trade was in truth exercised here.'[10]

This provides a salutary check to the widespread belief that, provided no sales contract is ever signed in the UK, trading cannot be held to be taking place here. That is simply not so. The identification of the place of trade will invariably necessitate an analysis of the nature and scope of a person's activities in the various territories concerned, with particular reference to where, in relation to those activities, the profits, in substance, arise.

1 At **4.17** above.
2 *Smidth & Co v Greenwood* (1922) 8 TC 193 at 204, per Atkin LJ.
3 (1860) 2 TC 149.
4 (1896) 3 TC 311.
5 (1922) 8 TC 193.
6 (1881) 1 TC 351.
7 (1888) 2 TC 402.
8 (1888) 2 TC 402 at 410–412.
9 *Smidth & Co v Greenwood* (1922) 8 TC 193.
10 *Smidth & Co v Greenwood* (1922) 8 TC 193 at 204.

4.19 Employments

The condition which must be fulfilled before a person who works full-time in an office or employment will become entitled to have his residence status decided without regard to any place of abode which he maintains in the UK is contained in ITA 2007 s 830(4) and is that 'if all its duties are performed outside the UK'.

The employment however is also foreign if it meets the provisions of s 830(5), that is, the duties are in substance performed outside the UK and the only duties performed in the UK are incidental to the foreign duties.

In *Robson v Dixon*,[1] Pennycuick V-C expressed doubt as to whether the requirement of substance had any meaning if viewed as anything but an adjunct to the question whether the duties were incidental:

'The words 'in substance' are extremely vague in their import. Moreover, it is extremely difficult to see in what circumstances that requirement could be of any significance independently of the second requirement in the subsection. The Special Commissioners skated over the first requirement. I think they were quite right to do so, and I propose to follow their example. The sole question is whether the second requirement is performed.'[2]

It is suggested, however, that that opinion (and its last sentence in particular) should not be taken as an absolute dismissal of the term 'in substance' but merely as the Vice-Chancellor's own assessment of its relevance in the context of the *Robson* case, coloured as that case was by his own particular interpretation of the word 'incidental'. HMRC would seem to have indicated a way in which the term might well be of significance independently of the question as to whether the duties are incidental when it states in its guidance notes:

'It is normally the nature of the duties performed in the United Kingdom, rather than the amount of time spent on them, that is important, but if the total time you spend working in the United Kingdom is more than 91 days a year, the work you do will not be treated as incidental.'[3]

HMRC, it seems, regards the requirement of 'substance' as establishing a *quantitative* trip-wire which will close the door to the benefits of the section if ever UK duties *qualitatively* incidental to overseas duties occupy a disproportionate amount of a person's time. In the Revenue's eyes, an employment of which duties other than overseas duties involve periods in the UK amounting to 91 days or more in the year is not 'in substance one of which the duties fall . . . to be performed outside the UK', and, once that is the case, no concession can be made under ITA 2007 s 830 even if the UK duties are, in qualitative terms, 'merely incidental' to the overseas duties.

---

1 (1972) 48 TC 527.
2 (1972) 48 TC 527 at 534.
3 IR20 (July 2008), para 5.7, see **Appendix 1** below.

4.20 Incidental duties

The discussion in the previous paragraph brings us to the words 'merely incidental' which are central in ITA 2007 s 830(5)(b). Unfortunately for the taxpayer, these words have been given a judicial definition which is not only exceedingly narrow but which must surely be at variance with the understanding of that term in the mind of 'the man on the Clapham omnibus':[1]

The expression 'merely incidental to' is a striking one, and effect must be given to the natural meaning of those words. The words 'merely incidental to' are upon their ordinary use apt to denote an activity (here the performance of duties) which does not serve any independent purpose but is carried out in order to further some other purpose.[2]

4.20 *Arrivals and departures*

Although that definition must presently be adhered to, it is interesting to compare it with the definition of 'incidental' provided by *Chambers Dictionary*[3] – 'liable to occur: naturally attached: accompanying: concomitant: occasional, casual' – and to observe, as this discussion proceeds, that had any one of those meanings been adopted by Pennycuick V-C in the *Robson* case, its outcome would undoubtedly have been quite different.

Having said that, it must be admitted that Pennycuick V-C's understanding of the term does not actually invalidate the examples of 'incidental duties' offered by the Royal Commission on the Taxation of Profits and Income when, in 1955, it recommended that 'there should be a saving qualification to the effect that work is not the less to be treated as performed wholly in one country because certain merely incidental duties such as returning for report, to collect samples, etc., are carried out in another'.[4] In a parliamentary debate, however, it was said that:

'... if a man were in this country, perhaps on leave, for a month during the year, and was called to the London office to give an opinion on something, or received instructions,'[5]

his performance of those duties could be regarded incidental to the duties he performed abroad. That first example is surely beyond the narrow scope of the Vice-Chancellor's definition, for the giving of an opinion would surely serve a purpose independent of the purpose of the person's overseas duties.

It should also be noted that all the examples given concern occurrences of short *duration* which merely break briefly into the long-term pattern of overseas activity. This could be taken as indicating that Parliament, at least, understood the word 'incidental' to be expressive of temporariness, and it was this factor that was, Mr Robson argued, of paramount importance in deciding whether or not duties performed in the UK were merely incidental to duties performed abroad.

Mr Robson was a pilot employed by KLM, a Dutch airline, and was based at Schipol Airport in Amsterdam, although he and his wife and children had their home in Chorleywood, Hertfordshire. So far as his employment allowed him to do so, he commuted between Chorleywood and Schipol, travelling at preferential rates on passenger flights to and from Heathrow Airport. During the years 1961–62 to 1966–67 (for which he had been assessed to tax as a person resident in the UK), his regular duty was to fly aircraft on scheduled journeys between Amsterdam and various worldwide locations, in particular North and South America. Of the 811 take-offs and landings which he made during the years in question, 38 landings took place in the UK, but none related to flights beginning here, and of the 38 landings 16 were on charter services which were outside his regular duties. Landings in the UK generally involved a wait of 45 to 60 minutes before taking-off again, though there would be a further hour or so delay if refuelling was necessary. In each of the relevant years, Mr Robson spent less than 60 days in the UK, excluding days on which he had landed here as described, and he contended, therefore, that his residence status should have been decided without regard to his home in Chorleywood. As he saw it, he worked full-time in an employment of which all the duties were performed outside the UK apart from duties which 'were of short duration by contrast with the substantial periods spent outside the UK'[6] and which were therefore merely incidental to the performance of his duties outside the UK. Accordingly, in his opinion, he came within the ambit of FA 1956 s 11 (now ITA 2007 s 830). Pennycuick V-C could not agree:

> 'With the best will in the world, I find it impossible to say that the activities carried on in or over England are merely incidental to the performance of the comparable duties carried on in or over Holland or in or over the ultimate destination in America. The activities are precisely co-ordinate, and I cannot see how it can properly be said that the activities in England are in some way incidental to the other activities. Going back to the words of the section, when one asks, 'What exactly are the other duties outside the United Kingdom to which the performance of the duties are incidental?' no satisfactory answer can be given. The other duties are simply co-ordinate duties.'[7]

If one were to take the dictionary definition of 'incidental' quoted earlier, one could retort, 'But co-ordinate duties *are* incidental duties; no satisfactory answer can be given to your question because of the particular way in which you have chosen to define the word "incidental"; and you are not "going back to the words of the section" but to the extremely narrow interpretation you have given to the words of the section.' It is, however, no part of the Inland Revenue's duties to dilute the strength of a favourable judicial decision, however open to criticism that decision might be, and, accordingly, it has merely taken-up and amplified the Vice-Chancellor's dicta in its guidance notes relating to this matter.[8]

Commenting on the construction of TA 1970 s 50(3) (now ITA 2007 s 830(5)) advanced by Mr Robson, the Vice-Chancellor said:

> 'I think it is impossible to construe subsection three ... as indicating merely relatively short periods of employment in the United Kingdom in relation to the period of employment outside the United Kingdom. It would have been quite simple for the section so to provide; and it may well be that if the condition were imported only by the expression 'in substance' that would be the result. But the second requirement is expressed in quite different terms and cannot, I think, be treated as referring merely to what has been described as a quantitative, in contradistinction to a qualitative, basis.'[9]

Again it must be said that, had the Vice-Chancellor attached a more usual meaning to the word 'incidental', there would have been no divergence between the words of the first and second requirements and Mr Robson's contention could have been upheld. As matters now stand, however, the amount of time occupied by duties performed in the UK must be regarded as being of no significance for the purpose of deciding whether or not those duties are 'merely incidental', and, in consequence, great care will need to be taken by anyone who works full-time abroad to ensure that he does not inadvertently place himself beyond the ambit of ITA 2007 s 830

4.20 *Arrivals and departures*

by allowing his normal duties to bring him, however fleetingly, into the UK. Having said that, it must, however, be added that an isolated performance of duties in the UK which are qualitatively no different from the duties performed overseas will not always preclude the operation of the section. In the *Robson* case, the Vice-Chancellor made it clear that, so far as a pilot is concerned,

> '... it is accepted on behalf of the Crown that a landing in the United Kingdom by reason of some emergency, such as weather conditions or mechanical trouble, might be regarded as incidental to the performance of duties outside the United Kingdom,'[10]

and he not only thought that was right but outlined other situations which, though he could express no view on them, clearly commended themselves to him as cases for leniency:

> '... the position of *de minimis* – a single landing ... the position if a pilot's normal route did not touch on the United Kingdom but on one or two occasions he had landed in the United Kingdom while acting as a substitute for some other pilot who was ill. Those might well be borderline questions.'[11]

In the event, the Crown accepted that the *de minimis* principle[12] should be applied as regards 1961–62, a year in which Mr Robson made only one landing and take-off in the UK, and, three years after the *Robson* case, it was confirmed in an answer to a parliamentary question concerning airline pilots that:

> 'In practice, where only a single take-off and landing in this country occurred in a year, the Inland Revenue would normally disregard this on *de minimis* grounds in considering whether any duties were performed in this country.'[13]

Although the circumstances in the *Robson* case served to highlight the particular problems which airline pilots may encounter in attempting to fulfil the 'incidental duties' requirement, there would seem to be no obvious argument which HMRC could advance were the *de minimis* principle to be pleaded in relation to a single transgression of the rules by a member of any other class of overseas employee.

---

1 An expression coined by Lord Devlin.
2 *Robson v Dixon* (1972) 48 TC 527 at 534, per Pennycuick V-C.
3 1998 edition.
4 Final Report, 1955, Cmd 9474, para 300.
5 *Hansard*, 7 June 1956, col 1456.
6 *Robson v Dixon* (1972) 48 TC 527 at 530.
7 *Robson v Dixon* (1972) 48 TC 527 at 534.
8 IR20 (July 2008), paras 5.7, 5.8 and 5.5, see Appendix 1 below.
9 *Robson v Dixon* (1972) 48 TC 527 at 535.
10 *Robson v Dixon* (1972) 48 TC 527 at 535.
11 *Robson v Dixon* (1972) 48 TC 527 at 535.
12 *De minimis non curat lex*: the law does not concern itself with trifles.
13 *Hansard*, 28 October 1975, vol 898, no. 187, col 431. Contained in Statement of Practice A10.

4.21 Capital gains tax: temporary non-residence

Section 127(1) of the Finance Act 1998 introduced a new s 10A to the TCGA Act 1992 amending the capital gains tax rules where taxpayers go abroad for temporary periods in order to sell assets which would otherwise be chargeable to capital gains tax. The new rules apply to individuals who cease to be resident or ordinarily resident in the UK on or after 17 March 1998 or to those who become resident or ordinarily resident on or after 6 April 1998.

Individuals who have been tax resident in the UK for any part of, at least, four out of seven tax years immediately preceding the year of departure, and became not resident and not ordinarily resident for a period of less than five tax years, and own assets before they leave the UK will be liable to tax on any gains realised on those assets after departure from the UK. Gains made by such an individual in the year of assessment in which he or she leaves the country will be chargeable for that year. Gains made after that will be chargeable in the year of assessment in which the taxpayer resumes residence in the UK. Losses will be allowable on the same basis as gains are chargeable. Section 10A was amended by F(No 2)A 2005 s 32 to prevent temporarily neither resident nor ordinarily resident in the UK, but were resident or in another country from benefiting from exemption from tax on disposal under the terms of a tax treaty if they returned before five full tax years had elapsed.

4.22 Remittance basis: temporary non-residence

Finance Act 2008 Sch 7 para 52 inserting ITA 2007 s 832A extends the same temporary non-residence regime to non-domiciled individuals who cease to be resident but return before five full tax years have elapsed. Amounts remitted during the five-year period will be deemed to be remitted to the UK in the year the individual returns to resume residence.

CHAPTER 5

Residence of trusts and estates

5.01 Introduction

A trust is, in law, a relationship rather than a person. It is the equitable obligation which is created when one person (the settlor) transfers assets (the trust property) to another person (the trustee) who is to hold, control and deal with those assets for the benefit of third parties (the beneficiaries) of whom the trustee himself may be one and any one of whom may enforce the obligation. If the trust is created by the settlor *inter vivos* it is usually referred to as a settlement and the trust property is known as settled property.

Residence, on the other hand, is a personal attribute – a quality which a person attracts to himself by virtue of the strength of his association with a particular place or country. The liability to tax in relation to trusts is by reference to the persons concerned as a result. In the case of the trustees, their personal residence will thus determine their fiscal affiliation as the representative owners of the trust property.

Prior to Finance Act 2006 the position was unsystematic and problematic where there were resident and non-resident trustees. Different rules applied for income tax and capital gains tax. In relation to income tax, in *Dawson v IRC*[1] the House of Lords ruled that, where the general administration of the trust was ordinarily carried on outside the UK and a majority of the trustees was non-resident, a UK resident trustee was not assessable under Schedule D in respect of income derived from sources outside the UK. It was held that the trust income did not accrue to an individual trustee in his personal capacity and that he had no right of control over it except, in conjunction with his co-trustees, to see that it was applied in accordance with the terms of the trust.[2]

Finance Act 2006[3] aimed at a structured and systematic treatment of the subject. For the first time it made the tests to be applied to determine the residence status of the trustees of a settlement identical for income tax and capital gains tax. The present rules in ITA 2007 ss 474–476 for income tax are effective from 5 April 2007 and follow the latest efforts of the Tax Law Rewrite Project replacing the wording in FA 2006. The capital gains tax equivalent provisions are TCGA 1992 s 69(1) and (2).

5.01 *Residence of trusts and estates*

The Finance Act 2006 also provided that the trustees of a settlement are to be treated as a single person for the purposes of the Taxes Act unless the context requires otherwise. Also, the meaning of 'settled property' and, for most purposes, of 'settlement' and 'settlor' are now identical for the two taxes.

1 [1989] STC 473.
2 [1989] STC 473 at 479, per Lord Keith.
3 Sch 13 (income tax) and Pt 1 of Sch 12 (capital gains tax).

Trusts

5.02 Residence and ordinary residence

The new rules start by bestowing a collective legal personality on the trustees. Thus, the trustees of a settlement are to be treated as a single 'deemed person' for the purposes of the Taxes Act unless the context requires otherwise.[1] If different parts of the settled property in relation to a settlement are vested in different bodies of trustees, the residence rules still apply in relation to the different bodies as if they were all one body.[2] As part of the process of rationalisation and simplification, the meaning of 'settled property' and, for most purposes, of 'settlement' and 'settlor', are also identical for the two taxes.

1 ITA 2007 s 474(1).
2 ITA 2007 s 474(2)).

5.03 Single residence trustees

Where all the trustees are resident in the UK, the position is straightforward. The trustees (that is, the 'deemed person') is treated for income tax and capital gains tax purposes as resident and ordinarily resident in the UK. Where all the trustees are not resident in the UK, then conversely the trustees are neither resident nor ordinarily resident in the UK.

5.04 Mixed residence trustees

Where there are trustees who are resident and trustees who are non-resident in the UK, then the residence of the persons who comprise the deemed person does not determine the residence of that deemed person. The focus of attention shifts to the settlor. This is the case where at least one trustee is resident in the UK and at least one is not. If there is at least one of each, then it does not matter how many more trustees may be resident or non-resident. Thus, a majority of non-resident trustees does not make the deemed person non-resident, and neither does a majority of resident trustees make for a resident trust.

Instead, the residence and ordinary residence of the deemed person is decided by whether the settlor was resident, ordinarily resident, or domiciled in the UK at the 'relevant time'.[1] If, at a time when the Settlor made the settlement (or is treated for income tax or capital gains tax purposes as making the settlement) he was UK resident, ordinarily UK resident or domiciled in the UK, then the trustees are resident and ordinarily resident in the UK from the time the settlement is made.[2]

A transfer of property between settlements can affect the residence of the trustees. Thus, if there is a transfer of property between settlements, and a settlor is treated as a settlor in relation to the transferee settlement[3] as a result, and immediately before the transfer, that settlor meets the residence, ordinary residence or domicile condition as a settlor in relation to the transferring settlement then he also meets that condition as a settlor in relation to the transferee settlement from the time he becomes such a settlor until he ceases to be such a settlor.[4]

Trusts taking effect on death require a determination of the settlor's status at that time. If the settlement arose on the settlor's death, whether by will or intestacy or in any other way, and immediately before the Settlor's death, he was UK resident, ordinarily UK resident or domiciled in the UK, then the trustees are resident and ordinarily resident in the UK from the date of death of the settlor.[5]

The trustees will be neither resident nor ordinarily resident in the UK in cases where the settlor is not UK resident, ordinarily UK resident or domiciled in the UK at the relevant time. Furthermore where the settlor has met these conditions at the relevant time, the trustees will cease to be resident and ordinarily resident when the settlor ceases to be treated as a settlor in relation to the settlement.

It will be apparent that these statutory provisions, in effect, abolish the possibility of a distinction between residence and ordinary residence for trustees. The residence *simpliciter* of the trustees and the status of the settlor determine the residence and ordinary residence of the trustees at a single stroke.

---

1 'Condition C' see s ITA 2007 s 476.
2 ITA 2007 s 476(3).
3 Under ITA 2007 s 470.
4 ITA 2007 s 476(4).
5 ITA 2007 s 476(2).

5.05 Non-resident trustees with a UK permanent establishment

As has been seen, the residence of the single deemed person constituting the trustees is in part determined by examining the residence of the trustees who make up that deemed person. The residence of each trustee is determined by reference to the rules applicable to in the case of individual trustees in Chapter 2 and in the case of corporate trustees in Chapter 6. An

5.05 Residence of trusts and estates

exception is made in the case of non-resident trustees operating in the UK. ITA 2007 s 475(6) reads:

> '475(6) If at a time a person ('T') who is a trustee of the settlement acts as trustee in the course of a business which T carries on in the United Kingdom through a branch, agency or permanent establishment there, then for the purposes of subsections (4) and (5) assume that T is UK resident at that time.'

The expression 'branch or agency' is now used only in relation to income tax to determine the extent of any UK representative's liability in respect of a trade carried on in the UK by a non-resident individual,[1] as well as the limit on liability to income tax of non-UK residents[2] and capital gains tax.[3]

Permanent establishment is the equivalent expression in relation to non-resident companies carrying on a trade in the UK[4] introduced by Finance Act 2003 s 148. In general:

> '148(1) For the purposes of the Tax Acts a company has a permanent establishment in a territory if, and only if–
> (a) it has a fixed place of business there through which the business of the company is wholly or partly carried on, or
> (b) an agent acting on behalf of the company has and habitually exercises there authority to do business on behalf of the company.'

The consequence of a non-resident trustee acting as such in the course of a business is that such trustee is treated as resident in the UK for the purpose of determining the residence and ordinary residence of the single deemed person.

---

1 FA 1995 s 126(8).
2 ITA 2007 s 811.
3 TCGA 1992 s 9.
4 ICTA 1988 s 11(1).

5.06 Residence for tax treaties

As is the case with any other person, the trustees may be treated as resident in the UK under its laws but at the same time treated as a resident in another country for the purposes of its tax laws. Qualification as a person and a resident will normally bring with it access to treaty benefits under treaties patterned on the OECD Model:

> '4(1) For the purposes of this Convention, the term 'resident of a Contracting State' means any person who, under the laws of that State, is liable to tax therein by reason of his domicile, residence, place of management or any other criterion of a similar nature, and also includes that State and any political subdivision or local authority thereof. This term, however, does not include any person who is liable to tax in that State in respect only of income from sources in that State or capital situated therein.'

Where a tax treaty is in place, such dual residence may be resolved for the purposes of the treaty by the following mechanism:

'4(3) Where by reason of the provisions of paragraph 1 a person other than an individual is a resident of both Contracting States, then it shall be deemed to be a resident only of the State in which its place of effective management is situated.'

The commentary to the OECD Model does not directly consider the postion of trusts. However, the Special Commissioners have considered the meaning of the expression 'place of effective management' in two decisions. In *Trustees of Wensleydale's Settlement v IR Commrs*[1] the success or failure simple of a capital gains tax avoidance scheme turned entirely upon whether in fact the trustees of a settlement were deemed to be a resident of the Republic of Ireland for the reason that they, being 'a person other than an individual' and a resident of both the Republic of Ireland and of the UK, 'its place of effective management was situated' in the Republic. In the absence of much guidance the Special Commissioner considered that 'effective' implies realistic, positive management. On the evidence he found that she was a trustee in name rather than in reality, signing all the documents placed before her and on this basis held that the place of effective management of the trust was not in the Republic of Ireland.

A similar conclusion was reached in *Trevor Smallwood Trust v R & C Commrs*[2] which also concerned a not dissimilar tax avoidance scheme where a trust moved from the UK to Mauritius. The Special Commissioners believed 'effective' should be understood in the sense of the French *effective* (*siège de direction effective*) which connotes real, French being the other official version of the OECD Model. Having regard to the ordinary meaning of the words in their context and in the light of their object and purpose, the place of effective management depended on where the real top-level management (or the realistic, positive management) of the trustee, as trustee, was to be found. They accepted that the administration of the trust moved to Mauritius, but in their view the 'key' decisions were made in the UK and consequently, the trust's 'place of effective management' was in the UK.

---

1 (1996) Sp C 73.
2 *Trevor Smallwood & Mary Caroline Smallwood Trustees of the Trevor Smallwood Trust v R & C Commrs; Trevor Smallwood Settlor of the Trevor Smallwood Trust v R & C Commrs* [2008] UKSPC 669.

5.07 Residence of estates

Unlike the residence of trustees, the residence of personal representatives of deceased estates was not comprehensively reformed by the Finance Act 2006. Legislation only addresses the case of mixed personal representantives. HMRC takes the position that the personal representatives are deemed to have the same residence, ordinary residence and domicile status as the deceased had at the date of death.[1]

The statutory treatment of personal representatives of a deceased person is somewhat similar in the case of mixed residence personal

5.07 *Residence of trusts and estates*

representatives to that of trustees. For income tax purposes, if the personal representatives of a deceased person include one or more persons who are UK resident and one or more persons who are non-UK resident, then if the deceased died resident, ordinarily resident or domiciled in the UK, the UK resident persons are treated, in their capacity as personal representatives, as UK resident. In contrast then if the deceased died not resident, ordinarily resident or domiciled in the UK, the UK resident persons are treated, in their capacity as personal representatives, as not UK resident.[2] For capital gains tax purposes, 'resident' and 'ordinarily resident' have the same meanings in TCGA 1992 as in the Income Tax Acts.[3]

---

1 HMRC Capital Gains Manual CG30650.
2 ITA 2007, s 834.
3 TCGA 1992 s 9(1).

CHAPTER 6

Residence of companies

A Company Limited? What may that be?
The term, I rather think, is new to me.

Sir W. S. Gilbert *Utopia Limited* Finale

6.01 Introduction

A corporation is a legal entity. It is, under the law, an artificial person, separate and distinct from its members and endowed with an existence independent of their existence.[1]

Although a corporation's personality is artificial, it is not fictitious. Since 1889 the word 'person' in any Act of Parliament has included 'a body of persons corporate' unless the contrary intention appears,[2] and a corporation may, accordingly, be fined for contempt of court,[3] be convicted of an offence involving a fraudulent intent,[4] and be a 'respectable and responsible person' to whom to assign a lease.[5] This chapter examines the residence of companies. The term 'company' is not, of course, descriptive only of a limited company but, under ICTA 1988 s 832(1), must be taken to mean, in this context, 'any body corporate or unincorporated association' excluding 'a partnership, a local authority or a local authority association'. More to the point, it may possess the status of residence and ordinary residence:

> 'Now the definition of the word "residence" is founded upon the habits and relations of the natural man, and is therefore inapplicable to the artificial and legal person whom we call a corporation. But for the purpose of giving effect to the words of the Legislature an artificial residence must be assigned to this artificial person, and one formed on the analogy of natural persons.'[6]

The territorial basis of taxation applies to companies who are chargeable to corporation tax on their profits.[7] Profits for this purpose means income and chargeable gains.[8] A company is chargeable to corporation tax on all its profits wherever arising,[9] but a company not resident in the UK is not within the charge to corporation tax unless it carries on a trade in the UK through a permanent establishment there.[10] Where it does so, it is chargeable to corporation tax only on profits attributable to the permanent

113

6.01 Residence of companies

establishment and on trading income and chargeable gains relating to assets used or held by or for the permanent establishment.[11] A company that is not resident in the United Kingdom may also be liable to income tax on certain income from sources within the UK not attributable to a permanent establishment.[12]

Until 1988 there was no statutory defintion of residence for companies. Although HMRC has published practice in this area (principally Statement of Practice SP 1/90, the more thoughtful International Tax Manual, Chapter 3 and the International Manual INTM 120000 and following), the application of this practice has not given rise to the same difficulties faced in the individual residence area. As will be explained,[13] the courts have been required to interpret the expression and a substantial body of case law has resulted.

---

1 *Salomon v Salomon & Co* [1897] AC 22.
2 Interpretation Act 1978 s 5 and Sch 1.
3 *R v J G Hammond & Co* [1914] 2 KB 866.
4 *R v ICR Haulage Ltd* [1944] KB 551.
5 *Ideal Film Renting Co v Nielson* [1921] 1 Ch 575.
6 *Calcutta Jute Mills Co Ltd v Nicholson* (1876) 1 TC 83 at 103, per Huddleston B.
7 ICTA 1988 s 6(1).
8 ICTA 1988 s 6(1).
9 ICTA 1988 s 8(1).
10 ICTA 1988 s 11(1).
11 ICTA 1988 s 11 (2) and 2(A).
12 FA 2003 s 150.
13 **6.03** and following.

6.02 UK incorporated companies

Section 66 of the Finance Act 1988 provides that as from 15 March 1988 any company incorporated in the UK is deemed to be resident in the UK. Any other rule determining residence is excluded. The case law which determined the test of residence on the basis of the location of a company's central control and management is of no relevance to any company which is incorporated in the UK. Although the term residence continues to be applied to such companies, the ordinary meaning of the term has been suspended in favour of a formal test. Thus the tax liability of companies incorporated in the UK is determined by the place of incorporation and not any factual enquiry as to where or how it conducts its business.[1]

There is a limited exception to the incorporation rule. This operates firstly, if the company was carrying on business before 15 March 1988 and had become non-resident before then, pursuant to a general or a specific Treasury consent obtained under what was ICTA 1988 s 765(1)(a) or its predecessors.[2]

If the consent was a specific consent, the company can remain non-resident regardless of where it is based, and it only becomes UK resident if it in fact becomes resident under the central management and control test.

If the consent was a general consent, a further condition has to be satisfied. This condition is that a company was taxable in a foreign territory. By 'taxable' is meant being liable to tax on income by reason of domicile, residence or place of management but not simply being liable to a flat rate sum or fee. Provided that a company which registered before 15 March 1988 pursuant to general consent was taxable in a foreign state it may remain non-resident, but only so long as it is so taxable.

The second application of the exception for companies which become non-resident pursuant to a specific consent applies also to companies which became non-resident on or after 15 March 1988 pursuant to a specific consent applied for before then. Such a company does however have to have commenced business before then. If it ceases to carry on business, the exception will cease to apply.

---

1 See **6.03** below.
2 Originally introduced as in FA 1951 s 36.

6.03 Foreign incorporated companies

The test of central control and management is now only in most cases applicable to foreign registered companies. Thus, a foreign registered company will be resident in the UK if the central management and control of the company is exercised in the UK.

The phrase 'central management and control' was coined not by Parliament but by Lord Loreburn in one of the earliest of all the cases concerning company residence, *De Beers Consolidated Mines v Howe*,[1] at the beginning of the 20th century. The head office was formally at Kimberley, and the general meetings were held there. Profits were made out of diamonds raised in South Africa, and sold under annual contracts for delivery in South Africa. Further, some of the directors and Life Governors lived in South Africa, and there were directors' meetings at Kimberley as well as in London. But the majority of directors and Life Governors lived in England. The directors' meetings in London were the meetings where the real control was always exercised in practically all the important business of the company, except the mining operations. London always controlled the negotiation of the contracts with the syndicates to whom the diamonds were sold, determined policy in the disposal of diamonds and other assets, the working and development of mines, the application of profits, and the appointment of directors. London also always controlled matters that required to be determined by the majority of all the directors, which included all questions of expenditure except wages, materials, and such like at the mines, and a limited sum which might be spent by the directors at Kimberley. In finding the company resident in the UK, Lord Loreburn formulated the principle as:

> 'A company resides, for the purposes of Income Tax, where its real business is carried on ... I regard that as the true rule; and the real business is carried on where the central management and control actually abides'.

6.03 *Residence of companies*

In *Bullock v Unit Construction Co Ltd*,² Lord Radcliffe summarised the position as it existed in 1959 as:³

> '... the necessity of establishing some common standard for the treatment of different taxpayers meant that the Courts of Law were bound in course of time to produce and apply some general principle of their own to form an acceptable test of residence ... [T]he principle was adopted that a company is resident where its central management and control abide: words which, according to the decision of the House of Lords that finally propounded the test, *De Beers Consolidated Mines Ltd v Howe*,⁴ are equivalent to saying that a company's residence is where its 'real business' is carried on....
>
> ... as precise and unequivocal as a positive statutory injunction ... I do not know of any other test which has either been substituted for that of central management and control, or has been defined with sufficient precision to be regarded as an acceptable alternative to it. To me ... it seems impossible to read Lord Loreburn's words without seeing that he regarded the formula he was propounding as constituting the test of residence.'

---

1 *De Beers Consolidated Mines Ltd v Howe* (1906) 5 TC 198 at 213.
2 (1959) 38 TC 712.
3 (1959) 38 TC 712, per Lord Radcliffe at 738.
4 (1906) 5 TC 198.

6.04 The *Untelrab* synthesis

From a practical perspective, a brief statement of principles is most desirable. In *Untelrab Ltd & Ors v McGregor* (HMIT),¹ the first published decision of the Special Commissioners dealing with company residence, an attempt was made to synthesise the principles developed in a large number of cases over more than a century as follows:

> ' From these authorities we have identified the following principles:
> – that the residence of a company is where the directors meet and transact their business and exercise the powers conferred upon them;
> – that if the directors meet in two places then the company's residence is where its real business is carried on and the real business is carried on where the central management and control actually abides;
> – that a determination as to whether a case falls within that rule is a pure question of fact to be determined by a scrutiny of the course of business and trading;
> – that the actual place of management, and not the place where a company ought to be managed, fixes the place of residence of a company;
> – that it is an exceptional case for a parent company to usurp control from its subsidiaries; a parent company usually operates through the boards of its subsidiaries;
> – that although a board might do what it was told to do it did not follow that the control and management of the company lay with another, so long as the board exercised their discretion when coming to their decisions and would have refused to carry out an improper or unwise transaction; and
> – that when deciding the issue of residence one should stand back from the detail and make up one's mind from the picture which the whole of the evidence presents.'²

The case is one that represents two modern circumstances where arguments between companies and the Revenue have been most acute. The first, as in *Untelrab*, is where a company forms part of an international group of companies and the operations of group members are affected to a greater or lesser extent by group policies led from the parent company. The second is in relation to privately-owned companies where it claimed that the power of a dominant shareholder prevails. Very often these are special purpose vehicles set up to perform a specific function within a corporate group or in organising an individual's affairs.

Untelrab concerned subsidiaries of a UK resident public company incorporated in the Channel Islands and Bermuda. Their directors were lawyers and accountants resident in those territories. Board meetings were held there and the day-to-day management of the companies undertaken there. Although managed overseas, in certain respects, they adopted group policy as formulated by the parent company. The Special Commissioners found that the board of Untelrab met in Bermuda and transacted the company's business there. At board meetings proposals were discussed and decisions were made by the directors in the best interests of the company. They would have refused to carry out any proposal which was improper or unreasonable. The UK resident parent company did not control the board in the exercise of their powers. It could have taken steps to remove the directors but could not control them in their conduct of Untelrab's business.[3] The decision was not appealed. It was however endorsed by Park J in the High Court in *Wood v Holden*.[4]

1 (1995) SpC 55.
2 *Untelrab Ltd & Ors v McGregor* (HMIT) (1995) SpC 55 at para 74.
3 *Untelrab Ltd & Ors v McGregor* (HMIT) (1995) SpC 55 at para 73.
4 [2005] EWHC 547 (Ch) at para 26.

6.05 A question of fact

In relation to the application of the central management and control test, Lord Loreburn, having formulated the rule,[1] continued in *De Beers*:

> 'It remains to be considered whether the present case falls within that rule. This is a pure question of fact, to be determined, not according to the construction of this or that regulation or byelaw, but upon a scrutiny of the course of business and trading.'[2]

Although the enquiry into exercise of central management and control is a factual enquiry, special considerations apply in the context of a legal person. Early case law proceeded by analogy with individuals. Thus in the seminal decision in *De Beers*, Lord Loreburn said:

> 'In applying the conception of residence to a Company, we ought, I think, to proceed as nearly as we can upon the analogy of an individual. A Company cannot eat or sleep, but it can keep house and do business. We ought, therefore, to see whether it really keeps house and does business. An individual may be of foreign nationality, and yet reside in the United Kingdom. So may a Company.'[3]

6.05 *Residence of companies*

While the habits and lifestyle of an individual form the obvious fact base, in the case of companies, the question as to which facts ought to be examined is less obvious and has been controversial. Case law and administrative practice has focussed on identifying, what is meant by 'central management and control', who exercises it and where that exercise takes place. These elements are interrelated but may be considered individually for ease of analysis.

Because the residence of a company is to be determined by the location of its central management and control, and because that location is a question of fact, a finding by the Commissioners that a company is resident in this place or that will be unassailable provided the Commissioners have before them evidence from which their finding can be made and providing they do not misdirect themselves in law.[4] The court's approach is well-illustrated by Lord Loreburn's conclusion in the *De Beers* case:[5]

> 'The Commissioners, after sifting the evidence, arrived at the two following conclusions, viz: ... (2) That the head and seat and directing power of the affairs of the Appellant Company were at the office in London, from whence the chief operations of the Company, both in the United Kingdom and elsewhere, were, in fact, controlled, managed and directed. That conclusion of fact cannot be impugned, and it follows that this Company was resident within the United Kingdom for the purposes of Income Tax.'[6]

---

1 See **6.02**.
2 *De Beers Consolidated Mines v Howe* (1906) 5 TC 198 at 213.
3 *De Beers Consolidated Mines v Howe* (1906) 5 TC 198 at 212.
4 See **2.03** above.
5 *De Beers Consolidated Mines v Howe* (1906) 5 TC 198.
6 *De Beers Consolidated Mines v Howe* (1906) 5 TC 198 at 213–214.

6.06 Who exercises central management and control?

Bullock v Unit Construction Co Ltd[1] has for many years formed the basis of a very broad approach to the factual enquiry by the Revenue. There, Unit Construction Company Ltd, a UK resident subsidiary of Alfred Booth & Co Ltd, a UK resident parent company, made subvention payments to three of its fellow subsidiary companies in Kenya and claimed that those payments were, under FA 1953 s 20, permissible deductions in arriving at its profits for tax purposes. This would have been so only if the three Kenyan subsidiaries also were resident in the UK, but the Inland Revenue contended that they were not. The three subsidiaries had been incorporated in Kenya and their articles of association expressly placed their management and control in the hands of their directors and required directors' meetings to be held outside the UK. That being so, the three Kenyan subsidiaries must, said the Revenue, be resident outside the UK. The Commissioners found as a *fact*, however, that, due to trading difficulties which the subsidiaries had encountered,

> '... at the material times ... the boards of directors of the African subsidiaries ... were standing aside in all matters of real importance and in many matters of

Who exercises central management and control? **6.06**

minor importance affecting the central management and control, and ... the real control and management was being exercised by the board of directors of Alfred Booth & Co Ltd in London.'[2]

Accordingly, the Commissioners found that each of the African subsidiaries was resident in the UK, and their finding was ultimately upheld in the House of Lords. Referring to the reversals the decision had suffered at the hands of the High Court and the Court of Appeal, Viscount Simonds said:

> '... the contention of learned Counsel for the Crown which has so far found favour with the courts is no less than this, that if by the constitution of the company, that is, by its memorandum and articles of association interpreted in the light of the relevant law, that is, in this case the law of Kenya, the management of the company's business is contemplated as being exercised, and ought therefore to be exercised, in Kenya or at any rate outside the United Kingdom, then for the purpose of British Income Tax law the facts are to be disregarded and the control and management which as a fact are found to abide in the United Kingdom are to be regarded as abiding outside it. There is no doubt, I think, that the management of the African subsidiaries, which were incorporated in Kenya under the Kenya Companies Ordinance and registered in Nairobi, was placed in the hands of their directors and that their articles of association expressly provided that directors' meetings might be held anywhere outside the United Kingdom. Nor can there be any doubt – for this is the unchallengeable finding of the Commissioners – that the management of the business of the companies was not exercised in the manner contemplated. Whence it follows that the business was conducted in a manner irregular, unauthorised and perhaps unlawful ...
>
> My Lords, I should certainly be prepared to admit that the many Judges who in the past have pronounced upon this question had not in mind such a case as this. But, with great respect to those who take a different view, the present case does not seem to lie outside the principle underlying their judgment. Nothing can be more factual and concrete than the acts of management which enable a Court to find as a fact that central management and control is exercised in one country or another. It does not in any way alter their character that in greater or less degree they are irregular or unauthorised or unlawful. The business is not the less managed in London because it ought to be managed in Kenya. Its residence is determined by the solid facts, not by the terms of its constitution, however imperative. If indeed I must disregard the facts as they are, because they are irregular, I find a company without any central management at all. For, though I may disregard existing facts, I cannot invent facts which do not exist and say that the company's business is managed in Kenya. Yet it is the place of central management which, however much or little weight ought to be given to other factors, essentially determines its residence. I come, therefore, to the conclusion ... that it is the actual place of management, not the place in which it ought to be managed, which fixes the residence of a company.'[3]

The broad approach is highlighted in the HMRC Statement of Practice on company residence:

> 'In some cases ... central management and control is exercised by a single individual. This may happen when a chairman or managing director exercises

powers formally conferred by the company's Articles and the other board members are little more than cyphers, or by reason of a dominant shareholding or for some other reason. In those cases the residence of the company is where the controlling individual exercises his powers.[4]

Generally, however, where doubts arise about a particular company's residence status, the Inland Revenue adopt the following approach:
(i) They first try to ascertain whether the directors of the company in fact exercise central management and control.
(ii) If so, they seek to determine where the directors exercise this central management and control (which is not necessarily where they meet).
(iii) In cases where the directors apparently do not exercise central management and control of the company, the Revenue then look to establish where and by whom it is exercised.[5]

The full extent to which this approach is considered to apply is illustrated in *Wood v Holden (Inspector of Taxes)*[6] where the Court of Appeal affirmed the decision of the High Court judge who had overruled the Special Commissioners' conclusion that a Netherlands company was resident in the UK.

The case arose from a scheme to avoid capital gains tax on the sale of trading companies by two UK resident individuals. The scheme had been designed by a firm of accountants who also attended to its implementation. The shares in the trading companies came to be held by a Netherlands-incorporated company itself owned by a British Virgin Islands company which was in turn owned by trustees of offshore family trusts. The sole director of the Netherlands company was a Dutch trust company. HMRC argued that the company registered in the Netherlands (but surprisingly, not the BVI company) was nevertheless resident in the UK. The HMRC case was that the Dutch corporate director did not in fact take the decisions but did what it was told to do by Mr Wood or by the firm of UK-based chartered accountants acting on his behalf. This contention was upheld by the Special Commissioners[7] but not by the High Court or the Court of Appeal. The House of Lords refused leave to appeal. In the Court of Appeal Chadwick LJ said at para 27:

'In my view the judge was correct in his analysis of the law. In seeking to determine where "central management and control" of a company incorporated outside the United Kingdom lies, it is essential to recognise the distinction between cases where management and control of the company is exercised through its own constitutional organs (the board of directors or the general meeting) and cases where the functions of those constitutional organs are "usurped" – in the sense that management and control is exercised independently of, or without regard to, those constitutional organs. And, in cases which fall within the former class, it is essential to recognise the distinction (in concept, at least) between the role of an "outsider" in proposing, advising and influencing the decisions which the constitutional organs take in fulfilling their functions and the role of an outsider who dictates the decisions which are to be taken. In that context an "outsider" is a person who is not, himself, a participant in the formal process (a board meeting or a general meeting) through which the relevant constitutional organ fulfils its function.'

The Netherlands company's directors had not been bypassed and they had not stood aside. They had also decided to accept the agreement proposed by the accountants and had made the decision to sign and execute the documents. Theirs was an effective decision by a constitutional organ, exercising management and control.

This reveals two categories of management pattern to consider. The first category is where management and control of the company is exercised by its own constitutional organs. The second category concerns where the functions of those constitutional organs are 'usurped'. Where it is determined that management and control is exercised by the company's constitutional organs, it is necessary to examine what and where those organs do. Where management and control is usurped, the place and nature of the usurper's action must be the focus of attention.

---

1 (1959) 38 TC 712.
2 (1959) 38 TC 712 at 721–722.
3 (1959) 38 TC 712 at 735–736.
4 SP 1/90, para 13.
5 SP 1/90 para 15.
6 2006 STC 443.
7 *Sub nom R & Anor v Holden (HM Inspector of Taxes)* [2004] UK SPC422.

6.07 Delegated management and control

Delegated management and control and *central* management and control are mutually exclusive concepts. Indeed delegation is itself an exercise of management and control.

In *Calcutta Jute Mills v Nicholson*,[1] Huddleston B held that the central management and control of the Calcutta Jute Mills, though ostensibly exercised by a director in India, was actually exercised from the company's office in London where the board of directors met:

> 'From that office would issue all the orders to the managing director in Calcutta. No doubt, until he received orders to the contrary, he would have full power and discretion to do what he liked in Calcutta; but at any moment, from this head office, they might have revoked his authority, or altered any arrangement which he had made connected with the working of the company.'[2]

The director in Calcutta was, for all his powers, a mere delegate and one had, therefore, to look beyond him to the delegators from whom his powers had been derived and by whom they were being sustained.

In *American Thread Company v Joyce*[3] the delegation of powers to the American Thread Co Ltd was ostensibly managed and controlled by an executive committee of directors in New York. The Master of the Rolls was, however, quite clear that central management and control lay in Manchester, England:

> 'Now the current business the daily purchasing and selling of raw materials and making them into thread is, no doubt, carried out by the executive committee in New York, the executive committee of three. Who appoint them? The English

board. It must be done by the English board where the majority of the directors, four out of seven, reside. They are appointed by them, their salary is fixed by them, in fact the whole control of the machine, so to say, is kept and carefully kept at Manchester.'[4]

In *News Datacom Ltd & News Data Security Products Ltd v Revenue & Customs*,[5] an executive committee of the board of directors existed as permitted by the Articles of Association. It was concerned with day-to-day operational matters and seven of its nine meetings were in the UK. HMRC argued that it, rather than the Board, exercised central management and control. The Special Commissioners found that the Executive Committee exercised no part in the 'controlling brain' of the company.

What all these cases illustrate, therefore, is that, in determining the location of a company's central management and control, it is necessary to ask of those who appear to be exercising such control, 'To whom do you look over your shoulder? From whom do you derive your powers and who is able to modify or withdraw them?' If the answer is, 'No one. We derive our powers from the shareholders who appointed us and, short of the shareholders removing us from office, no-one can interfere with our powers', identification of those who exercise central management and control will have been made.[6] If the answer is otherwise it will provide a pointer either to those who truly exercise central management and control or to a person or persons who are one step nearer to the centre than those to whom the question was addressed.

---

1 (1876) 1 TC 83.
2 (1876) 1 TC 83 at 107.
3 (1913) 6 TC 163.
4 (1913) 6 TC 163.
5 [2006] UKSPC SPC561.
6 The distinction between shareholder control and central management and control is discussed at **6.08** below.

6.08 Shareholder control

It must be stressed that the test of corporate residence involves the identification of the place of central management *and* (not *or*) control. In other words, the control in question is that which relates to the highest level of management of a company's business and must not, therefore, be confused with the control which vests in a company's shareholders *per se*. The distinction was stressed by Moulton LJ in *Stanley v Gramophone and Typewriter Ltd*[1] when he said:

> '... the individual corporator does not carry on the business of the corporation; he is only entitled to the profits of that business to a certain extent, fixed and ascertained in a certain way, depending upon the constitution of the corporation and his holding in it. This legal proposition ... is not weakened by the fact that the extent of his interest in it entitles him to exercise a greater or lesser amount of control over the manner in which the business is carried on. Such control is inseparable from his position as a corporator, and is a wholly

different thing both in fact and in law from carrying on the business himself. The Directors and employees of the corporation are not his agents, and he has no power of giving directions to them which they must obey. It has been decided by this court in the *Automatic Self-cleaning Filter Syndicate Co Ltd v Cunninghame*[2] that in an English Company by whose Articles of Association certain powers were placed in the hands of the Directors the shareholders could not interfere with the exercise of those powers by the Directors even by a majority in General Meeting. Their course is to obtain the requisite majority to remove the Directors and put persons in their place who agree to their policy. This shows that the control of individual corporators is something wholly different from the management of the business itself. Nor is this principle less true when the holding of the individual corporator is so large that he is able to override the wishes of the other corporators in matters relating to the control of the business of the Company. The extent but not the nature of his power is changed by the magnitude of his holding.'[3]

It follows, therefore, that a company whose business is, in fact, managed and controlled by a board of directors in, say, London, will none the less be resident in England even if, say, 98 per cent of its shares are owned by an individual resident in France. This proposition was specifically approved by the Court of Appeal in *Bullock v Unit Construction Co Ltd*[4] and still stands. The Court of Appeal also assented to the proposition, however, that:

'... a shareholder who holds sufficient in a company can *de facto* control its affairs by his ability to remove directors who disagree with his policy and to vote others into their places.'[5]

The significance of a shareholder's power was given detailed consideration in *American Thread Co v Joyce*.[6] There, the Crown contended that the operations of the American company were controlled from Manchester not merely because a majority of directors met there but also because the English parent company owned the entire share capital of the American company.

In the Court of Appeal, Buckley LJ went to some lengths to emphasise that it was not shareholder control on which the finding that the American company was resident in the UK rested:

'The shareholders can, no doubt, by virtue of their votes control the corporation; they can compel directors ... to do their will, but it does not follow that the corporators are managing the corporation. The contrary is the truth; they are not. It is the directors who are managing the affairs of the corporation ... [T]he executive committee in New York were in fact controlled ... on this side in extraordinary sessions of the Board which were held once a fortnight, and the real control, the head and seat and directing power of the affairs of the Company were here. It was in that sense that the control was here....'[7]

Before leaving the question of shareholder control, attention must – for the sake of completeness – be drawn to *Apthorpe v Peter Schoenhoffen Brewing Co Ltd*[8] which concerned the wholly-owned American brewing subsidiary of an English company. The directors of the English company had full

6.08 *Residence of companies*

power of management and control of the affairs of the American company but they delegated these powers to a committee of management in Chicago. The Commissioners found that:

> '... the head and seat and directing power of the [English] Company were at the [English] Company's registered office in the City of London, and that if the business at Chicago and the profits made thereby were technically the business and profits of the American company the American company was for such purpose the agent of the [English] Company.'[9]

In its statement of practice, the Revenue declares its position on wholly-owned subsidiaries to be as follows:

> 'It is particularly difficult to apply the "central management and control" test in the situation where a subsidiary company and its parent operate in different territories. In this situation, the parent will normally influence, to a greater or lesser extent, the actions of the subsidiary. Where that influence is exerted by the parent exercising the powers which a sole or majority shareholder has in general meetings of the subsidiary, for example to appoint or dismiss members of the board of the subsidiary and to initiate or approve alterations to its financial structure, the Revenue would not seek to argue that central control and management of the subsidiary is located where the parent company is resident. However, in cases where the parent usurps the functions of the board of the subsidiary (such as *Unit Construction* itself) or where that board merely rubber stamps the parent company's decisions without giving them any independent consideration of its own, the Revenue draw the conclusion that the subsidiary has the same residence for tax purposes as its parent.[10]

This may reflect the case law described in this chapter if it is read as going no further than *Untelrab* and *Wood v Holden*. However, the statement then goes on to say that:

> 'The Revenue recognise that there may be many cases where a company is a member of a group having its ultimate holding company in another country which will not fall readily into either of the categories referred to above. In considering whether the board of such a subsidiary company exercises central management and control of the subsidiary's business, they have regard to the degree of autonomy which those directors have in conducting the company's business. Matters (among others) that may be taken into account are the extent to which the directors of the subsidiary take decisions on their own authority as to investment, production, marketing and procurement without reference to the parent.'[11]

This is plainly at odds with the current state of the law but remains unamended.

---

1 (1908) 5 TC 358.
2 [1906] 2 Ch 34.
3 (1908) 5 TC 358 at 376.
4 (1959) 38 TC 712 at 729–730, per Romer LJ.
5 (1959) 38 TC 712 at 730.
6 (1913) 6 TC 163.
7 (1913) 6 TC 163.

8 (1899) 4 TC 41.
9 (1899) 4 TC 41 at 46.
10 SP 1/90, para 16.
11 SP 1/90, para 17.

6.09 Elements of central management and control

In the two cases in which the test was first established,[1] all business activities of the companies concerned were carried out, and largely controlled, overseas. Calcutta Jute Mills Co manufactured and sold jute in India and the Cesena Sulphur Co manufactured and sold sulphur in Italy. All Calcutta's property was situated in India – indeed the directors of Calcutta did not have even an office in the UK but met in that belonging to one of their number! – and Cesena's main books, accounts and banking accounts were maintained in Italy. Yet, on the basis of the 'real business' test, the court held that both companies were resident in the UK. Clearly, therefore, it cannot have been the day-to-day management and control of the business activities of those companies which Kelly CB and Huddleston B had in mind when they decided that the 'real business' of those companies was carried on, not overseas, but in the UK.

The clue as to what they did have in mind is provided by Kelly CB who said that:

'... the answer to the question, Where does a joint stock company reside? is, ... where its governing body is to be met with and found, and where its governing body exercises the powers conferred upon it by the Act of Parliament, and by the Articles of Association, where it meets and is in bodily and personal presence for the purposes of the concern.'[2]

The 'real business' of Calcutta Jute Mills Ltd and of Cesena Sulphur Co Ltd was, in other words, carried on, not in India or Italy, but in the place from which the decision to carry out operations in India or Italy had emanated. As Huddleston B said of the Cesena Sulphur Co Ltd's business:

'No doubt the manufacturing part may be done and was done in Italy; so supposing that in another part of the world they found sulphur and carried on their business there, the manufacturing part of the business would be carried on there, no doubt; but the administrative part of the business would be carried on at the place from which all the orders came, from which all the directions flowed, and where the appointments were made, where the appointments of the officers were revoked, where the agents were nominated, where their powers were recalled, where the money was received (whatever may have been sent), where the dividends were payable, and where the dividends were declared. We find that all these Acts are performed in London. I cannot help thinking that the main place of business of the Company is in England....'[3]

The place of central management and control is, then, not necessarily the place in which a company's manufacturing or trading activities take place but the place in which the parameters governing those activities are set and the place in which the fundamental policies to be implemented in the UK or elsewhere are conceived and adopted.

1 *Calcutta Jute Mills Co Ltd v Nicholson* (1876) 1 TC 83 and *Cesena Sulphur Co Ltd v Nicholson* (1876) 1 TC 88.
2 (1876) 1 TC 83 at 95.
3 (1876) 1 TC 88 at 107.

6.10 Finance as a key element

If, as has been demonstrated at **6.09** above, policy-making is the primary expression of central management and control, the raising and allocation of the funds without which a company's policies could not be implemented must be an almost equally important manifestation of such management and control.

In *American Thread Co v Joyce*,[1] for instance, the Master of the Rolls noted that the business of the New York company was one in which seasonable purchases of cotton had to be made, and commented:

> 'Those purchases of cotton necessarily involve considerable financing. The whole policy depends really upon aye or no, shall we finance to the extent of, I think in one case it appears, £300,000. The New York people cannot do that at all. The whole purse-strings in the sense of money coming in by borrowing are kept most zealously at Manchester, and by means of those purse strings they are able to control and do control the policy of the Company and the mode in which they carry on their business of buying and selling.'[2]

Similarly, in *De Beers Consolidated Mines Ltd v Howe*,[3] the Lord Chancellor took as evidence that the company was resident in the UK the fact that:

> 'London has ... always controlled ... all questions of expenditure except wages, materials, and such like at the mines, and a limited sum which may be spent by the Directors at Kimberley.'[4]

A further factor to be considered – though one which alone is not, it seems, determinative of central management and control[5] – is the declaration of dividends. In *Calcutta Jute Mills Co Ltd v Nicholson*,[6] it was asserted (in support of the proposition that the company was resident in India) that the activities of the company in England were minimal, consisting of little more than the dividing between the English shareholders of the amount, less expenses, remitted to this country from India. Huddleston B refuted such a contention by pointing out that:

> 'The operation of the Company in London was, not to divide the amount sent among the shareholders, but it was to "declare" the amount; and I apprehend that, within the meaning of that clause, the directors in London, who had full power, might say, "Well, we do not approve of this system upon which the division has been made, and we shall require a different dividend for the future", or something of that kind, – showing plainly that they exercise the authority, and that they are the persons who are the principal body. . . .'[7]

Similarly, in the *American Thread Company* case,[8] one of the factors which led Hamilton J to uphold the finding of the Commissioners that the central management and control of the American company rested with the English directors was that:

> 'In each year the directors, sitting in extraordinary session in England, recommend what the dividend on the common stock should be ... But in the year 1904, when the dividend was 16 per cent, though the Board by resolution recommended that rate, the gentleman who sent the cablegram to the American directors said that the Board had decided that the dividend should be 16 per cent, and went on to say: "Arrange for usual formal resolutions as regards dividends on preferred shares and common stock without delay". Accordingly, the 16 per cent was announced. . . .'[9]

These words of Hamilton J make it clear that, so far as dividends are concerned, the person or group of persons who actually decides upon the quantum of the dividend, that is the directors and not the persons who formally resolve to pay it or give their formal approval to its declaration, that is, the shareholders.

---

1 (1913) 6 TC 163.
2 (1913) 6 TC 163.
3 (1906) 5 TC 198.
4 (1906) 5 TC 198 at 213.
5 In *Egyptian Hotels Ltd v Mitchell* (1914) 6 TC 542 at 552 Lord Sumner said that 'The mere declaration and payment of a dividend here out of profits earned in a business otherwise wholly carried on abroad, does not prevent the business in which the profits have already been earned from having been wholly carried on abroad. To say that part of a Company's business is to pay dividends, if it has earned them, seems to me to be a play upon words.'
6 (1876) 1 TC 83.
7 (1876) 1 TC 83 at 107.
8 (1913) 6 TC 163.
9 (1913) 6 TC 163.

6.11 Degree of activity

The degree of activity does not form part of the test and must be put in context. In *Wood v Holden (Inspector of Taxes)*[1] in the Court of Appeal Chadwick LJ[2] adopted the analysis of Park J in the High Court as compelling where he said:

> '[64] ... The making of the board resolutions and the signing and execution of documents which the Commissioners say were the only acts of management and control of Eulalia all took place in the Netherlands. A company is resident where its central management and control are situated. How, therefore, can Eulalia have been resident in the United Kingdom? How can it have been resident anywhere other than the Netherlands?
> [65] ... What [the Commissioners] seem really to be saying is that, although the only acts of control and management took place outside the United Kingdom, there was not much involved in them. But the test of a company's residence is still the central control and management test: it is not the law that that test is superseded by some different test if the business of a company is such that not

a great deal is required for central control and management of its business to be carried out.'

'[66] ... If directors of an overseas company sign documents mindlessly, without even thinking what the documents are, I accept that it would be difficult to say that the national jurisdiction in which the directors do that is the jurisdiction of residence of the company. But if they apply their minds to whether or not to sign the documents, the authorities ... indicate that it is a very different matter. ...'

Park J also rejected the notion that 'effective decisions ... require some minimum level of information' with the implication that decisions taken by a director that were not informed somehow did not count.

1 [2006] EWCA Civ 26.
2 At paras [35] and [36].

6.12 Administrative functions

The undertaking of activities to comply with company law such as those of a company secretary are not indications of residence.[1] More recently in *News Datacom*,[2] the Special Commissioners concluded that a single meeting in the UK was concerned only with ministerial matters and matters of good housekeeping. The meeting was not concerned with policy, strategic, or management matters relating to the conduct of the business of the company. It did not reflect a manifestation of the controlling brain or where the business of the company was really carried on. It was not an exercise of central management and control. It was the tidying up operation, conducted by alternate directors. The circumstances are unusual and the extent to which any principle is established is questionable.

1 *Todd v Egyptian Delta Land and Investment Co Ltd* (1929) 14 TC 119, contrary to *Swedish Central Railway Co Ltd v Thompson* (1925) 9 TC 342.
2 *News Datacom Ltd & News Data Security Products Ltd v Revenue & Customs* [2006] UKSPC SPC561.

6.13 Influence compared with management and control

Influencing of company policy by persons who are not authorised to make decisions as part of the constitutional organs of the company is not an exercise of central management and control, at least in cases where the functions of those organs have not been 'usurped'. As Chadwick LJ said at para 27 in *Wood v Holden*:

'[I]t is essential to recognise the distinction (in concept, at least) between the role of an "outsider" in proposing, advising and influencing the decisions which the constitutional organs take in fulfilling their functions and the role of an outsider who dictates the decisions which are to be taken. In that context an "outsider" is a person who is not, himself, a participant in the formal process (a board meeting or a general meeting) through which the relevant constitutional organ fulfils its function.'

Thus the design and superintending of the transaction by the accountants on behalf of their client did not constitute an exercise of central management and control.

6.14 Location of central management and control

Identification of the person or group of persons who exercise *de facto* central management and control of a company does not, of course, conclude the question of a company's residence. There remains the final step of identifying the place from which they exercise that central management and control.

Where, as will usually be the case, full powers of management and control are vested in the directors of a company and those powers are exercised by the directors or delegated to others under their control,[1] the place where the directors habitually meet to make their decisions on policy, finance and related matters will be the place of central management and control. This is stressed in case after case.

In *Calcutta Jute Mills Co v Nicholson*,[2] for example, Kelly CB says that a company resides

'... where its governing body is to be met with and found, and where its governing body exercises the powers conferred upon it ... where it meets and is in bodily and personal presence for the purposes of the concern ... at the office or place of dwelling ... where the directors meet'.[3]

Similarly, in *De Beers Consolidated Mines Ltd v Howe*,[4] the Lord Chancellor said:

'... it is clearly established ... that the Directors' Meetings in London are the meetings where the real control is exercised in practically all the important business of the Company....'[5]

This recurrent emphasis on the place of directors' meetings must not, however, lead one to suppose that the location of directors' meetings is *the* test of company residence. As Lord Radcliffe pointed out in *Bullock v Unit Construction Co Ltd*:[6]

'... the necessity of establishing some common standard for the treatment of different tax payers meant that the Courts of Law were bound in course of time to produce and apply some general principles of their own to form an acceptable test of residence. No doubt it might have taken a variety of forms ... the site of meetings of the directors' board [was a] possible candidate ... for selection as the criterion. In fact, as we know, the principle was adopted that a company is resident where its central control and management abide....'[7]

6.14 *Residence of companies*

Even if central management and control is in the hands of the directors because their role has not been usurped, their place of meeting may not determine the company's place of residence if their meetings there are merely a matter of form. The Revenue Statement of Practice[8] puts it as follows:

> 'In general the place of directors' meetings is significant only in so far as those meetings constitute the medium through which central management and control is exercised. If, for example, the directors of a company were engaged together actively in the United Kingdom in the complete running of a business which was wholly in the United Kingdom, the company would not be regarded as resident outside the United Kingdom merely because the directors held formal board meetings outside the United Kingdom.[9]

This statement is now limited to those extreme cases where the directors as a matter of proper exercise of their functions have already made the decisions that constitute central management and control in the UK but hold meetings pretending that the decisions are made eleswhere. In *Wood v Holden*, Park J said,[10] 'that the principle almost always followed is that a company is resident in the jurisdiction where its board of directors meets. [22] In the previous sentence I have said "almost always" because it is possible for a company to be resident in one territory even if it does not hold directors' meetings there' (where the board's function is usurped).

Such judicial statements have not deterred HMRC from pressing the point. The HMRC position was argued in *News Datacorp* thus:

> '129. Mr Brennan QC submitted that the test of corporate residence is the *De Beers* test. This required the questions to be asked where is the real business of the company carried on and where does central management and control actually abide?
>
> 130. These questions were to be answered in all cases by reference to the course of business and trading.
>
> 131. The test of central management and control is not to be treated as a test which depends solely on the location where the directors meet. The search is for the principal seat of business – it is there where the central management and control actually abides (see *the Calcutta Jute* case at page 96). This carries with it connotations of continuity because of the use of phrases such as 'actually abides', 'carries on business', 'keeping house'. It is not sufficient, therefore, to look simply at the period during July 1992 when the relevant transactions were carried out: instead it is necessary to consider the overall pattern of conduct established over a period of time – residence does not change on every occasion where there is short-term change in the location of board meetings.
>
> 132. The location of directors meetings could have been but was not chosen as the test for corporate residence (see Lord Radcliffe in *Unit Construction* [1960] AC 351 at 365).'

The correct approach now in the case of legal persons is to pay attention to the legal framework and constitution that gives them life. There have thus far been no cases concerning companies where the board does not function through meetings but via written resolutions or where meetings are held by telephone or video conference.

The residence of a company is where the directors perform the functions that constitute central management and control, not where they reside. In *John Hood & Co Ltd v Magee*,[11] for instance, Mr Hood was the sole director of a company incorporated in Belfast and registered in New York. The Commissioners found that, although the company traded in both Ireland and America, it kept house and did its real business in Belfast where Mr Hood held the majority of his board 'meetings'. Kenny J said: 'It is a mere accident that Mr Hood resides in New York.'[12]

Gibson, J put it thus:

'The residence of the company cannot be determined by Mr Hood's choice of his own residence. No doubt, wherever he went, he carried his functions with him... All the same, he was not the company, it owned his brain and capacity as well as the business. The tap-root of the fruit-bearing tree was at Belfast.'[13]

Clearly, the residence of individual directors may be of some significance from an evidentiary perspective.

---

1 See **6.07** above.
2 (1876) 1 TC 83.
3 (1876) 1 TC 83 at 95–96.
4 (1906) 5 TC 198.
5 (1906) 5 TC 198 at 213.
6 (1959) 38 TC 712.
7 (1959) 38 TC 712 at 738.
8 SP 1/90.
9 SP 1/90 para 14.
10 SP 1/90 para 21.
11 (1918) 7 TC 327.
12 (1918) 7 TC 327 at 358.
13 (1918) 7 TC 327 at p 350.

6.15 Dual or multiple residence

In this chapter the quest hitherto has been that, no matter how complex the affairs of a company or how dispersed over the face of the earth its activities might be, it may be possible to find the place of central management and control exercised in the UK. Exceptionally, that place may not be the UK exclusively. As Lord Radcliffe says in *Bullock v Unit Construction Co Ltd*:[1]

'... the facts of individual cases have not always so arranged themselves as to make it possible to identify any one country as the seat of central management and control at all. Though such instances must be rare, the management and control may be divided or even, at any rate in theory, peripatetic. Situations of this kind do not arise just to tease the minds of Judges: they are the product of some peculiar necessity, political or otherwise.'[2]

Such a division of management and control will necessitate a finding of dual residence, and, although the first such finding was not made until 1925, the possibility of such a finding had been admitted earlier.

6.15 Residence of companies

In 1915, *Mitchell v Egyptian Hotels Ltd*[3] came before the court and, in an oblique way, the matter was moved forward a stage. Egyptian Hotels Ltd had admitted to being resident in the UK and its residence status was, therefore, not in question. It was held, however, that the company was managed and controlled in Egypt so as to be liable to tax on its profits under Schedule D, Case V. Viscount Cave saw this decision as being a tacit acceptance of the principle of dual residence:

> '... the facts ... were sufficient ... to establish residence in Egypt, so that, if a company can have but one residence – namely, the place where its control and management abides, it must have been held that the company being resident in Egypt was not resident here, and accordingly was not taxable at all; but no such suggestion was made either by counsel or by any member of the tribunals by which the decision was given and upheld. This being so, while the case does not expressly decide that a company may have two residences for income tax purposes, the decision appears to be inconsistent with any other view.'[4]

This opinion was expressed by Viscount Cave LC in the context of his judgment in *Swedish Central Rly Co Ltd v Thompson*,[5] the first case in which an actual finding of dual residence was made and upheld. The decision in that case was, however, later described as 'unfortunate ... having regard to the course of authority both before and after its date',[6] and the facts reveal why. The company concerned had been incorporated in England for the purpose of constructing, maintaining and leasing a railway between Frovi and Ludvika in Sweden. During the period with which the case was concerned the company had fulfilled all these objectives and was merely drawing an annual rental under a lease granted to a Swedish traffic company. The registered office of the company was maintained in London and there the company seal was kept, formal administrative business was dealt with by a committee of three directors, transfers of shares were made and registered, and the accounts were drawn up and audited. All directors' and shareholders' meetings were, however, held in Stockholm and there the minimal business activity of the company (the receipt of rents) was carried on. It was found as a fact by the Special Commissioners that the central control and management was in Sweden but that the company was also resident in the UK, and their findings were upheld in the House of Lords. In another part of the speech from which the earlier quotation is taken, Viscount Cave LC said that:

> '... when the central management and control of a company abides in a particular place the company is held for the purposes of income tax to have a residence in that place; but it does not follow that it cannot have a residence elsewhere. An individual may clearly have more than one residence (see *Cooper v Cadwalader*[7]); and in principle there appears to be no reason why a company should not be in the same position. The central management and control may be divided and it may 'keep house and do business' in more than one place; and if so it may have more than one residence.[8]

The finding of the Commissioners, however, had been not that central management and control was divided, but that it lay in Sweden. Once upheld by the House of Lords, therefore, the case began to be regarded as an authority for the proposition that, while central management and control was one test of corporate residence, there was another test also: that of the location of administrative control. This was the approach taken by the Crown in *Egyptian Delta Land and Investment Co Ltd v Todd*,[9] but, there, in the House of Lords, Viscount Sumner went to great lengths to stamp out the idea and to forestall any endorsement of it by his brethren:

> 'All that was decided in the *Swedish Central Railway* case was that the company could have two residences, one in England as well as one in Sweden. Your Lordships were not asked to decide more. It is true that by admission the controlling power over the business was in Sweden, but other business was done in London the character and importance of which, though set out in the Case, was not discussed at the Bar. It was a matter of degree on the facts and your Lordships cannot be deemed to have come to some unexpressed conclusion on that ground merely because you did not for yourselves declare ... that there was no evidence of business carried on in England ... Nor is it decisive of the point to say now that the business done in England was only administrative. It was in fact a good deal more, and in the static condition of the company's affairs it was not much less important than the Swedish part. If new questions arose the Swedish directors could settle them, but as things were little had to be done anywhere except "administration" ... and that was fairly divided between the two countries.'[10]

In other words, the question whether the Swedish Central Railway Co Ltd had more than one residence had been a question of fact for the Commissioners to determine, and the House of Lords, having held that there was some evidence on which the Commissioners' finding of dual residence could have been made, had felt itself unable to interfere with that finding. That did not mean, however, that the control of administrative duties (which was the only control the London board appeared to exercise) was an alternative test of residence. It was not, and the Law Lords had never said it was. Central control and management remained the only test and one must reconcile that with the Commissioners' decision by assuming a finding of divided central management and control.

Viscount Sumner's speech was a skilful piece of oratory – verbally shoring-up the meagre facts until they were able (if only just) to carry the weighty conclusion the Commissioners had placed on them – and it was much needed, for the facts in the *Egyptian Delta* case[11] then before the House of Lords, though not, on the face of it, dissimilar from the facts in the *Swedish Railway* case,[12] had led the Commissioners to find that Egyptian Delta Land and Investment Co Ltd was resident in Egypt only!

Viscount Sumner contrived a distinction between the two findings by declaring that such management and control as there was in the *Swedish Railway* case[13] was almost equally divided between London and Stockholm while, in the *Egyptian Delta* case,[14] the whole of the central management and control was situated in Cairo. This method of reconciling the apparently irreconcilable found such favour with Lord Radcliffe that, in *Bullock v Unit Construction Co Ltd*,[15] he declared:

6.15 *Residence of companies*

'I am myself of the opinion that the best way of treating the matter is to regard the *Swedish Central Railway Company* and the *Egyptian Delta Land Company* decisions as if they were in effect one decision of the House and the speech of Viscount Sumner in the later case as affording an authoritative commentary on the significance of the earlier. He was party to both of them. If this is done much of the difficulty disappears; for it is clear that Lord Sumner wished it to be understood that the Swedish Central Railway Company's business and administration were of such a nature that what managing and controlling had to be done was in fact done as much on English as on Swedish soil. He regarded the key of the earlier decision as being contained in the words of Lord Cave: "The central management and control of a company may be divided, and it may 'keep house and do business' in more than one place; and if so it may have more than one residence".[16] On this basis the 1925 decision of the House is ... a decision on that special class of case[17] ... where the facts themselves are genuinely such as to not to admit of a finding that central management and control are exercised in or from any one country.'[18]

The second case in which a finding of dual residence was made was *Union Corpn Ltd v IRC*.[19] The case concerned a company which had been incorporated in South Africa but which carried on its activities partly in London and partly in South Africa. Management and control at the highest level was divided between the directors in the UK and those in South Africa but final and supreme authority lay with the directors in London. On those facts, therefore, the Commissioners found that the company was resident in the UK. That finding was rejected by the Court of Appeal as being wrong in law.

Sir Raymond Evershed MR found himself in difficulties but derived assistance from the Australian case of *Koitaki Para Rubber Estates Ltd v Federal Comr of Taxation*[20] in which Dixon J had said:

'... a finding that a company is a resident of more than one country ought not to be made unless the control of the general affairs of the company is not centred in one country but is divided or distributed among two or more countries. The matter must always be one of degree and residence may be constituted by a combination of various factors, but one factor to be looked for is the existence in the place claimed as a residence of some part of the superior or directing authority by means of which the affairs of the company are controlled.'[21]

In the light of this judgment, and of the English authorities, Sir Raymond Evershed MR rejected the Special Commissioners' view and arrived at the conclusion that:

'... there must, in order to constitute residence, be not only some substantial business operations in any given country but also present some part of the superior and directing authority ... [T]he question of the extent of the superior or directing authority required (as well as of the business operations being performed) is one of fact to be determined by the Special Commissioners.'[22]

In other words, final and supreme arbitrating authority is not the same thing as central management and control and if the latter is found to be divided to a significant degree between two or more territories a finding of multiple residence must be made – even if in one of those territories is a person or group of persons with the power of ultimate arbitrament.

It is important to understand that the decision in *Union Corpn Ltd v IRC*[23] has not established a new or modified test of residence but has merely provided a basis for decision where *the* test of residence ('Where does the central control and management of this company abide?') will not admit of the single-territory answer which the word 'central' in the test question demands. Sir Raymond Evershed's solution was to 'fragment' the principle underlying the test of residence and to 'establish a residence for tax purposes wherever the exercise of some portion of controlling power and authority can be identified'.[24] Lord Radcliffe suggested this solution might still be open to question,[25] but the remainder of his dicta in *Bullock v Unit Construction Co Ltd*[26] make it clear that any basis for decision which involved a concept other than central management and control could never be countenanced.

---

1 (1959) 38 TC 712.
2 (1959) 38 TC 712 at 739.
3 (1915) 6 TC 542.
4 (1925) 9 TC 342 at 374.
5 (1925) 9 TC 342 at 374.
6 *Bullock v Unit Construction Co Ltd* (1959) 38 TC 712 at 740, per Lord Radcliffe.
7 (1904) 5 TC 101. See **2.09** above.
8 *Swedish Central Rly Co Ltd v Thompson* (1925) 9 TC 342 at 372.
9 (1929) 14 TC 119.
10 (1929) 14 TC 119 at 143.
11 (1929) 14 TC 119.
12 (1925) 9 TC 342.
13 (1925) 9 TC 342.
14 (1929) 14 TC 119.
15 (1959) 38 TC 712.
16 *Swedish Central Rly Co Ltd v Thompson* (1925) 9 TC 342 at 372.
17 *Swedish Central Rly Co Ltd v Thompson* (1925) 9 TC 342 at 372.
18 *Bullock v Unit Construction Co Ltd* (1959) 38 TC 712 at 740.
19 (1952) 34 TC 207.
20 (1940) 64 CLR 15.
21 (1952) 34 TC 207 at 241.
22 (1952) 34 TC 207 at 275.
23 (1952) 34 TC 207 at 275.
24 *Bullock v Unit Construction Co Ltd* (1959) 38 TC 712 at 739, per Lord Radcliffe.
25 *Bullock v Unit Construction Co Ltd* (1959) 38 TC 712 at 739, per Lord Radcliffe.
26 (1959) 38 TC 712.

6.16 Residence for tax treaty purposes

The purpose and effect of double taxation treaties has already been described at **2.22** above. In relation to companies, Art 4(1) of the OECD Model provides:

> '4(1) For the purposes of this Convention, the term "resident of a Contracting State" means any person who, under the laws of that State, is liable to tax therein by reason of his domicile, residence, place of management or any other

6.16 *Residence of companies*

criterion of a similar nature, and also includes that State and any political subdivision or local authority thereof. This term, however, does not include any person who is liable to tax in that State in respect only of income from sources in that State or capital situated therein.'

Thus a company may be treated as a resident under domestic law on the basis of the place of incorporation (domicile). 'Residence or place of management' will generally suffice to cover the place where central management and control are exercised. Thus, prima facie, a company incorporated in the UK or one whose central management and control is exercised there will be a resident of a contracting state, that is the UK, for treaty purposes. Where a tax treaty is in place, such dual residence may be resolved for the purposes of the treaty by the following mechanism:

'4(3) Where by reason of the provisions of paragraph 1 a person other than an individual is a resident of both Contracting States, then it shall be deemed to be a resident only of the State in which its place of effective management is situated.'

Whether the company is also at the same time resident of the other contracting state will depend on the domestic tax law of that state. Thus a finding of dual residence as described at **6.15** above will not itself entail dual residence for treaty purposes.

There has been little consensus internationally on the meaning of 'place of effective management' and recent attempts by the English courts to interpret and apply it to companies have not been entirely satisfactory.

The OECD Commentary on Art 4(3) has itself been controversial. Its latest version found in the 2008 OECD Model treaty reads:

'24.1 An entity may have more than one place of management, but it can have only one place of effective management at any one time.
24.2 The place of effective management is the place where the key management and commercial decisions that are necessary for the conduct of the entity's business are in substance made., *i.e.* the place where the actions to be taken by the entity as a whole are, *in fact*, determined and all. *All the* relevant facts and circumstances must be examined to determine the place of effective management.
24.3 The place of effective management will ordinarily be the place where the most senior person or group of persons (for example a board of directors) makes its decisions, which normally corresponds to where it meets. There are cases, however, where the key management and commercial decisions necessary for the conduct of the entity's business are in substance made in one place somewhere by a person or group of persons but are formally finalized somewhere else by it or by another person or group of persons. In such cases, it will be necessary to consider other factors. Depending on the circumstances, these other factors could include:
 – Where a board of directors formally finalizes key management and commercial decisions necessary for the conduct of the entity's business at meetings held in one State but these decisions are in substance made in another State, the place of effective management will be in the latter State.
 – If there is a person such as a controlling interest holder (e.g. a parent company or associated enterprise) that effectively makes the key

management and commercial decisions that are necessary for the conduct of the entity's business, the place of effective management will be where that person makes these key decisions. For that to be the case, however, the key decisions made by that person must go beyond decisions related to the normal management and policy formulation of a group's activities (e.g. the type of decisions that a parent company of a multinational group would be expected to take as regards the direction, co-ordination and supervision of the activities of each part of the group).
– Where a board of directors routinely approves the commercial and strategic decisions made by the executive officers, the place where the executive officers perform their functions would be important in determining the place of effective management of the entity. In distinguishing between a place where a decision is made as opposed to where it is merely approved, one should consider the place where advice on recommendations or options relating to the decisions were considered and where the decisions were ultimately developed.'

Indofood International Finance Ltd v JP Morgan Chase Bank NA[1] involved the Indonesia-Netherlands tax treaty in a commercial dispute governed by English law. The court was asked to deal with what an Indonesian court would have decided was the place of effective management of a hypothetical Dutch company. Two judges in the Court of Appeal declined to decide the case on this point but Sir Andrew Morritt, the Chancellor expressed the following views

'As counsel for the issuer pointed out the test, as elaborated by the OECD commentary, refers to the place where "key" decisions are taken. The provisions of the trust deed and, more particularly, of the note conditions show clearly that they must be taken by the parent guarantor. Whilst I do not doubt that the board of directors of Newco would be permitted to determine what to do with the handling charges and equity capital and would be responsible for complying with the requirements of Dutch law, those are hardly the "key" decisions. Let it be assumed that the issuer and Newco are otherwise resident in Holland and the question arose whether to interpose Newco it is, in my view, plain beyond doubt that such a decision and the terms of any interposition would not be left to the issuer or Newco but would be decided by the board of the parent guarantor. In particular it would not be left to the board of the issuer or of Newco to decide whether to assign or to accept the benefit of the loan agreement between the parent guarantor and the issuer and if so on what terms. Questions in relation to any subsequent migration, substitution or interposition of another company between the parent guarantor and Newco or between Newco and the issuer would be decided by the board of the parent guarantor. In my view it is plain that the place of effective management of the issuer is Indonesia and that the place of effective management of Newco, if interposed between the parent guarantor and the issuer, would be Indonesia too.'[2]

These comments cast little light on the expression as the key decisions refered to are shareholder issues rather than those relating to the management of the hypothetical company.

In *Wood v Holden* the Commissioners accepted the HMRC submission that in the present context there is no difference between central management and control and the place of effective management.[3] Park J said:

6.16 Residence of companies

'Article 4(3) requires there to be identified a "place" of effective management, and it has to be a place situated in one of the two States'[4] and 'when it comes to applying the detailed wording of article 4(3) what was the "place ... situated" in the United Kingdom which was Eulalia's "place of effective management"?'[5] The Court of Appeal[6] did not address the issue.

In *Trevor Smallwood Trust v R & C Comrs*[7] the Special Commissioners reviewed this case and the OECD commenatary as it applies to companies but ultimately merely concluded that 'having regard to the ordinary meaning of the words in their context and in the light of their object and purpose, we should approach the issue of POEM as considering in which state the real top level management is found.'[8]

---

1 [2006] EWCA Civ 158.
2 At para 57.
3 At para 146.
4 [2005] EWHC 547 (Ch) para 77.
5 At para 78.
6 [2006] EWCA Civ 26.
7 *Trevor Smallwood & Mary Caroline Smallwood Trustees of the Trevor Smallwood Trust v R & C Comrs; Trevor Smallwood Settlor of the Trevor Smallwood Trust v R & C Comrs*, [2008] UKSPC 669.
8 At para 130, see **5.06** above.

6.17 Transfer of residence abroad

Following the decision of the courts that the place of a company's central management and control was the sole determinant of its place of residence, it became commonplace for companies engaged extensively in overseas activities to amend their articles of association and to transfer their central management and control abroad once the burden of UK taxation became significantly greater than that which would be imposed were they to be resident overseas. Of the companies involved in the cases discussed in this chapter, two, at least, changed their place of residence in this way: The Cesena Sulphur Company became resident in Italy and The American Thread Company became resident in America,[1] and, in 1928, when the validity of The Egyptian Delta Land and Investment Co Ltd's change of residence was being challenged, Viscount Sumner was able to affirm that:

> 'Many companies have, at the cost of some trouble and expense, transferred their control and management abroad on the faith of decisions, or if you will, *dicta*, to the effect that by so doing they could legitimately reduce the burden of their taxation.'[2]

A company incorporated outside the UK may cease to be resident there by moving its central management and control outside the territory. A company incorporated in the UK will only cease to be resident if it is able to benefit from tax treaty under which it is treated as resident in the other contracting state by application of the tie-breaker in Article 4(3) or equivalent provisions.

1 See paras 3 and 4 of the case stated in *Bradbury v English Sewing Cotton Co Ltd* (1923) 8 TC 481 at 482.
2 *Egyptian Delta Land and Investment Co Ltd v Todd* (1929) 14 TC 119 at 156.

6.18 Treaty non-resident companies

Under s 249 of the Finance Act 1994 a company which would otherwise be regarded as resident in the UK and is regarded for the purpose of any double taxation relief arrangements as resident in a territory outside the UK and not resident in the UK is treated as from 30 November 1993 as non-resident for all UK tax purposes.

6.19 European Company

The European Company Regulation[1] came into force on 8 October 2004. The Regulation permitted the formation of a European Company (SE) which would be subject to the tax law of the country within the EU in which it was resident. A SE which transfers its registered office to the UK in accordance with Art 8 of the Council Regulation, upon registration there is regarded for the purposes of the Taxes Acts as resident in the UK; the central management and control test is displaced by registration.[2] However, a SE does not cease to be regarded as resident in the UK by reason only of the subsequent transfer from the UK of its registered office.[3] This would suggest that a transfer out of the registration must be accompanied by the exercise of central management and control outside the UK.

1 Council Regulation (EC) 2157/2001 on the Statute for a European Company (Societas Europaea).
2 FA 1988 s 66A(2).
3 FA 1988 s 66A(3).

6.20 Residence for special statutory purposes

For most corporation tax purposes, a single question is posed: is the company a resident of the UK or not? If it is not, then the corporation tax system does not care where its residence may be found.[1] This indifference is replaced with specific statutory measures in relation to three elements of the corporation tax system, namely group relief, controlled foreign companies and transfer pricing. Each of these has its own mechanism for identifying the territory of residence of a non-UK resident company. In the case of the controlled foreign companies and transfer pricing rules, the mechanisms include determining which of two or more foreign territories the company in question is resident in for those purposes.

1 *News Datacom Ltd v Atkinson* (HMIT) [2006] UKSPC 561 para 123.

6.21 Group relief

Losses and certain other amounts incurred in one member of a group of UK resident companies may be set off by way of group relief against profits in other UK resident companies[1] if, in the material accounting period of the company which would otherwise be the surrendering company, that company is a 'dual resident investing company' no such losses or other amounts may be surrendered by it.[2] Dual resident company is defined as follows:

> '404(4) A company is for the purposes of this section a dual resident company in any accounting period in which–
> (a) it is resident in the United Kingdom; and
> (b) it is also within a charge to tax under the laws of a territory outside the United Kingdom–
>   (i) because it derives its status as a company from those laws; or
>   (ii) because its place of management is in that territory; or
>   (iii) because under those laws it is for any other reason regarded as resident in that territory for the purposes of that charge.'

In the case of dual resident investing companies the inability to surrender group relief occurs if the company is liable to tax in another territory under foreign law. The language of s 404(4)(b) borrows from Art 4(1) of the OECD Model treaty in specifying that if the company is within the foreign tax charge by reason of its place of incorporation or place of management, then it is treated as a dual resident. The same is true if the territory applies some other residence test. A place of management in this sense is likely not limited to the UK 'central management and control' test. It is, however, insufficient that the company be regarded as dual resident for UK corporation tax purposes. A company is only dual resident for this purpose if it is also a resident of another territory under the tax laws of that territory. It does not matter for these purposes if the company is resident in more than one foreign territory under more than one foreign law.

1 ICTA 1988 s 403.
2 ICTA 1988 s 404(1).

6.22 Controlled Foreign Companies

If a company is resident in a territory outside the UK where it is subject to a level of taxation less than three-quarters of the UK rate, and is controlled by UK resident persons, then it is a CFC the Controlled Foreign Companies provisions apply. In such a case the chargeable profits of that CFC and its creditable tax (if any) for that period are apportioned among its shareholders and taxed in the hands of UK resident corporate shareholders with at least a 25 per cent interest in that company.[1]

As is the case with dual resident companies, the basic residence test borrows heavily from Art 4(1) of the OECD Model:

'749(1) Subject to subsections (2) to (4) and (6) below, in any accounting period in which a company is resident outside the United Kingdom, it shall be regarded for the purposes of this Chapter as resident in that territory in which, throughout that period, it is liable to tax by reason of domicile, residence or place of management.'

The residence of a CFC in a particular territory if it is resident in more than one foreign territory under more than one foreign law will determine whether it is subject to a lower rate of taxation and whether it qualifies for certain exemptions. Resolution of the foreign dual or multiple residence is addressed through a series of tests.

Dual or multiple foreign residence is determined initially as being at the place of effective management of the company.[2] The legislation thus adopts the language of Art 4(3) of the OECD Model.[3] The draftsperson, however, misunderstood the meaning of 'place of effective management' in Art 4(3) as is demonstrated by a rule which addresses the case where the place of effective management is in two or more territories.[4]

In such a case, it is said, that the company is resident in the territory where the greater amount of its assets are situated.

The territory where the greater amount of its assets are situated is likewise deemed to be where the company is resident if its place of effective management is in none of the territories under whose laws it is resident.[5]

If none of these results in a single territory of residence, the company may elect to be treated as resident in a particular territory.[6] Where an election has not been made within the statutory time limit the Board may 'justly and reasonably' designate the territory of residence.[7]

A company with no territory of residence, for example, because it is only in a country with no system of corporate taxation or one which imposes tax on companies not by reference to domicile, residence or place of management, is that it is conclusively presumed to be subject to a lower level of taxation. For the purposes of the Excluded Countries Regulations[8] a company which has no territory of residence under those Regulations is treated as resident in the country where it is incorporated.

1 See generally ICTA 1988 Pt XVII Ch IV.
2 Section 749(3)(a).
3 See para 6.16 above.
4 Section 749(3)(b).
5 Section 749(3)(c).
6 Section 749(3)(d).
7 Section 794(3)(e).
8 SI 1998/3081.

6.23 Transfer pricing – exemption for small or medium-sized enterprises

Profits of persons where there is common participation in the management control or capital fall to be adjusted in relation to transactions beteween them that are not on arm's-length terms.[1] This rule does not apply generally to small enterprises and is modified in the case of medium-sized

6.23 *Residence of companies*

enterprises.² These exceptions do not apply to transactions with persons resident in a 'non-qualifying territory'.³ The exception applies whether or not that person is also a resident of a qualifying territory. For this purpose 'resident', in relation to a territory,

(a) means a person who, under the laws of that territory, is liable to tax there by reason of his domicile, residence or place of management, but
(b) does not include a person who is liable to tax in that territory in respect only of income from sources in that territory or capital situated there.⁴

---

1 ICTA 1988 Sched 28AA(1).
2 ICTA 1988 Sched 28AA(5A–D).
3 ICTA 1988 Sched 28AA(5B)(4).
4 ICTA 1988 Sched 28AA(5B)(6).

CHAPTER 7

Domicile

> *If I should die, think only this of me:*
> *That there's some corner of a foreign field*
> *That is for ever England ...*
>
> Rupert Brooke *The Soldier*

7.01 Introduction

The purpose of this chapter is to explore the concept of domicile as a determinant of liability to inheritance tax and as a modifying factor in relation to other taxes, and to explain how a person's domicile may be identified.

Since publication of the decisions of the Special Commissioners started in 1995, several cases have been reported concerning the domicile of individuals.[1] Only one[2] has been appealed (unsuccessfully) to the High Court, and none have grappled with the essential elements of the law of domicile which has shown much stability. In *Gaines-Cooper* it was argued that the Special Commissioners made an error of law if their conclusion was not the only true and reasonable conclusion on the basis of the facts found *and the unchallenged evidence*. This was not found to be the case. Arguments on the law of domicile advanced by the taxpayer were likewise rejected. All have turned on the facts and surrounding circumstances examined in great detail by the Commissioners. They all make interesting reading, but a comparison of the facts of one domicile case with the facts of another domicile case is of limited assistance in deciding the domicile of any particular person.[3]

---

1 *Anderson (executor of Anderson dec'd) v IRC* (1997) Sp C 147; *F & Anor (as personal representatives of F deceased) v Commissioners of Inland Revenue* (1999) Sp C 219; *Civil Engineer v IRC* (2001) Sp C 299; *Surveyor v IRC* (2002) Sp C 339; *Executors of Moore dec'd v IRC* [2002] UKSC SPC335; *Executors of Winifred Johnson Dec'd v HMRC* (2005) Sp C 481; *Gaines-Cooper v HMRC* [2006] UKSPC SPC568.
2 *Gaines-Cooper v HMRC* [2007] EWHC 2617 (Ch).
3 Cf Lord Justice Mummery in *Agulian & Anor v Cyganik* [2006] EWCA Civ 129 para 49.

The nature of domicile

7.02 Historical background

The concept of domicile (or domicil, as some prefer to call it) originated in the Roman Empire when, following the downfall of the Republic, Italy was divided into a number of individual townships known as *municipia* and the Empire was fragmented into numerous provinces. Each province and *municipium* possessed its own jurisdiction and, to a large extent, its own divergent internal law which was administered and enforced by magistrates. Most inhabitants of the Empire were connected by citizenship with one or more of these provincial or municipal communities and/or with Rome itself.

The link of citizenship could arise in various ways – by *origo* (the place within the Empire to which a person's father or, if he was illegitimate, his mother belonged), by adoption, by election or by manumission – and that presented three possibilities. A person might be a citizen of one place, a citizen of more than one place[1] or a citizen of none. This, inevitably, created difficulties. Given that, as stated, each province or *municipium* had its own system of law, to which system should a man in each of those situations be subject? The answer supplied by Rome was, in the first situation, the law of the man's place of citizenship, and, in the second situation, the law of his *origo*. In the third situation, however, a different determinant was needed and the determinant created was 'domicile' – the place in which a person had made his permanent home.

That concept of domicile was one of the concepts of Roman law, which, in the thirteenth century, was enthusiastically revived by the 'post-glossators' jurists who were attached to the Italian universities and who were engaged in developing the Roman law to meet the nation's changing needs.[2] Italy had by then emerged from the barbarism and feudalism into which the civilised world had been plunged following the fall of the Roman Empire in the fifth century and had become a land of independent, cosmopolitan cities – Bologna, Florence, Genoa, Milan, Padua, Pisa etc – all of which were subject generally to Roman law, but each of which had diverse laws of its own which gave rise to conflict as commercial intercourse between the cities increased. As a basis for the resolution of such conflicts, the post-glossators developed a set of principles, known to legal historians as 'statute theory', and it was into these that the revived concept of domicile was introduced.

A 'statute' in the terminology of the post-glossators was any legislative or customary local law which was found to be contrary to Roman law in general; and the statute theory proceeded from the premise that all such laws were either 'real', 'personal' or 'mixed'. A law which concerned things other than moveables was 'real',[3] a law which concerned persons and moveables was 'personal', and a law which concerned acts (such as the making of a contract) was 'mixed' as it generally concerned both persons and things. Real statutes were seen as essentially territorial and as having no application beyond the territorial bounds of the locality in which they were found. Mixed statutes were seen as partially territorial in that they applied to all acts done within the territorial bounds of the locality in which they were found but could give rise to litigation elsewhere. Personal statutes, on the other hand, were seen as non-territorial and as applicable to any person *domiciled* within the locality in which the laws were found, wherever that person might be. Thus a Bologna-born merchant whose permanent home was in Florence would remain subject to Florentine personal laws while visiting, say, Padua, and neither Bolognan nor Paduan personal laws would apply to him.

The statute theory – the basis of today's 'private international law' or 'conflict of laws' as it is often called – was neither as simple nor as effective as it might appear and it was much refined by French jurists in the sixteenth century and Dutch jurists in the seventeenth century. Its subsequent development is beyond the scope of this work and it is sufficient to say that, despite all the changes which have taken place and despite the English and Scottish developments of the conflict of laws in the nineteenth century, the concept of domicile, and its use as the determinant of the system of personal law to which a person should be subject wherever he might be, has remained intact to the present day in the common law jurisdictions of the UK, the Commonwealth and the United States of America. To such nations, possessing as they do within their territorial boundaries a number of diverse legal systems, domicile still presents, as it once presented to Italy, the best determinant of the relevant personal law. Ironically, in the nineteenth century, Italy itself and most other countries in Europe rejected the test of domicile in favour of the test of nationality, and Japan and many South American states followed suit.

---

1 St Paul, for example, was a citizen of Tarsus in Cilicia and a citizen of Rome (Acts 21: 39; 22: 27).
2 In the eleventh century the jurists of Italy had taken the *Corpus Juris* – the Justinian code of Roman law – and added to it *glossae* – explanatory notes. The jurists themselves came to be known as the 'glossators' and the revived and expanded Roman law became the general law throughout Italy and the legal code on which the post-glossators then worked.
3 From late Latin *realis* (Latin *res*), a thing.

7.03 The two roles of domicile

The brief picture of domicile's origins given at **7.02** above should have sufficed to show that domicile is essentially a conflict of laws concept employed in determining the system of personal law which should be applied where a person has connections with more than one jurisdiction. Personal law is that part of law which, to some degree, governs the validity of marriage, the effect of marriage on the proprietory rights of husband and wife, divorce and nullity of marriage, legitimacy, legitimation and adoption, wills of moveables and intestate succession to moveables. It follows, therefore, that, whenever a question arises in the English courts concerning any of these matters, it must be determined according to the law of the domicile of the person concerned and not (unless English law happens to be the law of his domicile) according to English law, the law of the territory in which he happens to be, or the law of the nation of which he is a citizen.

Example

Alan, a citizen of Eriador (where wills require the attestation of three witnesses), dies on holiday in Mordor (where wills require the attestation of four witnesses) but, at the time of his death, is domiciled in Gondor under whose laws he has made a will attested by only one witness as is permitted under Gondorian law. His will is contested in the English courts on the grounds that two witnesses are required under English law or, alternatively, that three are required under Eriadorian law or, alternatively, that four are required under Mordorian law. The suit fails.[1]

The rationale for this lies in the fact that (conceptually, at any rate) domicile, at any given moment in a person's life or at the moment of his death, singles out, from among all the territories in the world, the one territory in which – irrespective of where he happens to be or where he happens to reside or ordinarily reside – that person has his real home; and, once that person's real home has been identified, the law of that territory, and of no other, is the law which should be applied in all matters which relate to him as a person.

One of those matters is the transfer of capital to another – dispositions which reduce the value of a person's estate upon his death or, in certain circumstances, during his lifetime – and it is upon such transfers of value that, under UK revenue law, inheritance tax is charged. It is entirely appropriate, therefore, that – except as regards any part of a person's estate which is situated in the UK – the determinant of liability to tax on capital transfers should be the same as the determinant of the personal law governing those transfers, ie domicile.

There is, however, a second and more cogent reason why a person's domicile is a more appropriate determinant of liability to inheritance tax than residence. Inheritance tax is a cumulative charge on transfers of value made by a person upon his death *and* during the previous seven years, and there is also a seven-year cumulation period in respect of chargeable transfers during his lifetime.[2] The effectiveness of the inheritance tax system depends, therefore, on a link of the greatest possible strength being used to attach a person to the UK, and domicile is just such a link. Residence may easily be snapped, ordinary residence is only a little stronger, but the bonds of domicile are very difficult to break – and, as is explained later,[3] even if a person should succeed in breaking those bonds, he may nonetheless find himself attributed with a *deemed* domicile under rules which Parliament has enacted to cover just such a contingency.

The confinement of UK taxation of income and capital gains to the taxation of remittances in the case of income and gains generated overseas by a person who is not domiciled in the UK is further parliamentary recognition of the strength of the link between person and territory which domicile represents.

1 The territories used in this example are some of the fictitious territories created by J R R Tolkien as a setting for *The Lord of the Rings*.
2 IHTA 1984 s 7 as amended by FA 1986.
3 At **7.16** below.

7.04 The five principles of domicile

Domicile, being a common law concept, is not defined in the Taxes Acts. In 1858, however, Lord Cranworth said: 'By domicile we mean home, the permanent home,'[1] and, ever since, that has been regarded as a basic (if deceptively simple) definition of the term. Although the idea of a permanent home is indeed central to the concept of domicile, the meaning of 'permanent home' in this context is not necessarily the meaning which the man on the Clapham omnibus would give to the term. There are, as will be shown, instances in which the courts will decide that a person's permanent home is in some faraway territory in which he has never set foot and with which, so far as he is aware, he has never had any connection. This is because domicile, though founded on fact, is not merely a finding of fact but a conclusion of law which is reached by application of a set of legal principles.

The principles referred to are five in number, and the first is that no one shall, at any time, be without a domicile.[2] The necessity for this becomes apparent once we remind ourselves that domicile is, in English law, the sole determinant of the personal law to which a person is to be subject. Indeed, it is one of the weaknesses of legal systems which have opted for nationality as a determinant of the personal law that a person may be stateless and may thus not possess the required connecting link. This is not to say, of course, that assigning a domicile to every person never presents difficulties: it frequently does, but the courts have developed additional principles to overcome these problems.

The second principle is that no one can simultaneously have more than one operative domicile.[3] The justification for this is that domicile, being the sole determinant of the personal law, must, by its very nature, be exclusive, otherwise a further determinant will be needed. This exposes another weakness in systems which have taken nationality as the determinant of the personal law, for many persons have dual nationality. The adjective 'operative' has been introduced into the above statement of principle because, as will be explained,[4] there are three kinds of domicile and one of these, domicile of origin, will, if displaced by either of the others, become dormant but will, in the event of either of the others being lost, instantly revive. It should be noted that, in English law, domicile is regarded as a purely objective concept which remains unaffected by the subject matter of the point at issue.[5] In theory, therefore, there should be no question, in English law, of a person having one domicile for taxation purposes and another for, say, the purposes of divorce. As explained below, however, there are certain situations in which that may be possible – though not through any abandonment of the objective approach.

7.04 *Domicile*

The third principle is said to be that domicile must relate to a territory subject to a single system of law, whether or not the limits of that territory coincide with national boundaries. This, so far as the UK is concerned, would mean that a domicile could arise only in Northern Ireland, Scotland or England and Wales.

However, the Taxes Acts speak not of domicile in Northern Ireland or Scotland or England and Wales but of domicile 'in the United Kingdom'.[6]

The fourth principle is that a change of domicile may never be presumed.[7] As Jenkins LJ has said:

> 'Change of domicile, particularly where the change is from the domicile of origin to a domicile of choice (as distinct from a change from one domicile of choice to another) has always been regarded as a serious step which is only to be imputed to a person upon clear and unequivocal evidence.'[8]

In other words, a change of domicile will always have to be proved and, as Lord Chelmsford has said:

> '... the burden of proof unquestionably lies upon the party who asserts the change.'[9]

The question of the degree of proof required is considered at **7.15** below.

The fifth principle is that domicile must be determined according to the English concept of domicile. As Lindley MR said in *Re Martin*:[10]

> 'The domicil ... must be determined by the English Court ... according to those legal principles applicable to domicil which are recognised in this country and are part of its law.'[11]

The significance of this rule lies in the fact that 'domicile' does not have a precise and universally accepted meaning. Not all jurisdictions accept the objective approach to domicile, others (such as Australia, New Zealand and the United States of America) do not accept English doctrines such as that of the revival of the domicile of origin,[12] and under some international conventions domicile is equated with habitual residence.[13]

---

1 *Whicker v Hume* (1858) 7 HL Cas 124 at 160.
2 *Udny v Udny* (1869) Lr 1 Sc & Div 441 at 457, per Lord Westbury.
3 *IRC v Bullock* [1976] STC 409 at 414, per Buckley LJ.
4 See **7.06** below.
5 It is understood that a subjective or 'multiple concept' view of domicile is increasingly being adopted in the United States of America.
6 Eg, ICTA 1988 ss 65(4), 192 and 207 and TCGA 1992 s 12(1).
7 See *Moorhouse v Lord* (1863) 10 HL Cas 272 at 286, per Lord Chelmsford.
8 *Travers v Holley* [1953] P 246 at 252.
9 *Moorhouse v Lord* (1863) 10 HL Cas 272 at 286.
10 [1900] P 211.
11 [1900] P 211 at 227.
12 See **7.06** below.
13 Article 5 of the 1955 Hague Convention to Regulate Conflicts between the Law of Nationality and the Law of Domicile attributes domicile with this meaning.

Domicile of origin

7.05 Acquisition

English law recognises three kinds of domicile: domicile of origin, domicile of dependence and domicile of choice. Every person will possess the first of these, and may, at different times, possess either of the others.

The domicile of origin is the form of domicile which is imposed on every person at the moment of his birth. It is a link, forged by the law, which attaches a person to a particular system of law and which retains its hold on him throughout his life. Should he acquire a domicile of dependence or a domicile of choice, the link will be removed, but not destroyed; rather it will be held at readiness to reattach him instantly to the original system of law should his domicile of dependence cease or his domicile of choice be abandoned.

Except in the case of a foundling (when the domicile of origin imposed is that of the place where the child is found), the basis of imposition of a domicile of origin is parentage. If a child is born legitimate and during his father's lifetime, the domicile of origin imposed on him is that of his father at the time of the child's birth.[1] If a child is born illegitimate,[2] or born legitimate but after his father's death,[3] the domicile of origin imposed on him is that of his mother.

One problem which could arise in this connection springs from the fact that the question of legitimacy is itself a matter of personal law. As the determinant of the appropriate person law is the child's domicile and as the child's domicile cannot be determined until the question of its legitimacy has been settled, it can be seen that, unless both parents are of the same domicile, an endless legal loop is created. Various solutions to the problem have been proposed[4] but there is no authority on the question in English law.

It seems clear that in the event of an illegitimate child being legitimated the child's domicile of origin will remain unaffected since, under the Legitimacy Acts, legitimation does not operate retrospectively.[5] In the event of a child becoming adopted, however, it would appear that a new domicile of origin will be acquired since adoption involves the complete severance of the legal relationship between parent and child and the establishment of a new one between child and the adoptive parent.[6]

The Law Commission and the Scottish Law Commission have recommended that the domicile of origin be abolished and that, in future, a child's domicile should be determined from the outset under revised domicile of dependence rules.[7]

---

1 *Udny v Udny* (1869) LR 1 Sc & Div 441 at 457, per Lord Westbury.
2 *Udny v Udny* (1869) LR 1 Sc & Div 441 at 457, per Lord Westbury.
3 This is apparently unsupported by any English authority.
4 Eg, by R H Graveson in *Private International Law* (7th edn, Sweet and Maxwell) at pp 195–196.
5 See **7.08** below for the domicile of dependence which legitimation creates.
6 *Bromley's Family Law* (Oxford Univeristy Press, 10th edn) p 408.

7.05 *Domicile*

7 The Law Commission Working Paper No 88 and the Scottish Law Commission Consultative Memorandum No 63, 'Private International Law, The Law of Domicile' (1985), para 4.22. See **7.08** below.

7.06 Displacement and revival

A domicile of origin, being a domicile imposed by operation of law independently of a person's will, can never be extinguished by an act of will or by mere abandonment. It will continue to be operative, whether its possessor wishes it to be operative or not, until it is displaced by the acquisition of either a domicile of dependency or a domicile of choice. This is well illustrated by the leading case of *Bell v Kennedy*.[1]

Mr Bell was born in 1802 of Scottish parents who were domiciled by choice in the island of Jamaica. Accordingly, he possessed a Jamaican domicile of origin. Following the death of his mother, Bell, at the age of two, was sent to Scotland to be cared for and educated. When he was 10 years old his father died and left him his Jamaican estate. Mr Bell completed his education in Scotland, travelled for a while in Europe, then, shortly after reaching his majority, returned to Jamaica to cultivate the estate that had been left to him. The estate prospered and Mr Bell became a wealthy and important personage, attaining membership of the island's Legislative Assembly. He married and fathered three children. In 1834, however, the law was changed with regard to slavery and the change was to culminate in the complete emancipation of slaves in 1838. Mr Bell strongly disapproved of the change and that, coupled with his failing health, decided him upon a permanent return to the UK. Accordingly, in 1837, he sold the estate and left the island for good. Initially, he and his immediate family resided with his mother-in-law in Edinburgh and Mr Bell set about finding a suitable estate, preferably in Scotland but possibly across the border, in England, which he could purchase and in which he and his family could settle down. Before he had succeeded in this, however, his wife died. At that time, a woman acquired the domicile of her husband upon marriage and, accordingly, in order to resolve a dispute which had arisen concerning Mr and Mrs Bell's daughter's succession to Mrs Bell's share in goods held in common between Mr and Mrs Bell at the date of Mrs Bell's death, it became necessary to determine Mr Bell's domicile at the date of his wife's death. The court held that his domicile was his domicile of origin, ie, Jamaica. Lord Cairns said:

> 'The birth-domicile of [Bell] in Jamaica continued, at all events till 1837, and the onus lies upon those who desire to shew that there was a change in this domicile . . . to prove that that change took place. The law is, beyond all doubt, clear with regard to the domicile of birth, that the personal status indicated by that term clings and adheres to the subject of it until an actual change is made by which the personal status of another domicile is acquired . . . It appears to me . . . that so far from [Mr and Mrs Bell's daughter and her husband] having discharged the onus which lies upon them to prove the adoption of a Scottish domicile, they have entirely failed in discharging that burden of proof, and that the evidence leads quite in the opposite direction. There is nothing in it to shew that [Bell's]

personal status of domicile as a native and inhabitant of Jamaica has been changed on coming here by that which alone could change it, his assumption of domicile in another country.'[2]

Lord Colonsay had this to say:

'I think it is very clear that Mr Bell left Jamaica with the intention of never returning ... But I do not think that his having sailed from Jamaica with that intent extinguished his Jamaica domicile ... He could not so displace the effect which law gives to the domicile of origin, and which continues to attach until a new domicile is acquired *animo et facto*.'[3]

Once a person has, however, *animo et facto* or through the act of the person on whom he is dependent, acquired a new domicile, his domicile of origin, though displaced, still does not die. It lives on within him, dormant but ready to awake and come back into operation in the instant any other domicile is voluntarily abandoned. As Lord Westbury has said in *Udny v Udny*:[4]

'When another domicile is put on, the domicile of origin is for that purpose relinquished, and remains in abeyance during the continuance of the domicile of choice; but as the domicile of origin is the creature of law, and independent of the will of the party, it would be inconsistent with the principles on which it is by law created and ascribed to suppose that it is capable of being by the act of the party entirely obliterated and extinguished.'[5]

Colonel Udny acquired a domicile of origin in Scotland when he was born there of Scottish parents in 1779. His childhood was spent in Scotland but, after serving as an officer in the Guards, in 1812, he married and settled in London. There he resided for the next 32 years. In 1844, however, the Colonel 'having been involved for some time in pecuniary difficulties (owing chiefly to his connection with the turf) was compelled to leave England in order to avoid his creditors'.[6] He first went to Scotland and from there he arranged for the sale of the lease of the London house and 'everything that was in the house, including what had belonged to his mother, his sister, and his ... wife';[7] he then fled to Boulogne. It was in Boulogne that he formed the illicit attachment that resulted in the birth of a child whose legitimation was in question.

Some doubt was expressed by the court whether Colonel Udny had ever, in fact, acquired an English domicile of choice. Nevertheless, the Lord Chancellor was of the opinion that:

'... the English domicil of Colonel Udny, if it were ever acquired, was formally and completely abandoned in 1844 when he sold his house and broke up his English establishment with the intention never to return. And, indeed, his return to that country was barred against him by the continued threat of process by his creditors. I think that on such abandonment his domicil of origin revived. It is clear that by our law a man must have some domicil, and must have a single domicil. It is clear, on the evidence, that the Colonel did not contemplate residing in France ... Why should not the domicil of origin cast on him by no choice of his own, and changed for a time, be the state to which he naturally falls back when his first choice has been abandoned *animo et facto*, and whilst he is deliberating before he makes a second choice.'[8]

Both the Private International Law Committee[9] and now the Law Commission and the Scottish Law Commission[10] have recommended that the principle of revival be discarded and that an existing domicile should continue until a new domicile is acquired. This is the rule in the United States of America,[11] New Zealand[12] and Australia.[13]

The question of the precise point at which the domicile of origin will revive upon a domicile of choice being abandoned is fully discussed at **7.15** below.

---

1 *Bell v Kennedy* (1868) LR 1 Sc & Div 307.
2 *Bell v Kennedy* (1868) LR 1 Sc & Div 307 at 310, 316–317.
3 *Bell v Kennedy* (1868) LR 1 Sc & Div 307 at 323.
4 (1869) LR 1 Sc & Div 441.
5 (1869) LR 1 Sc & Div 441 at 458.
6 (1869) LR 1 Sc & Div 441 at 445.
7 (1869) LR 1 Sc & Div 441 at 445.
8 (1869) LR 1 Sc & Div 441 at 448.
9 First Report (1954) Cmd 9068, para 14.
10 The Law Commission Working Paper No 88 and the Scottish Law Commission Consultative Memorandum No 63, 'Private International Law, The Law of Domicile' (1985, HMSO), para 5.22.
11 *Re Jones' Estate* 192 Iowa 78, 182 NW 227 (1921).
12 Domicile Act 1976 s 11 (New Zealand).
13 Domicile Act 1982 s 7 (Australia).

Domicile of dependence

7.07 Married women

Until 1 January 1974 there were three classes of persons who could or would acquire a domicile of dependence: children, mentally disordered persons and married women. Now, only the first two classes remain, for, by the Domicile and Matrimonial Proceedings Act 1973 s 1, the rule at common law that every woman acquired from her husband his domicile immediately upon her marriage was swept away. The Act provides that the domicile of a married woman as at any time on or after 1 January 1974:

> '... shall, instead of being the same as her husband's by virtue only of marriage, be ascertained by reference to the same factors as in the case of any other individual capable of having an independent domicile.'[1]

So far as any woman who married on, or has married since, 1 January 1974 is concerned, the position is quite straightforward. As the subsection quoted makes plain, the woman has the same capacity as her husband or any other non-dependent person for acquiring a domicile of choice. It will, of course, usually be the case that the domicile of a husband and his wife will be the same, but this will now merely be because of their independent choice to live together permanently in the same place. Such a choice is not always made at the time of the marriage, or if made then, may not be implemented by residence until later. In that event, each may, under the Act, retain different domiciles.

Example

Marie-Louise is domiciled in Belgium. While attending art college in Manchester in 1985 she marries a fellow student, Henri, who is domiciled in France. Upon the completion of their respective courses they are resolved to settle permanently in Monaco. Until that decision is implemented by residence in Monaco, Marie-Louise will retain her Belgian domicile and Henri will retain his French domicile. Thereafter they will each acquire a Monagesque domicile of choice. Had they married before 1 January 1974, Marie-Louise would, upon her marriage, have acquired a French domicile of dependence and then, when they settled in Monaco, a Monagesque domicile of dependence.

The position of a woman who married before 1 January 1974 is set out in subsection (2) of the Act:

> 'Where immediately before [1 January 1974] a woman was married and then had her husband's domicile by dependence, she is to be treated as retaining that domicile (as a domicile of choice, if it is not also her domicile of origin) unless and until it is changed by acquisition or revival of another domicile on or after [1 January 1974].'[2]

The principal difficulty to which this provision gives rise was dealt with in *IRC v Duchess of Portland*.[3] In 1948, the taxpayer, a Canadian citizen with a domicile of origin in Quebec, married Lord William Cavendish-Bentinck (subsequently the Duke of Portland) in England and became Lady William Cavendish-Bentinck (subsequently the Duchess of Portland). Thereupon she acquired from her husband an English domicile of dependence which displaced her Quebec domicile of origin, but she was resolved to return to live in Canada should her husband predecease her and she hoped to persuade him to live in Canada on his retirement. Throughout her marriage, the Duchess of Portland maintained her links with Canada, returning there to visit friends and relatives for between 10 and 12 weeks each year and (since about 1964) owning and maintaining there at her own expense her family home in Metis Beach, Quebec. The Duchess of Portland's first visit to Canada following the enactment of the Domicile and Matrimonial Proceedings Act 1973 was in July 1974, and following that visit she claimed that, under s 1(2) of the Act, her domicile of dependence had been changed by the revival of her Quebec domicile of origin. Had her claim succeeded she would have become exempt under ICTA 1970 s 122(2)(a) from liability to tax on income accruing to her in Canada but not remitted to the UK.

7.07 *Domicile*

The basis of the Duchess of Portland's claim was that the domicile of choice which, under DMPA 1973 s 1(2), she acquired on 1 January 1974 was merely a *deemed* domicile of choice and that the strict test applicable to the abandonment of a true domicile of choice should not be applied in deciding whether or not her deemed domicile of choice had been abandoned. Instead, she claimed, the more lenient test applicable to the abandonment of a domicile of dependency was appropriate. Nourse J agreed that DMPA 1973 s 1(2) was a deeming provision but said:

> '... that which is deemed in a case where the domicile of dependency is not the same as the domicile of origin is the retention of the domicile of dependency as a domicile of choice. I think that that must mean that the effect of the subsection is to reimpose the domicile of dependency as a domicile of choice. The concept of an imposed domicile of choice is not one which it is very easy to grasp, but the force of the subsection requires me to do the best I can. It requires me to treat the taxpayer as if she had acquired an English domicile of choice, even though the facts found by the commissioners tell me that that would have been an impossibility in the real world. In my judgment it necessarily follows that the question whether, after 1 January 1974, the taxpayer abandoned her deemed English domicile of choice must be determined by reference to the test appropriate to the abandonment of a domicile of choice and not by reference to the more lenient test appropriate to the abandonment of one of dependency.'[4]

It was pointed out in *IRC v Duchess of Portland* that, if the Duke and Duchess had married on or after 1 January 1974 the effect of DMPA 1973 s 1(1) would have been to preserve the Duchess's domicile of origin. Nourse J admitted that it was so and said:

> 'It seems clear that a woman living in England with her husband who was married before 1 January 1974 can only free herself from the shackles of dependency by choosing to leave her husband for permanent residence in another country. That is a very limited freedom and it is less than that available under s 1(1) to those who marry on or after 1 January 1974. Be that as it may, Parliament did not, as it might have done, provide that a woman who was married before 1 January 1974 was to be treated as if she had never acquired her domicile of dependency. Section 1(2) having taken the form which it has, by treating the married woman as retaining her domicile of dependency as a domicile of choice, I regret that I have no choice but to attach to it all the consequences which the law has long recognised the latter domicile to have.'[5]

A second difficulty which arises in relation to DMPA 1973 s 1(2) concerns the position after 1 January 1974 of a woman who, having married before that date, had left or had been abandoned by her husband before that date and had settled permanently in some country other than that of her domicile of dependence. In the absence of some new act on her part on or after 1 January 1974, does the woman retain her domicile of dependence as her domicile of choice or does she immediately acquire as her domicile of choice the country in which she settled permanently during her domicile of dependency? This question was also answered, albeit *obiter*, in *IRC v Duchess of Portland*. The problem, said Nourse J, is to be resolved 'consistently with the rule which would have applied if the husband had died before 1 January 1974'.[6] The rule he referred to was established in *Re Cooke's Trustees*[7] and *Re Scullard*[8] and is that where a husband and wife have been living apart, the intent and act of the wife in permanently making her home elsewhere creates a domicile of choice upon the death of her husband without the need for any additional act on her part, or, if the country in which she has settled is her domicile of origin, revives her domicile of origin without the need for any such act. The application of the rule is straightforward.

Example

In 1952, Tom, who was, and continued to be, domiciled in England, married Ingrid, who had a domicile of origin in Germany. In 1968 Ingrid left Tom and made her permanent home in Switzerland. Upon her marriage, Ingrid acquired an English domicile of dependence. This endured until 1 January 1974, but, on that date, in accordance with the rule in *Re Scullard's Estate*,[9] she automatically acquired a domicile of choice in Switzerland. Had Ingrid, upon leaving Tom, made her permanent home in Germany rather than Switzerland, her domicile of origin would have automatically revived on 1 January 1974.

Nourse J summed up as follows the procedure which DMPA 1973 s 1(2) requires one to adopt in determining the domicile of a woman who was married before 1 January 1974:

'... first ... look at the state of affairs prevailing on 1 January 1974 to see whether there has been any automatic change on that date [as in the above example]. If there has not ... look at events after that date in order to see whether any change has occurred subsequently.'[10]

---

1 DMPA 1973 s 1(1).
2 DMPA 1973 s 1(2).
3 [1982] STC 149.
4 [1982] STC 149 at 154.
5 [1982] STC 149 at 156.
6 [1982] STC 149 at 155.
7 (1887) 56 LT 737.
8 [1956] 3 All ER 898.
9 [1956] 3 All ER 898.
10 *IRC v Duchess of Portland* [1982] STC 149 at 155.

7.08 Children

Until 1 January 1974, it was the rule at common law that a minor, whether married or not, was totally incapable of acquiring by his own act an independent domicile of choice.[1] A female child who, before then, married before attaining her majority acquired her husband's domicile as a domicile of dependence and, if widowed before that date, reacquired the domicile she had immediately before her marriage.[2]

7.08 *Domicile*

On 1 January 1974, however, the Domicile and Matrimonial Proceedings Act 1973 came into effect and, with application only to England and Wales and Northern Ireland,[3] confined this rule to unmarried children under the age of 16.[4] Since then, any child reaching the age of 16 or marrying under that age, has been capable of acquiring an independent domicile of choice; and the same applied to any child who, at that date, was already over the age of 16 or, if then still under the age of 16, was then already married.[5]

The present position is, then, that every child acquires at birth a domicile of origin[6] and cannot, so long as they remain unmarried and below the age of 16, displace that domicile of origin by a domicile of choice acquired by their own act of will. There is, however, nothing to prevent their domicile of origin being displaced by an act of will on the part of one of their parents, and if this occurs the new domicile they acquire will be a domicile of dependence.

The primary rule is that, upon any change in the domicile of a child's father after the child's birth, a legitimate or adopted child will acquire their father's new domicile as a domicile of dependence unless their parents[7] are living apart and they either have then a home with their mother and not with their father or having had a home with their mother have not since then had a home with their father.[8] This is because, upon a separation, a child acquires a domicile of dependence from the parent with whom they make their home and, should they subsequently make their home with the other parent, they will (subject to a mother's right *not* to communicate her domicile to a child who is dependent upon her – see next paragraph) acquire a new domicile of dependence from that parent, but, should they cease to have a home with either parent, their last-acquired domicile of dependence will continue. A legitimate, legitimated or adopted child who shares their time between the homes of both parents will acquire and retain throughout the arrangement the domicile of their father.

Where a child is illegitimate or was born after the death of their father, they will prima facie acquire as a domicile of dependence any new domicile acquired by their mother whether they have a home with her or not,[9] unless the mother elects, bona fide and in the interests of the child, that the child's domicile shall not change with her domicile.[10]

Where one or both of a child's parents die during a child's period of dependency, the rules are as follows.

Where a legitimate or adopted child's father dies after the child is born, the child acquires (if they have not acquired it already[11]) the domicile of their mother as a domicile of dependence[12] which will then change as her domicile changes – subject, as explained above, to her right to elect that it shall not be so. The same will be true of an illegitimate child who, before their father's death, has been legitimated, for such a child will, upon legitimation, have received their father's domicile as a domicile of dependence. The death of the father of an illegitimate child who has not been legitimated will have no effect.

Where a child's mother dies, the death will have no effect on the child's domicile unless the child was either born illegitimate and has never been legitimated or has (or last had) a home with their mother following a separation of their parents. In either event, the child will continue to have their dead mother's domicile as a domicile of dependence unless and until, in the case of a legitimate or legitimated or adopted child only, they make a home with their father.[13]

Where a child's parents both die, the domicile of dependence which the child possessed at the date of their deaths will continue; though a child's guardian has no capacity to change the domicile of their ward.[14]

A domicile of dependence will continue until *animo et facto* they abandon the country of that domicile. Thereupon their domicile of origin will revive until it is displaced by a domicile of choice.[15]

Example

Susan is born of an English domiciled father and thus acquires an English domicile of origin by operation of law. When she is eight years old she and her parents move to Denmark and her father acquires there a domicile of choice which is then automatically communicated to Susan as a domicile of dependence. Susan continues to live with her parents until she is 24 when she marries a Norwegian and moves to Oslo where she intends to spend the rest of her life. Her Danish domicile of dependence will endure until she leaves Danish territorial waters, whereupon her English domicile of origin will revive. Upon arriving in Norway, however, her domicile of origin will be displaced by her Norwegian domicile of choice.

It should be noted that it is usually easier to establish the abandonment of a domicile of dependence than to establish the abandonment of a domicile of choice.[16]

The Law Commission and the Scottish Law Commission have proposed that the domicile of any person under the age of 16 should be determined according to where the child has their home. If their home is with both parents, their domicile, they say, should be the same as, and change with, that of their parents if their domiciles are the same, or with that of their mother if their domiciles are different. If their home is with only one parent, their domicile, they say, should be the same as, and change with, the domicile of that parent. And in any other case, the child's domicile should, they say, be the country with which they are, for the time being, most closely connected.[17]

---

1 *Forbes v Forbes* (1854) Kay 341; *Harrison v Harrison* [1953] 1 WLR 865.
2 *Shekleton v Shekleton* [1972] 2 NSWR 675.
3 Not Scotland. Under Scottish law the relevant respective ages are 14 in the case of a boy, 12 in the case of a girl.
4 DMPA 1973, s 3.
5 Because no English domiciled child has the capacity to marry below that age, however, the parts of the rule which relate to persons who are married under the age of 16 is of application only to foreign domiciled children whose marriages are recognised by the courts in this country – as, for example in *Mohamed v Knott* [1968] 2 All ER 563.
6 See **7.05** above.
7 Adoptive parents in the case of an adopted child (Children Act 1975 Sch 1, para 3 as repealed and re-enacted in the Adoption Act 1976 s 39(1) and the Adoption (Scotland) Act 1978 s 39(1)).

8 *D'Etchegoyen v D'Etchegoyen* (1888) 13 PD 132, DMPA 1973 s 4(1)–(2).
9 DMPA 1973, s 4(4) and *Johnstone v Beattie* (1843) 10 Cl & Fin 42.
10 In *Re Beaumont* [1893] 3 Ch 490 at 496, Stirling J said, 'Change in the domicile of an infant which ... may follow from a change of domicile on the part of the mother, is not to be regarded as the necessary consequence of a change of the mother's domicile, but as the result of the exercise by her of a power vested in her for the welfare of the infants, which in their interest she may abstain from exercising, even when she changes her own domicile.' Where, however, a mother exercises her power in her own interest, eg to take advantage of a law of succession more beneficial to herself, such an exercise of her power will be ineffective (*Potinger v Wightman* (1817) 3 Mer 67).
11 The child might already have acquired their mother's domicile as a domicile of dependence if their parents had separated before their father's death and if the child had, upon the separation, made their home with their mother.
12 *Potinger v Wightman* (1817) 3 Mer 67.
13 DMPA 1973 s 4(3).
14 See Dicey and Morris, *The Conflict of Laws* (13th edn), (Sweet & Maxwell), Vol 1, p 141.
15 *Re Macreight, Paxton v Macreight* (1885) 30 ChD 165.
16 *Harrison v Harrison* [1953] 1 WLR 865.
17 The Law Commission Working Paper No 88 and the Scottish Law Commission Consultative Memorandum No 63, 'Private International Law, The Law of Domicile' (1985, HMSO), para 4.18.

7.09 Persons suffering from mental disorder

The position of a person suffering from mental disorder is lacking in direct authority so far as the question of their domicile is concerned. Until a child reaches the age of 16 or marries under that age, the rules governing their domicile will be those already discussed at **7.05** and **7.08** above. If, however, a child becomes insane and their insanity continues beyond their sixteenth[1] birthday, the law would appear to be that their domicile will continue to change with the parent from whom they last acquired a domicile of dependence, but that where they become of unsound mind after they have attained the age of 16 or married under that age, they will permanently retain whatever domicile they then possessed and that domicile will be incapable of change either by their own act or by that of those who are entrusted with their care.[2] The degree of mental unsoundness which is required before these rules will have effect is not settled, but it is arguable that the test to be applied should be whether or not the person is capable of forming the necessary intention to bring about a change in domicile.[3]

The Law Commission and the Scottish Law Commission have recommended that the domicile of an adult *incapax* should not be frozen at the onset of their incapacity but should be changed as necessary so that their domicile is always that of the country with which they are at any time most closely connected.[4]

1 In Scotland, 14 in the case of a boy, 12 in the case of a girl.
2 *Sharpe v Crispin* (1869) LR 1 P & D 611 at 615, per Sir J. P. Wilde.
3 See **7.12** below.
4 The Law Commission Working Paper No 88 and the Scottish Law Commission Consultative Memorandum No 63, 'Private International Law, The Law of Domicile' (1985, HMSO), para 6.9.

Domicile of choice

7.10 Acquisition

As has been explained at **7.07** to **7.09** above, a domicile of choice can be acquired only by a person who is not incapacitated either by age or by unsoundness of mind. There are no formal steps to be taken for a person of full age and capacity to acquire a domicile of choice. As the Inland Revenue guidance note puts it:

> 'To do so, you must broadly leave your current country of domicile and settle in another country. You need to provide strong evidence that you intend to live there permanently or indefinitely.'[1]

In *Udny v Udny*,[2] Lord Westbury described a domicile of choice as:

> '... a conclusion or inference which the law derives from the fact of a man fixing voluntarily his sole or chief residence in a particular place, with the intention of continuing to reside there for an unlimited time.'[3]

Both elements must be present. As Lord Chelmsford put it in *Bell v Kennedy*:[4]

> '... a new domicile is not acquired until there is not only a fixed intention of establishing a permanent residence in some other country, but until also this intention has been carried out by actual residence there.'[5]

These two elements are known, respectively, as the *animus manendi* (the intention to remain) and the *factum* (the fact of residence) and, as foregoing dicta make clear, both are essential. Before considering each element individually, however, one point must be made. The 'country' to which both the *animus* and the *factum* relate must, for the purpose of determining whether a domicile of choice has been acquired under common law, be 'a territory subject to a distinctive legal system.'[6]

This follows from the third principle of domicile discussed at **7.04** above but, as explained there, the problem which arises when discussing domicile in the context of UK taxation is that, under the Taxes Acts, the question to be determined is whether a person is domiciled 'in the UK', ie, a territory which is *not* subject to a distinctive legal system. It is important to refer to the earlier discussion, therefore, and to bear in mind that where a reference is made to a 'country' or 'territory' in the following paragraphs, it is possible that, for the purposes of this work, the country or territory referred to may be the UK collectively and not necessarily Northern Ireland, Scotland or England and Wales individually.

---

1 IR20 (July 2008), para 4.5, see **Appendix 1** below.
2 (1869) LR 1 Sc & Div 441.
3 (1869) LR 1 Sc & Div 441 at 458.
4 (1868) LR 1 Sc & Div 307.
5 (1868) LR 1 Sc & Div 307 at 319.

6 *Re Fuld's Estate (No. 3)* [1968] P 675 at 684, per Scarman J reiterating the formula in *Henderson v Henderson* [1967] P 77 at 79.

7.11 Residence

The meaning of the term 'residence' has already been explored at some depth in the earlier chapters of this work but here a distinction must be drawn between residence as a connecting factor in its own right for the purposes of UK taxation and residence in the context of the acquisition of the connecting factor of domicile. In *IRC v Duchess of Portland*,[1] Nourse J said:

> 'Residence in a country for the purposes of the law of domicile is physical presence in that country as an inhabitant of it ... [I]n a case where the domiciliary divides his physical presence between two countries at a time ... it is necessary to look at all the facts in order to decide which of the two countries is the one he inhabits.'[2]

The Duchess of Portland had claimed that, by spending some 10 to 12 weeks each year in Quebec visiting relatives and maintaining her links with Canada (the land of her birth and the country to which she hoped eventually to return), she had acquired a domicile of choice in Canada. She spent the rest of her time living with her husband in England. Nourse J said:

> 'On those facts it appears clear to me that since 1948 the taxpayer has been physically present in this country as an inhabitant of it. Her physical presence in Quebec has been for periods of limited duration and for the purpose of maintaining her links with the country to which it is her intention ultimately to return. That is not enough to have made her an inhabitant of Quebec. In my judgment it is clear that she was resident in England on 1 January 1974 and that that residence was not displaced when she went to Canada in July 1974 or at any other time during the material period.'[3]

It has been shown that residence for tax purposes, ie, as a territorial connecting link *per se*, is a quality of the person which – despite judicial asseverations to the contrary – may be attributed to a person not according to its ordinary meaning in the speech of plain men but according to a special, forensic meaning derived from case law precedents and Revenue practice. It will be recalled, for instance, that the celebrated Mr Lysaght, who had a settled place of residence in Ireland, was attributed with UK residence status merely by reason of his regular monthly business trips to the UK during the course of which he stayed with his brother or at the Spa Hotel in Bath.[4] It has also been demonstrated that, because residence in its taxation context is a qualitative attribute, a person may (as in the case of Lysaght) be resident in two or more countries at the same time.[5] It is clear from the judgment of Nourse J, however, that neither of these possibilities is open so far as residence in the context of the acquisition of a domicile of choice is concerned. A person *may* be resident in a particular country for both taxation purposes *and* domicile purposes, but he will not necessarily be so. Residence for domicile purposes involves actual inhabitance of a country,[6] dwelling within its borders rather than merely paying it visits, however extensive and regular those visits might be: and where a person inhabits two different countries, the only one in which he will be regarded as resident for domicile purposes is the one in which, on the balance of the facts, he is shown to have his 'chief residence'.[7]

The length of a person's residence in a particular country may be of great importance in determining whether or not a person has acquired a domicile of choice in that country, but it is not in itself determinative of the matter. As Lord Chelmsford said in *Bell v Kennedy*:[8]

'It may be conceded that if the intention of permanently residing in a place exists, a residence in pursuance of that intention, however short, will establish domicile.'[9]

This principle was reiterated (with the insertion of an interesting additional clause) by Nourse J in *Re Clore (No 2)*:[10]

'... if the evidence [of intention] is there, particularly perhaps where the motive is the avoidance of taxes, the necessary intention will not be held to be missing merely because the period of actual residence is a short one.'[11]

The fact of residence does, however, raise a presumption of domicile in the country of residence[12] and this presumption grows with the length of the period of residence so that, in some instances, it will be sufficient to override declarations of contrary intention[13] and will require a person's actual removal elsewhere if it is to be rebutted.[14] In *Udny v Udny*,[15] Lord Chelmsford said:

'Time is always a material element in questions of domicil; and if there is nothing to counteract its effect, it may be conclusive upon the subject.'[16]

Anderson v Laneuville[17] provides an interesting illustration of the point. The case concerned Anderson, a person born in 1768 with an Irish domicile of origin who, at the age of 67 (by which time he had acquired an English domicile of choice) traced, and thereafter until his death some 24 years later, cohabited with, in France, a widow, Madame Laneuville, who, some 46 years earlier, had risked her life in helping him to escape the Terror of the revolution in France where he was then being educated. Anderson had, it seems, expressed some intention of returning to England should Madame Laneuville have predeceased him, but on appeal from the Prerogative Court of Canterbury, that one fact was held to carry insufficient weight to counteract the effect of the length of Anderson's residence in France, and that long period of residence was held to lead inevitably to the conclusion that Anderson had died domiciled in France.

Thus it was in the more recent case of *Re Furse, Furse v IRC*.[18] William King Furse was born in Rhode Island in 1883 and had a Rhode Island domicile of origin. At the age of four, he was brought to England by his father but, after completing his education here, he returned to America, married and remained in employment there until 1916. He then left

7.11 Domicile

America to serve in the British army in the 1914–18 war. Upon demobilisation in 1919 he returned to New York where his wife had purchased a house and he found employment there. In 1923 Furse and his wife and children moved to England and bought a farm in West Hoathly. There Furse lived until his death 40 years later. From time to time between 1923 and the early 1950s, Furse and his wife contemplated a return to America and in the 1940s actually inspected a farm in Maryland. In the early 1950s Furse decided, however, that he would not return to America unless he became incapable of leading an active life on his farm in England. Fox J, declaring that Furse died domiciled in England, said:

> '... the facts ... show a man deeply settled in England. He came to England at the age of four; he died in England at the age of 80. Of the intervening 76 years he spent 58 in England (in the sense that England was his normal place of abode in those years) and three or four in the British army ... [He] was wholly integrated into the English community in which he lived. There is no doubt at all, as I see it, that the life which he was living in England was the life he wanted to go on living to the end of his life ... In my view, by the time of his death, the balance of probabilities is that he can have had no real intention of leaving; a fact which is emphasised by the vagueness of his expressed intentions.'[19]

There was, to use Lord Chelmsford's words, nothing (or nothing sufficiently concrete in the way of intention or surrounding circumstances) to counteract the effect of time, and time was, therefore, conclusive on the subject. This is not to say, however, that residence of long duration will alone suffice to establish domicile. It will not. As the Inland Revenue guidance note points out:

> 'Living in another country for a long time, although an important factor, is not enough in itself to prove you have acquired a new domicile.'[20]

This follows from what Cottenham LC said in *Munro v Munro*:[21]

> 'Residence alone has no effect, per se, though it may be most important as a ground from which to infer intention.'[22]

In both *Anderson v Laneuville*[23] and *Re Furse, Furse v IRC*,[24] that was where the significance of the long residence of Anderson and Furse lay. All the evidence suggested that, despite their vague assertions of a possible return to their native lands, Anderson and Furse would have remained where they were, however long they had lived; and the courts, therefore, permitted the *animus* of true intention to be inferred from the *factum* of residence.

Where, however, there is evidence to the contrary – something sufficiently concrete to counteract the effect of the duration of residence – the duration of residence will not be conclusive upon the subject as *Ramsay v Liverpool Royal Infirmary*[25] illustrates. George Bowie (the validity of whose will was in question) was born in Glasgow in 1845 and acquired from his father a Scottish domicile of origin. Upon reaching the age of 37 he gave up his employment as a commercial traveller and steadfastly refused to work again throughout the remainder of his life. For

10 years he 'lived on the bounty' of his mother and sisters in Glasgow, then, in 1892, he moved to lodgings in Liverpool and for the next 21 years sponged instead on his brother. Upon his brother's death, Bowie moved into his brother's house and for the next eight years sponged on his sister until she died in 1920. He remained at his brother's house and died in Liverpool (where he had arranged to be buried) seven years later. Bowie boasted of being a Glasgow man but during the 36 years he lived in England he refused to return to Scotland, even for his mother's funeral. He left England only twice, once to visit America and once to holiday in the Isle of Man. On those facts, the House of Lords held unanimously that Bowie had *not* acquired a domicile of choice in England but that his Scottish domicile of origin was still operative at the date of his death. Their lordships were convinced that declarations by Bowie to the effect that he would never return to Scotland were mere posturing and that, had Bowie's source of funds dried up, he would, in fact, have gone back there. That, plus the fact that there was no evidence to show that Bowie had made his permanent home in England was, in their view, sufficient to quash the inference of intention to which Bowie's 36 years of residence in England would otherwise have given rise. Lord Macmillan said:

> 'Prolonged actual residence is an important item of evidence of ... volition, but it must be supplemented by other facts and circumstances indicative of intention. The residence must answer a qualitative as well as a quantitative test.'[26]

IRC v Bullock[27] provides a modern (and much more convincing) illustration of the application of this principle. Group Captain Bullock had a domicile of origin in Nova Scotia but came to England in 1932 and joined the Royal Air Force. He intended to return to Canada on completing his service but, in 1946, he married an Englishwoman some three years his junior. Between then and 1960, Bullock and his wife made several trips to Canada and, upon leaving the RAF in 1959, Bullock would have liked them to move there permanently. His wife did not wish to do so, however, so Bullock took up civilian employment in England until 1961 when an inheritance enabled him to retire completely. Until 1966, Bullock continued to try to persuade his wife to move with him to Canada, but thereafter resigned himself to the fact that she would never do so. In that year, however, he made a will under Nova Scotia law in which he declared that his domicile was and would continue to be the Province of Nova Scotia and that he would return and remain there upon his wife's death. Bullock retained his Canadian nationality and passport, never acquired British nationality or a British passport, refused to vote in local or parliamentary elections, maintained close contact with Canadian relatives and friends, and was a regular reader of a Toronto newspaper. On these facts the Commissioners found that Bullock was not domiciled in England and the Court of Appeal (reversing Brightman J's judgment in the High Court) upheld the Commissioners' finding. Bullock's residence in England, though over 40 years in duration, was accompanied at all times by a clear and definite intention to return to Canada upon the substantial possibility

7.11 *Domicile*

of his wife predeceasing him, and that was sufficient to counteract the effect of the element of time.

---

1 [1982] STC 149.
2 [1982] STC 149 at 155.
3 [1982] STC 149 at 155–156.
4 See **2.13** above.
5 See **2.09** above.
6 *IRC v Duchess of Portland* [1982] STC 149 at 155, per Nourse J.
7 *Re Fuld's Estate (No 3)* [1968] P 675 at 682, per Scarman J.
8 (1868) LR 1 Sc & Div 307.
9 (1868) LR 1 Sc & Div 307 at 319.
10 [1984] STC 609.
11 [1984] STC 609 at 615.
12 *Bruce v Bruce* (1790) 2 Bos & P 229; *Bempde v Johnstone* (1796) 3 Ves 198.
13 *Stanley v Bernes* (1830) 3 Hagg Ecc 373; *Re Marrett, Chalmers v Wingfield* (1887) 36 Ch D 400.
14 *Hodgson v De Beauchesne* (1858) 12 Moo PC 285.
15 (1869) LR 1 Sc & Div 441.
16 (1869) LR 1 Sc & Div 441 at 455.
17 (1854) 9 Moo PC 325.
18 [1980] STC 596.
19 [1980] STC 596 at 606.
20 IR20 (July 2008), para 4.5, see **Appendix 1** below.
21 (1840) 7 Cl & Fin 842.
22 (1840) 7 Cl & Fin 842 at 877.
23 (1854) 9 Moo PC 325.
24 [1980] STC 596.
25 [1930] AC 588.
26 [1930] AC 588 at 598.
27 [1976] STC 409. See also *IRC v Cohen* (1937) 21 TC 301 where a person with an English domicile of origin who went to Australia at the age of 18 and did not return to England until 32 years later was nonetheless held to have retained his English domicile of origin throughout. Overturning the Commissioners' finding that Henry Cohen had acquired an Australian domicile of choice and never abandoned it, Finlay J held (at 315) that the true inference from the facts was that Henry Cohen 'intended to reside and to reside for a long time in Australia, but . . . he intended to reside there so long only as his business made that necessary, and his business connection with Australia ceased in 1911'.

7.12 Intention

The acquisition of a domicile of choice requires not only residence (in the sense of actual habitation of the chosen territory) but also an intention to make that territory 'the permanent home'.[1] The problem of what is meant by 'permanent' has lain at the root of many a case concerning domicile. Lord Chelmsford took a strict view of the matter. In *Moorhouse v Lord*[2] he said:

> 'The present intention of making a place a person's permanent home can exist only where he has no other idea than to continue there without looking forward to any event, certain or uncertain, which might induce him to change his residence. If he has in contemplation some event upon the happening of which residence will cease, it is not correct to call this even a present intention of making it a permanent home. It is rather a present intention of making it a temporary home, though for a period indefinite and contingent.'[3]

But others thought that far too strict. In *A-G v Pottinger*,[4] Bramwell B said:

> 'There is not a man who has not contingent intentions to do something that would be very much to his benefit if the occasion arises. But if every such intention or expression of intention prevented a man having a fixed domicil, no man would ever have a domicil at all, except his domicil of origin.'[5]

The less absolute view of the nature of the necessary intention may be discerned in Lord Westbury's statement in *Udny v Udny*[6] that the residence which is the other necessary element in the acquisition of a domicile of choice:

> '... must be a residence not for a limited period or particular purpose, but general and indefinite in its future contemplation.'[7]

It emerged even more openly when, in *Gulbenkian v Gulbenkian*,[8] Langton J said:

> 'The intention must be a present intention to reside permanently, but it does not mean that such intention must be irrevocable. It must be an intention unlimited in period, but not irrevocable in character.'[9]

And it is clearly discernible in the two widely-approved propositions concerning the acquisition of a domicile of choice made by Scarman J in *Re Fuld's Estate (No 3)*:[10]

> '... a domicile of choice is acquired when a man fixes voluntarily his sole or chief residence in a particular place with an intention of continuing to reside there for an unlimited time.'[11]

> 'A domicile of choice is acquired only if it be affirmatively shown that the *propositus* is resident within a territory subject to a distinctive legal system with the intention, formed independently of external pressures, of residing there indefinitely.'[12]

'Permanent', it will be noted, has become 'indefinite' or 'unlimited' and the difference that brings about may clearly be seen by comparing the dictum of Lord Cairns in *Bell v Kennedy*[13] and that of Buckley LJ in *IRC v Bullock*.[14] Lord Cairns said:

> 'The question ... is ... Whether [Bell] ... had determined to make, and had made, Scotland his home, with the intention of establishing himself and his family there, and ending his days in that country.'[15]

Buckley LJ said:

> 'I do not think that it is necessary to show that the intention to make a home in the new country is irrevocable or that the person whose intention is under consideration believes that for reasons of health or otherwise he will have no opportunity to change his mind. In my judgment, the true test is whether he intends to make his home in the new country until the end of his days *unless and until something happens to make him change his mind.*'[16]

Buckley LJ had not only the authority of Bramwell B to rely on in adding those final 11 words. In *Aikman v Aikman*,[17] Campbell LC (another nineteenth century judge) had said that a mere intention to return to a man's native country on a doubtful contingency would not prevent residence in a foreign country putting an end to his domicile of origin.

Given that Scarman J and Buckley J have accurately stated the current judicial view of intention for domicile of choice purposes, however, the question then arises: what constitutes a 'doubtful contingency'; what is the 'something' which a person might have in contemplation without the necessary intention of indefinite or unlimited residence being found lacking? Scarman J has answered the question thus:

'If a man intends to return to the land of his birth upon a clearly foreseen and reasonably anticipated contingency, eg the end of his job, the intention required by law is lacking: but if he has in mind only a vague possibility, such as making a fortune (a modern example might be winning a football pool) or some sentiment about dying in the land of his fathers, such a state of mind is consistent with the intention required by law. But no clear line can be drawn; the ultimate decision in each case is one of fact.'[18]

And Buckley LJ has answered it in a similar manner:

'No doubt, if a man who has made his home in a country other than his domicile of origin has expressed an intention to return to his domicile of origin or to remove to some third country on an event or condition of an indefinite kind (for example 'if I make a fortune' or 'when I've had enough of it'), it might be hard, if not impossible, to conclude that he retained any real intention of so returning or removing. Such a man, in the graphic language of James LJ in *Doucet v Geoghegan*,[19] is like a man who expects to reach the horizon; he finds it at last no nearer than it was at the beginning of his journey.'[20]

In both these passages, however, the contingency contemplated is of a 'pipe dream' character. What if the contingency contemplated is something more specific? In the event, said Buckley LJ, the question to be asked is:

'... is there a sufficiently substantial possibility of the contingency happening to justify regarding the intention to return as a real determination to do so on the contingency occurring rather than a vague hope or aspiration?'[21]

The facts of the case of *IRC v Bullock*[22] in which that test was propounded, have already been set out at **7.11** above and it is clear from those facts that the single contingency upon which Group Captain Bullock intended to return to Canada was the death of his wife. It was only his wife's refusal to live in Canada which was keeping the Group Captain here, and, as his wife was only two or three years his junior, there was a substantial possibility that she would predecease him. Accordingly, Buckley LJ held that his test question could be answered affirmatively: Group Captain Bullock did not have the necessary intention to make England his domicile of choice. When applied to the facts in *Re Furse, Furse v IRC*[23] (also set out at **7.11** above), however, Buckley LJ's test produced the opposite answer. William

Furse was happy and content in England and the only contingency upon which he intended to return to America was his becoming physically incapable of taking an active interest in his farm. Fox J said:

> 'It seems to me that the intention of [Furse] was indeed to continue to reside in England for an unlimited period. His intention was to continue to live here for the rest of his life, save on the contingency which he expressed. That contingency is so vague that I do not think it can be regarded as imposing any clear limitation on the period of his residence. I do not believe that he was ever prepared to face up to such a limitation. The contingency is of the sort which Simon P in *Qureshi v Qureshi*[24] described as 'open-ended'... I think that, when [Furse] died in his 81st year, still in England and still with no arrangements made for leaving England, one could not realistically regard his permanent home as other than in England. He intended to live out his days here, save on a contingency so vaguely expressed that I do not think, against the history of his life, it could be regarded for practical purposes as limiting that intention.'[25]

It will have been noted that in many of the extracts from judgments given in this section the words 'present intention' are used. The force of the adjective 'present' emphasises that what must be considered is the state of a person's mind at the time when the acquisition of a domicile of choice is alleged to have taken place. Subsequent variations in that intention are irrelevant[26] unless accompanied or followed by appropriate action.[27]

It should not be overlooked, however, that evidence of a subsequent change of mind might, in some instances, lead the court to infer that the original intention to remain indefinitely in the country of choice was not as settled as the evidence of that original intention indicated.

Although actual residence and the intention to reside indefinitely must concur before a domicile of choice can be created, the intention may precede or succeed the commencement of residence. The person who decides to emigrate to Quebec will possess the intention which is one element in the creation of a Quebec domicile of choice before he establishes the residence which is the other essential element. The refugee escaping persecution may, on the other hand, establish residence before he acquires the intention to remain indefinitely in the land in which he resides.

The only remaining point to be made concerning intention is that it is only the intention to remain indefinitely in a country which is relevant to the acquisition of a domicile of choice. If a person has that intention and there comes a time when the intention coincides with actual residence, a domicile of choice is acquired whether it was also the person's intention to acquire a domicile of choice or not. Thus, in *Re Steer*,[28] Mr Steer, an Englishman who established his permanent home in Hamburg and died there 50 years later, was held to have died domiciled in Germany even though, on one of his temporary visits to England, he had made a will in which he declared that although he was returning to Hamburg he had no intention of renouncing his English domicile of origin. The principle governing this matter was succinctly stated over a century ago:

> 'If the intention [to reside indefinitely in a particular country] exists and if it is sufficiently carried into effect certain legal consequences follow from it, whether

7.12 *Domicile*

such consequences are intended or not and perhaps even though the person in question may have intended the exact opposite.'[29]

---

1 *Whicker v Hume* (1858) 7 HL Cas 124 at 160, per Lord Cranworth.
2 (1863) 10 HL Cas 272.
3 (1863) 10 HL Cas 272 at 285–286.
4 (1861) 30 LJ Ex 284.
5 (1861) 30 LJ Ex 284 at 292.
6 (1869) LR 1 Sc & Div 441.
7 (1869) LR 1 Sc & Div 441 at 458.
8 [1937] 4 All ER 618.
9 [1937] 4 All ER 618 at 627.
10 [1968] P 675.
11 [1968] P 675 at 682.
12 [1968] P 675 at 684.
13 (1868) LR 1 Sc & Div 307.
14 [1976] STC 409.
15 *Bell v Kennedy* (1868) LR 1 Sc & Div 307 at 311.
16 *IRC v Bullock* [1976] STC 409 at 415. Author's italics.
17 (1861) 4 LT 374 at 376.
18 *Re Fuld's Estate (No 3)* [1968] P 675 at 685, per Scarman J.
19 (1878) 9 Ch D 441 at 457.
20 *IRC v Bullock* [1976] STC 409 at 416.
21 *IRC v Bullock* [1976] STC 409 at 416.
22 [1976] STC 409.
23 [1980] STC 596.
24 [1971] 1 All ER 325 at 340.
25 *Re Furse, Furse v IRC* [1980] STC 596 at 606.
26 *Re Marrett, Chalmers v Wingfield* (1887) 36 Ch D 400.
27 See **7.15** below.
28 (1858) 3 H & N 594. See also *Re Lawton* discussed at **7.14** below.
29 *Douglas v Douglas* (1871) LR 12 Eq 617 at 644–645.

7.13 Motive as evidence of intention

It will have been noted that the first of Scarman J's two propositions concerning the acquisition of a domicile of choice, quoted at **7.12** above contains the words 'fixes *voluntarily* his sole or chief residence', and that the second contains the words 'with the intention, *formed independently of external pressures*, of residing'. Those words draw attention to the fact that the acquisition of a domicile of choice presupposes a freedom of choice. As Lord Westbury put it in *Udny v Udny*:[1]

> 'There must be a residence freely chosen, and not prescribed or dictated by any external necessity....'[2]

If it can be shown that a person resides where he does, not by choice but by constraint, the necessary intention will be lacking and no change of domicile will be imputed to the involuntary exile.

The most obvious example of residence by constraint rather than through choice is imprisonment in some country other than that of the existing domicile. No prisoner, during the term of his imprisonment, will acquire a new domicile in the country of his imprisonment, even if the imprisonment is for a very long term, for his residence is not a matter of choice.³

Another example of constraint is the persecution which may impel a person to flee his existing country of domicile for some other country. Although the residence in the country of refuge will be a matter of free choice, the inference at law will be that the refugee will return to his homeland upon it being safe for him to do so and he will, therefore, prima facie lack the intention to reside permanently in the country of refuge which would be necessary in order to attribute him with a domicile of choice in that country. It might be, of course, that a refugee will acquire such an intention during the course of his exile.⁴

A fugitive from justice is in much the same position as the refugee except that, if his crime is such that he will always (or for a very long time) be liable to proceedings in the country from which he has fled, there will be a presumption at law that he has selected his country of refuge with the intention of residing there indefinitely.⁵ His departure will have been a matter of constraint but his establishment of residence elsewhere will have been a matter of free choice.

'The demands of creditors' was one of Lord Westbury's examples of an external necessity which might result in a person residing where he would not otherwise reside.⁶ So it was with Colonel Udny and his residence in France. But the fact that a person has fled the country to escape his creditors will not necessarily mean that he cannot acquire a domicile of choice in the country to which he has fled. It will depend on circumstances: the size of the debts, the likelihood of them ultimately being met, how long their discharge is likely to take, and the imminence of recovery proceedings.

The invalid who, although in no immediate danger of untimely death, settles for the sake of his health in a country other than the country of his existing domicile is regarded at law as doing so out of choice rather than out of constraint. In the case of *Hoskins v Matthews*,⁷ for example, Turner LJ said that Mr Matthews, an Englishman who, at the age of 60, had gone to Florence suffering from a spinal injury and had died there 12 years later, was not, when he first took up residence in Florence,

> '... in any immediate danger or apprehension. He was, no doubt, out of health, and he went abroad for the purpose of trying the effect of other remedies and other climates. That he would have preferred settling in England I have little doubt, but I think he was not driven to settle in Italy by any cogent necessity. I think that in settling there he was exercising a preference, and not acting upon a necessity, and I cannot venture to hold that in such a case the domicil cannot be changed.'⁸

If, however, the change of environment is a matter of life or death, or if, death being imminent and inevitable, the change of climate will alleviate suffering, there will, it seems, be no presumption of a change in domicile.⁹

The 'tax exile' who, in order to escape the incidence of taxation in the country of his existing domicile, settles in a country with a less harsh tax regime, will, it seems, be presumed to intend to remain in the new country permanently. In *Re Clore (No 2)*,¹⁰ Nourse J said that even a short period of residence would be sufficient to establish a domicile of choice 'if the evidence is there, particularly perhaps where the motive is the avoidance of taxes.'[11]

In the *Clore* case, there were, according to Nourse J, three areas where the evidence supported Sir Charles Clore's acquisition of a domicile of choice in Monaco. One was the severance of the more important of his connections with England where Sir Charles had his domicile of origin. Another was the establishment of connections with Monaco including residence there. But the most important, in Nourse J's eyes, was that:

> '... the professional advice which Sir Charles received was given not solely with the immediate object of his acquiring a non-resident status for income and capital gains tax purposes, but with the long-term objective of his acquiring a foreign domicile. Further, unless the operation was to be at least partially counter-productive, it was essential that the new country should be one where no tax was payable. Monaco was chosen because it was the only tax haven with which Sir Charles was familiar and the only one which could have been acceptable to him.'[12]

Against the evidence in those three areas, however, was the evidence of four of his close friends who were unanimous in their testimony that Sir Charles was unhappy in Monaco and had never, in his heart of hearts, abandoned England. All his actions from mid-1978 until his death in London on 26 July 1979 were tentative and, right up to the time of his death, he was showing an interest in acquiring residential properties in France and Israel. Accordingly, Nourse J held that Sir Charles died domiciled in England. That decision must not, however, be allowed to obscure the fact that, because Sir Charles had resided in Monaco and his motive for residing there was tax avoidance, Nourse J accepted that there was a presumption at law that a domicile of choice had been acquired in Monaco. As with any presumption at law, however, the presumption to which a tax avoidance motive will give rise may be rebutted by other evidence, and in the *Clore* case it was rebutted by the evidence of parol declarations made by Sir Charles in his final years and testified to by his four friends.

It must finally be pointed out that the residence of a person in a country other than the country of his existing domicile will give rise to no presumption that a domicile of choice has been acquired in the new country if the person is there in pursuit of what Lord Westbury called 'the duties of office'.[13] These have been held to include the duties of a consul,[14] chief justice,[15] embassy attaché,[16] naval officer,[17] and army officer.[18] Such a negative presumption may, of course, be rebutted by evidence to the contrary.[19]

---

1 (1869) LR 1 Sc & Div 441.
2 (1869) LR 1 Sc & Div 441 at 458.
3 *Re the late Emperor Napoleon Bonaparte* (1853) 2 Rob Eccl 606.
4 *De Bonneval v De Bonneval* (1838) 1 Curt 856. See also *Steiner v IRC* (1973) 49 TC 13 where a refugee from the Nazi persecution of Jews made his home in England in 1939 but was held not to have acquired an English domicile of choice here until about 1950 when the facts were such as to indicate that he had formed the intention of remaining permanently in England.
5 *Re Martin, Loustalan v Loustalan* [1900] P 211.

6 *Udny v Udny* (1869) LR 1 Sc & Div 441 at 458.
7 (1856) 8 De GM & G 13.
8 (1856) 8 De GM & G 13 at 28–29.
9 See Lord Kingsdown's comments in *Moorhouse v Lord* (1863) 10 HL Cas 272 at 292.
10 [1984] STC 609.
11 [1984] STC 609 at 615.
12 [1984] STC 609 at 614.
13 *Udny v Udny* (1869) LR 1 Sc & Div 441 at 458.
14 *Sharpe v Crispin* (1869) LR 1 P & D 611.
15 *A-G v Lady Rowe* (1862) 1 H & C 31.
16 *A-G v Kent* (1862) 31 LJ Ex 391.
17 *Re Patten's Goods* (1860) 6 Jur NS 151.
18 *Firebrace v Firebrace* (1878) 4 PD 63.
19 *Donaldson v Donaldson* [1949] P 363.

7.14 Proof of intention

As Scarman J said in *Re Fuld's Estate (No 3)*:[1]

> 'It is beyond doubt that the burden of proving the abandonment of a domicile of origin and the acquisition of a domicile of choice is upon the party asserting the change. But it is not so clear what is the standard of proof: is it to be proved beyond reasonable doubt or upon the balance of probabilities, or does the standard vary according to whether one seeks to establish abandonment of domicile of origin or merely a switch from one domicile of choice to another? Or is there some other standard? ... The formula of proof beyond reasonable doubt is not frequently used in probate cases and I do not propose to give it currency. It is enough that the authorities emphasise that the conscience of the court ... must be satisfied by the evidence. The weight to be attached to evidence, the inferences to be drawn, the facts justifying the exclusion of doubt and the expression of satisfaction will vary according to the nature of the case. Two things are clear – first, that unless the judicial conscience is satisfied by evidence of change, the domicile of origin persists: and secondly, that the acquisition of a domicile of choice is a serious matter not to be lightly inferred from slight indications or casual words.'[2]

Those statements were later endorsed by Orr LJ who, in *Buswell v IRC*,[3] said:

> 'I ... accept the statements as accurate and would only add that in referring to the judicial conscience I am satisfied that Scarman J was not recognising the existence of some general standard of proof intermediate between the criminal and civil standards but was merely emphasising that in the application of the civil standard the degree of proof required will vary with the subject-matter of the case.'[4]

The approach to assessing evidence of intention was neatly expressed by Mummery LJ in *Agulian & Anor v Cyganik*:[5]

> '(1) Although it is helpful to trace ... life events chronologically and to halt on the journey from time to time to take stock, this question cannot be decided in stages. [T]he court must look back at the whole of the deceased's life, at what he had done with his life, at what life had done to him and at what were his inferred

7.14 *Domicile*

intentions in order to decide whether he had acquired a domicile of choice in England by the date of his death. Soren Kierkegaard's aphorism that 'Life must be lived forwards, but can only be understood backwards' resonates in the biographical data of domicile disputes.
(2) Secondly, special care must be taken in the analysis of the evidence about isolating individual factors from all the other factors present over time and treating a particular factor as decisive.'

If the judicial conscience is to be satisfied that a change in domicile has taken place, the courts must subject every department of a person's life to the most searching scrutiny. The length and nature of his residence in the country in which it is asserted that he has acquired a domicile will, of course, be a factor of particular interest since, as has been explained,[6] residence gives rise at law to a presumption of domicile, and intention may be inferred from residence if the residence is of sufficient length and there is other evidence to support such an inference. His motives too must be examined for, as has been explained at **7.13** above, a person's motive in taking up residence in a country other than that of his existing domicile may give rise to a presumption of, or against, a change in domicile. But the court's concern is never confined merely to residence and the motive for residence. As Lord Atkinson said of *Winans v A-G*[7] in *Casdagli v Casdagli*:[8]

> '... the tastes, habits, conduct, actions, ambitions, health, hopes, and projects of Mr Winans deceased were all considered as keys to his intention to make a home in England.[9]

It is often said that if a person wishes to ensure that his change of domicile will withstand the scrutiny of the courts he must not only take up residence in the country of choice but should purchase a property there and dispose of any property he has in the country he has abandoned, that he should apply for citizenship of the new country, obtain a passport in the new country and relinquish his existing passport, close all bank accounts in the abandoned country and open new accounts in the country of choice, relinquish credit cards and obtain new ones in the country of choice, resign any directorships in the country he has abandoned and acquire business interests in the country of choice, sever membership of clubs, societies, religious organisations etc in the abandoned country and join clubs etc in the country of choice, vote in the new country's elections, become involved in its politics and socially integrated into its life, educate his children in its schools, have his will drawn up under its laws and make arrangements to be buried or cremated there. Such a checklist has a certain value, being a list of factors to which particular significance has been attached in cases which have come before the courts at different times. But the approach is wrong. A person who has genuinely made his 'permanent home' in a new country will, in those and many other ways, manifest the reality of his intention to live out his days as an inhabitant of the land to which he has gone; but the person who is engaged in nothing more than a cosmetic exercise designed to conceal the fact that 'in spite of all temptations to belong to other nations, he remains an Englishman'[10] is likely to betray his lack of genuine intention no matter how scrupulously he adheres to a list of 'dos and don'ts'. No one factor will, in itself, be decisive, and even a factor which seems of supreme significance when viewed in isolation may carry little weight when set against all other factors. Thus, for example, in *Wahl v A-G*,[11] the fact that a person with a German domicile of origin and German nationality had become a naturalised British subject was not regarded as being at all conclusive:

> 'I am far from saying that an application for naturalisation is not a matter to be carefully considered as part of the evidence in a case of domicile, but it must be regarded as one of the totality of facts and it cannot assume the dominant importance attached to it in the judgment of the trial judge ... It is not the law either that a change of domicile is a condition of naturalisation, or that naturalisation involves necessarily a change of domicile.'[12]

In making his application for naturalisation, Wahl had made a statutory declaration to the effect that he intended to continue to reside permanently within the UK. That too formed part of the evidence of his intention and, since such declarations are frequently made by persons changing their domicile, their value must now be considered. In *F v IRC*[13] the executor of F, a former Iranian national who had died in 1993, appealed against the determination of the Revenue that he had been domiciled in the UK for the years of assessment 1986–87 to 1992–93 inclusive. F had operated an accountancy business in Iran. He had bought land with a view to developing it, owned three houses and had constructed a large family home. At the time of the Iranian revolution he had sent his wife and children to live in the UK while remaining himself in Iran. At the time of the US hostage crisis F had decided to remain outside Iran at the same time he had been placed on an exit barred list due to alleged outstanding tax liabilities. In 1980 he had been granted indefinite leave to remain in the UK. He had subsequently applied for naturalisation, falsely claiming that he had left Iran to escape religious persecution. Up until the time of his death, F had made efforts at getting the exit bar removed. He had continued to consider Iran as his home. The Court in allowing the appeal held that the Revenue had not discharged the burden of proof to demonstrate that F had not abandoned his Iranian domicile. Having regard to the evidence, it had always been F's intention to return to Iran permanently during the relevant years for assessment. His acquisition of British citizenship and a British passport had not affected his domicile of origin in Iran, and so *Wahl v A-G* applied. He had been keen to gain the necessary documentation that would enable him to continue to travel freely in the furtherance of his business interests and had been willing to lie in order to gain such documentation. His return to Iran had been precluded by the exit bar. Such external pressures had prevented F from forming a free intention to acquire another domicile.

An example of the difficulties to which a written declaration might give rise is found in *Buswell v IRC*.[14] Leslie Buswell had a Transvaal domicile of origin acquired from his father who had a Transvaal domicile of choice. In 1928, when Buswell was seven years old, he and his parents moved to England so that Buswell could be educated here. Following his education and a brief period which Buswell spent as a teacher in Tenbury Wells, he was called-up in 1941 and served in the Royal Indian Navy. Upon demobilisation in 1945, he took employment in India and remained there until 1952 when he returned to England where his father was living in a poor state of health. Once in England, he took employment with a publishing firm for six months, then obtained a position with British Olivetti Ltd which he held until 1963. In 1955, Buswell obtained a South African passport and elected for South African nationality when South Africa left the Commonwealth, and, in 1958, wrote to a cousin in South Africa saying he intended to return there one day. In 1961, he married an Englishwoman of means who was agreeable to settling eventually in South Africa, and, by her, had children who were educated in England but were registered as South African nationals. In 1968, Buswell and his wife visited South Africa (Buswell's first visit there for 40 years) and bought a property in which they thereafter spent some three months of each year. Buswell claimed that, for the years 1961–62 to 1967–68, he was 'not domiciled in the UK' for the purposes of ITA 1952 s 132 (now ICTA 1988 s 65(4)). That claim was resisted by the Inland Revenue on the grounds that, on 11 November 1952, Buswell had completed a Revenue questionnaire (Form P86) by answering 'Yes' to the question 'Do you propose to remain permanently in the UK?' and inserting a dash in answer to the next question: 'If not, how long do you expect to remain in this country?' The Commissioners attached great weight to those replies and accordingly found that Buswell had acquired an English domicile of choice. The High Court upheld the Commissioners' finding on appeal, but the Court of Appeal reversed it. Orr LJ said.

> 'The crucial question ... is ... whether the Commissioners, in coming to their conclusion, attributed to the answers on Form P86 a weight which in all the circumstances they could not reasonably bear. For this purpose it is necessary to consider both the terms of the questions asked on the form and the circumstances in which it may reasonably be supposed that [Buswell] answered them ... [T]he form was not intended by the Revenue to ascertain domicile and it nowhere used that word ... A person faced with ... mutually exclusive questions, would, I think, be very likely to consider that he was not expected to say "I do not know" in answer to the second question, an answer which would have to be given if he said "No" to the first ... I find ... that, in attributing a decisive importance to [Buswell's] answers on the Form P86, given at a time when he had been back in this country for less than five months after an absence of ten years, and against the background to which I have referred, the Commissioners acted "upon a view of the facts which could not reasonably be entertained".'[15]

Often a written declaration of intention will appear in a person's will, taking a form similar to that appearing in the will of Frank Lawton in *Re Lawton*:[16]

> 'Inasmuch as I am a British subject having my original domicile in England (which domicile I have never relinquished or abandoned) it is my wish and intention that this my will ... shall be construed and operate so far as the case admits as if I were now and remained until my death domiciled in England.'[17]

The value of such a declaration was assessed by Romer LJ in *A-G v Yule and Mercantile Bank of India*[18] as follows:

> 'For myself, I am not prepared to attach any importance to a declaration by a man as to his domicile unless there is some evidence to show that the man knew what 'domicile' means. A declaration by a man made orally or in writing that he intends to remain in a certain country will, if not inconsistent with the facts, be of assistance in determining the question whether he has become domiciled there. Domicile is, however, a legal conception on which the views of a layman are not of much assistance.'[19]

Lawton had, in fact, left England before he had attained the age of 21 and, having lived and worked in Argentina and Spain, retired to France where he died some 63 years later. Upjohn J held that, despite the declaration in his will, Lawton died domiciled in France.

Where the assertion of intention as to residence has been made orally, the testimony of the person to whom it was made is admissible as evidence of intention but, if made long after the assertion itself was made, will be treated with caution:

> 'To entitle such declarations to any weight, the court must be satisfied not only of the veracity of the witnesses who depose to such declarations, but of the accuracy of their memory, and that the declarations contain a real expression of the intention of the deceased.'[20]

Where the assertion is actually made by the person whose domicile is being determined during the court proceedings at which the determination of his domicile is to be made, the assertion will, of course, carry very little weight indeed. In *Bell v Kennedy*[21] the Lord Chancellor said of Bell's own testimony:

> '... it is to be accepted with very considerable reserve. An Appellant has naturally, on an issue like the present, a very strong bias calculated to influence his mind, and he is, moreover, speaking of what was his intention some twenty-five years ago.'[22]

---

1 [1968] P 675.
2 [1968] P 675 at 685–686.
3 [1974] STC 266.
4 [1974] STC 266 at 273.
5 [2006] EWCA Civ 129 at para 49.
6 See **7.11** above.
7 [1904] AC 287.
8 [1919] AC 145.
9 [1919] AC 145 at 178.
10 W S Gilbert, *HMS Pinafore*, Act II.
11 (1932) 147 LT 382.
12 (1932) 147 LT 382 at 385, per Lord Atkin.
13 [2000] 1 WTLR 505.
14 (1974) 49 TC 334.
15 (1974) 49 TC 334 at 362–363.
16 (1958) 37 ATC 216. See also *Re Steer* discussed at **7.12** above.
17 (1958) 37 ATC 216 at 218.
18 (1931) 145 LT 9.
19 (1931) 145 LT 9 at 17.

20 *Hodgson v De Beauchesne* (1858) 12 Moo PC 285 at 325.
21 (1868) LR 1 Sc & Div 307.
22 (1868) LR 1 Sc & Div 307 at 313.

7.15 Change of domicile of choice

It should by now have become clear that the courts will not easily be satisfied that a domicile of origin has been replaced by a domicile of choice. The presumption of a domicile of origin's continuance is of the utmost strength and, compared with a domicile of choice:

'... its character is more enduring, its hold stronger and less easily shaken off.'[1]

This is because a domicile of origin is conferred on a person by operation of law whereas, as has been explained,[2] a domicile of choice is acquired merely *animo et facto*. Once acquired, however, a domicile of choice may be extinguished *animo et facto* also, ie, by an intention and an act. The act is the leaving of the country of the domicile of choice and the intention is the intention not to resume permanent residence there. This last is technically referred to as an *animus non revertendi*. Such an *animus* does not, it should be noted, include within it a decision to reside permanently elsewhere. In *Udny v Udny*,[3] the Lord Chancellor summed up the whole matter as follows:

'... if the choice of a new abode and actual settlement there constitute a change of the original domicil, then the exact converse of such a procedure, viz the intention to abandon the new domicil, and an actual abandonment of it, ought to be equally effective to destroy the new domicil. That which may be acquired may surely be abandoned, and though a man cannot, for civil reasons, be left without a domicil, no such difficulty arises if it be simply held that the original domicil revives. That original domicil depended not on choice but attached itself to its subject on his birth, and it seems to be consonant both to convenience and to the currency of the whole law of domicil to hold that the man born with a domicil may shift and vary it as often as he pleases, indicating each change by intention and act, whether in its acquisition or abandonment; and, further, to hold that every acquired domicil is capable of simple abandonment *animo et facto* the process by which it was acquired, without its being necessary that a new one should be at the same time chosen, otherwise one is driven to the absurdity of asserting a person to be domiciled in a country which he has resolutely forsaken and cast off, simply because he may (perhaps for years) be deliberating before he settles himself elsewhere.'[4]

Just as a domicile of choice cannot be acquired *animo solo*, however, a domicile of choice cannot be abandoned unless the intention to leave the territory of the existing domicile of choice for good is accompanied by an actual departure from that territory. As Cotton LJ said in *Re Marrett*:[5]

'... in order to lose the domicil of choice once acquired, it is not only necessary that a man should be dissatisfied with his domicil of choice, and form an intention to leave it, but he must have left it, with the intention of leaving it permanently.'[6]

The application of this principle is to be found in *Zanelli v Zanelli*.[7] The case concerned an Italian who, having married an Englishwoman and lived with her in England, deserted her and returned to Italy. The wife petitioned for divorce in England claiming that the English courts had jurisdiction because immediately before deserting her, her husband was domiciled in England within the terms of the Matrimonial Causes Act 1973 s 13. The question before the court was whether that was so. It was accepted that, following the marriage, the woman's husband had acquired a domicile of choice in England and it was accepted also that, by the time of his desertion, he had formed the intention to return permanently to Italy. But did that bring about a loss of domicile of choice? Lord du Parcq decided that no, it did not:

'... although the husband may have given up an intention to reside here, he certainly had not given up residence here. The *factum* had not occurred.'[8]

Accordingly, the woman's petition was granted and her divorce (which would not have been permitted under Italian law) was granted under English law.

The question when the *factum* of departure does occur is not always an easy question to answer as *Re Raffenel's Goods*[9] illustrates. Madame Raffenel had a domicile of origin in England but, upon marrying a French naval officer, had acquired a French domicile of dependence. Following her husband's death, she decided to return permanently to England. She boarded ship at Calais with her children and baggage, having closed down her establishment in Dunkirk, but, before the ship left the harbour, became so ill that she had to disembark. She returned to Dunkirk where she later died. Sir Cresswell Cresswell said:

'I cannot think that the French domicil was abandoned so long as the deceased remained in the territory of France. It must be admitted that she never left France, and that intention alone is not sufficient.'[10]

Although that case was concerned with abandonment of a domicile of dependence, Lord du Parcq, in the case of *Zanelli v Zanelli*[11] which (as explained above) concerned the abandonment of a domicile of choice, expressly approved the decision in *Re Raffenel's Goods*[12] and drew no distinction between the two types of domicile in this connection. Speaking of Zanelli's desertion of his wife he said:

'... he cannot be said to have lost his domicile of choice even at the moment when he stepped into the train with his ticket in his pocket. Having regard to what was decided ... in *Re Raffenel's Goods* ... I do not think that, even when he stepped on board the ship which was to carry him to the Continent, he had yet lost his domicile of choice.'[13]

It should be noted, however, that in that case, Asquith LJ went even further:

'To change an English domicile of choice there must be both *animus* and *factum*, the *animus* being the formation of the intention, and the *factum*

7.15 *Domicile*

consisting in some outward and visible act evincing it such as leaving this country or, *perhaps more accurately, arriving in another.*'[14]

And on the strength of that dictum, Baker J held, in *Leon v Leon*,[15] that a person who had displaced his domicile of origin in British Guiana (now Guyana) by a domicile of choice in England but had then left England for good and returned to British Guiana, had:

'... kept his English domicile until he reverted to his domicile of origin on his arrival in British Guiana in August 1964.'[16]

This, it is suggested, was stretching Sir Cresswell Cresswell's dicta in *Re Raffenel's Goods*[17] too far. Surely, the domicile of origin of both Zanelli and Leon revived as soon as their respective ships left the territorial waters of the UK, not when they docked on the shores of their respective homelands.

It was said at the outset of this section that the *animus* required to effect the abandonment of a domicile of choice is an *animus non revertendi*, ie, an intention not to return. It must now be emphasised that (despite recent indications of some relaxation in this view)[18] such an *animus* does *not* cover a case of mere irresolution (*sine animo revertendi*). A person who leaves the country of his existing domicile of choice in a state of indecision as to whether or not he will return there retains his existing domicile of choice until such time as his indecision hardens into a decision never to return. This is illustrated by *Fielden v IRC*.[19] Fielden had an English domicile of origin but, in or about 1935, this was displaced by a Michigan domicile of choice when he married a Michigan resident and settled in that state of America with the intention of remaining there permanently. In 1943, Fielden and his wife moved to Burnley in Lancashire with the intention of helping in his father's ailing business, and they bought a house there. In 1947, Fielden became a director of his father's company and later became chairman and managing director. It seems that he then decided that he owed it to his father to remain in England until he was satisfied the business could continue successfully without him, but he asserted that, upon his retirement, he would return to America, though not necessarily to Michigan. At the time the case was heard, however, he was still living in Burnley, 22 years after leaving America. The Commissioners decided that, by 1954–55, the first of the years for which his domicile was in question, Fielden's English domicile of origin had revived, but they also found that his Michigan domicile of choice had been retained for some years after his return to England, probably until 1947. This was, it is suggested, because for those years he was merely *sine animo revertendi* to Michigan, not *animo non revertendi* to Michigan. Later, however, his intention to return to America in general became too vague to prevent him being regarded as *animo non revertendi* and thereupon his domicile of origin revived. The Commissioners' findings were upheld by Cross J who said:

'... it is not necessary, in order to retain a domicile of choice after a change of residence, to have an unwavering intention of returning to live in the place of domicile in all circumstances ... When [Fielden] came to England in 1943, he came under the stress of circumstances. He wanted to help his country and his father in the war; and the Commissioners have found – I think quite rightly found – that he did not there and then lose his Michigan domicile of choice. It would not, I think, matter for this purpose whether he then had an intention to go back as soon as possible to Michigan after the war, or simply to go back to some place in the United States after the war. But then one finds that after the war he buys a house here, that when he goes to the United States it is only for a short stay, and that he remains here continuously until the present time ... [H]e re-acquired his English domicile of origin about 1947 ... because ... such intention as he may thereafter have had of going to live somewhere in the United States after his retirement was really too vague and uncertain to prevent the re-acquisition of his English domicile of origin.'[20]

If a person leaves his domicile of choice *animo revertendi* but subsequently abandons his intention to return, his domicile of origin will, of course, thereupon revive.[21]

Finally, it should be noted that where a person *animo et facto* abandons one domicile of choice and *animo et facto* acquires another, his domicile of origin will revive for the duration of the interval, however brief, between the abandonment and the acquisition.[22]

---

1 *Winans v A-G* [1904] AC 287 at 290, per Lord Macnaghten; *F (F's Personal Representatives v IRC)* [2000] STC (SCD) 1.
2 See **7.10** above.
3 (1869) LR 1 Sc & Div 441.
4 (1869) LR 1 Sc & Div 441 at 450.
5 (1887) 36 Ch D 400.
6 (1887) 36 Ch D 400 at 407.
7 (1948) 64 TLR 556.
8 (1948) 64 TLR 556.
9 (1863) 3 Sw & Tr 49.
10 (1863) 3 Sw & Tr 49.
11 (1948) 64 TLR 556.
12 (1863) 3 Sw & Tr 49.
13 (1948) 64 TLR 556.
14 (1948) 64 TLR 556 at 557. Author's italics.
15 [1967] P 275.
16 [1967] P 275 at 282. These words must not be taken as some sort of authority for the proposition that presence in the domicile of origin is necessary for that domicile's revival. As *Tee v Tee* [1974] 1 WLR 213 clearly shows, it is not.
17 (1863) 3 Sw & Tr 49.
18 In *Re Flynn* [1968] 1 WLR 103 Megarry J said (*obiter* at 113) that 'mere negative absence of any intention' to resume residence, rather than a positive intention not to return, would suffice to bring a domicile of choice to an end, and this was approved in *Qureshi v Qureshi* [1971] 2 WLR 518 at 530; but see *Executors of Winifred Johnson Dec'd v HMRC* [2005] UKSPC 481.
19 (1965) 42 TC 501.
20 (1965) 42 TC 501 at 507–508.
21 *Tee v Tee* [1973] 3 All ER 1105.
22 *Harrison v Harrison* [1953] 1 WLR 865. The proposal of The Law Commission and the Scottish Law Commission is that this should cease to be so and that an abandoned domicile of choice should continue until a new domicile is acquired (Working Paper No 88 and Consultative Memorandum No 63, para 5.22).

7.16 Deemed domicile

In introducing the capital transfer tax (which has now been renamed 'inheritance tax'), the Finance Act 1975 s 45 provided that, under any of three sets of circumstances a person who was not domiciled in the UK under the common law rules described in this chapter was nevertheless to be treated as domiciled in the UK for most purposes of the tax. The provision relating to one of those three sets of circumstances was repealed by Finance (No 2) Act 1983 s 12 and the provisions describing the remaining two sets of circumstances have now been substantially re-enacted as the Inheritance Tax Act 1984 s 267(1)(a) and (b).

Section 267(1)(a) and (3) provides that a person not domiciled in the UK at the time of a transfer of value etc ('the relevant time') is to be treated as domiciled in the UK at that time if he was domiciled in the UK on or after 10 December 1974 and within the three years immediately preceding the relevant time.

In the absence of statutory definition to the contrary, 'year' means a period of 12 calendar months consisting of 365 days or 366 days in a leap year.[1]

The effect of this provision is to postpone (for inheritance tax purposes only) a person's acquisition of a domicile in some country outside the UK to a date three years after the date on which, according to common law rules, the acquisition of the new domicile actually took place. Thus, any transfer of value made by the person within the three years immediately following his acquisition of an overseas domicile will remain potentially subject to inheritance tax regardless of the *situs* of the asset.

This rule has no rational basis and is a transparently directed at keeping within the inheritance tax net for a period of time anyone who leaves the UK permanently. Superficially, it parallels a Revenue practice regarding the residence status of a person who leaves the UK for permanent residence abroad, ie that a decision on that person's claim to have become non-resident and not ordinarily resident in the UK will be postponed for three years and that during those three years the person's tax liabilities will be calculated on the basis that he remains a UK resident; but, in the case of residence, a decision at the end of three years that the person had become non-resident on his departure is then applied retrospectively to the date of departure and all assessments are revised accordingly. There is, however, nothing similarly provisional about the three year postponement of non-domiciled status.

Unlike s 267(1)(a), s 267(1)(b) is a rational piece of legislation which is designed to place a non-domiciled person who has lived in the UK for a long number of years on an equal footing with the UK domiciled taxpayer.[2] It (and s 267(3)) provides that a person not domiciled in the UK at the time a transfer of value etc takes place ('the relevant time') is to be treated as domiciled in the UK at that time if he was resident in the UK on or after 10 December 1974 and in not less than 17 of the 20 years of assessment ending with the year of assessment in which the relevant time falls. It should be noted, however, that, for the purposes of this provision:

'... the question of whether a person was resident in the UK in any year of assessment shall be determined as for the purposes of income tax.'[3]

Chapters 2 and 4 should, therefore, be studied in this context, in particular sections **2.08** to **2.10** and **4.06** and **4.07** above. A person will thus be likely to acquire residence status if his presence in the UK is of sufficiently long duration during a tax year for a territorial link to be established (183 days or more in the opinion of HMRC) *or* if the pattern of his visits to the UK in years prior to and subsequent to the tax year in question, though not in themselves of significant length, nevertheless establish a similar territorial link (an average of three or more months a year over a period of four or more tax years in the Revenue's view) *or* if visits to the UK which would otherwise be insignificant are given by ties such as nationality, family and business a significance sufficient to establish the kind of territorial link which residence status connotes.

The provision itself has two effects. The first is to bring persons who have never been domiciled in the UK into the inheritance tax net. The second (and often overlooked) effect is, unless the change of domicile takes place on 6 April, to keep a person who has been, but is no longer, domiciled in the UK within the inheritance tax net for up to almost a year longer than s 267(1)(a) will keep him there.

1 *IRC v Hobhouse* [1956] 1 WLR 1393.
2 See Official Report, Standing Committee A, 13 February 1975, cols 1645–1646.
3 IHTA 1984 s 267(4).

7.17 Domicile for tax treaty purposes

It should be noted that where (whether under these deemed domicile rules or not) a person is regarded under UK law as domiciled in the UK but is regarded under the law of a foreign state with which the UK has a double tax treaty covering estate and inheritance taxes as domiciled in that foreign state, the provisions of the treaty will apply so as to ensure that the person is treated by both the UK and the foreign state as being domiciled in one of the territories only for the purpose of that treaty.[1] Article 4(2) of the OECD 1982 draft double taxation convention on estates and inheritances provides for this to be achieved by a series of tests identical with those applied to determine fiscal residence as described at **2.22** above. A number of these treaties are, however, old and contain a variety of provisions addressing fiscal domicile quite differently from the OECD Model.

1 IHTA 1984 ss 158 and 267(2).

CHAPTER 8

Compliance and appeals

> *'The bell'*, said Noggs, as though in explanation; *'at home?'*
> *'Yes.'*
> *'To anybody?'*
> *'Yes.'*
> *'To the tax-gatherer?'*
> *'No! Let him call again.'*
>
> Dickens *Nicholas Nickleby* Ch 2

8.01 Introduction

Absence from the territory of the UK does not relieve compliance obligations or provide a defence against proceedings in the UK for the recovery of tax payable under an assessment. Any person chargeable to income tax or capital gains tax for a year of assessment and who has not received a notice requiring a return for that year of his total income and gains, must give to an officer of HMRC notice that he is so chargeable within six months from the end of that year.[1] Notice is not required in respect of certain classes of income where tax is deducted at source.[2] In *Whitney v IRC*,[3] Lord Wrenbury considered the obligation which ITA 1918 s 7(3) imposed on every person chargeable with supertax (a form of income taxation which no longer exists) to give notice that he was so chargeable, and said of Mr Whitney, an American citizen and a resident of New York who had received dividends in respect of shares in a UK corporation:

> If ... I am right in thinking that the non-resident alien is chargeable in respect of property in the UK, it was his duty to give that notice.[4]

In *IRC v Huni*,[5] for example, a Swiss national who was not resident in the UK argued that a notice to make a return for supertax purposes served on him at his Paris address was invalid since it had been served outside the territory of the UK. It followed, he said, that he could not have failed to make a return within the terms of the legislation (FA 1910 in relation to supertax) and that the Commissioners had, therefore, no jurisdiction to make an assessment to the best of their judgment. Furthermore, he contended, irrespective of the validity of the assessment, the notice of

183

assessment (also served on him at his Paris address) was as invalid (on the same grounds) as had been the notice requiring him to make a return. Rowlatt J did not agree. He said:

> 'A great deal has been said in the course of this argument about a non-resident and about an alien, but I think I am confronted with the question as to the operation of this Statute without the realm ... In the words of the Statute there is no distinction drawn between aliens or residents or non-residents or anything of that sort; the question really is as to whether the Statute is to be cut down so as not to serve notices abroad. Now the principle involved here is the principle that Acts of Parliament are prima facie not to be construed so as to assume jurisdiction without the realm – extra-territorial jurisdiction – so as to make the jurisdiction extra-territorial. And of course where it comes to the case of creating a duty abroad or creating an offence abroad – both of which of course can be done by Parliament – ... the Courts are bound to look narrowly at the Statute to see whether that is what is meant. But I apprehend there is no difficulty of that sort in the way if what the Statute really directs is the mere service of a notice, and that is all it is. There is no international difficulty in serving a notice abroad ... It may have consequences, but it is a mere notice ... I think there is involved in this machinery the mere giving of a notice as a preliminary to the Commissioners proceeding to do something which they are entitled to do ... and that I ought not to limit the words of this Section so as to make this notice as a mere notice null and void.'[6]

That being so, the assessment which followed Mr Huni's failure to make the return required of him was valid. Accordingly Rowlatt J turned to the question of the notice of assessment:

> 'The Respondent says that the notice of assessment is bad too, because it was served on him abroad. That I cannot think is bad. If a man has been validly assessed in England, what principle of international law is to be invoked by way of reflection to limit the words of the Statute which says that he may be told he has been assessed, I cannot conceive.'[7]

This judgment was approved by the House of Lords in the *Whitney* case[8] where Mr Whitney had advanced arguments against his assessability similar to those which had been advanced by Mr Huni. Lord Wrenbury said:

> 'There was sent to the Appellant by post addressed to him in the United States a notice under Section 7(2) requiring him to make a return. It is contended that there was no right to send him a notice so addressed. The case, it is contended, is similar to the case of service of a writ out of the jurisdiction. I do not agree ... It is not a step in a judicial proceeding, but a step which will create *inter partes* a state of things in which judicial proceedings can subsequently be taken in default of compliance. I think the notice was duly served. In my opinion *IRC v Huni* was rightly decided.'[9]

If notice is to be served validly under the Taxes Acts, therefore, all that is required is that it be served at the 'usual or last known place of residence' of the person on whom it is served, whether that place of residence be in the UK or an address overseas.[10]

The provisions described above relate to income tax and capital gains tax, but similar provisions exist in relation to corporation tax and inheritance tax.

1   TMA 1970 s 7.
2   TMA 1970 s 7(3).
3   (1924) 10 TC 88.
4   (1924) 10 TC 88 at 114.
5   (1923) 8 TC 466.
6   (1923) 8 TC 466 at 474.
7   (1923) 8 TC 466 at 474.
8   (1924) 10 TC 88.
9   (1924) 10 TC 88 at 113.
10 TMA 1970 s 115.

8.02   Assessment of non-residents

Notwithstanding the above, the UK adopts two domestic law mechanisms of ensuring compliance with its direct tax laws in the international context by imposing obligations on persons other than the taxpayer. Firstly, in the case of non-residents, a UK representative may be jointly liable with the non-resident in relation to trade income.[1] Secondly, the system of deduction of tax at source by the payer of certain items of income is extended to persons whose 'usual place of abode' is outside the UK which often, but not always, coincides with non-residence.

1   FA 1995 s 126 for non-corporates and FA 2003 s 150 for companies.

8.03   Deduction of tax at source – 'usual place of abode'

ITA 2007 imposes obligations on payers to deduct tax at source on certain amounts paid to persons whose 'usual place of abode is outside the UK.' This includes certain yearly interest[1], royalties, or sums payable periodically, in respect of a relevant intellectual property right[2], and 'Non-resident landlord income'.[3] The expression is not defined in the legislation and, like its counterpart expressions, residence, ordinary residence and domicile requires interpretation.

HMRC practice in this area is somewhat imprecise with slightly different expositions of their practice in different parts of their published guidance.

HMRC International Tax Manual explains that '[th]e term 'usual place of abode' is used in the legislation because the purpose of the legislation is to provide an effective way of collecting tax due from someone who is usually outside the UK and/or does not have a taxable presence in the UK.[4] Usual place of abode, it says, 'means principal place of business or the place where the person is normally to be found. It is not the same as tax residence.' The HMRC Property Income Manual suggests: 'Usual place of abode' is not identical in meaning to residence, or ordinary residence, but a person who is not resident in the UK should normally be treated as having their usual place of abode outside the UK'.[5]

One HMRC explanation of the usual place of abode in the context of 'non-resident' landlords in the Property Income Manual[6] reads:

8.03 *Compliance and appeals*

'1) Individuals have a usual place of abode outside the UK if they usually live outside the UK. You should still regard the term as applying to them even if in a particular year they are resident in the UK for tax purposes, as long as the usual place of abode is outside the UK. (For example the individual may count as resident in the UK in a particular year because of a six months' visit, or a visit of a shorter time when he has a place of abode available in the UK). Do not treat someone as having their usual place of abode outside the UK if they are only temporarily living outside the UK, say for six months or less.

2) Companies that have their main office or other place of business outside the UK, and companies incorporated outside the UK, will normally have a usual place of abode outside the UK. However if the company is treated as resident in the UK for tax purposes, do not treat it as having a usual place of abode outside the UK.

3) Trustees have a usual place of abode outside the UK if all the trustees have a usual place of abode outside the UK.'

In relation to interest payments, the HMRC Savings Income Manual comments in relation to trustees:

'Trustees, including personal representatives, have a usual place of abode abroad if each trustee, considered as an individual or a company as the case may be, has a usual place of abode there. So if one trustee does not have a usual place of abode abroad, neither does the trust.'[7]

While it may be true that a person whose usual place of abode is in the UK is resident in the UK,[8] it does not follow that a person whose usual place of abode is outside the UK is *not* resident in the UK.[9] In imposing a test of 'usual place of abode' (rather than a test of residence) in this context, it may be observed that a person on whom it places the onus of applying the test (ie any person making payment) will rarely be in possession of such facts as are required for the determination of the residence status of the person to whom payment is being made, whereas the determination of such a person's usual place of abode may arguably be capable of determination by mere enquiry and observation.

In *Haslope v Thorne*,[10] Lord Ellenborough CJ considered the term 'place of abode' in the context of a rule of court which required the place of abode of the deponent of an affidavit to be inserted in the affidavit and came to the conclusion that it meant 'the place where the deponent was most usually to be found'.[11] Thus, the place where a man 'lives with his family and sleeps at night' will always be 'his place of abode in the full sense of that expression'.[12] That does not presuppose, however, that the living and sleeping will take place in a house or flat or even an hotel room: a yacht,[13] a caravan,[14] a tent or bender,[15] and even a car[16] may constitute a person's place of abode!

---

1 ITA 2007 s 874.
2 ITA 2007 s 906.
3 ITA 2007 s 971.

4 INTM505020.
5 PIM4810 with PIM4800
6 PIM4810 with PIM4800. Cf the International Manual INTM370060. Also see Savings Income Manual re interest SAIM9080.
7 SAIM9080.
8 See **2.08** above.
9 See **2.11–2.19** above.
10 (1813) 1 M & S 103.
11 (1813) 1 M & S 103 at 104. In accordance with that principle, the usual place of abode of a company will presumably be its principal place of business.
12 *R v Hammond* (1852) 17 QB 772 at 780, 781, per Lord Campbell CJ.
13 In *Bayard Brown v Burt* (1911) 5 TC 667, it was accepted that an ocean-going yacht anchored in territorial waters was the place of abode of Mr Bayard Brown, its owner and occupier.
14 In *Makins v Elson* [1977] STC 46, it was held that a wheeled caravan jacked up and resting on bricks, with water, electricity and telephone services installed, was a dwelling house.
15 In *Hipperson v Electoral Registration Officer for the District of Newbury* [1985] 2 All ER 456, Sir John Donaldson MR (at 462) rejected the submission that women living in tents, vehicles and benders (a form of tent) on Greenham Common in furtherance of their protest concerning cruise missiles could not be said to have a home in the camp: 'It may be unusual to make one's home in a tent, bender or vehicle, but we can see no reason in law why it should be impossible.'
16 In *R v Bundy* [1977] 2 All ER 382, the motor car in which a certain Mr Bundy had been living rough was held to be his place of abode when sited but not while in transit. The court held, at 384, that the term '"place of abode" ... connotes, first of all, a site. That is the ordinary meaning of the word "place". It is a site at which the occupier intends to abide. So there are two elements in the phrase "place of abode", the element of site and the element of intention. When the appellant took the motor car to a site with the intention of abiding there, then his motor car on that site could be said to be his "place of abode", but when he took it from that site to move it to another site where he intended to abide, the motor car could not be said to be his "place of abode" during transit.'

8.04 Claiming not ordinarily resident or non-domiciled status

For income and capital gains tax purposes, following the Finance Act 2008 it is normally necessary for an individual who is resident but either not ordinarily resident or not domiciled in the UK to claim such status (ITA 2007 s 809B). Where such individuals are liable to notify chargeability to tax, they will in consequence normally be required to complete a self-assessment tax return. Where a return is to be filed, the claim must be made in the return.[1] Provision for the making of such claims is made in the 'non-residence' pages of the return.

1 TMA 1970 s 42.

8.05 Appeals

Up to the tax year 2007–08, a special procedure for dealing with disputes as to domicile or ordinary residence[1] required the Commissioners of Revenue and Customs to determine such disputed domicile or ordinary residence. Their decision was then subject to appeal to the Special Commissioners. This procedure was repealed.[2] For the tax years 2008–09

8.05 *Compliance and appeals*

and thereafter, appeals in relation to these issues will be dealt with under normal self-assessment provisions and appeal.

1   ITEPA 2003 Pt 2 and Ch 6, TCGA 1992 s 9(2).
2   FA 2008 Sch 7, paras 23, 54 and 77.

8.06 Evidential burden on appeal

As early as 1876, in *Cesena Sulphur Co Ltd v Nicholson*[1] the court held that the burden of proof to show that a company was resident in the UK was on the Revenue and said, at p 105:

> 'I admit that the onus of proving residence lies upon the Crown...and if the Crown fails to satisfy the Court that the place of residence is within the jurisdiction, or within the area of taxation, you cannot say that the company should be taxed.'

Several recent cases have involved a consideration of the evidential burden. The Revenue have unsuccessfully argued that the burden of proof simply lies with the taxpayer, relying on s 50(6) of the Taxes Management Act 1970 which provides:

> '56(6) If, on an appeal, it appears to the majority of the Commissioners present at the hearing, by examination of the appellant on oath or affirmation, or by other lawful evidence, that the appellant is overcharged by any assessment, the assessment shall be reduced accordingly, but otherwise every such assessment shall stand good.'

Firstly, in *Untelrab Ltd & Ors v McGregor (HMIT)*[2] the Special Commissioners, on the authority of *Cesena* concluded that the burden of proving residence lies on the Crown. In their view s 50(6) was not relevant in the context of that appeal because it was not a case where the Appellants were saying that they had been overcharged by an assessment but where they are saying that the Revenue had no jurisdiction to assess them at all.[3]

Secondly, in *Wood v Holden*[4] the Court of Appeal upheld Park J in the High Court in relation to shifts in the evidentiary burden even where TMA 1970 s 50(6) applies. Once the taxpayer, on appeal has 'done enough to raise a case that [the company] is not resident in the UK', the burden must then pass to the Revenue to produce some material to show that, despite what appears from everything which the taxpayer has produced, the company is actually resident in the UK. Chadwick LJ said this:[5]

> 'It is a feature of tax litigation – not least where the litigation arises from a tax avoidance scheme – that, in the first instance, the facts are likely to be known only to the taxpayer and his advisers. The revenue will not have been party to the transaction; and will know only those facts which have been disclosed by the taxpayer or others; following, perhaps, the exercise of the Revenue's investigatory powers. I have no doubt that there are cases in which the evidence before the special commissioners is so unsatisfactory that the only just course for them to take is to hold that the taxpayer has not discharged the burden of

proof which section 50(6) of TMA 1970 has placed upon him. But, equally, I have no doubt that the judge was correct, for the reasons which he gave, to hold that the present case was not one of those cases. There was no reason to think that the material facts had not been disclosed; and the commissioners did not hold that it was for that reason that they were unable to decide the question of residence.'

In *News Datacom Ltd v Atkinson (HMIT)*[6] the Special Commissioners followed the guidance of Chadwick LJ in *Wood v Holden* and accordingly, proceeded on the basis that it was for the appellants there to show that the assessments had been wrongly made. They accepted that the evidential burden can shift to HMRC but did not reach a decision purely on grounds relating to the burden of proof in the *Wood v Holden* sense. They held the company to be not resident in the UK without a failure to discharge the evidential burden.[7]

1 (1876) 1 TC 88.
2 (1995) Sp C 55.
3 At para 68.
4 [2006] EWCA Civ 26.
5 [2006] EWCA Civ 26, at para 33.
6 (2006) Sp C 561.
7 See para 155.

8.07 Role of court on appeal

Residence and domicile are essentially factual in nature. The right of appeal from a decision of the Special Commissioners is on points of law only.[1] Only one reported decision of the Special Commissioners on domicile[2] has been appealed. In *Agulian & Anor v Cyganik*[3] the Court of Appeal was faced with the contention that the appeal was essentially against a finding or findings of fact by the court below and that it was not entitled to substitute its own assessment of the evidence for that of the deputy judge, who heard and saw the witnesses, preferred the evidence of his client and made a finding corroborated by independent evidence. Mummery LJ explained the normal role of the appellate court as follows:

> 'Further, this was not an appeal against the exercise of a discretion by the lower court nor was it a case in which the lower court was applying a fairly flexible and imprecise standard involving an evaluation of all the facts... In those cases the appellate court is more reluctant to interfere with the trial judge's decision than in the case of a finding of primary fact or an inference from primary facts. This is an appeal contesting the correctness of an inference as to Andreas's relevant intentions between 1995 and 1999. The function of the appellate court is to decide whether the inference is wrong, making proper allowances for any advantages that the trial judge would have had and an appellate court would not have and not interfering with inferences which the judge could reasonably have made.'[4]

In appeals from the Special Commissioners, by contrast, the appeal court has no such power. It must be satisfied, not that the Special

8.07 *Compliance and appeals*

Commissioners' evaluation of the facts was wrong, but that they made an error of law.[5]

Such a re-evaluation of the facts on appeal is only possible where there is a question of mixed fact and law as in *Edwards v Bairstow*[6] in which Lord Radcliffe said:

> 'If the case contains anything ex facie which is bad law and which bears upon the determination, it is, obviously, erroneous in point of law. But, without any such misconception appearing ex facie, it may be that the facts found are such that no person acting judicially and properly instructed as to the relevant law could have come to the determination under appeal. In those circumstances, too, the court must intervene. It has no option but to assume that there has been some misconception of the law and that, this has been responsible for the determination. So there, too, there has been error in point of law. I do not think that it much matters whether this state of affairs is described as one in which there is no evidence to support the determination or as one in which the evidence is inconsistent with and contradictory of the determination, or as one in which the true and only reasonable conclusion contradicts the determination. Rightly understood, each phrase propounds the same test. For my part, I prefer the last of the three, since I think that it is rather misleading to speak of there being no evidence to support a conclusion when in cases such as these many of the facts are likely to be neutral in themselves, and only to take their colour from the combination of circumstances in which they are found to occur.'

In *Gaines-Cooper*, that the Special Commissioners did not accept certain of Mr Gaines-Cooper's evidence, or that 'in one short paragraph they utterly fail to do justice' to the evidence of witnesses as well as a number of other factual criticisms, was held on appeal to reveal no error of law. A general assertion that the tribunal's conclusion was against the weight of the evidence and was therefore wrong was held impermissible in an appeal restricted to questions of law.

---

1 TMA 1970 s 56A(1). (Any question before the General Commissioners may be considered by the High Court on a case stated for their opinion under s 56.)
2 See **7.01** above.
3 [2006] EWCA Civ 129.
4 At para 12.
5 *Gaines-Cooper v Revenue and Customs Commissioners* [2007] EWHC 2617 (Ch) at para 27.
6 [1956] AC 14; 36 TC 207.

CHAPTER 9

Residence, nationality and discrimination in the European Union

9.01 Introduction

The Treaty establishing the European Communities grants important rights to citizens of the Member States and the European Union and to businesses established in the Community. These are:

'**Article 12**
Within the scope of application of this Treaty, and without prejudice to any special provisions contained therein, any discrimination on grounds of nationality shall be prohibited.'

'**Article 18**
(1) Every citizen of the Union shall have the right to move and reside freely within the territory of the Member States, subject to the limitations and conditions laid down in this Treaty and by the measures adopted to give it effect.'[1]

'**Article 39**
(1) Freedom of movement for workers shall be secured within the Community.
(2) Such freedom of movement shall entail the abolition of any discrimination based on nationality between workers of the Member States as regards employment, remuneration and other conditions of work and employment.
(3) It shall entail the right, subject to limitations justified on grounds of public policy, public security or public health:
 (a) to accept offers of employment actually made;
 (b) to move freely within the territory of Member States for this purpose;
 (c) to stay in a Member State for the purpose of employment in accordance with the provisions governing the employment of nationals of that State laid down by law, regulation or administrative action;'

'**Article 43**
Within the framework of the provisions set out below, restrictions on the freedom of establishment of nationals of a Member State in the territory of another Member State shall be prohibited. Such prohibition shall also apply to

restrictions on the setting up of agencies, branches or subsidiaries by nationals of any Member State established in the territory of any Member State.

Freedom of establishment shall include the right to take up and pursue activities as self-employed persons and to set up and manage undertakings, in particular companies or firms within the meaning of the second paragraph of article 58, under the conditions laid down for its own nationals by the law of the country where such establishment is effected subject to the provisions of the chapter relating to capital.'

'**Article 48**
Companies or firms formed in accordance with the law of a Member State and having their registered office, central administration or principal place of business within the Community shall, for the purposes of this Chapter, be treated in the same way as natural persons who are nationals of Member States.

'Companies or firms' means companies or firms constituted under civil or commercial law, including co-operative societies, and other legal persons governed by public or private law, save for those which are non-profit-making.'

'**Article 49**
Within the framework of the provisions set out below, restrictions on freedom to provide services within the Community shall be prohibited in respect of nationals of Member States who are established in a State of the Community other than that of the person for whom the services are intended.'

'**Article 56**
(1) Within the framework of the provisions set out in this Chapter, all restrictions on the movement of capital between Member States and between Member States and third countries shall be prohibited.
(2) Within the framework of the provisions set out in this Chapter, all restrictions on payments between Member States and between Member States and third countries shall be prohibited.'

'**Article 58**
(1) The provisions of Article 56 shall be without prejudice to the right of Member States:
    (a) to apply the relevant provisions of their tax law which distinguish between taxpayers who are not in the same situation with regard to their place of residence or with regard to the place where their capital is invested;
    (b) to take all requisite measures to prevent infringements of national law and regulations, in particular in the field of taxation and the prudential supervision of financial institutions, or to lay down procedures for the declaration of capital movements for purposes of administrative or statistical information, or to take measures which are justified on grounds of public policy or public security.
(2) The provisions of this Chapter shall be without prejudice to the applicability of restrictions on the right of establishment which are compatible with this Treaty.
(3) The measures and procedures referred to in paragraphs 1 and 2 shall not constitute a means of arbitrary discrimination or a disguised restriction on the free movement of capital and payments as defined in Article 56.'

Direct taxation does not at present fall within the purview of the European

Community, but the powers over direct taxation which are retained by Member States must be exercised consistently with the EC Treaty.

Since the mid-1980s the European Court of Justice (ECJ) has increasingly been called upon to hear cases where taxpayers who have argued that the national tax laws of Member States infringe the rights granted by Community law.

EC Treaty rights are not, in principle, determined by reference to residence. The general prohibition against discrimination is on the basis of nationality.[2] The freedom of establishment and to provide cross-border services are also guaranteed to nationals of Member States.[3] In the case of freedom of movement for workers, this entails the abolition of all discrimination based on nationality.[4] The concept of residence makes an appearance in the broad right of free movement for citizens of the European Union. The right to move feely and *reside* in the territory of Member States is a key right of European citizens.[5]

On the other hand, the prohibition on the free movement of capital is, in principle, granted not by reference to persons but in respect of the capital itself.[6] This prohibition is not absolute and Member States may, in certain circumstances, apply the relevant provisions of their tax law which distinguish between taxpayers who are not in the same situation with regard to their place of residence.[7]

The UK, in common with other Member States has not adopted nationality as a significant connecting factor for tax purposes. Despite the lack of direct reference to residence, the central territorial connecting factor in taxation, in the enumeration of EC Treaty rights, there have been over 100 direct tax cases in which the ECJ has examined differences in Member State treatment, many based on residence. The vast majority have been found to infringe Community rights.

---

1 European citizenship is established by Art 17.
2 Art 12(1).
3 Arts 43 and 49.
4 Art 39(2).
5 Art 18(1).
6 Art 56(1).
7 Art 58(a).

9.02 Individual nationality and tax residence

In *Giovanni Maria Sotgiu v Deutsche Bundespost*[1] the Court was asked to consider the relationship between residence and nationality in this context. In other words, whether the non-discrimination article was to be interpreted as containing a prohibition not only against treating a worker differently because he is a national of another Member State, but also against treating him differently because he is resident in another Member State. The ECJ ruled that regarding equality of treatment in the treaty, not only overt discrimination by reason of nationality was forbidden, but also all covert forms of discrimination which, by the application of other criteria of differentiation, lead in fact to the same result. This interpretation, which is necessary to ensure the effective working of one of the fundamental principles of the community which requires that equality of treatment of workers shall be ensured 'in fact and in law'. Therefore, criteria such as residence of a worker may, according to circumstances, be tantamount, as regards their practical effect, to discrimination on the grounds of nationality, such as is prohibited by the treaty. The rules regarding equality of treatment forbid not only overt discrimination by reason of nationality but also all covert forms of discrimination which, by the application of other criteria of differentiation, lead in fact to the same result. The approach in *Sotgiu* was adopted by the Court in *Finanzamt Köln-Altstadt v Roland Schumacker*[2] and has been consistently applied since then. Thus where there is no objective difference between the situations of such a non-resident and a resident engaged in comparable activity such as to justify different treatment this is regarded as an unacceptable restriction on the fundamental freedoms granted to nationals of Member States.

1 *Giovanni Maria Sotgiu v Deutsche Bundespost* (152–73) [1974] ECR 153.
2 *Finanzant v Schumacher (C-279/93)* [1995] STC 306 at 314.

9.03 Corporate nationality and tax residence

The residence of companies, as legal persons, is not identical to that of individuals. Article 48 of the EC treaty provides for companies or firms formed in accordance with the law of a Member State and having their registered office, central administration or principal place of business within the Community to be treated in the same way as natural persons who are nationals of Member States for the purpose of the right of establishment. The adoption of the place of incorporation test in the Finance Act 1988, s 66[1] has the effect of granting UK incorporated companies the notional nationality for these purposes.

In *EC Commission v France*,[2] with regard to the right of establishment of companies, the Court noted in the context of Art 48 that it is their 'seat' that serves as the connecting factor within the legal system of a particular State, like nationality in the case of natural persons. In the same judgment the Court held that acceptance of the proposition that the Member State in which a company seeks to establish itself may freely apply to it different treatment solely by reason of the fact that its seat is situated in another Member State would deprive the provision of all meaning.

In *R v Inland Revenue Commissioners, ex parte Commerzbank AG*[3] the Court considered the impact of tax residence explicitly in relation to indirect discrimination on grounds of nationality. Commerzbank AG was a company incorporated under German law with its registered office in Germany. It had a branch in the UK through which it granted loans to a number of US companies and it paid tax in the UK on the interest received from those companies. It was discovered that because of a provision in the UK/US Double Taxation Convention the interest was not properly taxable since Commerzbank was not resident in the UK. The tax was accordingly repaid to it.

Commerzbank then claimed a 'repayment supplement' under ICTA 1988 s 825. That section enabled resident companies to recover interest on tax overpaid and the Revenue refused the claim accordingly. Commerzbank argued succesfully in the ECJ that the residence requirement infringed the right of establishment. In following the *Sotgiu* judgment the ECJ ruled that equality of treatment forbids not only overt discrimination by reason of nationality or, in the case of a company, its seat, but all covert forms of discrimination which, by the application of other criteria of differentiation, lead in fact to the same result.The issue of tax residence was addressed thus:

'Although it applies independently of a company's seat, the use of the criterion of fiscal residence within national territory for the purpose of granting repayment supplement on overpaid tax is liable to work more particularly to the disadvantage of companies having their seat in other Member States. Indeed, it is most often those companies which are resident for tax purposes outside the territory of the Member State in question.'[4]

The Court does not as a result seek to apply a residence test but rather tests the Member State laws including where appropriate, tax residence for compliance with Community law.

1 See **6.02** above.
2 Case C-270/83 [1987] 1 CMLR 401.
3 Case C-330/91 [1993] ECR I-4017.
4 At para 15.

9.04 Change of residence and exit taxes

The ECJ has twice ruled on the legality of taxes levied on individuals by reason of a change in residence. In *Hughes de Lasteyrie du Saillant v Ministère de l'Économie, des Finances et de l'Industrie*[1] Mr de Lasteyrie left France to settle in Belgium for the purpose of carrying on his profession there. He was deemed to dispose of shares in a family owned company at market value on the date of departure under French law.

The ECJ ruled that a taxpayer wishing to transfer his tax residence in exercise of the right of freedom of establishment is subjected to disadvantageous treatment in comparison with a person who maintains his residence in that State where he becomes liable, simply by reason of such a transfer, to tax on unrealised gains, whereas, if he remained in that State, increases in value would become taxable only when, and to the extent that, they were actually realised.

Thus, the Court held that Art 43 of the EC Treaty must be interpreted as precluding a Member State from taxing latent, unrealised, increases in value of company shares, where a taxpayer transfers his tax residence outside that State. The difference in treatment cannot be justified (as the French Government argued) by the aim of preventing tax avoidance, since tax avoidance or evasion cannot be inferred generally from the fact that the tax residence of a physical person has been transferred to another Member State.

The identical conclusion was reached in *N v Inspecteur van de Belastingdienst Oost/kantoor Almelo*,[2] this time examining not only the right of establishment in Art 43 but also the right of free movement for European citizens in Art 18.

Although not strictly a case on exit taxes, *R v HM Treasury and Commissioners of Inland Revenue, ex parte Daily Mail and General Trust plc*[3] concerned the right of a legal person to leave its Member State of origin.

At that time, Treasury consent was a prerequisite for a company resident in the UK to cease to be resident.[4] As a company incorporated under English law and having its registered office in the UK it could establish its central management and control outside the UK and cease to be resident for tax purposes without losing legal personality or ceasing to be a company incorporated in the UK.

The company applied for consent to transfer its central management and control to the Netherlands. The principal reason for the proposed transfer of central management and control was to enable the company to sell a significant part of its assets and to use the proceeds of that sale to buy its own shares, without having to pay the UK tax on these transactions. The company would be subject to Netherlands corporation tax, but the transactions envisaged would be taxed only on the basis of capital gains on increases in value accrued after the transfer of its residence for tax purposes. The Treasury, in negotiations with the company, proposed that it should sell at least part of the assets before transferring its residence out of the UK. This would have defeated the object of the exercise.

The Court concluded that the state of Community law at that time conferred no right on a company incorporated under the legislation of a Member State and having its registered office there to transfer its central management and control to another Member State. This was based on the then Art 220 of the Treaty which provides for the conclusion of agreements between Member States with a view to securing inter alia the retention of legal personality in the event of transfer of the registered office of companies from one country to another. No convention in this area had yet come into force. Even if this decision is assumed to be correct, it gives little support to the argument that exit taxes for companies are not contrary to Community law. The European Commission in its communication 'Exit taxation and the need for co-ordination of Member States' tax policies'[5] regards corporate exit taxes as infringing Community law.

---

1 *Hughes de Lasteyrie du Saillant v Ministère de l'Économie, des Finances et de l'Industrie* (C-9/02) [2004] ECR I-2409.
2 *N v Inspecteur van de Belastingdienst Oost/kantoor Almelo* (C-470/04).
3 *R v HM Treasury and Commissioners of Inland Revenue, ex parte Daily Mail and General Trust plc* (81/87) [1988] ECR 273.
4 ICTA 1970 s 482(1)(a).
5 COM(2006) 825.

APPENDIX 1

Inland Revenue Bulletin IR20 (2008)

HMRC Description

Residents and non-residents. Liability to tax in the United Kingdom

This booklet was updated earlier in 2008. It has now been updated again, in line with the undertaking we gave to our customers, to include guidance on the changes brought about by FA 2008 to the residence rules and how customers use the remittance basis. We are now able to provide this guidance as FA 2008 has received Royal Assent.

We have only made additions to the existing guidance where they are required to cover the changes brought about by FA 2008 as we are currently preparing replacement guidance on residence and domicile issues. We shall be launching a consultation exercise to obtain customer views on the replacement guidance we are preparing to ensure that it meets our customers' needs. When the replacement guidance is published, the current guidance will be withdrawn. In the meantime, this guidance can still be used to help customers understand their position on residence and domicile matters.

July 2008

Appendix 1

IR20 - Residents and non-residents
Liability to tax in the United Kingdom

Contents

Preface

Introduction

    General
    Definitions used in this booklet
    Contacting HM Revenue & Customs

Part I Meaning of 'residence', 'ordinary residence' and 'domicile' for tax purposes

1. Residence and ordinary residence

    Residence
    Ordinary residence
    Residence in both the UK and another country
    Leaving, or coming to, the UK part way through a tax year

2. Leaving the UK

    Short absences
    Working abroad
    Meaning of 'full-time'
    Accompanying spouse
    Leaving the UK permanently or indefinitely
    Calculating annual average visits
    Contacting HM Revenue & Customs
    Tax treatment after leaving the UK
    Special classes of employees

3. Coming to the UK

    Coming to the UK permanently or indefinitely
    Visitors to the UK
    Short term visitors
    Calculating annual average visits
    Longer term visitors
    Contacting HM Revenue & Customs
    Tax treatment after arrival in the UK

Inland Revenue Bulletin IR20 (2008)

4. Domicile

Domicile of origin
Domicile of dependency
Domicile of choice
Married women
Overseas electors
Tax treatment of those not domiciled in the UK

Part II Liability to UK tax

5. Earned income

Basis of liability
Earnings of those who come to, or leave, the UK part way through a tax year
Where your duties are performed
Incidental duties
Earned income arising outside the UK
Change of location of a trade, profession or vocation
UK social security benefits
Lump sums from overseas pension schemes and provident funds
Offshore oil and gas workers
Partnerships
Scope of liability to income tax of earnings
Scope of liability to income tax on individuals receiving pensions
Scope of liability to income tax on profits of individuals carrying on a trade or profession

6. Investment income

General
Investment income arising in the UK
Investment income arising outside the UK
Investment income of those who leave, or come to, the UK part way through a tax year
Scope of liability to income tax on individuals receiving investment income

7. Tax allowances and reliefs

Allowances for UK residents
Allowances for non-UK residents
Allowances for those coming to, or leaving, the UK part way through a tax year
Mortgage interest relief
How to claim tax allowances

Appendix 1

<ins>8. Capital gains tax</ins>

    Basis of liability
    Gains by those who leave, or come to, the UK part way through a tax year
    Temporary non-residence
    Non-residents with a UK branch or agency
    Overseas assets
    Gains in a foreign currency
    Exempt assets
    Further information
    Scope of liability to capital gains tax

<ins>9. Double taxation relief</ins>

    Non-residents and residents of more than one country
    Earnings from employment and professional services
    Teachers and researchers
    Students and apprentices
    Entertainers and sportsmen/women
    Dividends
    Capital gains
    UK residents
    List of the UK's double taxation agreements

<ins>10. Appeals</ins>

<ins>Part III Payment of UK National Insurance contributions</ins>

<ins>11. National Insurance contributions</ins>

    General
    Going abroad
    Arriving from abroad

Inland Revenue Bulletin IR20 (2008)

Preface

This current update of booklet IR20, which was last published in December 1999 and was subject to an update in February 2008, is only interim guidance. The only substantive amendments being made in **this** update of the booklet are to cover the changes to the residence and domicile rules resulting from the 2008 Budget and incorporated in statute in the Finance Act 2008. We recognise that the rest of this guidance needs updating and **we expect to publish full replacement guidance soon, at which point the IR20 will be withdrawn**. However, our customers said they would like IR20 to be updated to reflect the changes brought about by the 2008 Finance Act and this interim update provides that.

The notes below are not binding in law and do not affect rights of appeal about your own tax.

Some of the guidance originally included in the booklet published in December 1999 was removed when the guidance was updated in February 2008 as it is no longer relevant. No information has been removed from this latest update of the booklet and we have only made additions to cover the changes made by the 2008 Finance Act.

You should bear in mind that the booklet offers general guidance on how the rules apply, but whether the guidance is appropriate in a particular case will depend on all the facts of that case. If you have any difficulty in applying the rules in your own case, you should consult an HM Revenue & Customs Tax Office - see paragraphs 7-9 of the Introduction on contacting HM Revenue & Customs.

Some practices explained in this booklet are concessions made by HM Revenue & Customs. **A concession will not be given in any case where an attempt is made to use it for tax avoidance**.

Appendix 1

Introduction

General

1. Broadly, the United Kingdom (UK) charges tax on

    - income arising in the UK, whether or not the person to whom it belongs is resident in the UK

    - income arising outside the UK which belongs to people resident in the UK

    - gains accruing on the disposal of assets anywhere in the world which belong to people resident or ordinarily resident in the UK.

2. Special rules apply in some circumstances, but generally the amount of income tax and Capital Gains Tax you have to pay depends on whether you are **resident** and/or **ordinarily resident** in the UK, and in some cases on your **domicile**.

3. The first part of this booklet explains what is meant by **'residence', 'ordinary residence'** and **'domicile'**. The second part explains how these factors affect how much income tax and Capital Gains Tax you have to pay in the UK, and how the normal rules of taxation may be modified in some cases where a **double taxation agreement** applies.

4. The third part of the booklet outlines the rules for payment of UK **National Insurance contributions** for individuals going abroad or coming to the UK.

5. The booklet is only concerned with **individuals**. It does not cover the position of companies, trusts, clubs, societies or other legal persons. Nor does it deal with **Inheritance Tax**. The booklet, 'Customer Guide to Inheritance Tax', explains how your domicile can affect the Inheritance Tax position if you transfer property, normally on or within seven years of death.

Definitions used in this booklet

6. Several terms used in this booklet have a particular meaning, as follows

    Tax Year — The 12 months starting with 6 April in one year and ending with 5 April in the following year. For example, the tax year 2007-2008 runs from 6 April 2007 to 5 April 2008.

    United Kingdom — England, Wales, Scotland and Northern Ireland, including the territorial sea (that is, waters within 12 nautical miles of the shore).

    Abroad/overseas — Anywhere outside the UK. The Channel Islands and the Isle of Man are abroad (except in the limited context of certain bilateral Social Security Agreements - see paragraph 11.1).

Contacting HM Revenue & Customs

7. If you have any queries on your tax position, you should contact your Tax Office. Your employer will normally be able to tell you the address. If you have just come to the UK, or for any other reason you do not know which office deals with your tax affairs, you should write to your local Tax Office - the address is in *The Phone Book* under HM Revenue & Customs. If you have a UK National Insurance number, please give it in your letter.

8. A system of **Self Assessment** applies to individuals in the UK. This requires you to work out for yourself what tax you owe (calculating your own tax is, however, optional if you submit your tax return by a certain date, normally 30 September following the tax year). Initially, we will accept and process the figures in your return - except for any obvious

mistakes, which we will correct. After processing, we will check all cases and select some for further examination.

We will provide guidance to help you calculate your tax liability or make any claim. We will ask you to give sufficient detail of your income and circumstances to allow us to check your tax return.

9   In a number of places this booklet refers to matters that are dealt with by specialist offices of HM Revenue & Customs. These offices and their addresses are as follows

Charity, Assets & Residence **Bootle**	(Residency) St John's House Merton Road Liverpool England L75 1BB Phone **0845 070 0040** **From abroad** **Phone 44 151 210 2222**
Charity, Assets & Residence **Nottingham**	(Residency) Fitz Roy House PO Box 46 Nottingham England NG2 1BD Phone **0845 070 0040** From abroad Phone **44 151 210 2222**
HMRC South Wales	Government Buildings Ty-Glas Llanishen Cardiff Wales CF14 5YA Phone **0845 300 3949** **From abroad** **Phone 44 292 050 1290**
Foreign Compliance Compliance Centre 1	Queensway House East Kilbride Glasgow Scotland G79 1AA Phone **01355 275877 / 275733 / 275795**
Foreign Entertainers Unit	Charity, Assets and Residence St John's House Merton Road Liverpool England L75 1BB Phone **0151 472 6488**

Appendix 1

Charity, Assets & Residence　(Residency)
Newcastle　Benton Park View
Newcastle upon Tyne
NE98 1ZZ
Phone **0845 915 4811**
From abroad
Phone **44 191 225 4811**

Part I Meaning of 'residence', 'ordinary residence' and 'domicile' for tax purposes

1 Residence and ordinary residence

1.1 The terms '**residence**' and '**ordinary residence**' are not defined in the Taxes Acts. The guidelines to their meaning in this Chapter and in Chapters 2 (residence status of those leaving the UK) and 3 (those coming to the UK) are largely based on rulings of the Courts. This booklet sets out the main factors that are taken into account, but we can only make a decision on your residence status on the facts in your particular case.

As mentioned in paragraph 1.4, even if you are resident (or ordinarily resident) in the UK under these rules, the terms of a double taxation agreement with another country might affect your final tax position if, for example, you are resident in both that country and the UK.

Residence

1.2 To be regarded as **resident** in the UK you must normally be physically present in the country at some time in the tax year. You will always be resident if you are here for **183 days or more in the tax year. There are no exceptions to this**. You count the total number of days you spend in the UK - it does not matter if you come and go several times during the year or if you are here for one stay of 183 days or more. If you are here for less than 183 days, you may still be treated as resident for the year under other tests (see Chapter 3, and in particular paragraph 3.3).

For periods prior to 6 April 2008, the normal rule is that days of arrival in and departure from the UK are **ignored** in counting the days spent in the UK, in all the various cases where calculations have to be made to determine your residence position - see for example paragraphs 2.2, 3.3 and 3.4 and the examples in 2.10 and 3.6. (This rule is not relevant to the concessionary split year treatment described in paragraphs 1.5 -1.6, where a person coming to or leaving the UK part way through a tax year is resident from the date of arrival or to the date of departure.)

From 6 April 2008 onwards, when you are in the UK at the end of a day, i.e. at midnight, that day will count as a day of presence in the UK for residence purposes. An exemption is made for passengers who are in transit between two places outside the UK. Any day spent in transit through the UK (that is where you arrive in the UK in one day and depart to continue your journey on the next day); will not count as a day of presence in the UK for residence purposes. This exemption will only be given as long as you do not take part in any activity that is unrelated to your passage through the UK. This would include, for example, attending a business meeting, visiting friends or visiting a property which you own in the UK.

Inland Revenue Bulletin IR20 (2008)

Ordinary residence

1.3 If you are resident in the UK year after year, you are treated as **ordinarily resident** here. You may be resident but not ordinarily resident in the UK for a tax year if, for example, you normally live outside the UK but are in this country for 183 days or more in the year. Or you may be ordinarily resident but not resident for a tax year if, for example, you usually live in the UK but have gone abroad for a long holiday and do not set foot in the UK during that year.

Residence in both the UK and another country

1.4 It is possible to be resident (or ordinarily resident) in both the UK and some other country (or countries) at the same time. If you are resident (or ordinarily resident) in another country, this does **not** mean that you cannot **also** be resident (or ordinarily resident) in the UK. Where, however, you are resident both in the UK and a country with which the UK has a **double taxation agreement**, there may be special provisions in the agreement for treating you as a resident of only one of the countries for the purposes of the agreement (see paragraph 9.2).

Leaving or coming to the UK part way through a tax year

1.5 Strictly, you are taxed as a UK resident for the **whole** of a tax year if you are resident here for any part of it. But if you leave or come to the UK part way through a tax year, the year may, by concession (extra-statutory concession A11), be **split**. Where this applies, your tax liabilities on income which are affected by tax residence will be calculated on the basis of the period of your actual residence here during the year (see also paragraph 5.4). This has the same effect as splitting the tax year into resident and not resident periods.

There is a similar concession relating to the treatment of chargeable gains – see chapter 8

1.6 Split year treatment applies where

- you have been not ordinarily resident in the UK and you come to live here permanently or to stay for at least two years. You are taxed as a resident only from the date of your arrival; or
- you have been resident in the UK* and you leave to live abroad permanently or for a period of at least three years, and on your departure are not ordinarily resident in the UK. You are taxed as a resident only up to and including the date of your departure; or
- you have been resident in the UK* and you leave to take up full-time employment abroad, and you meet certain conditions (see paragraphs 2.2 -2.3). You are taxed as a resident only up to and including the date of your departure (and from the date when you return to the UK).

* **other than** resident only as a short term visitor - see paragraph 3.3.

1.7 For certain types of income of a non-resident the UK tax charged is limited to any tax deducted before payment (see paragraphs 5.15 and 6.3). This **only** applies, however, to complete years of non-residence. Where the tax year is split, the limitation does **not** apply to the part of the year for which you are treated as though you were not resident.

Split year treatment does not apply if you come to the UK as a short term visitor, or if you come for only limited periods with no intention to live here permanently or to stay for at least two years. (See paragraph 3.3 for details of the rules that apply in this case.)

Appendix 1

2   Leaving the UK

Short absences

2.1   You are **resident and ordinarily resident** in the UK if you usually live in this country and only go abroad for short periods - for example, on holiday or on business trips.

Working abroad

2.2   If you leave the UK to work full-time abroad under a contract of employment, you are treated as not resident and not ordinarily resident if you meet **all** the following conditions

- your absence from the UK and your employment abroad both last for at least a whole tax year

- during your absence any visits you make to the UK
    - total less than 183 days in any tax year, **and**
    - average less than 91 days a tax year. (The average is taken over the period of absence up to a maximum of four years - see paragraph 2.10. Any days spent in the UK because of exceptional circumstances beyond your control, for example the illness of yourself or a member of your immediate family, are not normally counted for this purpose.)

(Please see the Appendix at the end of this guidance for notes on a relevant case.)

2.3   If you meet all the conditions in paragraph 2.2, you are treated as not resident and not ordinarily resident in the UK from the day after you leave the UK to the day before you return to the UK at the end of your employment abroad. You are treated as coming to the UK permanently on the day you return from your employment abroad and as resident and ordinarily resident from that date.

If there is a break in full-time employment, or some other change in your circumstances during the period you are overseas, we would have to review the position to decide whether you still meet the conditions in paragraph 2.2. If at the end of one employment you returned temporarily to the UK, planning to go abroad again after a very short stay in this country, we may review your residence status in the light of all the circumstances of your employment abroad and your return to the UK.

If you do not meet all the conditions in paragraph 2.2, you remain resident and ordinarily resident unless paragraphs 2.8 - 2.9 apply to you. Special rules apply to employees of the European Community (see paragraph 2.14).

2.4   The treatment in paragraph 2.3 will also apply if you leave the UK to work full-time in a trade, profession or vocation and you meet conditions similar to those in paragraph 2.2.

Meaning of 'full-time'

2.5   There is no precise definition of when employment overseas is 'full-time', and a decision in a particular case will depend on all the facts. Where your employment involves a standard pattern of hours, we will regard it as full time if the hours you work each week clearly compare with those in a typical UK working week. If your job has no formal structure or no fixed number of working days, we will look at the nature of the job, local conditions and practices in the particular occupation to decide if the job is full-time.

If you have several part-time jobs overseas at the same time, we may be able to treat this as full-time employment. That might be so if, for example, you have several appointments with the same employer or group of companies, and perhaps also where you have simultaneous employment and self-employment overseas. But if you have a main employment abroad and some unconnected occupation in the UK at the same time, we will consider whether the extent of the UK activities was consistent with the overseas employment being full-time.

Accompanying spouse

2.6 If you are the husband or wife of someone who leaves the UK within the terms of paragraph 2.2 or 2.4 and you accompany or later join your spouse abroad, you may also by concession (extra-statutory concession A78) be treated as not resident and not ordinarily resident from the day after your departure to the day before your return, even if you are not yourself in full-time employment abroad. This applies where

- you are abroad for a complete tax year, and
- during your absence any visits you make to the UK
    - total less than 183 days in the tax year
    - average less than 91 days a tax year. (The average is taken over the period of absence up to a maximum of four years - see paragraph 2.10. Any days spent in the UK because of exceptional circumstances beyond your control, for example the illness of yourself or a member of your immediate family, are not normally counted for this purpose.)

Where the tax years of your departure or return are split in this way, your tax liabilities which are affected by residence status are calculated on the basis of the period you are treated as resident in the UK.

Leaving the UK permanently or indefinitely

2.7 If you go abroad permanently, you will be treated as remaining resident and ordinarily resident if your visits to the UK average 91 days or more a year - see paragraph 2.10. Any days spent in the UK because of exceptional circumstances beyond your control, for example the illness of yourself or your immediate family, are not normally counted for the purposes of averaging your visits.

2.8 If you claim that you are no longer resident and ordinarily resident, we may ask you to give some evidence that you have left the UK either permanently or to live outside the UK for three years or more. This evidence might be, for example, that you have taken steps to acquire accommodation abroad to live in as a permanent home, and if you continue to have property in the UK for your use, the reason is consistent with your stated aim of living abroad permanently or for three years or more. If you have left the UK permanently or for at least three years, you will be treated as not resident and not ordinarily resident from the day after the date of your departure providing

- your absence from the UK has covered at least a whole tax year, **and**
- your visits to the UK since leaving
    - have totalled less than 183 days in any tax year, and
    - have averaged less than 91 days a tax year. (The average is taken over the period of absence up to a maximum of four years - see paragraph 2.10. Any days spent in the UK because of exceptional circumstances beyond your control, for example the illness of yourself or a member of your immediate family, are not normally counted for this purpose.)

Appendix 1

2.9 If you do not have this evidence, but you have gone abroad for a settled purpose (this would include a fixed object or intention in which you are going to be engaged for an extended period of time), you will be treated as not resident and not ordinarily resident from the day after the date of your departure providing

- your absence from the UK has covered at least a whole tax year, **and**
- your visits to the UK since leaving
    - have totalled less than 183 days in any tax year, and
    - have averaged less than 91 days a tax year.

If you have not gone abroad for a settled purpose, you will be treated as remaining resident and ordinarily resident in the UK, but your status can be reviewed if

- your absence actually covers three years from your departure, or
- evidence becomes available to show that you have left the UK permanently

providing in either case your visits to the UK since leaving have totalled less than 183 days in any tax year and have averaged less than 91 days a tax year.

(Please see the Appendix at the end of this guidance for notes on a relevant case.)

Calculating annual average visits

2.10 If it is necessary to calculate your annual average visits to the UK, the method is as follows:

Total visits to the UK (in days) x 365 = annual average visits
Total period since leaving (in days)

For this purpose, days spent in the UK in the tax year before the date of your original departure are excluded.

Suppose, for example, you leave the UK on 5 October 2003. The first review of the average of your visits is made after 5 April 2005, and takes account of your visits between those two dates. If you visited the UK for 30 days between 6 October 2003 and 5 April 2004 and for 50 days in 2004-2005, the annual average is

$$\frac{30 + 50}{182 + 365} \times 365 = \frac{80}{547} \times 365 = 53.38 \text{ days}$$

If you continue to remain outside the UK, the annual average is calculated as follows in reviews after 5 April in subsequent years

- after 5 April 2006 - include visits from 5 October 2003 to 5 April 2006
- after 5 April 2007 - include visits from 5 October 2003 to 5 April 2007
- after 5 April 2008 - include visits from 6 April 2004 to 5 April 2008.

After the third review the year of departure is dropped from the calculation. At each subsequent review the oldest year is dropped, so that there is a rolling period of four years being reviewed.

However, if during your absence the pattern of your visits varied substantially year by year, it might be appropriate to look at the absence as being made up of separate

Inland Revenue Bulletin IR20 (2008)

periods for the purpose of calculating average visits. This might be necessary if, for example, a shift in the pattern of your visits suggested a change of circumstances, which altered how we viewed your residence status.

Contacting HM Revenue & Customs

2.11 You should let us know when you leave the UK (other than for short trips as in paragraph 2.1). You will normally be asked to complete form **P85**, which will help to determine your residence status.

Tax treatment after leaving the UK

2.12 For details of the tax treatment of your earned income (such as earnings from employment) after you have ceased to be resident in the UK, see Chapter 5 and in particular paragraphs 5.1 - 5.3 and the tables at 5.19 - 5.21. For similar details in the case of any investment income you may have (for example, interest arising in the UK), see Chapter 6 and in particular paragraph 6.3.

2.13 Some special provisions applying to those who leave the UK are dealt with as follows

- earnings of those who come to the UK
  part way through a tax year: paragraph 5.4

- earnings of those who leave the UK
  part way through a tax year: paragraph 5.4

- UK Government securities; interest
  arising in year of departure from UK: paragraph 6.7

- investment income of those leaving
  the UK part way through a tax year: paragraphs 6.15 - 6.16

- tax allowances: paragraph 7.4

- capital gains: paragraphs 8.3 - 8.6

Special classes of employees

2.14 Special rules apply to some employees working abroad. If one of the classes shown below applies to you, write to the HM Revenue & Customs office shown - the addresses appear in paragraph 9 of the Introduction. Please give your UK National Insurance number and details of your employment abroad. We will advise you of your tax position.

Class	Write to HM Revenue & Customs
Crown employees (e.g. civil servants, diplomats, members of the armed forces, etc.)	HMRC South Wales
European Union (EU) employees	CAR Residency, Bootle
Employees working in oil and gas exploration and extraction industries (where the employer is not resident in the UK)	Foreign Compliance, Compliance Centre 1
Merchant Navy seafarers	HMRC South Wales

Appendix 1

3 Coming to the UK

Coming to the UK permanently or indefinitely

3.1 You are treated as **resident and ordinarily resident** from the date you arrive if your home has been abroad and you intend

- to come to the UK to live here **permanently**, or
- to come and remain here for **three years or more.**

You 'remain' in the UK if you are here on a continuing basis and any departures are for holidays or short business trips. (The same applies for the other references in this Chapter to 'remaining' in the UK.)

Visitors to the UK

3.2 If you come to the UK other than to live here permanently as in paragraph 3.1, the guidelines in the rest of this Chapter will govern your residence and ordinary residence position in the UK.

The Chapter deals in turn with two main groups coming to this country

- **short term visitors** - where you visit the UK for only limited periods in one or more tax years, without any intention to remain for an extended period
- **longer term visitors** - where you come to the UK intending to remain indefinitely or for an extended period, perhaps stretching over several tax years.

At first you may fall within one of these categories and later move to the other, depending on your precise circumstances.

Short term visitors

Residence

3.3 You will be treated as **resident** for a tax year if

- you are in the UK for 183 days or more in the tax year (see paragraph 1.2), or
- you visit the UK regularly and after four tax years your visits during those years average 91 days or more a tax year - see paragraph 3.6. You are treated as resident from the fifth year. However

    - any days spent in the UK for exceptional circumstances beyond your control, for example the illness of yourself or a member of your immediate family, are not counted for this purpose

    - you are treated as resident from 6 April of the first year, if it is clear when you first come to the UK that you **intend** making such visits and you actually carry out your intention

    - you are treated as resident from 6 April of the tax year in which you **decide** that you will make such visits, where this decision is made before the start of the fifth tax year and you actually carry out your decision.

For example

- you come to the UK with no definite intentions, but your visits during the tax years 2007-2008 to 2010-2011 average at least 91 days a tax year; you are resident from

Inland Revenue Bulletin IR20 (2008)

6 April 2011

- you first come to the UK during 2007-2008, intending that between then and 5 April 2011 your visits will average at least 91 days a tax year; you are resident from 6 April 2007, provided that your visits in fact reach that level

- you first come to the UK during 2007-2008 with no definite intentions and you spend, say, 60 days here; you come again during 2008-2009 and decide you will come regularly in future years and your visits will average at least 91 days a tax year; you are resident from 6 April 2008, provided that your visits in fact reach that level.

Ordinary residence

3.4 You will be treated as **ordinarily resident** if you come to the UK regularly and your visits average 91 days or more a tax year - see paragraph 3.6. Any days spent in the UK for exceptional circumstances beyond your control, for example the illness of yourself or a member of your immediate family, are not normally counted for this purpose.

3.5 The date from which you are treated as ordinarily resident depends upon your intentions and whether you actually carry them out. You will be ordinarily resident

- from 6 April of the tax year of your first arrival, if it is clear when you first come here that you **intend** visiting the UK regularly for at least four tax years

- from 6 April of the fifth tax year after you have visited the UK over four years, if you originally came with no definite plans about the number of years you will visit

- from 6 April of the tax year in which you **decide** you will be visiting the UK regularly, if that decision is made before the start of the fifth tax year.

For example

- you first come to the UK during 2005-2006, you intend visiting regularly until at least 5 April 2009 and your visits will average at least 91 days a tax year. You are ordinarily resident from 6 April 2005

- you come to the UK with no definite intentions, but you visit regularly during the tax years 2005-2006 to 2008-2009 and your visits average at least 91 days a tax year. You are ordinarily resident from 6 April 2009

- you first come to the UK during 2005-2006 with no definite intentions; you come again in 2006-2007 and 2007-2008 during 2007-2008 you decide you will come regularly in future years, and your visits will average at least 91 days a tax year. You are ordinarily resident from 6 April 2007.

Appendix 1

Calculating annual average visits

3.6 Where it is necessary to calculate your annual average visits, the method is as follows:

Total visits to the UK (in days) x 365 = annual average visits
Relevant tax years (in days)

For example, suppose you visited the UK for 80 days in 2001-2002, 100 days in 2002-2003, 85 days in 2003-2004 and 105 days in 2004-2005. The annual average is

80+100+85+105 x 365 = 370 x 365 = 92.44 days
366+365+365+365   1461

Longer term visitors

Residence

3.7 You are treated as **resident** in the UK from the day you arrive to the day you leave (see paragraphs 1.5 - 1.6) if you come to the UK for a purpose (for example, employment) that will mean you remain here for at least **two years**. The same treatment will apply if you own or lease accommodation in the UK in the year you arrive here (see paragraph 3.11, first bullet).

In all other cases you will be treated as resident for the tax year if

- you spend 183 days or more in the UK in the tax year, or
- you own or lease accommodation in the UK (see paragraph 3.11, second bullet).

Ordinary residence

3.8 You will be treated as **ordinarily resident** in the UK from the date you arrive, whether to work here or not, if it is clear that you **intend** to stay for at least **three years**.

If you come to the UK **as a student** for an extended period of study or education, see paragraph 3.13.

3.9 You will be treated as ordinarily resident from the beginning of the tax year after the third anniversary of your arrival if you come to, and remain in, the UK, but you

- do not originally intend to stay for at least three years, and
- do not buy accommodation or acquire it on a lease of three years or more.

For example, if you arrive in the UK on 21 November 2005 and are still living in the UK on 6 April 2009, you are ordinarily resident from 6 April 2009.

3.10 If, after you have come to the UK, you **decide** to stay for at least **three years** from the date of your original arrival, you will be treated as ordinarily resident from

- the day you arrive if your decision is made in the tax year of arrival, or
- the beginning of the tax year in which you make your decision when this is after the year of arrival.

For example

- you arrive in the UK on 4 January 2006 and decide on 16 May 2006 to stay permanently. You are ordinarily resident from 6 April 2006
- you come to the UK to work on 14 July 2005 on a 2½ year contract of

Inland Revenue Bulletin IR20 (2008)

employment, but in December 2007 your assignment is changed and your contract is extended until after July 2008*. You are ordinarily resident from 6 April 2007.

* If there is a change in the circumstances of your assignment, but no formal change to the terms of a contract, whether you are treated as ordinarily resident - and from what date - will depend on the precise facts.

3.11 If you come to, and remain in, the UK, you will be treated as ordinarily resident

- from the day you arrive, if
    - you already own accommodation here
    - you buy accommodation during the tax year of arrival, or
    - you have or acquire accommodation on a lease of three years or more during the tax year of arrival; or

- from 6 April of the tax year in which such accommodation becomes available, when this occurs after the year of arrival.

3.12 If you are treated as ordinarily resident **solely** because you have accommodation here (paragraph 3.11) and you dispose of the accommodation and leave the UK within three years of your arrival, you may be treated as not ordinarily resident for the duration of your stay if this is to your advantage.

3.13 If you are a **student** who comes to the UK for a period of study or education and you will be here for less than **four years**, you will be treated as not ordinarily resident, providing

- you do not own or buy accommodation here, or acquire it on a lease of three years or more, and

- on leaving the UK you do not plan to return regularly for visits which average 91 days or more a tax year.

Contacting HM Revenue & Customs

3.14 You should let us know when you come to the UK. You will normally be asked to complete form **P86**, which will help to determine your residence status.

Tax treatment after arrival in the UK

3.15 For details of the tax treatment of your earned income both in the UK and abroad (such as earnings from employments) after you have become resident in the UK, see Chapter 5 and in particular paragraphs 5.1 - 5.3, 5.9 - 5.12 and the tables at 5.19 - 5.21. For details of the treatment of any investment income you may have, see Chapter 6 and in particular paragraph 6.2.

213

Appendix 1

3.16 Some special provisions applying to those coming to the UK are dealt with as follows

- earnings of those who come to the UK part way through a tax year: paragraph 5.4

- lump sums from overseas pension schemes and provident funds: paragraph 5.16

- UK Government securities: interest arising in year of arrival in UK: paragraph 6.7

- investment income of those coming to the UK part way through a tax year: paragraphs 6.18 onwards

- tax allowances: paragraph 7.4

- capital gains: paragraphs 8.3 - 8.6

4 Domicile

4.1 Domicile is a general law concept. It is not possible to list all the factors that affect your domicile, but some of the main points are explained in this Chapter.

4.2 Broadly speaking, you are domiciled in the country where you have your permanent home. Domicile is distinct from nationality or residence. You can only have one domicile at any given time.

Domicile of origin

4.3 You normally acquire a **domicile of origin** from your father when you are born. It need not be the country in which you are born. For example, if you are born in France while your father is working there, but his permanent home is in the UK, your domicile of origin is in the UK.

Domicile of dependency

4.4 Until you have the legal capacity to change it - see paragraph 4.5 - your domicile will follow that of the person on whom you are legally dependent. If the domicile of that person changes, you automatically acquire the same domicile (a **domicile of dependency**), in place of your domicile of origin.

Domicile of choice

4.5 You have the legal capacity to acquire a new domicile (a **domicile of choice**) when you reach age 16. To do so, you must broadly leave your current country of domicile and settle in another country. You need to provide strong evidence that you intend to live there permanently or indefinitely. Living in another country for a long time, although an important factor, is not enough in itself to prove you have acquired a new domicile.

Married women

4.6 Before 1974, when you married you automatically acquired your husband's domicile. After marriage this domicile would change at the same time as your husband's domicile changed. If your marriage ended, you kept your husband's domicile until such time as you legally acquired a new domicile.
This rule is modified by the terms of the double taxation agreement between the UK and the USA. A marriage before 1974 between a woman who is a US national and a man

Inland Revenue Bulletin IR20 (2008)

domiciled within the UK is deemed to have taken place on 1 January 1974 for the purpose of determining her domicile on or after 6 April 1976 for UK tax purposes.

4.7 From 1 January 1974 your domicile is not necessarily the same as your husband's domicile. It is decided by the same factors as for any other individual who is able to have an independent domicile. If, however, you were married before 1974 and had acquired your husband's domicile (see paragraph 4.6), you **retain** this after 1 January 1974 until such time as you legally acquire a new domicile.

Overseas electors

4.8 From 6 April 1996 registering and voting as an overseas elector is not normally taken into account as one of the factors for determining whether you are domiciled in the UK, for the purpose of establishing your tax liability here.

Tax treatment of those not domiciled in the UK

4.9 Those who are resident in the UK but not domiciled here receive special tax treatment in respect of income and gains arising outside the UK. For details, see paragraphs 5.12 and 6.2 (income tax) and 8.8 (capital gains tax). We will consider the question of your domicile only where this will affect your current tax liability.

For inheritance tax purposes, see booklet, 'Customer Guide to Inheritance Tax'.

Part II Liability to UK tax

5 Earned income

Basis of liability

5.1 Finance Act 2008 introduced some new rules for remittance basis users, so for claims and remittances after 6 April 2008 you will need to consider whether these new rules (which are outlined in this chapter – particularly at 5.12) will apply to your circumstances.

If you are **resident in the UK** under the rules in Part I of this booklet, you will normally pay UK tax on all your earned income, wherever it arises. This is called the 'arising basis of taxation'. As well as earnings for employment, earned income includes items such as pensions and income from a trade, profession or vocation. You may, however, be entitled to a reduction in the UK tax you have to pay if you receive overseas earnings and spend long periods abroad (see paragraphs 5.9 - 5.10) or if you receive an overseas pension (see paragraph 5.11). In certain cases where you are resident but **not ordinarily resident** in the UK, or resident but **not domiciled** here, we may deal with your overseas income on the 'remittance basis' (see paragraphs 5.9, 5.11 - 5.12).

5.2 If you are **not resident in the UK**, we will generally tax you on any UK pensions or on earnings from employment the duties of which are carried on in this country. Where your duties are carried on partly in the UK and partly abroad, an allocation, based on days worked in the UK and days worked abroad, will normally be made to ascertain the earnings for duties carried on in this country which are liable for UK tax. We will not tax you on earnings from an employment which is carried on wholly abroad (see paragraph 5.5). See paragraph 5.4 for the position if you become resident in the UK part way through a tax year and 5.9 regarding overseas earnings taxable on the remittance basis. In some cases you may make a claim under a double taxation agreement for exemption from UK tax on your UK pension, or on earnings arising in this country (see Chapter 9 and in particular paragraphs 9.3, 9.4 and 9.6).

Appendix 1

We will tax you on the profits of a trade, profession or vocation which is not carried on wholly outside the UK.

5.3 The tables at the end of this Chapter show in more detail how your pensions, earnings from any office or employment or profits from a trade, profession or vocation will be taxed, depending on your residence status and the place where your duties are performed. You should ask your Tax Office if you need further information or advice about your own tax position (paragraph 7 of the Introduction).

Special rules apply in the case of Crown employees - see paragraph 2.14.

Earnings of those who come to, or leave, the UK part way through a tax year

5.4 If you come to the UK during a tax year and are treated as resident here from the date of your arrival, by concession (extra-statutory concession A11) you will not pay tax on earnings for the part of the year before you arrive here, where these are from an employment carried on wholly abroad.

A similar concession applies if you leave the UK during a tax year and are treated as resident here up to and including the date of your departure. You will not pay tax on earnings for the part of the year after you leave the UK, where these are from an employment carried on wholly abroad.

In the case of earned income **other than** earnings from employment, the rules are the same as those for unearned income - see paragraphs 6.15 - 6.20.

If you are paid for a period of leave spent in the UK following work abroad, we treat this 'terminal leave pay' as arising during the period to which it relates even if your entitlement to it was built up over a period of overseas employment. Leave pay is normally taxable in the UK where an individual is resident here. It may, however, be covered by the 'foreign earnings deduction' if the leave immediately follows a period abroad which is a 'qualifying period' (see paragraphs 5.9 - 5.10, and footnote 2 to the table at 5.19, on the foreign earnings deduction).

Where your duties are performed

5.5 The table at 5.19 shows that the place where your duties are performed is a key factor in deciding the tax treatment of your earnings. If your work is usually done abroad but some duties are performed in the UK, we will treat these as though they had been performed abroad as long as they are merely **incidental** to your overseas duties (see paragraphs 5.7 and 5.8).

5.6 Where you are a seafarer or a member of an aircraft crew, we normally treat your duties as performed in the UK if

- the voyage or flight does not extend to a place outside the UK, or
- you are resident in the UK and the voyage or flight begins or ends in the UK, or
- you are resident in the UK and embarked on part of a voyage or flight which begins or ends in the UK.

A different rule applies for the purposes of the foreign earnings deduction (see paragraphs 5.9 - 5.10 and footnote 2 to the table at 5.19).

Inland Revenue Bulletin IR20 (2008)

Incidental duties

5.7 Whether duties you perform in the UK are 'incidental' to your overseas duties (paragraph 5.5) depends on all the circumstances. If the work you do in the UK is of the same kind as, or of similar importance to, the work that you do abroad, it will **not** be merely incidental unless it can be shown to be ancillary or subordinate to that work. It is normally the nature of the duties performed in the UK rather than the amount of time spent on them that is important, but if the total time you spend working in the UK is more than 91 days in a year, the work will not be treated as incidental. Examples of duties which we do **not** normally regard as incidental are

- attendance at directors' meetings in the UK by a director of the company who normally works abroad
- visits to the UK as a member of the crew of a ship or aircraft
- visits to the UK in the course of work by a courier.

5.8 If the work you do in the UK has no importance in itself, but simply enables you to do your normal work abroad, it may be treated as incidental. We will decide after looking at all the circumstances in your case. Examples of duties which we regard as incidental are

- visits to the UK by an overseas representative of a UK employer to report to the employer or to receive fresh instructions
- training in the UK by an overseas employee as long as
  - the total time spent in the UK for training is not more than 91 days in a year, and
  - no productive work is done in the UK in that time.

Earned income arising outside the UK

5.9 In the case of **earnings from employment**, the table at 5.19 sets out the tax position. If you are resident in the UK, we will normally tax you on all earnings you receive from sources abroad. In certain circumstances, however, you may be entitled to a deduction of 100% on certain earnings from an employment performed wholly or partly overseas, if you are resident (and ordinarily resident) in the UK but spend a sufficient number of days abroad (see paragraph 5.10).

For all years up to and including the year ended 5 April 2008, the default position is that you will be taxed on the earnings from your overseas employment on the **remittance basis** (see also paragraph 5.12) if you are

- resident but not ordinarily resident in the UK, or
- resident and ordinarily resident but not domiciled in the UK - but only in the case of 'foreign emoluments' where the duties of the employment are performed wholly outside the UK (see footnote 1 to the table at 5.19).

For tax years from 6 April 2008, although the qualifying criteria for the remittance basis have not changed, it is no longer mandatory in respect of earnings from overseas employment; instead, most individuals who wish to be taxed on the remittance basis are required to make a claim for it (see paragraph 5.12). In some circumstances there are certain exceptions from this general requirement to make a claim (see paragraph 5.12a)

5.10 The **foreign earnings deduction** in certain circumstances provides a deduction of

Appendix 1

100% from the amount of earnings chargeable where the following conditions are met

- the duties of your employment are performed wholly or partly overseas
- you remain resident and ordinarily resident in the UK while working abroad
- the earnings are for a period which is part of a qualifying absence lasting 365 days or more.

Up to **16 March 1998** the Foreign Earnings Deduction could be claimed by all employees, but after that date it is **only available to seafarers**. 'Seafarers' are individuals who perform the duties of their employment on a ship. A 'ship' would not include offshore installations such as mobile offshore drilling rigs.

For further details of the current rules

- seafarers may contact HMRC South Wales (see paragraph 9 of the Introduction)
- workers in the oil and gas industry may obtain further information from Foreign Compliance, Compliance Centre 1 (see paragraph 9 of the Introduction and paragraph 5.17).

5.11 In the case of **other types of earned income**, such as **overseas pensions** and income from an overseas trade, profession or vocation, the tables at 5.20 and 5.21 set out the position. We will normally tax you on all the income you receive from overseas sources if you are resident in the UK. You may, however, be entitled to a 10% deduction from the amount chargeable in the case of overseas pensions.

For all years up to and including the year ended 5 April 2008 the default position is that you will be taxed on your other earned income from overseas sources on the **remittance basis** (see paragraph 5.12) if you are

- resident but not domiciled in the UK, or
- resident but not ordinarily resident in the UK,

For these years, the remittance basis does **not** apply to other types of earned income arising in the Republic of Ireland.

For tax years from 6 April 2008, although the qualifying criteria for the remittance basis have not changed, individuals who wish to be taxed on it are required to make a claim for it to apply (see also paragraph 5.12). In some circumstances there are certain exceptions from this general requirement to make a claim (see paragraph 5.12a).

For tax years from 6 April 2008 the remittance basis may also now apply to certain types of earned income arising in the Republic of Ireland.

5.12 Where the **remittance basis** applies, you are liable to UK tax on the amount of your overseas income that is remitted to the UK. Income is remitted if it is paid here or transmitted or brought to the UK in any way. In working out your tax liability, we include all income remitted to the UK.

Where you are taxed on the remittance basis, you will **not** be able to claim either the 100% deduction for foreign earnings (see paragraphs 5.9 - 5.10) or the deduction for overseas pensions (see paragraph 5.11).

The remittance basis may also apply to any overseas investment income you receive (see paragraph 6.2) and to capital gains arising overseas (see paragraph 8.8).

For years up to and including the tax year ending 5 April 2008, the default position is that you will be taxed on the remittance basis on your overseas employment income and overseas chargeable gains but you must claim it for other income. The remittance basis applies if you are

- resident but not domiciled in the UK: and/or
- resident but not ordinarily resident in the UK

However, if you qualify for the remittance basis because you are resident but not ordinarily resident in the UK then the remittance basis is only available for income, not capital gains. Only those not domiciled in the UK can claim the remittance basis on capital gains.

For tax years from 6 April 2008 onwards, although the basis of entitlement for the remittance basis has not changed, in most cases individuals who wish to use the remittance basis of taxation are required to make an annual claim for that basis to apply. There are some exceptions to this outlined in 5.12 (a) below.

a) If you have less than £2,000 unremitted overseas income and gains in a tax year, this change may not affect you. You will continue to have access to the remittance basis by default, that is, without making any claim. This allows you to pay UK tax on your UK income and gains and on any overseas income and gains which you remit to the UK. You will also;

- keep your entitlement to UK personal tax allowances and to the annual exempt amount for capital gains tax (AEA).
- not need to pay the Remittance Basis Charge (RBC) – see paragraph 5.12(d)

b) If you have more than £2,000 unremitted overseas income or gains in a tax year, you will need to make a claim for that year if you want the remittance basis to apply to you. If you do not make a claim for the remittance basis, you will be taxed on the arising basis (see paragraph 5.1) and will pay UK tax on all of your worldwide income, even if it remains outside the UK.

You make a claim for the remittance basis via the Self Assessment system. If you do not currently receive a Self Assessment return and want to claim the remittance basis, you will need to ask us for a return by contacting your tax office. If you do not have a tax office, contact your local HMRC tax office to arrange to have a return issued to you.

Appendix 1

However, if, in a tax year:

- you have no UK income and gains; and
- you have not remitted any overseas income or gains to the UK; and
- you have not been resident in the UK for this year and at least seven of the previous nine tax years;

you will not be required to complete a Self Assessment return, even if the level of your unremitted overseas income and gains arising in this tax year is £2,000 or more.

If you have more than £2,000 unremitted overseas income or gains in a tax year and you choose to claim the remittance basis, you will still need to pay UK tax on your UK income and gains and on any overseas income and gains which you remit to the UK. In addition

- you will lose your entitlement to UK personal tax allowances and the annual exempt amount for capital gains tax. UK personal allowances include the basic personal allowance; age related allowances, blind person's allowance, tax reductions for married couples and civil partners and relief for life insurance premiums

- you will need to pay the Remittance Basis Charge (RBC – see paragraph 5.12(c)) if you have been resident in the UK in the tax year that you make the claim for the remittance basis and for at least seven of the previous nine tax years. In counting the number of tax years you have been resident for this purpose, you include those tax years when you were resident in the UK prior to 6 April 2008.

If you choose not to claim the remittance basis you will be dealt with on the arising basis (see paragraph 5.1) and will pay UK tax on all of your worldwide income. You can decide on a year-by-year basis whether or not you want to claim the remittance basis or be taxed on the arising basis.

Depending on your circumstances, when you are taxed on the arising basis and have overseas tax deducted from overseas income and/or gains, you might be entitled to Foreign Tax Credit Relief in the UK. This will depend on the terms of any Double Taxation Agreement existing between the UK and the country where the tax was deducted. In some cases, where there is no Double Taxation agreement, the UK might give unilateral relief for overseas tax deducted.

If you choose to be taxed on the remittance basis it applies to *all* of your income and gains. You cannot decide to apply the remittance basis only to income and not gains or vice versa. However, as mentioned above, where you claim the remittance basis because you are not ordinarily resident in the UK, as opposed to not domicile in the UK, then the remittance basis applies only to income, not gains.

Inland Revenue Bulletin IR20 (2008)

c) The Remittance Basis Charge (RBC)

From 6 April 2008 the RBC will apply to some people who wish to use the remittance basis. The RBC is an annual tax charge of £30,000 in respect of overseas income and gains left outside the UK.

If you have £2,000 or more in a tax year from overseas income and/or gains which you have not remitted to the UK you will pay the RBC if:

- you make a claim to use the remittance basis

- you are resident in the UK in the year that you make your claim for the remittance basis and are aged 18 or over at the end of the tax year **and**

- you were resident in the UK for at least seven of the previous nine tax years. In counting the number of tax years you have been resident for this purpose, you include all tax years when you were resident in the UK prior to 6 April 2008 (even if you were under 18 years old in some of them).

A flow chart at Appendix 2 will help you decide if you need to pay the RBC. If you do not wish to pay the RBC you can choose not to claim the remittance basis. You will then be taxed on the arising basis instead and will pay UK tax on your worldwide income – see paragraph 5.1.

d) The nature of the Remittance Basis Charge (RBC)

The £30,000 RBC is an annual tax charge in respect of overseas income and gains left outside the UK. It is in addition to any UK tax due on either UK income and gains or overseas income and gains remitted to the UK. The charge is due if it is appropriate to your circumstances as declared on your Self Assessment return (see 5.12(b)).

The RBC will be Income Tax, Capital Gains Tax or a combination of the two; when you make your claim for the remittance basis you must nominate how much of your foreign income and/or how much of your foreign gains the £30,000 tax charge is in respect of. This is known as your 'nominated' foreign income or gains. As the RBC will be Income Tax, Capital Gains Tax or a combination of the two, the Income tax and Capital Gains Tax elements should be creditable under many Double Taxation Agreements. The Income Tax element will also be available to cover UK Gift Aid donations.

If any of the 'nominated' foreign income or gains on which you have paid the RBC are remitted to the UK at a later date, they will not be taxed again. However, there are ordering rules which provide that in any year, any previously unremitted foreign income and gains will be considered to have been remitted before any of the nominated foreign income and gains on which the £30,000 RBC has been paid.

If you pay the £30,000 RBC from outside the UK it will not be treated as a remittance provided the payment is made direct to HMRC by

- cheque

- electronic payment of funds

If the £30,000 is later repaid to you, it will be regarded as a remittance when the repayment is made and **will** be subject to UK tax.

Appendix 1

Change of location of a trade, profession or vocation

From 6 April 1997 (or from 6 April 1995 for businesses which started on or after 6 April 1994)

5.13 If you have been carrying on a business wholly or partly outside the UK and you either become resident in the UK or cease to be resident in the UK, we will treat you at that point as having discontinued one business and started a new one. This means that the special cessation provisions will apply up to the date of 'deemed' cessation and the special commencement provisions from the date of deemed commencement.

Cessation and commencement of residence (and therefore deemed cessation and commencement of trade) usually take place at the start of the tax year in which your change of residence occurs. However, if you satisfy the conditions set out in paragraphs 1.5 - 1.6, the deemed cessation and commencement will take place on your actual date of arrival or departure.

Despite the deemed cessation and commencement, any losses incurred before the change of residence can be carried forward and set against profits of the business, as long as it would have been the same business under the rules in paragraph 5.14.

Before 6 April 1997 (or, where appropriate, 6 April 1995)

5.14 Whether a change of residence triggers the discontinuance of one business and the commencement of another is a question of fact. It depends on where the business is carried on rather than where the proprietor resides. Most trades and professions are carried on in a particular location (for example a shop, office or factory), so that a significant change of business location (such as from one country to another) will normally mean that the new business is a different one from the old business. This means that the cessation provisions will apply to your old business and the commencement provisions to the new one. It also means that losses from your old business cannot be carried forward and set against profits of the new business.

A few businesses, mainly of professional people, are not localised in this way, but are carried on wherever in the world the person happens to be. Examples are international actors, musicians, authors and sportsmen/women. If you are carrying on this kind of profession and continue to carry it on in the same way after a change of residence, it will be the same profession, and neither the cessation nor the commencement provisions will apply. However, for the year of change of residence, we will only assess you on a proportion of your profits for the full year, reflecting the profits made in the period from the date of your arrival in the UK to the following 5 April (or in the period from the preceding 6 April to the date of departure from the UK).

UK social security benefits

5.15 Various UK social security benefits including, for example, National Insurance Retirement Pension and widow's payments, are liable to UK tax. However, some relief from UK tax may be due under the terms of a double taxation agreement if you are not resident in the UK (see also paragraph 9.3).

From the year 1996-97, if you are not resident in the UK for the whole of a tax year and do not claim relief under the terms of a double taxation agreement, your liability on taxable UK social security benefits is limited to the tax, if any, deducted before payment.

Lump sums from overseas pension schemes and provident funds

5.16 By concession (extra-statutory concession A10), we will not charge income tax (or we will charge it only on a reduced amount) if you receive lump sum retirement benefits, relating to an employment overseas, under an overseas pension scheme or provident fund.

Inland Revenue Bulletin IR20 (2008)

The level of relief will depend on the extent of your overseas service. You qualify for full exemption where in that employment

- at least 75% of your total service was overseas, or
- your total service exceeds 10 years and the whole of the last 10 years of service have been overseas, or
- your total service exceeds 20 years and not less than 50% of total service, including any 10 of the last 20 years, was overseas.

If you do not meet the conditions for full exemption, we will charge income tax only on that percentage of the lump sum equivalent to your non-overseas service in that employment.

Offshore oil and gas workers

5.17 If you work offshore in connection with the exploration or exploitation of UK oil or gas, the rules set out in the first part of this Chapter still normally apply to you. In this context 'offshore' means

- the territorial sea of the UK (see paragraph 6 of the Introduction), and
- the UK continental shelf outside the territorial sea.

If, however, you are a resident of a country with which the UK has a double taxation agreement, the normal rules may be affected by that agreement (see Chapter 9 on agreements generally). Some of these include provisions specific to offshore oil and gas activities. You should put any queries about your tax liabilities to your Tax Office, if your employer is resident in the UK; or to Foreign Compliance, Compliance Centre 1, if your employer is not resident in the UK.

Partnerships

5.18 If you carry on a trade or profession in a partnership, the table at 5.21 sets out the position. In those circumstances, the remittance basis (see paragraph 5.12) may apply to your overseas profit, where the trade

- is carried on wholly abroad, or
- is carried on partly abroad and the partnership is managed and controlled abroad

 and in either case you are a UK resident partner and are

- not domiciled in the UK, or
- not ordinarily resident in the UK.

Appendix 1

5.19 Scope of liability to income tax of earnings

		Duties of employment performed wholly or partly in the UK		Duties of employment performed wholly outside the UK
		In the UK	outside the UK	
Foreign emoluments[1]	Employee resident and ordinarily resident in the UK	Liable – less possible deduction[2]	Liable – less possible deduction[2]	Liable if received in the UK[3]
	Resident but not ordinarily resident	Liable	Liable if received in the UK[3]	Liable if received in the UK[3]
	Not resident	Liable	Not liable	Not liable
Other earnings	Resident and ordinarily resident	Liable – less possible deduction[2]	Liable – less possible deduction[2]	Liable – less possible deduction[2]
	Resident but not ordinarily resident	Liable	Liable if received in the UK[3]	Liable if received in the UK[3]
	Not resident	Liable	Not liable	Not liable

1. '**Foreign emoluments**' is the term used in the Taxes Acts to mean the earnings of someone who is not domiciled in the UK and whose employer is resident outside, and not resident in, the UK For all tax years up to and including the year ended 5 April 2008 only, this includes an employer not resident in the Republic of Ireland.

2. There may be a **foreign earnings deduction** of 100% in these cases from the amount chargeable, if the earnings are for a period which is part of a qualifying absence lasting 365 days or more - this means that such earnings for that period will be free from UK tax. See paragraphs 5.9 - 5.10 for further details, and a summary of the changes that were introduced from 17 March 1998.

3. This tax treatment changed with effect from 6 April 2008. See paragraph 5.12 for details.

5.20 Scope of liability to income tax on individuals receiving pensions

	Paid by on behalf of a person	
	in the UK	outside the UK (overseas pension)
Residence status and domicile		
Resident and ordinarily resident, and domiciled	Liable	Liable[1]
Resident and ordinarily resident, not domiciled	Liable	Liable but may claim the remittance basis (paragraph 5.12) [2]
Resident but not ordinarily resident, domiciled	Liable	Liable but may claim the remittance basis[2]
Resident but not ordinarily resident, not domiciled	Liable	Liable but may claim the remittance basis (paragraph 5.12) [2]
Not resident	Liable[3,4]	Not liable

1. Less 10% deduction.

2. If a claim for the remittance basis is made then the 10% deduction referred to at 1 is not available. Up to the year ended 5 April 2008 the remittance basis cannot be claimed for a pension arising in the Republic of Ireland but the 10% deduction is available. If the pension is from the Irish Government you are taxable only if you are a UK national without also being an Irish national.

3. See Chapter 9 about possible relief under a double taxation agreement.

4. See paragraph 5.15 in the case of UK social security benefits such as National Insurance Retirement Pension.

Appendix 1

5.21 Scope of liability to income tax on profits of individuals carrying on a trade or profession

Residence status and domicile	Trade or profession carried on wholly or partly in the UK	Trade or profession carried on wholly outside the UK
Resident and ordinarily resident, and domiciled	Liable	Liable
Residence and ordinarily resident, not domiciled	Liable	Liable but may claim the remittance basis (see paragraph 5.12) [1]
Resident but not ordinarily resident, domiciled	Liable	Liable but may claim the remittance basis[1]
Resident but not ordinarily resident, not domiciled	Liable	Liable but may claim the remittance basis (see paragraph 5.12) [1]
Not resident	Liable[2]	Not liable

1. Up to the year ended 5 April 2008 you are taxable on the whole of the income of a trade or profession carried on wholly in the Republic of Ireland. From 6 April 2008 no distinction is made for the Republic of Ireland.

2. You are liable on the profits of the part of the trade or profession carried on the UK.

6 Investment income

General

6.1 Broadly, investment income means any income which is not a pension and is not earned by you as an employee, or from carrying on your profession or from running your own business. Among the more common types are

- interest from bank and building society accounts
- dividends on shares (see also paragraphs 9.11 - 9.13)
- interest on stocks
- rental income (unless your business amounts to a trade).

6.2 If you are **resident in the UK,** you will normally pay UK tax on all your investment income, wherever it arises. For tax years up to and including 5 April 2008, the **remittance basis of assessment can be claimed in respect of** overseas investment income (other than investment income arising in the Republic of Ireland) if you are

- resident but not domiciled in the UK; and/or
- resident but not ordinarily resident in the UK.

Where the **remittance basis** applies, you are liable to UK tax on the amount of your overseas investment income that is remitted to the UK. Income is remitted if it is paid here or transmitted or brought to the UK in any way. In working out your tax liability, we include all income remitted to the UK.

For tax years from 6 April 2008, although the basis for entitlement to the remittance basis has not changed, the rules for applying the remittance basis to your offshore investment income have. Details on this and on how to make a claim (including the effects of your doing so such as the loss of your entitlement to certain allowances and reliefs) can be found at paragraph 5.12. Depending on your circumstances, you might also be required to pay the Remittance Basis Charge (RBC) – see paragraph 5.12(c).

6.3 If you are **not resident in the UK**, we will only charge UK tax on investment income arising in the UK. Except in the case of UK rental income, if you are not carrying on a trade, profession or vocation through a UK branch or agency, your liability on investment income from 1996-97 will be limited to the tax, if any, deducted at source. However, if you have other UK income which is fully taxable, any personal allowances will be set against your investment income first.

If you are a resident of a country with which the UK has a double taxation agreement (see Chapter 9), you may in some cases be able to claim exemption or partial relief from UK tax on investment income (other than rental income from property in the UK).

Investment income arising in the UK

Income from property in the UK

6.4 Any profits you make from letting property situated in the UK are taxable in the UK, even if you cease to be resident in the UK. The following guidance applies to UK rental income from 6 April 1996.

6.5 Deleted from this version of IR20

Appendix 1

6.6 If your usual place of abode is outside the UK

- where you receive rental income direct from the tenant, the tenant must first deduct tax at the basic rate and pay it to HM Revenue & Customs

- where a letting agent collects the rental income for you, the letting agent must deduct tax at the basic rate from the income received less the allowable expenses paid on your behalf.

In either case you can set off the tax against your UK income tax liability when you complete your tax return.

You can, however, apply to CAR at Bootle (see paragraph 9 of the Introduction) for approval for your property income to be paid without tax being deducted providing

- your UK tax affairs are up to date, or

- you have never had any UK tax obligations, or

- you do not expect to be liable to UK income tax

and in all cases you undertake to comply with all your UK tax obligations.

Booklet IR140 'The Non-residents Landlords Scheme' was withdrawn in March 2006. Further information can be obtained from our website at **www.hmrc.gov.uk**

UK Government securities

6.7 UK tax is not chargeable on interest arising on **UK Government 'FOTRA' securities**, if you are not ordinarily resident in the UK. 'FOTRA' stands for 'Free of Tax to Residents Abroad'. Where we treat you as becoming, or ceasing to be, ordinarily resident in the UK part way through the tax year, no tax will normally be charged on interest payable while you are not ordinarily resident - that is, before the date you arrive here or after the date you leave.

Before 6 April 1998 FOTRA status only applied to certain UK Government securities. Please write to CAR at Nottingham (see paragraph 9 of the Introduction) if you want a list of the securities that had FOTRA status before 6 April 1998, or a form to claim repayment of tax.

6.8 UK tax is, however, charged if the interest forms part of the profits of a trade or business carried on in the UK. It is also charged in cases where laws to prevent tax avoidance provide that the income is to be treated as belonging to another person.

6.9 If you hold securities with a nominal value of more than £5,000 during a tax year in which you are resident in the UK at any time, special tax provisions (known as the '**accrued income scheme**') normally apply when the securities are transferred. You are charged income tax on the interest that has built up over the period you owned the securities following the last interest payment, even if you were not resident in the UK for part of that period. The leaflet 'Accrued income scheme – Taxing Securities on transfer' gives further details.

Interest from building societies and banks

6.10 Building societies, banks and other deposit takers in the UK normally deduct UK tax from interest paid or credited to your account. But if you are not ordinarily resident in the UK, you may be able to have the interest paid or credited without tax deducted. You can arrange this - assuming it is an option under the terms and conditions of your account - by completing a 'not ordinarily resident' declaration.

Any interest you receive without tax deducted is still liable to UK tax.

If your account includes the facility to make a 'not ordinarily resident' declaration and you want to arrange for your interest to be paid or credited without deduction of tax

- ask the building society, bank or deposit taker for a declaration form R105.
- if your account is a joint account, you can complete the declaration only if **all** the people who are beneficially entitled to the interest are not ordinarily resident in the UK
- give the completed declaration form to your building society, bank or deposit taker
- the declaration will have effect from the date on which your building society, bank or deposit taker receives it. It cannot be backdated to cover earlier interest payments
- if you later become ordinarily resident in the UK (or, in the case of a joint account, if any of the people who are beneficially entitled to the interest becomes ordinarily resident in the UK), you must notify your building society, bank or deposit taker without delay.

From the year 1996-97, where you are not resident for the whole tax year, your liability on interest from a UK bank or building society is limited to the tax, if any, deducted before payment, provided that you meet certain conditions.

6.11 Deleted from this version of IR20

6.12 Deleted from this version of IR20

Investment income arising outside the UK

6.13 Some income from overseas sources may not have UK tax deducted before it is paid to you. If you are resident in the UK, you will have to pay the tax due. For all years from 6 April 1997 to 5 April 2008 the tax due will be calculated on the whole amount arising or, if the remittance basis applies (see paragraph 6.2), the amount received in the UK in the year concerned.

For tax years from 6 April 2008 onwards, although the basis for entitlement to the remittance basis has not changed, the rules for applying the remittance basis to your offshore investment income have. Details on this and on how to make a claim (including the effects of your doing so, such as the loss of your entitlement to certain allowances and reliefs) can be found at paragraph 5.12. Depending on your circumstances, you might also be required to pay the Remittance Basis Charge (RBC) – see paragraph 5.12(c).

6.14 Deleted from this version of IR20

Appendix 1

Investment income of those who leave, or come to, the UK part way through a tax year

Leaving the UK

6.15 For tax years up to the year ending 5 April 2008, for overseas investment income where you are **not** taxed on the remittance basis, you will pay tax on the smaller of

- the actual overseas investment income arising for the period from 6 April to the date of your departure, and

- the same fraction of your total overseas income for the year of departure as the fraction of the full tax year for which you are resident in this country. For example, if you are resident in the UK from 6 April until 6 October in the same tax year, i.e. 6 months, the fraction is 6/12.

For tax years from 6 April 2008 onwards, the same rules will apply, depending on your personal circumstances. If you have chosen not to claim the remittance basis in the tax year of your departure you will be liable to pay UK tax on all of your income, including your overseas investment income, up to your departure from the UK – see paragraph 5.12.

6.16 For overseas investment income where you are taxed on the **remittance basis** (see paragraph 6.2), you will pay tax on the smaller of

- the actual overseas investment income remitted to the UK in the period from 6 April to the date of your departure, and

the same fraction of the total overseas income you remit to the UK in the year of departure as the fraction of the full tax year for which you are resident in this country.

Coming to the UK

6.17 Deleted from this version of IR20

6.18 Paragraphs 6.19 and 6.20 apply for years before 6 April 1996 and after 5 April 1997. There are special rules for the tax year 1996-97. Please contact CAR Residency at Bootle if you need further information for these years.

Also, for tax years from 6 April 2008 onwards, although the basis for entitlement to the remittance basis has not changed, the rules for applying the remittance basis to your offshore investment income have so if you wish to use the remittance basis you will need to consider how these changes will apply to your circumstances. Details on these changes and on how to make a claim (including the effects of your doing so such as the loss of your entitlement to certain allowances and reliefs) can be found at paragraph 5.12. Depending on your circumstances, you might also be required to pay the Remittance Basis Charge (RBC) – see paragraph 5.12(c).

Years before 6 April 1996 and after 5 April 1997

6.19 For the tax year of your arrival, where you receive overseas investment income from which tax has not been deducted and you are **not** taxed on the remittance basis, the following rules apply

- you will not have to pay tax on income from a source which ceases before the date of your arrival

- where the source continues after your arrival, but ceases in the same tax year, you will only pay tax on the income arising from the date of your arrival to the date the source ceased

Inland Revenue Bulletin IR20 (2008)

- where the source ceases in the tax year following the year of your arrival, you may be charged to tax for **both** years

    - **for the year of arrival**, you will pay tax on the greater of

    a. the same fraction of your overseas investment income for the year of arrival as the fraction of the full tax year for which you are resident in this country, and

    b. for years before 6 April 1996 the same fraction as in a. of your overseas income for the year preceding the year of arrival if the source was in existence at 5 April 1994

    - **for the year following the year of arrival**, you will pay tax on the overseas income arising from 6 April in that year to the date when the source ceased

- where the source continues to the end of the tax year of your arrival and beyond, and income first arose

    - in the tax year of your arrival but before you became resident here, or

    - for years up to and including 1995-96, in the previous tax year if the source was in existence at 5 April 1994

    you will only pay tax on the same fraction of your total overseas income for the year of arrival as the fraction of the full tax year for which you are resident in this country.

    > Suppose, for example, you come to the UK on 6 August 1993, and are resident for the rest of the tax year of your arrival (ending 5 April 1994). Your investment income continues beyond 5 April 1994, and first arose at some time between 6 April 1992 and 5 August 1993 (that is, in the tax year 1992-1993 or the first part of the year of your arrival). You are resident for 8 months during 1993-1994, and are therefore taxed on 8/12 of the whole of your investment income for that year

- for years up to and including 1995-1996 where the source continued as in the previous example, but income first arose **earlier** than the tax year before the year of your arrival, the fraction of income on which tax was chargeable was worked out in the same way as in the previous example, but the income in question was that of the year before the year of your arrival if the source was in existence at 5 April 1994.

    > Suppose the facts are as in the previous example, but your investment income first arose before 6 April 1992. You are taxed in the year of your arrival, 1993-1994, on 8/12 of your investment income for the tax year 1992-1993.

6.20 For the tax year of arrival, where you receive overseas investment income from which tax has not been deducted and you are taxed on the **remittance basis** (see paragraph 6.2), the following rules apply

- for tax years up to and including 6 April 2008, you will not have to pay tax on overseas investment income you remit from a source which ceased before the date of your arrival (for example, a bank account which you have closed)

- for tax years from 6 April 2008 onwards, you will have to pay tax on overseas income you remit from an overseas source which existed on or after 5 April 2007 but which ceased before the date of your arrival

Appendix 1

- where the source continues after your arrival but ceases in the same tax year, you will pay tax on the **lesser** of

  - the total overseas investment income that you remit to the UK in the year, and

  - the overseas income arising from the date of your arrival to the date the source ceased

- where the source ceases in the tax year following the year of your arrival, you may be charged to tax for **both** years

  - **for the year of arrival**, you will pay tax on the **lesser** of

    a. the overseas investment income you remit to the UK in that year (if the source was already in existence at 5 April 1994, the income remitted to the UK in the previous year if this is greater), and

    b. the same fraction of your total overseas income for the year of arrival (if the source was already in existence at 5 April 1994, the income remitted to the UK in the previous year if this is greater) as the fraction of the full tax year for which you are resident in this country

  - **for the year following the year of arrival**, you will pay tax on the overseas income you remit to the UK in that year, but reduced if necessary so that the sum taxed for the two years does not exceed the total of

    a. an amount worked out on the lines of b. above for the year of your arrival, and

    b. the amount of income arising from 6 April in the following year up to the date the source ceased.

6.21 Deleted from this version of IR20

6.22 Deleted from this version of IR20

6.23 Deleted from this version of IR20

6.24 Deleted from this version of IR20

6.25 Scope of liability to income tax on individuals receiving investment income

	Investment income arising in the UK	Investment income arising outside the UK	UK Government 'FOTRA' securities (see paragraph 6.7)
Residence status and domicile			
Resident and ordinarily resident, and domiciled	Liable	Liable	Liable
Resident and ordinarily resident, not domiciled	Liable	Liable, remittance basis may be claimed[1]	Liable
Resident but not ordinarily resident, domiciled	Liable	Liable, remittance basis may be claimed[1]	Not liable
resident but not ordinarily resident, not domiciled	Liable	Liable, remittance basis may be claimed[1]	Not liable
Not resident but ordinarily resident, domiciled	Liable[2]	Not liable	Liable
Not resident but ordinarily resident, not domiciled	Liable[2]	Not liable	Liable
Not resident and not ordinarily resident, domiciled	Liable[2]	Not liable	Not liable
Not resident and not ordinarily resident, not domiciled	Liable[2]	Not liable	Not liable

1. You are taxable on the whole of the income arising in the Republic of Ireland for all years up to and including 5 April 2008.

2. See Chapter 9 about possible relief under a double taxation agreement.

Appendix 1

7 Tax allowances and reliefs

Allowances for UK residents

7.1 If you are resident in the UK, you are entitled to certain allowances and reliefs, based on your personal circumstances, which reduce the amount of tax charged on your income.

However, from 6 April 2008, if you are resident in the UK and

- not domiciled in the UK and/or not ordinarily resident in the UK
- have £2000 or more in unremitted overseas income and/or gains
- are using the remittance basis – see paragraph 5.12

the legislation removes your entitlement to UK allowances and reliefs under domestic law.

7.2 UK residents who are employees have tax deducted at source from their wages or salaries under the 'Pay As You Earn' (PAYE) system. The employer deducts tax on the basis of code numbers issued for each employee by HM Revenue & Customs. These codes take account of the tax allowances and reliefs to which each individual is entitled. For more details, ask your Tax Office or HM Revenue & Customs Enquiry Centre.

From 6 April 2008 onwards, some people who use the remittance basis will not be entitled to UK personal tax allowances (see paragraphs 5.12 & 7.1). If you are not entitled to tax allowances because you use the remittance basis and you are continuing to receive them through the PAYE system, you will not be paying enough UK tax. You will need to complete a Self Assessment Return which will allow us to ensure that any tax you have underpaid is collected.

Allowances for non-UK residents

7.3 If you are **not resident** in the UK, you may claim tax allowances if you are any one of the following

- a Commonwealth citizen (this includes a British citizen)
- a citizen of a state within the European Economic Area (EEA), i.e. a citizen of a Member State of the European Union, Iceland, Liechtenstein or Norway (this includes a British citizen). For more details see 11.1
- a present or former employee of the British Crown (including a civil servant, member of the armed forces, etc.)
- a UK missionary society employee
- a civil servant in a territory under the protection of the British Crown
- a resident of the Isle of Man or the Channel Islands
- a former resident of the UK and you live abroad for the sake of your own health or the health of a member of your family who lives with you
- a widow, widower or the surviving civil partner of an employee of the British Crown
- a national and/or resident of a country with which the UK has a double taxation agreement which allows such a claim.

Allowances for those coming to, or leaving, the UK part way through a tax year

7.4 If you either become, or cease to be, resident in the UK during a tax year, you will be able to claim full allowances and reliefs for the year of arrival or departure (subject to 7.1 above).

7.5 Deleted from this version of IR20

How to claim tax allowances

7.6 If you wish to make a claim for tax allowances, you must do so within 5 years 10 months from the end of the tax year to which the claim relates. For example, if you wish to claim for the tax year 2001/2002 (6 April 2001 to 5 April 2002), you have until 31 January 2008.

7.7 UK residents may be sent a tax return. If you get one, you can use it to claim your allowances and reliefs. If you do not get a tax return, you can write to your Tax Office to claim allowances and reliefs if you are entitled to them.

7.8 If you are not resident in the UK, you should contact CAR at Bootle, **unless** you are an employee of the British Crown or receive a pension for Crown service, when you should contact HMRC South Wales. The addresses are in paragraph 9 of the Introduction.

8 Capital gains tax

Basis of liability

8.1 If you are either resident or ordinarily resident in the UK, you may be liable to capital gains tax on gains arising when you dispose of assets situated anywhere in the world. Disposing of an asset means selling, exchanging or transferring it, or giving it away, or realising a capital sum from it. Usually you will not pay capital gains tax

- on the transfer of an asset to your spouse

- on disposing of private motor vehicles

- on disposing of household goods and personal effects up to a value of £6,000 per item

- on disposing of a private home which has been treated as your only or main residence throughout the time you have owned it

- on gains arising from certain other assets - for example Save-As-You-Earn (SAYE) terminal bonuses, National Savings Certificates, Premium Bonds and investments held within an Individual Savings Account or Personal Equity Plan. Booklet 'Capital Gains Tax – An introduction' contains a fuller list.

If you have two or more residences, you can nominate one of them as your main residence for capital gains purposes by notifying your Tax Office. The residence you nominate need not be the same one as your main residence for mortgage interest tax relief purposes.

No tax is charged on the gains (after reliefs) you receive in any one year up to a certain amount. The 'annual exempt amount' for individuals is set at £9,200 for the tax year 2007-08. Husbands and wives are both entitled to their own annual exempt amount.

8.2 If you dispose of an asset you acquired before 31 March 1982, only the change in value since that date will generally be taken into account for determining the gain or loss. You may be able to make an election for this to apply in every case. An allowance is made for the effects of inflation up to April 1998 when computing gains. Taper relief, which reduces the amount of a gain which is chargeable to tax by reference to whole years of ownership, may be due for disposals on or after 6 April 1998. Booklet 'Capital Gains Tax - An introduction' gives more details.

Appendix 1

Gains by those who leave, or come to, the UK part way through a tax year

8.3 If you leave the UK during a tax year and cease to be resident or ordinarily resident in the UK, you may, by concession (extra-statutory concession D2), not be liable to capital gains tax on gains arising to you from disposals made after the date of your departure. However, if you leave the UK on or after 17 March 1998, you can qualify for this concession only if you were neither resident nor ordinarily resident in the UK for the whole of at least four of the seven tax years immediately preceding the tax year in which you leave the UK.

If you become resident in the UK during a tax year, having been neither resident nor ordinarily resident in the UK at any time during the five tax years immediately preceding that year, you are, by concession (extra-statutory concession D2), liable to capital gains tax only on gains arising from disposals made after the date of your arrival. If you arrived in the UK before 6 April 1998, the concession applied if you were neither resident nor ordinarily resident throughout the whole of the 36 months before the date of your arrival.

There is normally no charge to capital gains tax on your assets when you leave the UK if you do not actually make a disposal, nor is there any revaluation of assets when you come to the UK. However, in some cases, gains on which a charge has been held over or deferred, or which have been subject to a claim to reinvestment relief, may be brought back into charge if you become neither resident nor ordinarily resident in the UK. This charge will not apply if the reason you become neither resident nor ordinarily resident in the UK is that you are working abroad, provided that you become resident or ordinarily resident in the UK again within three years.

Temporary non-residence

8.4 If you have left the UK and dispose of assets while you are temporarily non-resident, special rules may apply for gains that would have been chargeable, and losses that would have been allowable, if you had been resident or ordinarily resident in the UK for the tax years in question. You are 'temporarily' non-resident if you have been neither resident nor ordinarily resident in the UK for fewer than five complete tax years.

The special rules have the effect of treating these gains and losses as though they arise in the tax year in which you return to the UK.
The special rules do **not** apply for gains and losses arising from disposals of any assets you acquired while you were temporarily non-resident, provided that the assets were not derived in some part from assets you held while you were resident or ordinarily resident in the UK.

8.5 The special rules apply **only** if **all** the following conditions are met

- there is a tax year (the 'year of return') for which you satisfy the residence requirements*

- you did not satisfy the residence requirements* for one or more tax years immediately preceding the year of return

- no more than four tax years fell between the most recent tax year for which you satisfied the residence requirements* (the 'year of departure') and the year of return

- you satisfied the residence requirements* for at least four of the seven tax years immediately preceding the year of departure.

* You satisfy the 'residence requirements' for a tax year if you are ordinarily resident in the UK during that year or if you are resident in the UK for any part of it.

Inland Revenue Bulletin IR20 (2008)

If any of these conditions is not **met**, there is no charge to capital gains tax on gains arising on the disposal of assets during your temporary non-residence. Similarly, losses arising in these circumstances will not be allowable losses for capital gains tax purposes.

8.6 Where the special rules apply, you may be able to claim relief from tax in the year in which you resume residence in the UK, if at the time you disposed of the assets you were a resident of a country with which the UK has a double taxation agreement. Any such relief (which may take the form of credit for the overseas tax or, in some cases, exemption from UK tax) will depend on the terms of the relevant agreement. In certain circumstances you may also be able to claim credit for overseas tax against UK tax where there is no double taxation agreement.

Non-residents with a UK branch or agency

8.7 If you are neither resident nor ordinarily resident in the UK and carry on a trade, profession or vocation through a branch or agency in the UK, you will be liable to capital gains tax on any gains on the disposal of assets in the UK which were used in the trade, profession or vocation, or by the branch or agency. You may also be liable to capital gains tax if the activity ceases or you transfer the assets outside the UK.

Overseas assets

8.8 An overseas asset is one situated outside the UK under the capital gains tax rules. For assets such as land and most types of movable property the asset is situated where it is located. For other assets (for example shares and securities) the rules are more complex. Your Tax Office will be able to advise you further.

If you are resident or ordinarily resident in the UK, and dispose of overseas assets, you will normally be liable to capital gains tax on any gains arising. But if you are not domiciled in the UK, and the remittance basis applies either by default (for years up to and including 6 April 2008) or, for years from 6 April 2008 onwards, because of an election you are taxed on such gains only to the extent that they are received in or remitted to the UK in a tax year for which you are resident or ordinarily resident in the UK. There is no capital gains tax charge on gains remitted to the UK before you become resident in the UK. (See also paragraph 5.12 on the **remittance basis**.) Where the proceeds of a disposal are remitted, an appropriate proportion of the proceeds is treated as a remittance of the gain.

Gains in a foreign currency

8.9 Where prices are expressed in a currency other than sterling, we calculate gains on the basis of sterling equivalents of the considerations for acquisition and disposal, converted at the date of purchase or sale as appropriate. Except where it is for personal expenditure outside the UK, foreign currency is a chargeable asset for capital gains tax purposes. Its disposal in return for any other asset will normally give rise to a chargeable gain or allowable loss.

Exempt assets

8.10 Gains on the disposal of gilt-edged securities and qualifying corporate bonds are exempt from capital gains tax.

Appendix 1

Further information

8.11 In the space available in this Chapter it is only possible to offer general guidance on some of the more important topics. For more detailed information about capital gains tax you can obtain 'Capital Gains Tax - An introduction' from any Tax Office or HM Revenue & Customs Enquiry Centre.

8.12 Scope of liability to capital gains tax

Residence status and domicile	Gains on disposal of	
	UK assets[1]	Overseas assets
Resident and ordinarily resident, domiciled	Liable	Liable
Resident and ordinarily resident, not domiciled	Liable	Liable if remitted to the UK
Resident but not ordinarily resident, domiciled	Liable	Liable
Resident but not ordinarily resident, not domiciled	Liable	Liable if remitted to the UK
Not resident but ordinarily resident, domiciled	Liable[2]	Liable[2]
Not resident but ordinarily resident, not domiciled	Liable[2]	Liable if remitted to the UK[2]
Not resident and not ordinarily resident, domiciled	Not liable[3,4]	Not liable[4]
Not resident and not ordinarily resident, not domiciled	Not liable[3,4]	Not liable[4]

1. There is no liability if the disposal is of certain UK Government Securities.

2. See Chapter 9 about possible relief under a double taxation agreement.

3. Liability will arise if the assets were used or held for the purposes of a trade, profession or vocation carried on in the UK through a branch or agency or by the branch or agency.

4. Gains arising during a period of temporary non-residence may be chargeable (see paragraphs 8.4 - 8.6).

Inland Revenue Bulletin IR20 (2008)

9 Double taxation relief

9.1 If you have income or gains from a source in one country and are resident in another, you may be liable to pay tax in both countries under their tax laws. To avoid 'double taxation' in this situation, the UK has negotiated double taxation agreements with a large number of countries. A list of these is given at paragraph 9.16.

Non-residents, and residents of more than one country

9.2 If you are a resident of a country with which the UK has a double taxation agreement, you may be able to claim exemption or partial relief from UK tax on certain types of income from UK sources. You may also be able to claim exemption from capital gains tax on the disposal of assets. The precise conditions of exemption or relief can be found in the relevant agreement. It is not possible to give full details here as they vary from agreement to agreement. If you are resident both in the UK and a country with which the UK has a double taxation agreement, there may be special provisions in the agreement for treating you as a resident of only one of the countries **for the purposes of the agreement.**

9.3 Normally, you will receive some relief from UK tax on the following sources of income under an agreement

- pensions and some annuities (other than UK Government pensions)
- royalties
- dividends (paid before 6 April 1999)
- interest.

Some agreements state that you must be subject to tax in the other country on the income in question before you get relief from UK tax.

9.4 If you receive a pension paid by the UK for service to the UK Government or to a local authority in the UK, you will usually be taxed only by the UK.

9.5 If you are carrying on a trade or running a business through a permanent establishment in the UK, you may not qualify for any relief from UK tax on royalties, interest or dividends connected with the permanent establishment. A 'permanent establishment' includes, for example, a place of management, a branch or an office.

Earnings from employment and professional services

9.6 Under many double taxation agreements you may be able to claim exemption from UK tax on

- earnings from an employment, and
- profits or earnings for independent, personal or professional services

carried on in the UK, if you are a resident of the overseas country for the purposes of the agreement (see paragraph 9.2). The usual conditions to be met are

- in the case of employments

    - you must not be in the UK for more than 183 days in the period (often, twelve months) specified in the agreement, and

    - your remuneration must be paid by (or on behalf of) an employer who is not

239

Appendix 1

>resident in the UK, and it must not be borne by a UK branch of your employer

- in the case of independent, personal or professional services, you must not operate from a fixed base in the UK (or, in the case of some agreements, spend more than a specified number of days in the UK).

Teachers and researchers

9.7 Under some agreements, if you are a teacher or professor who comes to the UK to teach in a school, college, university or other educational establishment for a period of **two years or less**, you are exempt from UK tax on your earnings from the teaching post. Temporary absences from the UK during this period normally count as part of the two years.

Some agreements cover persons who engage in research. Where this is so, the rules are normally the same as for teachers.

9.8 If you stay for more than two years you cannot claim exemption and you will be liable to tax on the whole of your earnings from the date you arrived. Some agreements only allow exemptions to be given if the earnings are liable to tax in your home country. If you have already received exemption for a visit (or visits) of up to two years, some agreements will not allow you to claim the exemption again if you make a further visit at a later date.

Students and apprentices

9.9 Under most agreements, if you are an overseas student or apprentice visiting the UK solely for full-time education or training, you will not pay tax on payments from sources outside the UK for your maintenance, education or training.

A number of agreements also provide that students or apprentices visiting this country will be exempt from UK tax on certain earnings from employment here. Individual agreements impose various restrictions on this relief, including, for example, monetary limits and conditions as to the type of employment.

Entertainers and sportsmen/women

9.10 Under most agreements, if you are not resident in the UK and you come here as an entertainer or sportsman/woman, any payments you receive will be liable to UK tax. The exemption described in paragraph 9.6 will not apply. You should contact the Foreign Entertainers Unit (see paragraph 9 of the Introduction) for advice on how your income as an entertainer or sportsman/woman will be treated for tax purposes.

This includes, for example, actors and musicians performing on stage or screen and those participating in all kinds of sports.

Dividends

9.11 If you are **resident** in the UK, you are entitled to a **tax credit** when you receive a dividend from a company resident in the UK. We charge income tax on the total of the dividend and the tax credit. The tax credit is available to reduce your tax liability. The rate of the tax credit was reduced from 20% to 10% from 6 April 1999, reflecting the reduction in the rate of tax on dividend income from that date.

9.12 If you are **not resident** in the UK, the normal rule is that you are not entitled to a tax credit when you receive a dividend from a UK company. From 6 April 1996 you do not pay UK tax (and before that date you would have paid UK tax, if at all, only at the higher rate) on any dividends.

Inland Revenue Bulletin IR20 (2008)

You may, however, be entitled to a tax credit if you are a resident of a country with which the UK has a double taxation agreement, and the agreement provides for payment of the same tax credit as a UK resident would be entitled to receive. In that case, you are liable to income tax on the total of the dividend and tax credit, at the rate of tax laid down in the agreement.

From 6 April 1999, all double taxation agreements that provide for payment of a tax credit on dividends paid by UK companies continue to give a right to claim a tax credit in excess of the amount which the UK is entitled to retain. However, because the rate of tax credit has been reduced (see paragraph 9.11), the amount which the UK is entitled to retain under those agreements will in practice cover the whole of the tax credit. So if you make a claim under an agreement where a dividend has been paid on or after 6 April 1999, there will be **no** balance of tax credit left for us to pay to you.

9.13 You may also have the right to a tax credit if you receive UK tax allowances and reliefs through a claim in accordance with paragraph 7.3. But if you can only claim these allowances because of the terms of a double taxation agreement (the final category in paragraph 7.3), whether you are entitled to the tax credit will depend on the terms of the agreement.

Capital gains

9.14 Under many agreements, if you are a resident of another country for the purposes of the agreement, you will often be liable to tax only in the other country on any gains you make from disposing of assets. In that case, you will be exempt from capital gains tax in the UK even if you are ordinarily resident here. If, however, you are carrying on a trade or running a business through a permanent establishment in the UK, any gains you make from disposing of assets connected with the permanent establishment will continue to be chargeable to capital gains tax in the UK.

UK residents

9.15 If you are resident in the UK and have overseas income or gains which are taxable in both the UK and the country of origin, you may qualify for relief against UK tax for all or part of the overseas tax you have paid. Even if there is no double taxation agreement between the UK and the other country concerned, you may still be entitled to relief under special provisions in the UK's tax legislation.

List of the UK's double taxation agreements

9.16 Countries with which the UK has double taxation agreements in force covering taxes on income and/or capital gains (other than limited agreements concerned solely with air transport and shipping) at October 2007 were as follows

Antigua and Barbuda	Lithuania
Argentina	Luxembourg
Australia	Macedonia
Austria	Malawi
Azerbaijan	Malaysia
Bangladesh	Malta
Barbados	Mauritius
Belarus	Mexico
Belgium	Mongolia
Belize	Montenegro
Bolivia	Montserrat
Bosnia-Herzegovina	Morocco
Botswana	Myanmar (Burma)

Appendix 1

Brunei	Namibia
Bulgaria	Netherlands
Canada	New Zealand
Chile	Nigeria
China	Norway
Croatia	Oman
Cyprus	Pakistan
Czech Republic	Papua New Guinea
Denmark	Philippines
Egypt	Poland
Estonia	Portugal
Falkland Islands	Romania
Fiji	Russian Federation
Finland	St Kitts and Nevis
France	Serbia
Gambia	Sierra Leone
Georgia	Singapore
Germany	Slovak Republic (Slovakia)
Ghana	Slovenia
Greece	Solomon Islands
Grenada	South Africa
Guernsey	Spain
Guyana	Sri Lanka
Hungary	Sudan
Iceland	Swaziland
India	Sweden
Indonesia	Switzerland
Ireland (Republic of)	Taiwan
Isle of Man	Thailand
Israel	Trinidad and Tobago
Italy	Tunisia
Ivory Coast (Cote d'Ivoire)	Turkey
Jamaica	Turkmenistan
Japan	Tuvalu
Jersey	Uganda
Jordan	Ukraine
Kazakhstan	USA
Kenya	Uzbekistan
Kiribati	Venezuela
Korea (Republic of)	Vietnam
Kuwait	Zambia
Latvia	Zimbabwe
Lesotho	

Inland Revenue Bulletin IR20 (2008)

10 Appeals

10.1 If you have any dispute with HM Revenue & Customs about your residence, ordinary residence or domicile, or about any claim for relief from UK tax, and agreement cannot be reached, you have the right to have your case considered by an independent tribunal.

10.2 If HM Revenue & Customs write to you giving a formal decision, they will explain to you how you may appeal and how long you have for this purpose. You may choose to have an appeal heard by either the General Commissioners or the Special Commissioners in connection with your residence status and claims for relief. All appeals in connection with your ordinary residence status and domicile are heard by the Special Commissioners.

10.3 Both the General Commissioners and the Special Commissioners are independent of HM Revenue & Customs. Their decisions on questions of fact are final, but you can appeal against their decisions on questions of law to the High Court. Leaflet DCA 'Tax Appeals' explains procedures in full. It can be obtained from our website at www.hmrc.gov.uk or from any HM Revenue & Customs office or Enquiry Centre.

Part III Payment of UK National Insurance contributions

11 National Insurance contributions

General

11.1 This chapter deals briefly with the rules for payment of National Insurance contributions (NICs) for individuals leaving or coming to the UK. The position broadly depends on whether you are going to or arriving from an **EEA** country, a country with which the UK has a bilateral **Social Security Agreement** covering NICs, or some other country.

The EEA countries are Iceland, Liechtenstein, Norway and the Member States of the European Union. Switzerland is not a member of the EEA but as a result of an agreement with the EU, the EU rules on National Insurance and Social Security will also largely cover Switzerland.

At January 2008, in addition to the UK, the Member States of the European Union were:

Austria	Latvia
Belgium	Lithuania
Bulgaria	Luxembourg
Czech Republic	Malta
Denmark	Netherlands
Estonia	Poland
Finland	Portugal
France	Republic of Cyprus
Germany	Romania
Greece	Slovakia
Hungary	Slovenia
Ireland	Spain
Italy	Sweden

243

Appendix 1

The countries with which the UK[1] has a bilateral **Social Security Agreement** in force covering NICs at October 2007 were as follows

Barbados	Korea
Bermuda	Mauritius
Canada (excluding Quebec)	New Zealand
Isle of Man	Philippines
Israel	Turkey
Jamaica	USA
Japan	Yugoslavia (Federal Republic)[2]
Jersey/Guernsey	

1. Some agreements include the Isle of Man, Guernsey and Jersey as part of the UK; where that is the case the benefits and obligations of the agreement apply also to those countries.

2. The UK's agreement with Yugoslavia is to be regarded as in force between the UK and the former Yugoslav states of Bosnia-Herzegovina, Croatia and Macedonia. Slovenia is a Member State of the European Union and is treated in line with other EEA countries.

11.2 The terms 'resident' and 'ordinarily resident' in relation to NICs do **not** have the same meaning as they do for tax purposes. The tax rules set out in the first part of this booklet are not therefore relevant. Leaflet NI38 'Social Security abroad' gives guidance on the rules that apply for NI purposes.

11.3 If you want further information about paying UK NICs, or copies of leaflets mentioned in this Chapter, you should contact CAR Residency Newcastle (see paragraph 9 of the Introduction), or your local National Insurance Contributions Office.

Going abroad

EEA countries

11.4 If you are going to another EEA country, the European Community Social Security Regulations apply. The general rule is that you will be subject to the social security legislation of the country in which you work; but there are some exceptions, as explained in the following paragraphs. Leaflet SA29 'Your social security insurance, benefits and health care rights in the European Community, and in Iceland, Liechtenstein and Norway' gives further details.

11.5 If your UK employer sends you to work in another EEA country for not more than 12 months at the outset, you and your UK employer will usually continue paying UK NICs as if you were still in the UK. Your employer will need to apply on your behalf to CAR Residency Newcastle (see paragraph 9 of the introduction), for form E101. This confirms that you will continue to pay UK NICs while working in the other country and will ensure that you are not required to contribute to the other country's social security scheme.

The European Health Insurance Card (EHIC) provides for healthcare cover abroad for you and any family members who accompany you for the period of your employment in the other country. These are issued by the Prescription Pricing Authority (PPA) and application packs can be obtained from any UK Post Office. Alternatively you may apply on line at **www.dh.gov.uk/travellers** or by telephone on **0845 606 2030**.

11.6 If your job in the other EEA country lasts longer than 12 months - even though you did not expect it to - you and your UK employer may continue paying UK NICs, for not more than another 12 months. However, the social security authorities in the other country must first agree to this. Your UK employer must, before the end of the first 12 months, apply on forms E102 to the social security authorities in the other country. These forms can be obtained from CAR Residency Newcastle (see paragraph 9 of the introduction). If the social security authorities in the other country agree to the request, you will need

Inland Revenue Bulletin IR20 (2008)

to ensure that you have a valid EHIC to provide cover for healthcare for yourself and any family who accompany you for the period of employment in the other country.

There are also special arrangements that allow you to continue paying UK NICs for longer periods, but usually for no more than five years. The social security authorities in the other country must agree to this.

11.7 Similar rules apply if you are self-employed. You must obtain forms E101 & E102 from CAR Residency Newcastle. Application packs for EHIC's in respect of healthcare cover in any EEA countries are available as per the information provided at 11.5

11.8 Different rules apply if you belong to one of the following groups

- those who work in more than one country
- mariners
- transport workers
- civil servants
- members of the staff of diplomatic or consular posts
- those who work for a member of the staff of a diplomatic or consular post
- members of the staff of the European Communities
- members of Her Majesty's forces
- civilians who work for Her Majesty's forces in Germany, or for an organisation like NAAFI which serves Her Majesty's forces.

In many of these cases, you will continue to pay UK NICs.

11.9 If you work in another EEA country in any other circumstances (for example, for a foreign employer) or you intend to remain abroad indefinitely, you will probably have to pay social security contributions to the other country's scheme. If so, you will not be required to pay UK NICs. However, it may be possible for you to pay UK voluntary NICs to protect your UK basic pension rights. There are more details in leaflet NI38], which contains an application form to pay UK voluntary NICs.

Agreement countries

11.10 If you are going to a country with which the UK has a bilateral Social Security Agreement covering NICs, the position will depend on the terms of the particular agreement. The general rule is that you will be subject to the social security legislation of the country in which you work; but there are some exceptions to this rule, as explained in the following paragraphs. There are information leaflets for each country (see paragraph 11.3 on how to obtain copies).

11.11 If your UK employer sends you to work in a country with which the UK has an agreement, you may be required to continue paying UK NICs as if you were still in the UK. How long you continue to pay UK NICs depends on the particular agreement. Your employer will need to apply on your behalf to CAR Residency Newcastle (see paragraph 9 of the introduction) for a certificate confirming that UK NICs continue to be paid while you are working in the other country. This will ensure that you are not required to contribute to the other country's social security scheme.

Unlike the EEA, there is no general provision for healthcare arrangements in most of the bilateral agreements.

Some agreements include provisions which may allow you to continue paying UK NICs for longer than the normal period under the agreement.

11.12 Not all agreements cover the self-employed. In the case of those that do, similar rules apply as for those in employment.

Appendix 1

Certain agreements contain special rules for particular groups, such as civil servants, mariners or transport workers.

11.13 If you work in a country with which the UK has an agreement in any other circumstances, for example, for a foreign employer, or you intend to remain abroad indefinitely, you will probably have to pay social security contributions to the other's country scheme. If so, you will not be required to pay UK NICs. However, it may be possible for you to pay UK voluntary NICs to protect your UK basic pension rights. There are more details in leaflet NI38, which contains an application form to pay UK voluntary NICs.

Other countries

11.14 If you are going to any other country, the position will depend on the domestic rules there. Leaflet NI38 gives further information.

11.15 If your UK employer sends you to work in a country outside the EEA and not covered by a bilateral agreement, you will be required to continue paying UK NICs for the first 52 weeks of employment in the other country where all the following conditions apply

- your employer has a place of business in the UK
- you are ordinarily resident in the UK
- you were resident in the UK immediately before starting the work abroad.

11.16 No certificate is required to confirm that you continue to pay UK NICs. Some countries will require you, in addition to your UK NICs, to contribute to their social security scheme. After 52 weeks you are not required to continue paying UK NICs, but you may pay voluntary NICs to protect your UK basic pension rights. There are more details in leaflet NI38, which contains an application form to pay UK voluntary NICs.

Should you decide not to pay voluntary UK NICs, your UK National Insurance record will still be protected for certain social security benefits (but not retirement pension or widow's benefit) on your return to the UK.

Arriving from abroad

11.17 If you arrive here from abroad and take up employment with a UK employer, or take up self-employment, you will generally be required to pay UK NICs; but there are some exceptions to this rule, as explained in the following paragraphs.

EEA countries

11.18 If an employer in another EEA country sends you to work in the UK for up to 12 months (longer in special cases), you may be able to continue paying foreign social security contributions. If form E101 is issued by the foreign social security institution, confirming that you continue to contribute to the foreign scheme, you will not have to pay UK NICs. Similar provisions apply to self-employed people who are working temporarily in the UK. Leaflet SA29 gives further information.

Agreement countries

11.19 If you are sent to work temporarily in the UK by an employer in a country with which the UK has a bilateral Social Security Agreement covering NICs, you may be able to continue paying foreign social security contributions. If a certificate is issued by the foreign social security institution, confirming that you continue to contribute to the foreign scheme, you will not have to pay UK NICs.

The information leaflet for each country (see paragraph 11.10) gives further details, and also explains if there are provisions for the self-employed in a particular agreement.

Other countries

11.20 If you are sent to work temporarily in the UK by an employer in a country which is outside the EEA and not covered by a bilateral Social Security Agreement, the general rule is that neither you nor your employer has to pay UK NICs for the first 52 weeks of your employment in the UK. NICs are payable from the 53rd week. If the foreign employer does not have a place of business in the UK, NICs are due from the UK 'host' employer.

Appendix 1

Appendix 1

Interpretation of Gaines-Cooper decision

The published decision of the Special Commissioners in Robert Gaines-Cooper v HMRC (SpC 568, 31 October 2006) attracted some attention from tax practitioners and their clients. In particular, some commentators suggested that the decision meant that HMRC had changed the way it calculates the '91-day test'. This is incorrect.

The '91-day test' is set out in Chapters 2 (Leaving the UK) & 3 (Coming to the UK) of this guidance. The text makes it clear that the '91-day test' applies only to individuals who have either:

- left the UK and live elsewhere, or
- who visit the UK on a regular basis.

Where an individual has lived in the UK, the question of whether he has left the UK has to be decided first. Individuals who have left the UK will continue to be regarded as UK-resident if their visits to the UK average 91 days or more a tax year, taken over a maximum of up to 4 tax years. HMRC's normal practice, as set out in this guidance, is to disregard days of arrival and departure in calculating days under the '91-day test'.

In considering the issues of residence, ordinary residence and domicile in the Gaines-Cooper case, the Commissioners needed to build up a full picture of Mr Gaines-Cooper's life. A very important element of the picture was the pattern of his presence in the UK compared to the pattern of his presence overseas. The Commissioners decided that, in looking at these patterns, it would be misleading to wholly disregard days of arrival and departure. They used Mr Gaines-Cooper's patterns of presence in the UK as part of the evidence of his lifestyle and habits during the years in question. Based on this, and a wide range of other evidence, the Commissioners found that he had been continuously resident in the UK. The '91-day test' was therefore not relevant to the Gaines-Cooper case, since Mr Gaines-Cooper did not leave the UK.

There was no change to HMRC practice about residence and the '91-day test', either in relation to the Gaines-Cooper case or as a result of it. HMRC will continue to:

- follow its published guidance on residence issues, and apply this guidance fairly and consistently;
- treat an individual who has not left the UK as remaining resident here;
- consider all the relevant evidence, including the pattern of presence in the UK and elsewhere, in deciding whether or not an individual has left the UK;
- apply the '91-day test' (where HMRC is satisfied that an individual has actually left the UK) as outlined in this guidance, normally disregarding days of arrival and departure in calculating days under this 'test'.

Inland Revenue Bulletin IR20 (2008)

Appendix 2

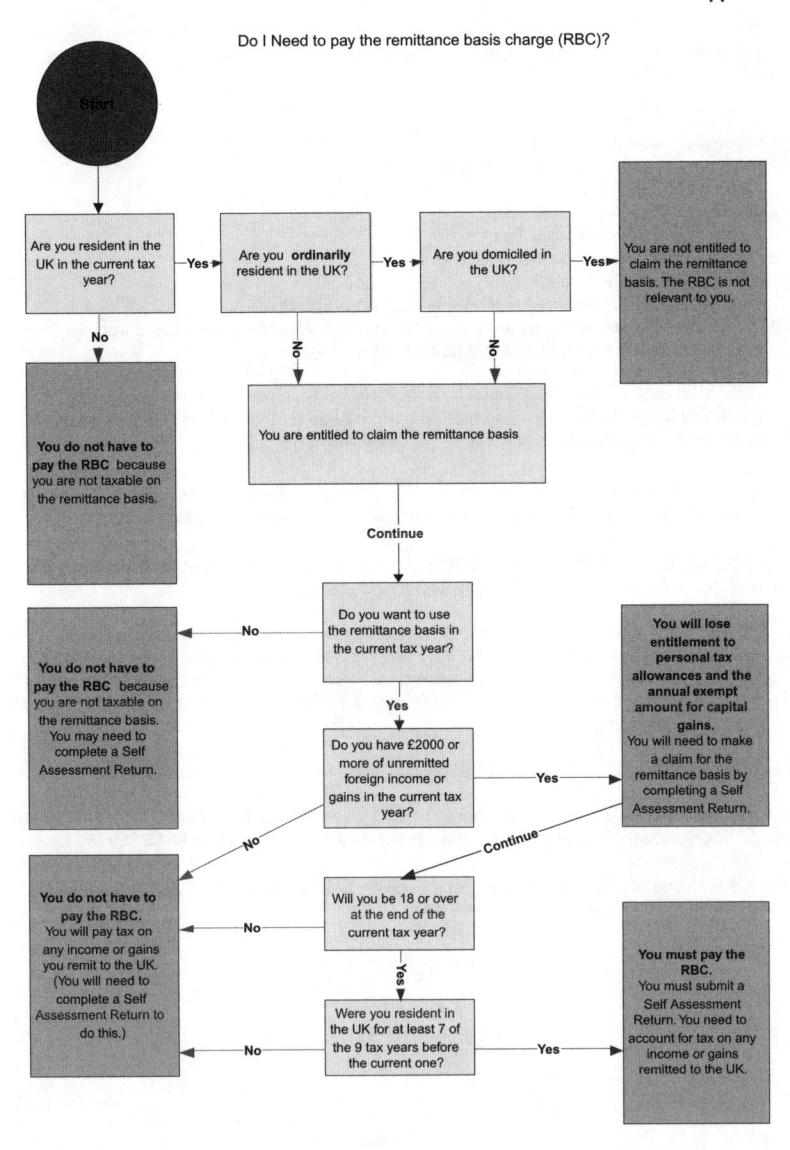

Do I Need to pay the remittance basis charge (RBC)?

Start

Are you resident in the UK in the current tax year?
- No → **You do not have to pay the RBC** because you are not taxable on the remittance basis.
- Yes → **Are you ordinarily resident in the UK?**
  - No → You are entitled to claim the remittance basis
  - Yes → **Are you domiciled in the UK?**
    - No → You are entitled to claim the remittance basis
    - Yes → **You are not entitled to claim the remittance basis. The RBC is not relevant to you.**

Continue

Do you want to use the remittance basis in the current tax year?
- No → **You do not have to pay the RBC** because you are not taxable on the remittance basis. You may need to complete a Self Assessment Return.
- Yes → **Do you have £2000 or more of unremitted foreign income or gains in the current tax year?**
  - No → **You do not have to pay the RBC.** You will pay tax on any income or gains you remit to the UK. (You will need to complete a Self Assessment Return to do this.)
  - Yes → **You will lose entitlement to personal tax allowances and the annual exempt amount for capital gains.** You will need to make a claim for the remittance basis by completing a Self Assessment Return.

Continue

Will you be 18 or over at the end of the current tax year?
- No → **You do not have to pay the RBC.** You will pay tax on any income or gains you remit to the UK. (You will need to complete a Self Assessment Return to do this.)
- Yes → **Were you resident in the UK for at least 7 of the 9 tax years before the current one?**
  - No → **You do not have to pay the RBC.** You will pay tax on any income or gains you remit to the UK. (You will need to complete a Self Assessment Return to do this.)
  - Yes → **You must pay the RBC.** You must submit a Self Assessment Return. You need to account for tax on any income or gains remitted to the UK.

Note: The flowchart is a broad guide to help you decide if you need to pay the Remittance Basis Charge. You have a choice each year whether to claim the remittance basis. If, in a particular year, it would be more beneficial for you to pay tax on your worldwide income and gains than to pay the RBC, you may choose not to claim the remittance basis.

Appendix 1

Guidance is available on the HMRC web site at **www.hmrc.gov.uk**

We also produce a wide range of leaflets and booklets, each designed to explain a different aspect of the tax system in plain English. Most of these are free. Some you might find useful are listed below.

ESC – Extra Statutory Concessions
DCA 'Appeals' leaflet
Accrued Income Scheme – Taxing Securities on Transfer
Property Income Manual
Capital Gains Tax - An introduction
Customer Guide to Inheritance Tax
SE1 – 'Are you thinking of working for yourself?'
NI38 – Social Security abroad
National Insurance for employers of people working abroad
SA29 - Your social security insurance, benefits and health care rights in the European Community, and in Iceland, Liechtenstein and Norway

Leaflet IR140 was withdrawn in March 2006. Information on the Non Residents Landlords Scheme can be obtained from our website at **www.hmrc.gov.uk**

Leaflet IR90 was withdrawn. Information on Tax Allowances and Reliefs can be obtained from our website at **www.hmrc.gov.uk** or from any HM Revenue & Customs Enquiry Centre

Our factsheet C/FS – 'Complaints and putting things right' tells you what you should do if you are unhappy with our service or the way we have treated you.

Our HMRC List 'Catalogue of leaflets and booklets' gives further information about our publications, most of which you can get from any HM Revenue & Customs Enquiry Centre or Tax Office. Their addresses are in your local phone book under 'HM Revenue & Customs'. Most offices are open to the public from 8.00am to 4.30pm, Monday to Friday, and some are also open outside these hours.

Your local library or Citizens' Advice Bureau may also have copies of our leaflets.

You can get most of our leaflets by phoning our Orderline on **0845 9000404** between 8.00am and 10.00pm, seven days a week (except Christmas Day), or by fax on **0845 9000604**.

When our offices are closed, you can get advice on **Self Assessment** by calling our Helpline, in the evenings or at weekends, on **0845 9000 444**.

Inland Revenue Bulletin IR20 (2008)

The guidance provided in this booklet is general in nature. If, on the facts of the matter, a dispute arises over the application of this general guidance and the parties cannot resolve their dispute by agreement, the Commissioners will determine any appeals. The Commissioners are bound to decide the legal issues by reference to statute and case law principles rather than HMRC guidance. Where a dispute relates to particular facts the Commissioners will consider the evidence and make findings of fact to which they will apply the law.

Customer Service

HM Revenue & Customs commitment
We aim to provide a high quality service with guidance that is simple, clear and accurate.

We will

- be professional and helpful
- act with integrity and fairness, and
- treat your affairs in strict confidence within the law.

We aim to handle your affairs promptly and accurately so that you receive or pay only the right amount due.

Putting things right
If you are not satisfied with our service, please let the person dealing with your affairs know what is wrong. We will work as quickly as possible to put things right and settle your complaint.

If you are still unhappy, ask for your complaint to be referred to the Complaints Manager.

Customers with particular needs
We offer a range of facilities for customers with particular needs, including

- wheelchair access to nearly all HMRC Enquiry Centres
- help with filling in forms
- for people with hearing difficulties
    - RNID Typetalk
    - Induction loops.

We can also arrange additional support, such as

- home visits, if you have limited mobility or caring responsibilities and cannot get to one of our Enquiry Centres
- services of an interpreter
- sign language interpretation
- leaflets in large print, Braille and audio.

For complete details please

- go online at **www.hmrc.gov.uk/enq**
  or
- contact us. You will find us in *The Phone Book* under HM Revenue & Customs.

Further information on customer service is available at HM Revenue & Customs local offices, set out in our Charters, complaints factsheet (Complaints and putting things right - C/FS) and Codes of Practice.

Appendix 1

These notes are for guidance only and reflect the position
at the time of writing. They do not affect any right of appeal.

Issued by
Customer Information Team
HM Revenue & Customs
July 2008
© Crown Copyright 2008

APPENDIX 2

Statements of Practice

SP 3/81 Individuals coming to the UK: ordinary residence

[10 April 1981]
A person who comes to the United Kingdom is not usually regarded as having become ordinarily resident here until he has been in this country for at least three years unless it is clear before then that he intends to be here for three years or more. But in general it is the Board's practice to regard someone who comes to the United Kingdom, whether to work here or not, as ordinarily resident for tax purposes–
(a) from the date of his arrival if he has, or acquires during the year of arrival, accommodation for his use in the United Kingdom which he occupies on a basis that implies a stay in this country of three years or more,
(b) from the beginning of the tax year in which such accommodation becomes available.

If, in the event, an individual, who has been regarded as ordinarily resident solely because he has accommodation here, disposes of the accommodation and leaves the UK within three years of his arrival he would normally be treated as not ordinarily resident for the duration of his stay if this were to his advantage.

[The text of SP 3/81 above is as it appears in IR 131 (2004).]

SP 1/90 Company residence

[9 January 1990]
1. Residence has always been a material factor, for companies as well as individuals, in determining tax liability. But statute law has never laid down comprehensive rules for determining where a company is resident and until 1988 the question was left solely to the Courts to decide. Section 66 FA 1988 introduced the rule that a company incorporated in the UK is resident there for the purposes of the Taxes Acts. Case law still applies in determining the residence of companies excepted from the incorporation rule or which are not incorporated in the UK.

Appendix 2

A. The incorporation rule

2. The incorporation rule applies to companies incorporated in the UK subject to the exceptions in Schedule 7 FA 1988 for some companies incorporated before 15 March 1988. (This legislation is reproduced for convenience as an Appendix to this Statement). Paragraphs 3 to 8 below explain how the Revenue interpret various terms used in the legislation.

Carrying on business

3. The exceptions from the incorporation test in Schedule 7 depend in part on the company carrying on business at a specified time or during a relevant period. The question whether a company carries on business is one of fact to be decided according to the particular circumstances of the company. Detailed guidance is not practicable but the Revenue take the view that 'business' has a wider meaning than 'trade'; it can include transactions, such as the purchase of stock, carried out for the purposes of a trade about to be commenced and the holding of investments including shares in a subsidiary company. Such a holding could consist of a single investment from which no income was derived.

4. A company such as a shelf company whose transactions have been limited to those formalities necessary to keep the company on the register of companies will not be regarded as carrying on business.

5. For the purpose of the case law test (see B below) the residence of a company is determined by the place where its real business is carried on. A company which can demonstrate that in these terms it is or was resident outside the UK will have carried on business for the purposes of Schedule 7.

'Taxable in a territory outside the UK'

6. A further condition for some companies for exception from the incorporation test is provided by Schedule 7 Para 1(1)(c) and Para 5(1). The company has to be taxable in a territory outside the UK. 'Taxable' means that the company is liable to tax on income by reason of domicile, residence or place of management. This is similar to the approach adopted in the residence provisions of many double 91 taxation agreements. Territories which impose tax on companies by reference to incorporation or registration or similar criteria are covered by the term 'domicile'. Territories which impose tax by reference to criteria such as 'effective management', 'central administration', 'head office' or 'principal place of business' are covered by the term 'place of management'.

7. A company has to be liable to tax on income so that a company which is, for example, liable only to a flat rate fee or lump sum duty does not fulfil the test. On the other hand a company is regarded as liable to tax in a particular territory if it is within the charge there even though it may pay no tax because, for example, it makes losses or claims double taxation relief.

'Treasury consent'

8. Before 15 March 1988 it was unlawful for a company to cease to be resident in the UK without the consent of the Treasury. Companies which

have ceased to be resident in pursuance of a Treasury consent, as defined in Schedule 7 Paragraph 5(1), are excepted from the incorporation rule subject to certain conditions. A few companies ceased to be resident without Treasury Consent but were informed subsequently by letter that the Treasury would take no action against them under the relevant legislation. Such letter is not a retrospective grant of consent and the companies concerned cannot benefit from the exceptions which depend on Treasury consent.

B. The law test

9. This test of company residence is that enunciated by Lord Loreburn in *De Beers Consolidated Mines v Howe* (5 TC 198) at the beginning of this century:

> 'A company resides, for the purposes of Income Tax, where its real business is carried on ... I regard that as the true rule; and the real business is carried on where the central management and control actually abides'.

10. The 'central management and control' test, as set out in *De Beers*, has been endorsed by a series of subsequent decisions. In particular, it was described by Lord Radcliffe in the 1959 case of *Bullock v Unit Construction Company* (38 TC 712) at p. 738 as being:

> 'as precise and unequivocal as a positive statutory injunction ... I do not know of any other test which has either been substituted for that of central management and control, or has been defined with sufficient precision to be regarded as an acceptable alternative to it. To me ... it seems impossible to read Lord Loreburn's words without seeing that he regarded the formula he was propounding as constituting the test of residence'.

Nothing which has happened since has in any way altered this basic principle for a company the residence of which is not governed by the incorporation rule; under current UK case law such a company is regarded as resident for tax purposes where central management and control is to be found.

Place of 'central management and control'

11. In determining whether or not an individual company outside the scope of the incorporation test is resident in the UK, it thus becomes necessary to locate its place of 'central management and control'. The case law concept of central management and control is, in broad terms, directed at the highest level of control of the business of a company. It is to be distinguished from the place where the main operations of a business are to be found, though those two places may often coincide. Moreover, the exercise of control does not necessarily demand any minimum standard of active involvement: it may, in appropriate circumstances, be exercised tacitly through passive oversight.

12. Successive decided cases have emphasised that the place of central management and control is wholly a question of fact. For example, Lord Radcliffe in Unit Construction said that 'the question where control and

Appendix 2

management abide must be treated as one of fact or "actuality"' (p 741). It follows that factors which together are decisive in one instance may individually carry little weight in another. Nevertheless the decided cases do give some pointers. In particular a series of decisions has attached importance to the place where the company's board of directors meet. There are very many cases in which the board meets in the same country as that in which the business operations take place, and central management and control is clearly located in that one place. In other cases central management and control may be exercised by directors in one country though the actual business operations may, perhaps under the immediate management of local directors, take place elsewhere.

13. But the location of board meetings, although important in the normal case, is not necessarily conclusive. Lord Radcliffe in Unit Construction pointed out (p 738) that the site of the meetings of the directors' board had not been chosen as 'the test' of company residence. In some cases, for example, central management and control is exercised by a single individual. This may happen when a chairman or managing director exercises powers formally conferred by the company's Articles and the other board members are little more than cyphers, or by reason of a dominant shareholding or for some other reason. In those cases the residence of the company is where the controlling individual exercises his powers.

14. In general the place of directors' meetings is significant only insofar as those meetings constitute the medium through which central management and control is exercised. If, for example, the directors of a company were engaged together actively in the UK in the complete running of a business which was wholly in the UK, the company would not be regarded as resident outside the UK merely because the directors held formal meetings outside the UK. While it is possible to identify extreme situations in which central management and control plainly is, or is not, exercised by directors in formal meetings, the conclusion in any case is wholly one of fact depending on the relative weight to be given to various factors. Any attempt to lay down rigid guidelines would only be misleading.

15. Generally, however, where doubts arise about a particular company's residence status, the Inland Revenue adopt the following approach:

(i) They first try to ascertain whether the directors of the company in fact exercise central management and control.

(ii) If so, they seek to determine where the directors exercise this central management and control (which is not necessarily where they meet).

(iii) In cases where the directors apparently do not exercise central management and control of the company, the Revenue then look to establish where and by whom it is exercised.

Parent/subsidiary relationship

16. It is particularly difficult to apply the 'central management and control' test in the situation where a subsidiary company and its parent operate in different territories. In this situation, the parent will normally influence, to a greater or lesser extent, the actions of the subsidiary. Where that influence is exerted by the parent exercising the powers which a sole or

majority shareholder has in general meetings of the subsidiary, for example to appoint and dismiss members of board of the subsidiary and to initiate or approve alterations to its financial structure, the Revenue would not seek to argue that central management and control of the subsidiary is located where the parent company is resident. However, in cases where the parent usurps the functions of the board of the subsidiary (such as Unit Construction itself) or where that board merely rubber stamps the parent company's decisions without giving them any independent consideration of its own, the Revenue draw the conclusion that the subsidiary has the same residence for tax purposes as its parent.

17. The Revenue recognise that there may be many cases where a company is a member of a group having its ultimate holding company in another country which will not fall readily into either of the categories referred to above. In considering whether the board of such a subsidiary company exercises central management and control of the subsidiary's business, they have regard to the degree of autonomy which those directors have in conducting the company's business. Matters (among others) that may be taken into account are the extent to which the directors of the subsidiary take decisions on their own authority as to investment, production, marketing and procurement without reference to the parent.

Conclusion
18. In outlining factors relevant to the application of the case law test, this statement assumes that they exist for genuine commercial reasons. Where, however, as may happen, it appears that a major objective underlying the existence of certain factors is the obtaining of tax benefits from residence or non-residence, the Revenue examine the facts particularly closely in order to see whether there has been an attempt to create the appearance of central management and control in a particular place without the reality.

19. The case law test examined in this Statement is not always easy to apply. The Courts have recognised that there may be difficulties where it is not possible to identify any one country as the seat of central management and control. The principles to apply in those circumstances have not been fully developed in case law. In addition, the last relevant case was decided almost 30 years ago, and there have been many developments in communications since then, which in particular may enable a company to be controlled from a place far distant from where the day-to-day management is carried on. As the Statement makes clear, while the general principle has been laid down by the Courts, its application must depend on the precise facts.

C. Double taxation agreements
20. In general our double taxation agreements do not affect the UK residence of a company as established for UK tax purposes. But where the partner country adopts a different definition of residence, it may happen that a UK resident company is treated, under the partner country's domestic law, as also resident there. In these cases, the agreement normally specifies what the tax consequences of this 'double' residence shall be.

21. Under the double taxation agreement with the United States, for

example, the UK residence of a company for UK tax purposes is unaffected. But where that company is also a US corporation, it is excluded from some of the reliefs conferred by the agreement. On the other hand, under a double taxation agreement which follows the 1977 OECD Model Taxation Convention, a company classed as resident by both the UK and the partner country is, for the purposes of the agreement, treated as resident where its 'place of effective management' is situated.

22. The Commentary in paragraph 3 of Article 4 of the OECD Model records the UK view that, in agreements (such as those with some Commonwealth countries) which treat a company as resident in a state in which 'its business is managed and controlled', this expression means 'the effective management of the enterprise'. More detailed consideration of the question in the light of the approach of Continental legal systems and of Community law to the question of company residence has led the Revenue to revise this view. It is now considered that effective management may, in some cases, be found at a place different from the place of central management and control. This could happen, for example, where a company is run by executives based abroad, but the final directing power rests with non-executive directors who meet in the UK. In such circumstances the company's place of effective management might well be abroad but, depending on the precise powers of the non-executive directors, it might be centrally managed and controlled (and therefore resident) in the UK.

23. The incorporation rule in Section 66(1) FA 1988 determines a residence which supersedes a different place 'given by any rule of law'. This incorporation rule determines residence under UK domestic law and is subject to the provisions of any applicable double taxation agreement. It does not override the provisions of a double taxation agreement which may make a UK incorporated company a resident of an overseas territory for the purposes of the agreement (see 20 and 21 above).

Appendix to SP 1/90
[The Appendix contains the text of FA 1988, s 66 and Sch 7 and is not reproduced here.]

SP 2/91 Residence in the UK: visits extended because of exceptional circumstances

[19 March 1991]
1. Under Section 336 of the Taxes Act, an individual is not regarded as resident in the UK in a year of assessment if, broadly,
(a) he is in this country for some temporary purpose only and without the intention of establishing his residence here; and
(b) he has not, in the aggregate, spent at least six months in the UK in that year.

2. In applying the first condition, one of the considerations is that an individual is regarded as resident in the UK if visits to the UK average at least three months in a tax year; the average is calculated over a maximum

of four years. Where this rule applies, any days which are spent in the UK because of exceptional circumstances beyond an individual's control, for example, illness, will be excluded from the calculation.

3. Each case where this relaxation of the normal rules may be appropriate will be considered in the light of its own facts. The statutory condition in paragraph 1(a) above must of course continue to be met, and the relaxation does not apply for the purposes of calculating the six months in paragraph 1(b) above.

APPENDIX 3

Extra-Statutory Concessions

A11 Residence in the United Kingdom: year of commencement or cessation of residence

The Income and Corporation Taxes Acts make no provision for splitting a tax year in relation to residence and an individual who is resident in the United Kingdom for any year of assessment is chargeable on the basis that he is resident for the whole year.

But where an individual
(a) comes to the United Kingdom to take up permanent residence or to stay for at least two years; or
(b) ceases to reside in the United Kingdom if he has left for permanent residence abroad;

liability to United Kingdom tax which is affected by residence is computed by reference to the period of his residence here during the year. It is a condition that the individual should satisfy the Board of Inland Revenue that prior to his arrival he was, or on his departure is, not ordinarily resident in the United Kingdom. The concession would not apply, for example, where an individual who had been ordinarily resident in the United Kingdom left for intended permanent residence abroad but returned to reside here before the end of the tax year following the tax year of departure.

This concession is extended to the years of departure and return where, subject to certain conditions, an individual goes abroad for full-time service under a contract of employment. These conditions are:
- the individual's absence from the United Kingdom and the employment itself both extend over a period covering a complete tax year; and
- any interim visits to the United Kingdom during the period do not amount to
  (i) 183 days or more in any tax year; or
  (ii) an average of 91 days or more in a tax year (the average is taken over the period of absence up to a maximum of four years); and
- for years up to and including 1992–93, all the duties of the employment are performed abroad or any duties the individual performs in the United Kingdom are incidental to duties abroad.

Appendix 3

Where the concession applies and the tax year is split, Section 128 FA 1995 (limit on income chargeable on non-residents: income tax) does not apply for the period for which an individual is treated as not resident. That section only applies to complete years of non-residence.

D2 Residence in the United Kingdom: year of commencement or cessation of residence: capital gains tax

1. An individual who comes to live in the United Kingdom and is treated as resident here for any year of assessment from the date of arrival is charged to capital gains tax only in respect of chargeable gains from disposals made after arrival, provided that the individual has not been resident or ordinarily resident in the United Kingdom at any time during the five years of assessment immediately preceding the year of assessment in which he or she arrived in the United Kingdom.
2. An individual who leaves the United Kingdom and is treated on departure as not resident and not ordinarily resident here is not charged to capital gains tax on gains from disposals made after the date of departure, provided that the individual was not resident and not ordinarily resident in the United Kingdom for the whole of at least four out of the seven years of assessment immediately preceding the year of assessment in which he or she left the United Kingdom.
3. This concession does not apply to any individual in relation to gains on the disposal of assets which are situated in the United Kingdom and which, at any time between the individual's departure from the United Kingdom and the end of the year of assessment, are either:
(i) used in or for the purposes of a trade, profession or vocation carried on by that individual in the United Kingdom through a branch or agency; or
(ii) used or held for, or acquired for use by or for the purposes of, such a branch or agency.
4. This concession does not apply to the trustees of a settlement who commence or cease residence in the United Kingdom or to a settlor of a settlement in relation to gains in respect of which the settlor is chargeable under sections 77–79 TCGA 1992, or section 86 and Schedule 5 TCGA 1992.
5. This revised concession applies to any individual who ceases to be resident or ordinarily resident in the United Kingdom on or after 17 March 1998, or becomes resident or ordinarily resident in the United Kingdom on or after 6 April 1998.

INDEX

[*References are to paragraph number and Appendices*]

91-day test
  arrivals in the UK, and, 4.05
  ordinary residence, and, 3.11
  physical presence, and, 2.13
  visits to UK 2.13
183-day test
  'actual residence', 4.08
  capital gains tax, and, 4.11–4.12
  changes, 4.03, 4.09
  examples (HMRC), 4.09
  passenger in transit, 4.09
  residence, for, 2.11, 4.03

A

Abandonment
  domicile of dependence, and, 7.06
Abode, place of 2.08–2.10
  arrival in the UK, and, 4.07
  deduction of tax at source, usual place outside UK, 8.02, 8.03
  habitual abode, and double taxation, 2.22
  multiple residence, 2.09
  occupation of dwelling, 2.08
  ordinary residence, and, 3.03
    available accommodation, 3.10
    voluntary adoption, 3.03, 3.04
  relevance of ownership, 2.10
  'usual', 8.03
Abroad, visiting 2.05, 4.13–4.15
Abroad, working 4.16–4.20, *see also* REMITTANCE BASIS
  'distinct break' from UK, proof of, 4.15
  foreign employment, 4.19, 4.20
  full-time work, 4.17
  generally, 4.16
  'incidental duties', 4.20
  residence, 4.16

Abroad, working – *contd*
  spouse later joining, concession for, 4.04, 4.16
  trades and professions, 4.18
Absence, temporary 2.07
Accommodation, *see also* ABODE, PLACE OF
  address in UK, 2.18
  available/availability, 2.10, 3.10, 4.06
    ignoring, 4.04, 4.05, 4.07, 4.12
  dwelling house, *see* HOME
Acquisition of domicile
  choice, of, 7.10
  dependence, of,
    children, 7.08
    married women, 7.07
    mentally disordered persons, 7.09
  inheritance tax anti-avoidance provisions, 7.16
  origin, of, 7.05
'Actual residence' 4.08
Address in UK 2.18
Adopted child
  domicile of dependence, 7.08
Airline pilot 1.26, 2.07, 2.12, 4.20
Allowances
Annual attribute
  ordinary residence, and, 3.11
  residence, 2.05
Appeal 8.05–8.07
  court role on, 8.07
  evidential burden, 8.06
  rules applying, 8.05
Arriving in the UK 4.01 *et seq*
  'actual residence', 4.08
  available living accommodation, ignoring, 4.04, 4.05, 4.07, 4.12
  capital gains tax test, 4.11
    comparison with ITA 2007 s 831, 4.12

263

Index

Arriving in the UK – *contd*
  conditional exemption, 4.04
  employment income, 4.04
  extra-statutory concessions, 4.01, 4.02, App 3
  intention of establishing residence, 4.06, 4.11
  ordinary residence (SP 3/81) App 2
  place of abode, 4.07
  short visit, 4.05
  183-day test (or six-month) test, 4.09
    capital gains tax, and, 4.11–4.12
    generally, 4.09
    Revenue guidance, 4.09
    tax year, period within, 4.10
  temporary purpose, 4.05
  view of establishing residence, 4.06, 4.11
Assessment
  income tax, and, 1.20, 2.05
  non-resident, 8.02, 8.04
  notice of, service abroad, 8.01
  'residence in UK for year of assessment', annual attribute, 2.05
  self-assessment, *see* TAX RETURN
Available accommodation, *see* ACCOMMODATION

B

Birthplace
  residence, and, 2.16
Body corporate 6.01, *see also* COMPANY
Business ties
  residence, and, 2.18

C

Capital gains tax
  183-day test, 4.11, 4.12
  annual exemption, 1.22
  assessment, *see* ASSESSMENT
  charge to, when arises, 1.22
  departing the UK temporarily, 4.21
  division of tax year, moving to or from UK, 4.02
  domicile, 1.22, 7.03
  ordinary residence, and chargeability, 1.10, 3.01, 3.03
  remittance basis, 1.15
  residence,
    outside UK, trade in UK, 1.22
    part of year of assessment only, 2.05
  split tax year, concession 4.02, App 3
  trusts, 5.01, 5.03, 5.06
  visits to UK, and liability to, 4.11, 4.12
Caravan 2.10, 8.03
'Care of' address
  residence, and, 2.18
Channel Islands 1.06
Chargeability to tax
  domicile, 1.12

Chargeability to tax – *contd*
  notice, 8.01
  ordinary residence, 1.11
  remittance basis, 1.15
  residence, 1.10
Child(ren)
  domicile of dependence, 7.08
  domicile of origin, 7.05
  ordinary residence of, 3.04
Choice, domicile of
  acquisition, 7.10
  change of, 7.15
  deemed, 7.16
  intention, 7.12–7.14
  residence, 7.11
Citizenship
  domicile, and, 7.02
Club membership
  residence, significance for, 2.19
Coming to the UK, *see* ARRIVING IN THE UK
Company 6.01 *et seq*
  'central management and control' test, 6.03–6.06, 6.08–6.14
    administrative functions not indicative, 6.12
    case coining phrase, 6.03
    degree of activity, 6.11
    delegation of powers, effect of, 6.07
    directors' meetings, 6.14
    fact, question of, 6.05, 6.06
    location of central management and control, 6.14
    policy-making decisions, 6.09, 6.12, 6.13
    raising and allocation of funds, 6.10
    'real business', where carried on, 6.09
    shareholder control contrasted, 6.08
    synthesis of principles applying, 6.04
    transfer of, 6.17
  chargeability, residence basis, 1.10
  chargeable gains, 6.01
  controlled foreign companies' charge, 1.21, 6.22
  domicile of origin, 7.05
  'dual resident investing company', 6.21
  European company, 6.19
  exit taxes and EC law, 9.04
  foreign registered, 6.03
  group relief, 6.21
  incorporation rule, 6.02
  non-resident, 6.03 *et seq*
    'central management and control' test, *see above*
    delegated management and control, 6.07
    double tax treaty, under, 6.16, 6.18
    group, 6.04, 6.08
    shareholder control, significance of, 6.08

264

Index

Company – *contd*
  profits, 1.21, 6.01
    common participation in management control, transfer pricing rules, 6.23
  residence, 1.10, 6.01 *et seq*, 9.03
    corporation tax, for, 6.20
    EC law, 9.03, 9.04
    foreign incorporated company, 6.03 *et seq, and see* 'non-resident' *above*
    multiple, 6.15
    personal attribute, 2.04, 6.01
    Statement of Practice (SP 1/90) 6.06, 6.08, App 2
    tax treaties, and, 6.16, 6.18
    transfer abroad, 6.17
    UK incorporated company, 6.02
    wholly-owned subsidiary, Revenue position on, 6.08
  right of establishment (EC law), 9.03
  transfer pricing, small and medium-sized enterprises, 6.23
Compliance 8.1–8.04
Concessions, *see* HMRC PRACTICES AND CONCESSIONS
Continuity of purpose
  ordinary residence, and, 3.03, 3.05
Controlled foreign company 1.21, 6.22
Corporation tax 1.21, 6.01, *see also* COMPANY
  permanent establishment in UK for, 6.01
  residence for purposes of, 6.20

D

Death
  estate of deceased, 5.07
  trust taking effect on, 5.04
Deduction of tax at source
  obligation, 8.03
  system of, 8.02, 8.03
  'usual place of abode', 8.03
Deemed domicile 7.16
Departing the UK 4.01 *et seq*
  capital gains tax, 4.21
  distinct break with UK, 4.15
  extra-statutory concessions, 4.01
  generally, 4.13
  occasional residence, 4.14
  temporarily, *see* TEMPORARY PURPOSE TEST
  working abroad, *see* ABROAD, WORKING
Dependence, domicile of
  children, 7.08
  married women, 7.07
  mentally disordered persons, 7.09
Discrimination
  covert, 9.02
  nationality ground, 9.01, 9.02
  residence ground, 1.09, 9.01, 9.02
    companies, 9.03

Displacement
  domicile of origin, and, 7.06
Domicile 7.1 *et seq*
  abandonment, 7.06
  acquisition,
    domicile of choice, 7.10
    domicile of origin, 7.05
    inheritance tax anti-avoidance provisions, 7.16
  adopted child, 7.08
  capital gains tax, and, 7.03
  change of,
    domicile of choice, 7.15
    general principle, 7.04
  children, 7.08
  choice, of,
    acquisition, 7.10
    change of, 7.15
    deemed, 7.16
    intention, 7.12–7.14
    residence, 7.11
  citizenship, and, 7.02
  claim that not domiciled in UK, 8.04
  deemed, 7.16
  dependence, of,
    children, 7.08
    married women, 7.07
    mentally disordered persons, 7.09
  displacement, 7.06
  dispute as to, *see* APPEAL
  double tax treaties, for purposes of, 7.17
  evidence, 7.14, 8.07
  foundlings, 7.05
  historical background, 7.02
  illegitimate child,
    domicile of dependence, 7.08
    domicile of origin, 7.05
  income tax, and, 7.03
  inheritance tax, and, 7.03, 7.16
    generally, 7.01
    introduction, 1.23
  intention,
    evidence, approach to assessing, 7.14
    generally, 7.12
    motive, and, 7.13
    proof, 7.14
  introduction, 7.01
  married women, 7.07
  mentally disordered persons, 7.09
  multiple domiciles, and, 7.04
  origin, of,
    acquisition, 7.05
    corporation, 7.05
    displacement, 7.06
    revival, 7.06
  principles, 7.04
  rationale, 7.03
  residence, 7.11
  revival, 7.06
  roles, 7.03

265

Index

Domicile – *contd*
  scope narrowed, 1.12
  territorial extent, 7.03
  transfer of capital for inheritance tax, 7.03
Double taxation
  domicile for tax treaty purposes, 7.17
  dual residence, and, 2.22
    non-resident company, 6.18
    trustees, 5.06
  protection from, 2.22, 6.16
Dual residence, *see* MULTIPLE RESIDENCE
'Dual resident investing company' 6.21
Duration of presence
  residence, for, 2.11
Dwelling, *see* HOME

E

Electoral roll
  place of abode, and, 2.10
Education
  residence, and, 2.20
Employment income 1.20, 3.01
  person arriving in UK, 4.04, 4.08
  working abroad, *see* ABROAD, WORKING
Enforcement 8.01–8.04
  introduction, 1.03, 1.04, 8.01
Estate of deceased
  residence of personal representative 5.07
European Community/Union 1.09
  change of residence, legality of taxes levied on, 9.04
  discrimination on nationality grounds, *see* DISCRIMINATION
  EC Treaty rights, and direct taxation, 9.01–9.03
  enforcement, mutual assistance in, 1.04
  equality of treatment, 9.02, 9.03
  exit taxes on change of residence, ECJ cases on legality, 9.04
  freedom of movement, 9.01, 9.04
  right of establishment, 9.03, 9.04
  tax residence of companies, cases, 9.03
European company
  residence of 6.19
Evidence
  appeal, re-evaluation of facts on, 8.07
  domicile of intention, as to, 7.14
  residence, proof of, 8.06
Extra-statutory concessions, *see* HMRC PRACTICES AND CONCESSIONS

F

Fact, question of
  appeal, 8.07
  ordinary residence, 2.03, 3.01
  residence, 2.03, 2.06, 8.07
    company, for, 6.05, 6.06
    question of law, circumstances, 2.03

Family ties
  residence, and, 2.17
Fiscal residence 2.22, 9.03
Foreign income 1.20, *see also* ABROAD, WORKING
Foreign registered company 6.03
Foundling
  domicile of origin, and, 7.05
Full-time work
  abroad, 4.17

G

Guidelines (HMRC) 1.14

H

Habitual abode, and double taxation 2.22
'Habitually and normally'
  ordinarily resident, meaning of, 3.02–3.03
HMRC guidelines 1.14
HMRC practices and concessions 1.26, *see also* IR20 BOOKLET
  application of and reliance on, 1.26
  division of tax year, moving to or from UK, 4.02, App 3
  effect and stature of, 1.26
  extra-statutory concessions set out, App 3
  ordinary residence, and,
    annual visits, 3.11
    available accommodation, 3.10
    defect in principles adopted, 3.09
    intention, 3.12
    year by year residence, 3.09
  presence, and, 2.13
  Statements of Practice App 2
Home
  caravan, 2.10, 8.03
  double tax treaties, for, 2.22
  multiple residence, 2.09, 2.22
  occupation of dwelling, 2.08
  ownership, relevance of, 2.10
  tent, 2.08, 2.21, 8.03
  'usual place of abode', 8.03
  yacht, 8.03, *see also* TERRITORIAL WATERS

I

Illegal presence
  residence, and, 2.21
Illegitimate child
  domicile of dependence, 7.08
  domicile of origin, 7.05
Incapacitated person
  domicile of dependence, and, 7.09
  ordinary residence of, 3.04
'Incidental duties'
  working abroad, and, 4.20
Income tax
  annual nature of, 1.20, 2.05
  assessment, *see* ASSESSMENT
  division of tax year, moving to or from UK, 4.02

Index

Income tax – *contd*
   domicile, and, 7.03
   estate of deceased, position of personal representative, 5.07
   legislation, 1.20, 4.03
   non-resident, 8.02
   ordinary residence, and chargeability, 3.03
   outline of, 1.20
   remittance basis, 1.15
   split tax year, concession 4.02, App 3
   trusts, and, 5.01, 5.03, 5.05

Individual taxpayer
   residence, 2.1 *et seq, see also* RESIDENCE

Inheritance tax
   domicile, and, 1.23, 7.01, 7.03, 7.16
   outline of, 1.23

Intellectual property right, sums payable periodically
   deduction of tax at source 8.03

Intention
   domicile, and,
     generally, 7.12
     motive, and, 7.13
     proof and evidence of, 7.14
   establishing residence, arrival in UK for, 4.06
   ordinary residence, and, 3.12
   residence, as to, 2.20

Interest, yearly
   deduction of tax at source, 8.03

Investment income 1.20

Involuntary presence
   residence, and, 2.20

IR20 booklet App 1
   application of, 1.26
   challenging, 2.02
   judicial attitude to, 1.26
   legal effect, 1.26
   refusal of HMRC to apply, 1.26

J

Jurisdiction
   service of notices abroad, 8.01
   sovereignty, and, 1.03
   tax treaties, allocation under, 2.22

L

Landlord income, non-resident
   deduction of tax at source, 8.03

Leaving the UK, *see* DEPARTING THE UK

Legality of presence
   residence, and, 2.21

Limited company, *see* COMPANY

M

Management and control, *see* COMPANY

Married women
   domicile of dependence, 7.07

Membership of clubs and societies
   residence, significance for, 2.19

Mentally disordered person
   domicile of dependence, 7.09
   ordinary residence, 3.04

Minor, *see* CHILD(REN)

Moving to the UK, *see* ARRIVING IN THE UK

Multiple residence 3.09
   company with, 6.15
   double tax treaties, protection under, 2.22
   generally, 2.09
   ordinary residence, 3.08

N

National Insurance Contributions (NICs) 1.24

Nationality
   birth ties, and residence, 2.16
   corporate, 9.03
   discrimination ground, 9.01, 9.02
   impact reduced, 1.13

Natural home 1.12

91-day test
   arrivals in the UK, and, 4.05
   ordinary residence, and, 3.11
   physical presence, and, 2.13
   visits to UK 2.13

Non-resident
   assessment of, 8.02, 8.04
   landlord, 8.03
   limited company, *see* COMPANY
   residence in UK, principles, *see* RESIDENCE
   temporary, *see* TEMPORARY NON-RESIDENCE REGIME
   trustee operating in UK 5.05

Northern Ireland 1.06

Notice requiring return 8.01

O

'Occasional residence abroad' 4.14

Occupation of dwelling
   residence, and, 2.08

183-day test
   'actual residence', 4.08
   capital gains tax, and, 4.11–4.12
   changes, 4.03, 4.09
   examples (HMRC), 4.09
   passenger in transit, 4.09
   residence, for, 2.11, 4.03

Ordinary residence 3.1 *et seq*
   see also **RESIDENCE**
   91-day test, 3.11
   acquisition, 3.03 *et seq*
   annual visits, 3.11
   anti-avoidance, and, 3.01
   available accommodation, 3.10
   breaking, 4.15
   chargeability to tax, and, 1.11, 3.01, 8.04
   children, 3.04

Index

Ordinary residence – *contd*
  claim that not ordinarily resident in UK, 8.04
  dispute as to, *see* APPEAL
  dual, 3.08
  elements,
    regular order of life, as part of, 3.06
    settled purpose, 3.05
    unlawful residence, 3.07
    voluntary adoption, 3.04
  fact, question of, 2.03, 3.01
  future intention, 3.12
  'habitually and normally', 3.02–3.03
  incapacitated persons, 3.04
  intention, 3.12
  introduction, 3.01
  liability determinant in special cases, 3.01
  meaning, 2.07, 3.01, 3.02
  multiple, 3.08
  none, 3.08
  personal attribute,
  place of abode,
    available accommodation, 3.10
    'regular order' of life, 3.06
    voluntary adoption, 3.03, 3.04
  regular order of life, 3.06
  residence, relationship with, 3.01, 3.03
  Revenue practice, 3.09–3.12
  settled purpose, 3.05
  short-term visitors, 3.11
  summary,
  unlawful residence, 3.07
  voluntary adoption, 3.04
  year by year arrangements, 3.09,
Origin, domicile of
  acquisition, 7.05
  displacement, 7.06
  revival, 7.06
Ownership
  dwelling, of, relevance to residence, 2.10

P

Pension 1.20
Permanent establishment
  corporation tax, for, 6.01
  trust, 5.05
Personal attribute
  ordinary residence as,
  residence as, 2.04
Personal belongings and chattels
  residence, significance for, 2.19
Personal representative 5.07
Person arriving in the UK, *see* ARRIVING IN THE UK
Persons departing the UK, *see* DEPARTING THE UK
Physical presence, *see* PRESENCE IN UK
Place of abode, *see* ABODE, PLACE OF

Practices and concessions, *see* HMRC PRACTICES AND CONCESSIONS
Presence in UK 2.01, 2.12–2.14, 4.14
  'actual residence', 4/08
  determining, 4.09
  duration, significance of, 2.11
  frequency of visits, 2.12
  future conduct, 2.14
  involuntary, 2.20
  limit before treated as resident, 4.09
  no establishment in UK, 2.11
  ordinary residence, 'regular order' of life for, 3.06
  previous history, 2.15
  regularity of visits, 2.12, 2.13
  residence, and, 2.01, 2.12–2.14, 4.14
  Revenue practice, 2.13
  unintentional, 2.20
  unlawful, 2.21
Previous history
  residence, and, 2.15
Profession
  working abroad, and, 4.18
Property income 1.20

Q

Qualitative attribute
  residence, and, 2.02

R

Recovery proceedings 8.01
Reforms 1.17–1.19
Registered company, *see* COMPANY
Regular order of life
  ordinary residence, and, 3.06
Religious observance
  residence, and ties of, 2.19
Remittance basis
  chargeability to tax, and, 1.15, 3.01
  claim basis, 1.13
  reform, 1.12, 1.16, 1.19
  temporary non-residence, 4.22
Representative in UK
  joint liability with non-resident (income tax), 8.02
Residence
  see also ORDINARY RESIDENCE
  183-day test, 2.11
  abode, place of, 2.08–2.10
  annual attribute, 2.05
  birth ties, 2.16
  business ties, 2.18
  cessation, see DEPARTING THE UK
  change of, legality of taxes levied (ECJ), 9.04
  chargeability to tax, and, 1.10, 2.01
  club memberships, 2.19
  commencement, *see* ARRIVING IN THE UK
  company or body corporate, *see* COMPANY

268

Residence – *contd*
connecting factors, 1.01
  birth ties, 2.16
  business ties, 2.18
  family ties, 2.17
  other UK ties, 2.19
constructive 4.06
discrimination as to, *see* DISCRIMINATION
domicile of choice, and, 7.11
double tax treaties, protection under, 2.22
duration of presence, 2.11
fact, question of, 2.03, 2.06
family ties, 2.17
fiscal, 2.22, 9.03
home,
  multiple residence, 2.09
  occupation of dwelling, 2.08
  ownership, relevance of, 2.10
intent, 2.20
involuntary presence, 2.19
judicial principles, 2.06
  synthesis of (*Shepherd*), 2.07
legality of, 2.21
meaning, 2.02, 2.03
membership of clubs and societies, 2.19
multiple, 2.09, 6.15
  double tax treaties, protection under, 2.22, 6.16
nature of,
  annual attribute, 2.05
  fact and degree, question of, 2.03, 2.06
  judicial principles, 2.06
  personal attribute, 2.04
  qualitative attribute, 2.02
occupation of dwelling, 2.08
ordinary residence contrasted, 3.01, 3.03
ownership of dwelling irrelevant, 2.10
part of year of assessment only, 2.05
personal attribute, 2.04
personal belongings and chattels, 2.19
physical presence, 2.11, *see also* PRESENCE IN UK
place of abode, *see* ABODE, PLACE OF
presence, *see* PRESENCE IN UK
question of fact and degree, 2.03, 2.06
reform proposals, 1.17–1.19
  principles underpinning, 1.18
religious observance ties, 2.19
six-month test, and, 2.11
split tax year, 4.02
spouses, and, 2.04
temporary purpose test, 2.10, 4.06
trusts, *see* TRUSTS
unintentional presence, 2.20
unlawful presence, 2.21
unlimited liability from, 1.01
visits to UK, 2.12–2.14
work abroad, during, 4.16
Return, *see* TAX RETURN

Revival
domicile of dependence, and, 7.06
Royalties
deduction of tax at source, 8.03

S

Scotland 1.06, 1.10
Self-assessment, *see* TAX RETURN
Settled purposes
ordinary residence, for, 3.05
Settlement 5.01 *et seq*, *see also* TRUSTS
Shareholder control
residence of company, and, 6.08
Short-term visitors, *see also* TEMPORARY PURPOSE TEST; VISITS TO UK
ordinary residence, and, 3.11
Six-month test 2.11, 4.03, *see now* 183-DAY TEST
Sovereignty 1.02–1.05
enforcement overseas, 1.04
jurisdictional limitations, 1.03
territorial sovereignty, 1.05, 1.08
Split tax year concession, *see* TAX YEAR
Spouses
inheritance tax exemption for transfer between 1.23
residence, and, 2.04
work abroad, concession for non-working spouse, 4.04, 4.16
Statements of Practice App 2

T

Tax return
compliance issues, 8.01
claim that not ordinarily resident/domiciled in UK in, 8.04
failure to make, 8.01
split year claim in 4.02
Tax year 4.10
183-day test, period within, 4.10
split, concessionary treatment, 4.02, App 3
claim for 4.02
Taxation, UK, *see* UK TAXATION
Temporary non-residence regime 4.11, 4.21, 4.22
Temporary purpose test 2.10, 4.06
arrivals in the UK, and, 4.05
capital gains tax, 4.11, 4.12, 4.21
Territorial sovereignty
extension, 1.08
generally, 1.05
Territorial waters 1.07
yacht moored in, 2.10, 2.20
Territory
European Community, 1.04
introduction, 1.01, 1.06
territorial waters, 1.07, 1.08
UK, meaning, 1.06

Index

Trades and professions
working abroad, and, 4.18
Trading income 1.20
Trading presence 1.05
Transfer pricing
small and medium-sized enterprises, 6.23
Trusts
background, 5.01
interest, and trustee's 'usual place of abode', 8.03
residence rules for trustees, 2.04, 5.01 *et seq*
capital gains tax, 5.01, 5.03, 5.06
'deemed person', trustees as, 5.02
income tax, 5.01,
mixed residence trustees, 5.04
non-resident trustees operating in UK, 5.05
ordinary residence, 5.02, 5.04
'permanent establishment' in UK, 5.05
residence of all trustees in UK, 5.03
'settled property', 5.01, 5.02
'settlor', 5.01, 5.02
tax treaties, and place of 'effective management', 5.06

U

UK taxation
determinants of chargeability,
complexity of rules, 1.14
domicile, 1.12, 1.14
nationality, 1.13
ordinary residence, 1.11
remittance basis, *see* REMITTANCE BASIS
residence, 1.10, 1.14
domicile, 1.12
enforcement, 1.03, 1.04
European Community law, effect on, 1.09
Finance Bill scrutiny, lack of, 1.02
jurisdiction, 1.03
liability, 1.14
ordinary residence, 1.11
Parliamentary control, 1.02
remittance basis, *see* REMITTANCE BASIS

UK taxation – *contd*
residence, 1.10
right to levy, 1.02
sovereignty, and, 1.02–1.05
territory, and, 1.06–1.09
Unincorporated association 6.01
Unintentional presence
residence, and, 2.20
Unlawful presence
residence, and, 2.21
Unlawful residence
ordinary residence, and, 3.07
Usual place of abode, *see* ABODE, PLACE OF

V

Value added tax 1.25
View of establishing residence
arrivals in the UK, and, 4.06
capital gains tax, 4.11
Visits abroad 2.05, 4.13–4.15
Visits to UK, *see also* 91-DAY TEST; 183-DAY TEST
annual 3.11
capital gains tax, liability to, 4.11, 4.12
extended because of exceptional circumstances (SP 2/91) App 2
ordinary residence, and, 3.03, 3.04, 3.06, 3.09, 3.11
residence, significance for, 2.12–2.14
temporary purpose, for, 4.05
Voluntary adoption
place of abode 3.03, 3.04

W

Wales 1.06
Working abroad, *see* ABROAD, WORKING

Y

Yacht
territorial waters, moored in, 2.10, 2.20
usual place of abode, 8.03
Year by year arrangements
ordinary residence, and, 3.09,
Year, tax, *see* TAX YEAR